First World War
and Army of Occupation
War Diary
France, Belgium and Germany

1 DIVISION
Divisional Troops
409 Field Company Royal Engineers
1 February 1917 - 30 September 1919

WO95/1254/1

The Naval & Military Press Ltd
www.nmarchive.com
Published in association with The National Archives

Published by

The Naval & Military Press Ltd

Unit 10 Ridgewood Industrial Park,
Uckfield, East Sussex,
TN22 5QE England
Tel: +44 (0) 1825 749494

www.naval-military-press.com
www.nmarchive.com

Contents

Document type	Place/Title	Date From	Date To
Heading	WO95/1254/1		
Heading	1st Division Roy. Engineers 409th Lowland Field Coy. R.E. (T) Feb-Dec 1917		
Heading	War Diary 409th. (Lowland) Field Coy. R.E. (T). 1st Division. February.1917		
Heading	War Diary of 409th (Lowland) Field Coy R.E. (T) From 1st February 1917 To 28th February 1917 (Volume No XXVI)		
War Diary	Warloy Coy In Billets less one Sctn	01/02/1917	02/02/1917
War Diary	2nd Section & Transport Lines at 1 Section at Chuiche 1 Section at Cerisy	03/02/1917	04/02/1917
War Diary	Coy (Less 1 Section) In Billets at Cerisy Remaining Setn at Chuiqnes	05/02/1917	05/02/1917
War Diary	Hd Qrs & 1 Section at Cerisy 1 Sectionlat Chuignes 2 Sections at chuicnolles	06/02/1917	06/02/1917
War Diary	Headqrs. & 1 Sct. at Re Dump Chuignolles 2 sections in Chuignoless 1 Section at Chuignes	07/02/1917	08/02/1917
War Diary	3 Sections & Transport Lines at Chuignolles 1 section at Chuignes	09/02/1917	09/02/1917
War Diary	Coy Less 1 Sect. in Billets at Chuignolles 1 Section in Billets at Chuignes	10/02/1917	16/02/1917
War Diary	Coy in forward area. 2 sections in Dugouts behind Support Line 2 section in Dugouts at Becquincourt, Transport Lines at Fontaine-Les-Cappy	17/02/1917	17/02/1917
War Diary	2 Sections in Dugouts Behind support line 2 sections in Dugouts near Becquincourt & Re dump. Transport Lines near Fontaine-Les-Cappy	18/02/1917	23/02/1917
War Diary	2 Section on Dugouts 2 Section in Dugouts at Becquincourt Transport Lines at Fontaine Les Cappy.	24/02/1917	24/02/1917
War Diary	2 Sections billeted in dugouts behind suppline 2 Seek one is Dugouts near RE Dump Becquineourt transport lines of fontaine-les-Cappy.	25/02/1917	25/02/1917
War Diary	2 Section us Dugouts behind suppline 2 seekone in Dugouts near Dump at Becquincourt Transport Lines as Fontaine Les-Cappy	26/02/1917	28/02/1917
Heading	War Diary 409th. Lowland Field Coy., R.E. 1st Division March 1917		
Heading	War Diary of 409th Lowland Field Coy RE From 1st March 1917 To 31st March 1917 Volume XXVII		
War Diary	2 Sections billeted behind Supp. Lane at N. 16 A 7-3 2 sections billeted near RE Dump Becquincourt Transport-Lines Near Fontaine-Les-Cappy	01/03/1917	06/03/1917
War Diary	2 Sections at Becquincourt 2 Sections at Chuicnolles Transport lines at Fontaine-Les-Cappy	06/03/1917	06/03/1917
War Diary	Whole Coy in billets at Chuignolles RE. Dump-less one Section billeted at Chuignes	07/03/1917	07/03/1917
War Diary	Coy billeted at RE Dump Chuicnolles less 1 Section billeted at Chuignes	08/03/1917	11/03/1917
War Diary	Whole Coy billeted at Chuignolles RE Dump less 1 Sectn billeted at Chuignes	12/03/1917	13/03/1917

War Diary	2 Sections billeted in Dugout behind Support line. 2 Sections in Dugo at (M 6 B 5.3) Transport Lines near Fontain-Les-Cappy	14/03/1917	17/03/1917
War Diary	Headqrs & 2 Sectons. billeted near assevillers (M 6 D 5.3) 2 Sections in forward ar a Transp at Lines near Fontaine-Les-Cappy	18/03/1917	18/03/1917
War Diary	Headquarters at M 6 D. 5.3 near Assevillers Transport Lanes near Fontaine Les-Cappy Les Sections in forward area near Brie	19/03/1917	20/03/1917
War Diary	Headqrs at M. 6 D. 5.3 near Assevillers Transport lines near Fontaine-Les-Cappy	21/03/1917	21/03/1917
War Diary	Whole Coy in billeted at Brie (027.C) sheet 62 SW edit 3 A	22/03/1917	31/03/1917
Heading	War Diary 409th. (Lowland) Field Coy. R.E. (T). 1st Division April 1917		
Heading	War Diary 409th (Lowland) Field Coy. R.E. (T) From 1st April 1917 to 30th April 1917 (Volume No XXVIII)		
War Diary	Whole Coy less 2 Sections billeted at Brie (027 C) Two Sections at La Flaque	01/04/1917	02/04/1917
War Diary	Whole Coy billeted at Brie (027C)-less 2 Sections at La-Flaque	03/04/1917	04/04/1917
War Diary	Whole Coy Billeted at Brie (027.C)	05/04/1917	08/04/1917
War Diary	Whole Coy in billeted at Brie (027C) sheet 62 S.W.	09/04/1917	09/04/1917
War Diary	Whole Coy in billeted at Brie (027.C)	10/04/1917	22/04/1917
War Diary	Coy in billets at Brie (027C)	23/04/1917	24/04/1917
War Diary	Whole Coy billeted at Brie (027C)	25/04/1917	27/04/1917
War Diary	Coy in Billets at Brie (027C)	28/04/1917	29/04/1917
War Diary	2 Sections in billets at Mericourt-Sur-Somme Remainder of Coy in billets at Brie (0.27.C.)	30/04/1917	30/04/1917
Heading	War Diary 409th (Lowland) Field Coy. R.E. (T). 1st Division. May 1917		
Heading	War Diary 409th (Lowland) Field Coy RE (T) From 1st May 1917 to 31st May 1917 Volume No. XXIX		
War Diary	Two Sections at Mericourt-Sur Somme Remainder of Coy at Brie (0.27 C.)	01/05/1917	01/05/1917
War Diary	Whole Coy in billets at Mericourt Sur Somme	02/05/1917	02/05/1917
War Diary	Coy in billets at Mericourt-Sur-Somme	03/05/1917	19/05/1917
War Diary	Whole Coy in billets at Villers Bretonneux	20/05/1917	21/05/1917
War Diary	Coy billets at Villers-Bretonneux	22/05/1917	27/05/1917
War Diary	Coy billeted near Bailleul (X.10P.4.8)	28/05/1917	31/05/1917
Heading	War Diary 409th. (Lowland) Field Coy. R.E. (T) 1st. Division June 1917		
Heading	DE Herewith War Diary Completed.		
Heading	War Diary of 409th (Lowland) Field Coy R.E. (T) From 1st June 1917 To 30th June 1917 (Volume No. XXX)		
War Diary	Coy billeted near Bailleul (X.10 P 4.8)	01/06/1917	07/06/1917
War Diary	Coy billeted at X10P.4.8. near Bailleul	08/06/1917	10/06/1917
War Diary	Coy billeted near Bailleul at (X.10.P.4.8)	11/06/1917	11/06/1917
War Diary	Coy in billets at O.30 near Queue-d"-oxelaere	12/06/1917	19/06/1917
War Diary	Coy billeted at Wormhoudt	20/06/1917	20/06/1917
War Diary	Coy at Wormhoudt	21/06/1917	21/06/1917
War Diary	Coy in billets at i. 8 D. 91 near rosendal	22/06/1917	22/06/1917
War Diary	Coy billeted near Rosendal at i.8 D.9.1.	23/06/1917	23/06/1917
War Diary	Coy billeted at R 32.B. near Coxyde-Baines	24/06/1917	25/06/1917
War Diary	Coy billeted in forward area Hqrs at R 27.C.4.0 near Coxyde-Baines	26/06/1917	27/06/1917

War Diary	Coy billeted near Rosendal I. 7. B. 1.3.	28/06/1917	29/06/1917
War Diary	Two Sections at I. 7. B. 1.3. near Rosendal Remainder of Coy Comped near Casino point-de-Gravelines	30/06/1917	30/06/1917
Heading	War Diary 409th. (Lowland) Field Coy. R.E. (T) 1st Division July 1917.		
Heading	War Diary of 409th (Lowland) Field Coy R.E. (T) From 1st July 1917 to 31st July 1917 (Volume no. XXXI)		
War Diary	The Coy (Less 2 sections) Casinno point-de-Gravelines Two sections billeted at Luarry near Dunkerque	01/07/1917	01/07/1917
War Diary	Coy-less two section-billeter near Casiiyo point-de-cravelines two seelious billeled at Luarry near Dunrerque	02/07/1917	02/07/1917
War Diary	The Coy-less 2 section-billeter near casino point-de-cravelines two seetions billeled at Luarry near Dunrerque	03/07/1917	03/07/1917
War Diary	Coy-less two section-billeter near Casiiyo point-de-cravelines two seelious billeled at Luarry near Dunrerque	04/07/1917	04/07/1917
War Diary	The Coy-less 2 section-billeter near casino point-de-cravelines two seetions billeled at Luarry near Dunrerque	05/07/1917	05/07/1917
War Diary	Coy-less 2 section-billeter near Casino point-de-cravelines two seelious billeled at Luarry near Dunrerque	06/07/1917	06/07/1917
War Diary	Coy-less 2 section-billeter near Casino at point-de-cravelines 2 seetions billeled at Luarry near Dunrerque	07/07/1917	07/07/1917
War Diary	Coy-less 1 section-billeter near Casino point-de-cravelines 1 seetions billeled at Luarry near Dunrerque	08/07/1917	08/07/1917
War Diary	Coy-less 1 section-billeter near Casino point-de-cravelines 1 seetions billeled at Luarry near Dunrerque	09/07/1917	09/07/1917
War Diary	Whole Coy-less 1 section-billeted near Casino Point-de-Gravelines 1 section camped at Luarry near Dunkerque	10/07/1917	11/07/1917
War Diary	The Coy-less 1 section-camped near Casino near point-de-Gravelines 1 section camped near Luarry at Dunkerque	12/07/1917	13/07/1917
War Diary	Coy less 1 section billeted near Casino near Point-de-Gravelines 1 section camped near Luarry at Dunkerque	14/07/1917	14/07/1917
War Diary	Coy billeted near Casino near point-de-Gravelines less 1 sectn. billeted near Luarry at Dunkerque	15/07/1917	16/07/1917
War Diary	Coy less 1 section billeted near Casino point-de-Gravelines 1 section at Railhead near Coy.	17/07/1917	17/07/1917
War Diary	Coy-less 1 section billeted near Casino point-de-Gravelines. Section billeted at Railhead near the remainder of the Coy.	18/07/1917	19/07/1917
War Diary	Coy-less 1 section billeled near Casino point-de-G"ravelines 1 seetion at Railhead near the Coy.	20/07/1917	20/07/1917
War Diary	Coy Camped near Casino near point-de-Gravelines less 1 section 1 section at Railhead near remainder of Company	21/07/1917	22/07/1917
War Diary	Whole Coy less 1 section Camped near the Casino at point-de-Grevelines 1 section at Railhead near the Coy.	23/07/1917	23/07/1917
War Diary	Coy less 1 section Camped near Casino near point-de-Gravelines. 1 section at Railhead near remainder of Company	24/07/1917	24/07/1917
War Diary	Coy Camped near Casino at point-de-Gravelines less 1 section working at Railhead near Coy.	25/07/1917	25/07/1917

War Diary	Coy less 1 section at Camp near point-de-Gravelines 1/2 section at Railhead near the Coy. One squad at Erin	26/07/1917	26/07/1917
War Diary	Coy less 1 section Camped at Casino near point-de-Gravelines. 1/2 section at Railhead near Coy. 1 squadel ERIN.	27/07/1917	31/07/1917
Heading	War Diary 409th (Lowland) Field Coy. R.E. (T) 1st Division August. 1917		
Heading	War Diary 409th (Lowland) Field Coy. R.E. (T) 1st Division September 1917		
Heading	War Diary of 409th (Lowland) Field Coy R.E. (T) From 1st August 1917 To 31st August 1917 (Volume No. XXXII)		
War Diary	Coy Camped near Casino C. 3.51.38 sheet 1 A Dunkerque 1/100000	01/08/1917	17/08/1917
War Diary	Coy Comped near Casino C. 3.51.38 sheet 1A Dunkerque 1/100,000	19/08/1917	31/08/1917
Miscellaneous			
Diagram etc	North & South Side		
Diagram etc	Revetting as in bull Nose Section.		
Heading	War Diary 409th (Lowland) Field Coy. R.E. (T) From 1st Sept. 1917 To 30th Sept. 1917 (Volume No. XXXIII)		
War Diary	Coy Camped near Casino	01/09/1917	01/09/1917
War Diary	Coy. Comped near Casino C. 3.51.38 sheet 1 A Dunkerque 1/100,000	02/09/1917	14/09/1917
War Diary	Coy Comped near Casino	15/09/1917	15/09/1917
War Diary	Coy Camped near Casino C. 3.51.38 sheet 1 A Dunkerque 1/100000	16/09/1917	16/09/1917
War Diary	Coy Camped near Casino C. 3.51.38	17/09/1917	17/09/1917
War Diary	Coy Camped near Casino C. 3.51.38 sheet 1 A Dunkerque 1/100,000	18/09/1917	27/09/1917
War Diary	Coy Camped near Casino C. 3.51.38	28/09/1917	28/09/1917
War Diary	Coy Camped near Casino C. 3.51.38 sheet 1 A Dunkerque 1/100,000	29/09/1917	29/09/1917
War Diary	Coy Camped at W 6 B. 26 sheet Furnes 1/40,000	30/09/1917	30/09/1917
Diagram etc	Section Third Centre		
Heading	War Diary 409th (Lowland) Field Coy. R.E. (T) 1st Division October 1917		
Heading	War Diary 409th (Lowland) Field Coy. R.E. (T) From 1st October 1917 To 31st October 1917 (Volume No. XXXIV)		
War Diary	Coxyde Bains [sheet 1/40,000 Furnes ref. W 6 & 2.6	01/10/1917	07/10/1917
War Diary	Conyde les Bains [Map Ref. 1/40,000 sheet Furnes W. 6. & 2.6.	08/10/1917	17/10/1917
War Diary	Conyde Bains	18/10/1917	26/10/1917
War Diary	East of Poperinghe sheet 27 1/40,000 L. 3.6.8.8.	27/10/1917	28/10/1917
War Diary	NE. of Ypres sheet 28 N.W. 1/10,000 C. 26. d. 7.7.	29/10/1917	31/10/1917
War Diary	Coxyde Bains	01/10/1917	01/10/1917
War Diary			
Heading	War Diary 409th (Lowland) Field Coy. R.E. (T) 1st Division November 1917		
War Diary	NE of Ypes	01/11/1917	06/11/1917
Miscellaneous			
War Diary	NE of Ypres Irish from Camp	07/11/1917	12/11/1917
War Diary	NE of Ypres	13/11/1917	23/11/1917
War Diary	Ypres Area	24/11/1917	30/11/1917

War Diary	N.E, of Ypres	30/10/1917	23/11/1917
Map			
Heading	War Diary 409th (Lowland) Field Coy. R.E. (T) 1st Division December 1917		
Heading	War Diary of 409th (Lowland) Field Coy. R.E. (T) From 1st Dec. 1917 To 31st Dec. 1917 (Volume No. XXXVI)		
War Diary	Woesten	01/12/1917	31/12/1917
Heading	1st Division Roy. Engineers 409th (Lowland) Field Coy. R.E. 1918 Jan.-1919 Sep.		
Heading	War Diary of 409th (Lowland) Field Coy R.E. (T) From 1st Jany. 1918 To 31st Jany. 1918 (Volume No. XXXVII)		
War Diary	Moulin a Vent Woeston	01/01/1918	24/01/1918
War Diary	Woeston	17/01/1918	31/01/1918
Map	Divnl Baths		
War Diary	H.Q. Woesten 2 Sects. in Shulter in Canal Bank near Bosinghe J. 1 Bridge	01/02/1918	03/02/1918
War Diary	Woesten	04/02/1918	08/02/1918
War Diary	Woesten to Irish Farm Camp.	09/02/1918	10/02/1918
War Diary	Irish Farm Camp NE of Ypres	11/02/1918	19/02/1918
War Diary	Kempton Park (C 15 a 11)	20/02/1918	28/02/1918
War Diary	Nth & Sth of Poelcapelle		
Heading	War Diary 409th (Lowland) Field Coy. R.E. (T) From 1st March 1918 To 31st March 1918 (Volume No. XXXIV)		
War Diary	Kempton Park (Sheet 28 NW 1/20000)	01/03/1918	12/03/1918
War Diary	NE of Ypres	13/03/1918	18/03/1918
War Diary	NE of Ypres Chiefty in Vicinity of Poelcappelle	01/03/1918	01/03/1918
War Diary	NE of Ypres	19/03/1918	21/03/1918
War Diary	NE of Ypres Ilminster Camp near English Farm	22/03/1918	26/03/1918
War Diary	Canal Bank Nth of Ypres	27/03/1918	31/03/1918
War Diary	N. of Ypres	22/04/1918	26/04/1918
War Diary		26/04/1918	31/04/1918
Heading	1st Divisional Engineers 409th (Lowland) Field Company R.E. April 1918		
War Diary	Canal Bank Immidiately North of Ypres Poel Cappelle Sector	01/04/1918	06/04/1918
War Diary	Canal Bank	07/04/1918	09/04/1918
War Diary	Annequin	10/04/1918	10/04/1918
War Diary	Cambrin Sector Billets on above	11/04/1918	15/04/1918
War Diary	Amnequin F 23 3.6.	16/04/1918	21/04/1918
War Diary	1st Annequin	22/04/1918	30/04/1918
Miscellaneous			
Miscellaneous	Report on Bridge Contracted at ? 22/4/18 by 409th Lowland Fd Coy RE	22/04/1918	22/04/1918
Miscellaneous			
Miscellaneous	Times strengths	26/04/1918	26/04/1918
Diagram etc	Diagram		
Diagram etc	Barrel Bridge P 14-59		
Miscellaneous	Lists of Material Reg.	24/04/1918	24/04/1918
War Diary	Annequin N.	01/05/1918	08/05/1918
War Diary	H.Q. 4 Sects Annequin N.	01/05/1918	08/05/1918
War Diary	Transports Mesnil-Ruitz About Bor 7 mile book	08/05/1918	11/05/1918
War Diary	Annequin	12/05/1918	14/05/1918
War Diary	Sailly La Bourse	14/05/1918	31/05/1918

Miscellaneous	Contact Mine		
Miscellaneous			
War Diary	Sailly		
Heading	War Diary of 409th (Lowland) Field Coy. R.E. (T) From 1st June 1918 To 30th June 1918 (Volume No. XLII)		
War Diary	Sailly La Bourse	01/06/1918	03/06/1918
War Diary	Annequin N	04/06/1918	30/06/1918
Heading	War Diary 409th (Lowland) Field Coy. R.E. (T) From 1st July 1918 To 31st July 1918 (Volume No. XLIII)		
War Diary	Annequin North Near Bethune	01/07/1918	16/07/1918
War Diary	Sailly La Bourse S E of Bethune	17/07/1918	20/07/1918
War Diary	Sailly La Bourse	24/07/1918	31/07/1918
Heading	War Diary of 409th (Lowland) Field Coy. R.E. (T) From 1st August 1918 To 31st August 1918 (Volume No. XLIV)		
Miscellaneous			
War Diary	Sailly-Labourse F 27 C 61 (Sheet 44 B.)	01/08/1918	05/08/1918
War Diary	Sailly Labourse	06/08/1918	06/08/1918
War Diary	Annequin	07/08/1918	22/08/1918
War Diary	Bajus 022 a 31	23/08/1918	23/08/1918
War Diary	Summary of Training	24/08/1918	30/08/1918
War Diary	Arras	31/08/1918	31/08/1918
Heading	War Diary of 409th (Lowland) Field Coy. R.E. (T) From 1st Sept. 918 To 30 Sept. 1918 (Volume No. XLV)		
Miscellaneous			
War Diary	Bajus	31/08/1918	31/08/1918
War Diary	Arras	01/09/1918	01/09/1918
War Diary	Neuville Vitasse	02/09/1918	02/09/1918
War Diary	1/40,000 sheet 51 (b) O 25 to about 1/2 mile W of Cherise	02/09/1918	02/09/1918
War Diary	O 25 to b W of Cherisy allt sheet 37th 1/40000 09 b 96	03/09/1918	04/09/1918
War Diary	Near Monchy in Preux 096b.9.6	05/09/1918	09/09/1918
War Diary	Tilloy Les Hermaville to Marcelcave & Chuignes	10/09/1918	16/09/1918
War Diary	Caulancourt	16/09/1918	17/09/1918
War Diary	N.E. of Vermana	17/09/1918	18/09/1918
War Diary	Vadencourt	19/09/1918	19/09/1918
War Diary	Cauleancourt	20/09/1918	24/09/1918
War Diary	Leaf Ward near Vermand	24/09/1918	25/09/1918
War Diary	Caulancourt	26/09/1918	29/09/1918
War Diary	Bihecourt	29/09/1918	30/09/1918
War Diary			
War Diary	Vadencourt		
War Diary	Out of H.Q.		
Heading	War Diary of 409th (Lowland) Field Coy. R.E. (T) 1st October 1918 To 31st October 1918 Volume XLVI		
War Diary	Pontruet	01/10/1918	05/10/1918
Miscellaneous	Transport	16/09/1918	16/09/1918
Miscellaneous	Special Parties		
Miscellaneous	Meals		
Miscellaneous	Company Order For 17-9-18		
War Diary	Ponture	06/10/1918	06/10/1918
War Diary	Caulancourt	07/10/1918	09/10/1918
War Diary	Bellenglise G 29 d 0 6	10/10/1918	11/11/1918
War Diary	Fresnoy Le Grand	12/11/1918	16/11/1918

War Diary	Fresnoy Le Grand to Bohain	16/10/1918	17/10/1918
War Diary	Vaux Andigny	17/10/1918	18/10/1918
War Diary	Vaux Andigny & Vallee Mulatre	19/10/1918	21/10/1918
War Diary	Vallee Mulatre	22/10/1918	31/10/1918
War Diary	Pontru Water Point	04/10/1918	04/10/1918
War Diary		29/09/1918	01/10/1918
War Diary		24/10/1918	30/10/1918
Diagram etc	Light Footbridge to Span Gap of Approx 17-0		
War Diary	Vallee Mulatre N. N.E. of Bohain	01/11/1918	02/11/1918
War Diary	Vallee Mulatre	03/11/1918	06/11/1918
War Diary	Fresnoy Le Grand	07/11/1918	13/11/1918
War Diary	Favril Area	13/11/1918	13/11/1918
War Diary	Sambreton	14/11/1918	15/11/1918
War Diary	Dompierres Area 14 Miles	15/11/1918	15/11/1918
War Diary	Sars Poteries 10 Mile	16/11/1918	16/11/1918
War Diary	Linlay	17/11/1918	17/11/1918
War Diary	Sara Poteries	18/11/1918	18/11/1918
War Diary	Donstiennes	19/11/1918	19/11/1918
War Diary	Prv.	20/11/1918	22/11/1918
War Diary	S. Aubin	23/11/1918	24/11/1918
War Diary	Fter	25/11/1918	30/11/1918
Miscellaneous			
War Diary			
Diagram etc	Diagram		
Diagram etc	Light Footbridge to Span Cap of Approx 17"0		
Diagram etc	Appendix A Part VII		
Miscellaneous	Appendix "A" Part VIII		
Miscellaneous	Appendix C		
War Diary			
Heading	War Diary of 409th (Lowland) Field Coy. R.E. for December 1918		
War Diary	Fter	01/12/1918	01/12/1918
War Diary	Rostenne	02/12/1918	02/12/1918
War Diary	Lavys	03/12/1918	03/12/1918
War Diary	Briquemont	04/12/1918	08/12/1918
War Diary	Haversion	09/12/1918	09/12/1918
War Diary	Hotton	10/12/1918	23/12/1918
War Diary	Ober-Drees	24/12/1918	31/12/1918
Miscellaneous	Pontru Water Point		
Heading	War Diary of 409th (Lowland) Field Coy. R.E. for January 1919		
War Diary	Ober-Drees, Germany sheet Germany 2 L 1/100,000 9 B. 45. 75	01/01/1919	21/01/1919
War Diary	Ober-Drees	01/01/1919	31/01/1919
Heading	War Diary of 409th (Lowland) Field Coy. R.E. (T) From 1st Feby. 1919 To 28th Feby. 1919 9 (Volume No. L)		
War Diary	Ober Drees	01/02/1919	17/03/1919
War Diary	Ober Drees to sochtem	01/03/1919	31/03/1919
War Diary		23/03/1919	08/04/1919
War Diary	Sechtem	01/04/1919	18/04/1919
War Diary	Rosberg Germany	19/04/1919	30/04/1919
War Diary	Rosberg	01/05/1919	31/05/1919
Heading	409th F Coy RE June 1919 Training		
War Diary	Rosberg	01/06/1919	30/06/1919
War Diary	Rosberg	01/06/1919	28/06/1919

Miscellaneous	Appendix B		
War Diary	Rosberg Germany	01/07/1919	19/07/1919
War Diary	Rosberg	20/07/1919	31/07/1919
Heading	War Diary for August 409th Fc Coy R.E.		
War Diary	Rosberg Germany	01/08/1919	26/08/1919
War Diary	In Train from Germany to Rhyll U.K.	26/08/1919	30/08/1919
War Diary	Kinmel Park Camp	30/08/1919	31/08/1919
Heading	Camp HQ Herewith last number of 409th Feb ? War Diary 01/10/19		
War Diary	Kinmel Pk Camp N. Wale	01/09/1919	16/09/1919
War Diary	Kinmel Pk	15/09/1919	30/09/1919

1ST DIVISION
ROY. ENGINEERS

~~1ST LOWLAND FIELD COY. R.E.(T)~~
JANUARY 1917.

409TH LOWLAND FIELD COY. R.E.(T)
FEB - DEC 1917

W A R   D I A R Y.

409th. (Lowland) Field Coy., R.E.(T).

1st. DIVISION.

FEBRUARY.1917.

Vol 26

CONFIDENTIAL

WAR DIARY

OF

409th (LOWLAND) FIELD COY R.E. (T)

from 1st February 1917 to 28th February 1917

(VOLUME No XXVI)

Army Form C. 2118.

Instructions regarding War Diaries and Intelligence Summaries are contained in F. S. Regs., Part II. and the Staff Manual respectively. Title pages will be prepared in manuscript.

WAR DIARY
or
~~INTELLIGENCE~~ SUMMARY.
(Erase heading not required.)

Place	Date	Hour	Summary of Events and Information	Remarks and references to Appendices
WARLOY. Coy. in Billets less one Sect.	1/2/17		During day the following programme of training carried out 8-45 AM to 9-15 Physical Drill 9-45 " " 12-0 Section & Coy. Drill 1-0 PM " 3-30 Route march in full marching order. One Section billeted in CHUIGNES & engaged on the erection of BATH-HOUSES there. Weather. Hard Frost — Dull.	WD
"	2/2/17		Contd the training programme thus 8-45 am to 9-15 Physical Drill 9-45 " " 12-0 Section & Coy. Drill. 1-0pm " 3-30 Short Route March in full marching order. One Section in billets at CHUIGNES & working on the erection of BATH-HOUSES Another Section left WARLOY, & marched to billets near CÉRISY Weather Clear — Keen frost & cold winds	WD

2353 Wt. W2544/1454 700,000 5/15 D. D. & L. A.D.S.S./Forms/C. 2118.

Instructions regarding War Diaries and Intelligence Summaries are contained in F. S. Regs., Part II. and the Staff Manual respectively. Title pages will be prepared in manuscript.

Army Form C. 2118.

WAR DIARY
or
~~INTELLIGENCE~~ SUMMARY.
(*Erase heading not required.*)

Place	Date	Hour	Summary of Events and Information	Remarks and references to Appendices
2 Sections & Transport Lines at WARLOY. 1 SECTION at CHUIGNES 1 SECTION at CERISY	3/2/17		The two Sections in WARLOY carried out the following training 8-45 AM to 9-15 Physical Drill 9:45 " " 12-0 Rifle Exercises 1-0 " " 3-30PM Packing stores etc + preparing for shift on the morrow. Section billeted at CERISY + preparing billets for remainder of Coy. coming on. Section billeted + working at CHUIGNES on BATH HOUSES. Weather. Very Keen Frost + Cold Winds.	WD
"	4/2/17		Remainder of Coy. in WARLOY packed up + moved off at 9-40AM arriving at CERISY 2 PMT joined section already there. Section billeted in CHUIGNES contd. work on the erecting of BATH-HOUSES there. Weather. Clear + Bright	WD

Army Form C. 2118.

WAR DIARY
or
~~INTELLIGENCE SUMMARY.~~
(Erase heading not required.)

Instructions regarding War Diaries and Intelligence Summaries are contained in F. S. Regs., Part II. and the Staff Manual respectively. Title pages will be prepared in manuscript.

Place	Date	Hour	Summary of Events and Information	Remarks and references to Appendices
Coy (less 1 Section) in Billets at CERISY. Remaining Sectn at CHUIGNES	5/2/17		One Section at CHUIGNES in billets. Contd work on BATH HOUSES there. Two " packed up & left CERISY for CHUIGNOLLES & went into billets there. The remaining Section engaged on the following during day Physical Drill Rifle Exercises Saluting Etc. Weather - Clear & Bright - Freezing Hard.	WD
Hd Qrs & 1 Section at CERISY. 1 Section at CHUIGNES. 2 Sections at CHUIGNOLLES	6/2/17		The Section in CHUIGNES contd work on BATH - HOUSES. Two Sections in CHUIGNOLLES engaged erecting NISSEN HUTS. Remainder of Coy. at CERISY packed up all stores & marched off at 10 AM to billets near CHUIGNOLLES, arriving there about mid-day. Wagons were all unloaded & billets improved so far as possible during afternoon. Weather - Very Cold Winds - Dry & Freezing.	WD

2353 Wt. W2544/1454 700,000 5/15 D. D. & L. A.D.S.S./Forms/C. 2118.

Instructions regarding War Diaries and Intelligence Summaries are contained in F. S. Regs., Part II. and the Staff Manual respectively. Title pages will be prepared in manuscript.

WAR DIARY
or
~~INTELLIGENCE SUMMARY.~~
(*Erase heading not required.*)

Army Form C. 2118.

Place	Date	Hour	Summary of Events and Information	Remarks and references to Appendices
Headqrs & 1 Sect at RE DUMP CHUIGNOLLES. 2 Sections in CHUIGNOLLES 1 Section at CHUIGNES	7/2/17		One Section engaged on the erecting of NISSEN HUTS for 1st Div. Eng. Headquarters, CHUIGNOLLES. " fitting out Divisional Headquarters in CHUIGNOLLES. " on the making of BATH-HOUSES at CHUIGNES. " on the erecting of NISSEN HUTS for C.R.A. at CHUIGNOLLES. Weather. Frosty - Hazy.	WD
"	8/2/17		(i) Contd work on NISSEN HUTS for C.R.A. CHUIGNOLLES. Two huts were completed with the exception of a dividing partition in each. One hut framed, floored, & 37 corrugated sheets fitted & another framed, floored, & 24 sheets fitted. (ii) Contd work on fitting Divisional Headqrs CHUIGNOLLES. The main partitions have been completed & the work of lining well in hand. The building was cleared of all beds etc left by previous occupants. (iii) BATHS at CHUIGNES. The section billeted there contd. work on these. (iv) 1st DE Headqrs CHUIGNOLLES. (NISSEN HUTS) One hut fully completed with exception of lining & doors. Preparing foundation for sides for 2nd Hut. (v) RE DUMP CHUIGNOLLES. Improved billets & horse-standings. Weather. Thaw - Very Foggy	WD

Instructions regarding War Diaries and Intelligence Summaries are contained in F. S. Regs., Part II. and the Staff Manual respectively. Title pages will be prepared in manuscript.

WAR DIARY
or
INTELLIGENCE SUMMARY.
(Erase heading not required.)

Army Form C. 2118.

Place	Date	Hour	Summary of Events and Information	Remarks and references to Appendices
3 Sections & Transport Lines at CHUIGNOLLES 1 SECTION at CHUIGNES	9/2/17		Contd. work on the following:- Erecting NISSEN HUTS for C.R.A. at CHUIGNOLLES. Completed sheeting for last two huts, also lining, with the exception of one bay. Made & rivetted on legs on stoves. Made two ladders & fitted framing for partitions in one hut. DIVISIONAL HEADQUARTERS, CHUIGNOLLES. Contd. work on lining over each vestibule. Floor joists fixed & a third of the flooring laid in the office. 1st D.E. Headqrs. CHUIGNOLLES (Erecting "NISSEN" HUTS) In one of the huts lining was completed, also door hung at either end. Piles for 2nd Hut put into position, framework erected & a start made with the roofing. BATHS at CHUIGNES. Work was contd on these. Benches & forms erected. Covering of roof completed & oil-cloth fitted into windows. Clothes bars made in dressing-room. Weather - Bright & Clear - Thaw.	WD

2353 Wt. W2544/1454 700,000 5/15 D. D. & L. A.D.S.S./Forms/C. 2118.

Instructions regarding War Diaries and Intelligence Summaries are contained in F. S. Regs., Part II. and the Staff Manual respectively. Title pages will be prepared in manuscript.

WAR DIARY
or
~~INTELLIGENCE SUMMARY.~~
(Erase heading not required.)

Army Form C. 2118.

Place	Date	Hour	Summary of Events and Information	Remarks and references to Appendices
Coy less 1 Sectn in billets at CHUIGNOLLES. 1 Section in billets at CHUIGNES	10/2/17.		Erecting NISSEN HUTS for 1st DE in CHUIGNOLLES continued. No 1 hut repaired two windows & fitted two latches. No 2 hut. Roofed: lined inside: fitted doors. A quantity of sandbags filled in preparation for revetting round bottoms of huts. The work was also contd on NISSEN HUTS for CRA in CHUIGNOLLES. The lining of huts completed. A partition was fitted in one of the huts. Made & fitted two doors & fixed one stove complete. Divisional Headquarters, CHUIGNOLLES. Work was continued on these Hrs & the flooring completed in Q Section. A quarter of the flooring laid in G Section. Made six doors for the entrances & partitions. Fitted one Armstrong Hut in site as ordered. Baths at CHUIGNES. Work also contd here. Slating up plant: making canvas screens: putting strips on roof. Brigade Head Qrs. Made shelves for Generals room & fixed oil-cloth into various windows. Supply Dumps: Fixed site of platform & commenced the driving in of piles for same. Weather – Freezing – Cold Wind	WD

2353 Wt. W2544/1454 700,000 5/15 D. D. & L. A.D.S.S./Forms/C. 2118.

Army Form C. 2118.

WAR DIARY
or
~~INTELLIGENCE SUMMARY.~~

(Erase heading not required.)

Instructions regarding War Diaries and Intelligence Summaries are contained in F. S. Regs., Part II. and the Staff Manual respectively. Title pages will be prepared in manuscript.

Place	Date	Hour	Summary of Events and Information	Remarks and references to Appendices
Coy. less one Sec. in billets at CHUIGNOLLES. 1 Section in billets in CHUIGNES	11/2/17		Divisional Head Qrs CHUIGNOLLES. Work was continued & the flooring of G Section completed. The intermediate strips for ceiling lining have all been fixed in both G & Q Sections & 400' of lining put up. Divisional Baths at CHUIGNES. Continued the making & fitting of straps to hold down felt on roof. Laid trench-boards where necessary. Commenced making & fitting shelves in storeroom. Made hoppers for dirty water. Brought up small motor-pump to bath-site. Brigade Head Qrs CHUIGNES. Made two tables & rebuilt fireplace. Fitted up a bed. Carried out repairs to door. ASC DUMP, CHUIGNES. Completed the digging of 21 holes in preparation for driving in piles for platform. NISSEN HUTS for CRA at CHUIGNOLLES. Completed the revetting around bottom of huts. No 1 HUT. Made & hung door & completed lining. Fixed coat hangers in all of the huts. 9 holes dug in preparation for piles for another hut. ADRIAN HUT (Church Army) CHUIGNOLLES. A start made with this hut, when a gable & one truss were bolted together. DE. Head Qrs CHUIGNOLLES. Erecting NISSEN HUTS. Revetted around foundations of all of the huts. Weather - Foggy - Keen Frost.	WD

2353 Wt. W2544/1454 700,000 5/15 D. D. & L. A.D.S.S./Forms/C. 2118.

Instructions regarding War Diaries and Intelligence Summaries are contained in F. S. Regs., Part II. and the Staff Manual respectively. Title pages will be prepared in manuscript.

WAR DIARY
or
~~INTELLIGENCE SUMMARY.~~
(Erase heading not required.)

Army Form C. 2118.

Place	Date	Hour	Summary of Events and Information	Remarks and references to Appendices
Coy. less 1 Sectn in Billets in CHUIGNOLLES 1 Section in Billets in CHUIGNES	12/3/17		Work continued on the erecting of NISSEN HUTS for 1st DE. Head Qrs. Fitted lines in window: Erected framework of partitions & half boarding completed. Continued work on revetting base of huts. Piles fixed in position for another hut & baulks, joists, & flooring laid. For the ARMSTRONG HUT, bearers & flooring laid, erected framework & lined half of hut with "Rubberite". DIVISIONAL HEADQUARTERS, CHUIGNOLLES The lining of ceiling in G & Q Sections was completed. Lining of various rooms continued. In the second hut joists have been laid for a half of the building & 90' of flooring laid. BATHS at CHUIGNES. Made & fitted shelves in store-room. Made stand & erected a 200 gln tank ASC DUMP. Completed pile holes for meat platform & a start made on the Grocery platform BRIGADE HEADQUARTERS, CHUIGNES. Repaired fire-place, made table for Generals room etc. Commenced the digging of holes for piles for NISSEN HUTS CRA. Headqrs CHUIGNOLLES. Contd work of sand-bagging around the huts. Fitted 2 stoves & piping complete. Lined half of HUTS 1 & 4 with canvas. Fixed 15 piles in position for another hut & fitted up framing flooring & two gable ends. ADRIAN HUT (Church Army) Fixed up eight medium trusses & one end truss. Made 10 beds for 1st Brigade Weather – Foggy – Mild	WD

2353 Wt. W2544/1454 700,000 5/15 D. D. & L. A.D.S.S./Forms/C. 2118.

Instructions regarding War Diaries and Intelligence Summaries are contained in F. S. Regs., Part II. and the Staff Manual respectively. Title pages will be prepared in manuscript.

WAR DIARY
or
~~INTELLIGENCE SUMMARY.~~
(Erase heading not required.)

Army Form C. 2118.

Place	Date	Hour	Summary of Events and Information	Remarks and references to Appendices
Coy. less one Section in billets in CHUIGNOLLES One Section billeted in CHUIGNES	13/2/17		BATHS at CHUIGNES. Work continued on these. Closed up entrances with boarding. Commenced painting the buildings. BDE HQrs " . One NISSEN HUT half erected. Lined Generals room with canvas. One table made for office. ASC DUMP CHUIGNES. About half of the piles cut & levelled off for meat platform. NISSEN HUTS for CRA at CHUIGNOLLES. Contd the lining on Huts 2 & 3. No5 was fitted with 39 corrugated sheets, door & lining complete. No 6 Hut. Made 15 holes to receive piles. CHURCH ARMY HUT. Excavated 40' x 9" to an average depth of 4' & erected the gable end of hut & two medium trusses. 1st DE Head Qrs CHUIGNOLLES. Office hut had partition completed. Mess Hut: framework, gables & 2/3 of roof fitted. Erected kicking boards in small stable. Made a ramp into stables. Large Stable. Erected 4 uprights & laid heavy rafters from these to wall [illegible] & purlins. Divisional Head Qrs, CHUIGNOLLES. The lining of C & Q Sections contd. & altogether 500 sq ft has been done. RE DUMP CHUIGNOLLES. Made 4 NOTICE BOARDS for Artillery & 3 for salvage. These boards were painted & lettered. Made 6 large tables for Divisional Head Qrs & four small ones. Weather — Dull & hazy – Dry	WD

2353 Wt. W2544/1454 700,000 5/15 D. D. & L. A.D.S.S./Forms/C. 2118.

Instructions regarding War Diaries and Intelligence Summaries are contained in F. S. Regs., Part II. and the Staff Manual respectively. Title pages will be prepared in manuscript.

WAR DIARY
or
~~INTELLIGENCE SUMMARY~~.

(Erase heading not required.)

Army Form C. 2118.

Place	Date	Hour	Summary of Events and Information	Remarks and references to Appendices
Coy. less 1 Sectn. and billets at CHUIGNOLLES. One Section in billets at CHUIGNES	11/2/17		Continued work on huts for CRA at CHUIGNOLLES. No 3 hut had gable end lined with canvas. No 4 hut, half lined partition with canvas & made & hung a door. Made & fitted 6 bends for stove piping, 2 [illegible] mud scrapers, also a ladder for No 5 hut. In the Officers cookhouse the floor was fitted.	
			BATTN HEADQRS CHUIGNOLLES. "NISSEN" HUT. Fitted 15 poles, framing & flooring, gable ends & six shelves.	
			CHURCH ARMY HUT " Excavated 32' x 9" to an average depth of 6" & erected four trusses.	
			BATHS at CHUIGNES. Fitted a floor in one room. Fitted hopper for dirty water.	
			ASC DUMP " Bread & Grocery platform nearly completed.	
			BDE HEADQRS " Completed hut with exception of a little inside lining.	
			1st DE HEADQRS CHUIGNOLLES. Continued the lining of ARMSTRONG HUT with canvas. Completed Mess hut. Fitted 2 stoves in Officers hut. Completed framework of large stable & half covered with corrugated iron. Erected part of framework & flooring for Officers cook house.	
			Divisional Headqrs CHUIGNOLLES. Continued the lining of ceiling, walls, & gable ends. 700' of lining has been put up in G & Q Sections. Window sills, jambs, doors & latches etc fitted.	
			No 2 hut, complete framing for half Nissen hut has been constructed & 400' of lining put up.	
			ARMSTRONG HUT. The Ruberoid work has been completed & the whole lined.	
			In Camp RE DUMP. CHUIGNOLLES ~~[illegible]~~. Made six sets of table legs and a drawing table etc.	
			Weather. Foggy	WD

2353 Wt. W2544/1454 700,000 5/15 D. D. & L. A.D.S.S./Forms/C. 2118.

Instructions regarding War Diaries and Intelligence Summaries are contained in F. S. Regs., Part II. and the Staff Manual respectively. Title pages will be prepared in manuscript.

WAR DIARY
or
~~INTELLIGENCE SUMMARY.~~

(Erase heading not required.)

Army Form C. 2118.

Place	Date	Hour	Summary of Events and Information	Remarks and references to Appendices
Coy. less one Sectn in billets at CHUIGNOLLES One Section in billets at CHUIGNES	15/2/17		Continued work at 1st Dn Headqrs CHUIGNOLLES. Erecting huts.	
			Continued lining: hanging doors: making latches: fitting stoves. A bedstead to hold sixmen was erected in the small stable. Roof completed on the large stable. Made & put up a throne on this stable.	
			Fitted 28 corrugated sheets on NISSEN HUT for Battn Headrs.	
			DIVISIONAL HEADQRS CHUIGNOLLES. The lining completed of G & Q Sections: stoves fitted & two partitions erected. The ARMSTRONG HUT was finished. A duck-board track laid also three boot scrapers made & fitted. A wind vane was made & set in position on Headqrs office	
			BATHS at CHUIGNES. Contd work of fitting rooms to hold dirty clothes.	
			BDE. HEADQRS Contd. work on NISSEN HUT for BRIGADE HEADQRS.	
			ASC DUMP. Contd. work on the meat & grocery platforms.	
			Two sections marched to forward area & relieved 2 sections of the 26th Field Coy. R.E.	
			Weather. Clear & Bright	WD

2353 Wt. W2544/1454 700,000 5/15 D. D. & L. A.D.S.S./Forms/C. 2118.

Instructions regarding War Diaries and Intelligence Summaries are contained in F. S. Regs., Part II. and the Staff Manual respectively. Title pages will be prepared in manuscript.

WAR DIARY
or
~~INTELLIGENCE~~ SUMMARY.
(*Erase heading not required.*)

Army Form C. 2118.

Place	Date	Hour	Summary of Events and Information	Remarks and references to Appendices
Coy less 1 Sch in Billets in CHUIGNOLLES 1 Section in Billets in CHUIGNES	16/2/17		Divisional Head Qrs CHUIGNOLLES. Work contd. here. Fitted 2 doors & erected tables in G & Q offices, & contd work on partitions in No. 2 hut, two rooms in which were almost completed. 1st DE Headqrs CHUIGNOLLES. Completed ARMSTRONG HUT. NISSEN HUT for Mess, boarded up gable over sleeping hut & hung partition door. COOKHOUSE. Made steps & fitted same, also put oiled linen into windows. SMALL STABLE. Strapped joints of head posts with iron. The Coy relieved the 26th Field Coy RE in the forward area at 12 noon. All work in Reserve Area handed over to 36th as complete. Work was continued in Dugouts at (N.11.B.4.6) & (N.11.C.0.5) & also in tunnel at (N.10.D.3.18). Weather Dull & Foggy	WD

2353 Wt. W2544/1454 700,000 5/15 D. D. & L. A.D.S.S./Forms/C. 2118.

Army Form C. 2118.

Instructions regarding War Diaries and Intelligence Summaries are contained in F. S. Regs., Part II. and the Staff Manual respectively. Title pages will be prepared in manuscript.

WAR DIARY
or
~~INTELLIGENCE SUMMARY.~~
(Erase heading not required.)

Place	Date	Hour	Summary of Events and Information	Remarks and references to Appendices
Coy. in forward area. 2 Sections in Dugouts behind SUPPORT LINE 2 Sections in Dugouts at BECQUINCOURT. Transport Lines at FONTAINE-LES-CAPPY.	17/2/17		Contd. work on Dugouts. At (N.11.C.0.5.) Excavated 5' x 4' x 3' & fitted one frame " (N.11.B.4.6.) Excavated 6' x 3'-6" x 5'-6" in Left entrance " 4' x 4' x 5'-6" " Right Tunnel at (N10.D.3.1½) One frame fitted & excavated 5' x 4' x 3' beyond frame. WORK AT TRANSPORT LINES, FONTAINE-LES-CAPPY. 75^x of framework for stables erected. 4 bays roofed with corrugated sheets. Ground cleared for sleeping hut 22' x 10' & framework erected & partially wired with netting WORK AT COY. HEADQRS, BECQUINCOURT RE DUMP. Carpenter's shop arranged in a lean-to in DUMP & a squad commenced making Notice-Boards. The various billets were improved. Cleaned up ground & commenced laying a duck-walk in camp. A ruined gable overhanging billets was pulled down. Weather - Foggy - Dry.	WD

2353 Wt. W2544/1454 700,000 5/15 D. D. & L. A.D.S.S./Forms/C. 2118.

Instructions regarding War Diaries and Intelligence Summaries are contained in F. S. Regs., Part II. and the Staff Manual respectively. Title pages will be prepared in manuscript.

WAR DIARY
or
~~INTELLIGENCE SUMMARY.~~
(Erase heading not required.)

Army Form C. 2118.

Place	Date	Hour	Summary of Events and Information	Remarks and references to Appendices
2 Sections in Dugouts behind Support line. 2 Sections at BECQUINCOURT & Head Qrs. TRANSPORT LINES at FONTAINE-LES-CAPPY	18/2/17		Contd. work on Dugouts:-	
			Tunnel (N10.D.3.1½) Excavated 9'×6'×3½'. Fitted one frame & filled 170 sandbags & emptied 150.	
			Work was delayed on account of a fall which took place at mouth of tunnel.	
			No1 Dugout (N11.C.0.5)	
			Left entrance excavated 8'×6'×2. Fitted 1 frame & filled & emptied 125 sandbags.	
			Right " " 7'×4'×1' " " " " " 170 "	
			No 2 Dugout (N11.B.4.6).	
			Left entrance excavated & 1 frame fitted & filled & emptied about 60 sandbags.	
			Right " " 1 " " " " " " " 70 "	
			Thru steps were fitted into each shaft.	
			WORK IN CAMP, RE DUMP, BECQUINCOURT.	
			34 Notice Boards were made & painted & 21 of these printed.	
			WORK ON BECQUINCOURT, HERBECOURT ROAD.	
			Water was drained from off road surface & worst holes filled with what brick etc could be got	
			WORK at TRANSPORT LINES of Coy. FONTAINE-LES-CAPPY. Contd work on sleeping hut, which was roofed floored & had a stove fitted. Contd works on stables. Erected post-props for hanging harness etc.	
			Weather — Foggy — Mild	WD

2353 Wt. W2544/1454 700,000 5/15 D. D. & L. A.D.S.S./Forms/C. 2118.

Instructions regarding War Diaries and Intelligence Summaries are contained in F. S. Regs., Part II. and the Staff Manual respectively. Title pages will be prepared in manuscript.

WAR DIARY
or
~~INTELLIGENCE~~ SUMMARY.

(Erase heading not required.)

Army Form C. 2118.

Place	Date	Hour	Summary of Events and Information	Remarks and references to Appendices
2 Sections in Dugouts behind Support Line. 2 Sections in dugouts at BECQUINCOURT TRANSPORT LINES at FONTAINE-LES CAPPY	19/2/17		Work continued on forward Dugouts	
			(N.10.D.3.1½) Tunnel. Excavated for & fitted 1 set of timber & sheeting. Revetted up part of roof.	
			(N.11.C.9.5) No 1 Dugout. The right entrance excavated & fitted 2 sets of timber & a set of sheeting	
			(N.11.B.4.6) No 2 " The left entrance excavated & fitted a temporary set of timber.	
			130 sandbags filled & emptied.	
			The right entrance a large stone was removed & the roof revetted up.	
			WORK IN CAMP RE DUMP, BECQUINCOURT. 20 Notice Boards were painted for 5th Bde	
			Work contd on the BECQUINCOURT HERBECOURT ROAD. Several small drains were cut & water run off the most flooded part of road near the DUMP at BECQUINCOURT.	
			Mud was cleared out of the worst holes & these filled with brick etc.	
			WORK at Transport Lines of Coy near FONTAINE-LES-CAPPY.	
			Stable roof extended on one side to a length of 80'. This was covered with sheeting. Transport Lines improved & all debris cleared away.	
			A platform was erected at C.Q.M.S. store for the cutting up of beef.	
			Weather - Foggy - Dry	WD

2353 Wt. W2544/1454 700,000 5/15 D. D. & L. A.D.S.S./Forms/C. 2118.

Instructions regarding War Diaries and Intelligence Summaries are contained in F. S. Regs., Part II. and the Staff Manual respectively. Title pages will be prepared in manuscript.

WAR DIARY
or
~~INTELLIGENCE SUMMARY.~~
(Erase heading not required.)

Army Form C. 2118.

Place	Date	Hour	Summary of Events and Information	Remarks and references to Appendices
2 Sections in Dugouts behind support line. 2 Sections in dugouts at BECQUINCOURT. TRANSPORT LINES AT FONTAINE-LES CAPPY.	20/2/17		Work contd on forward Dugouts. Tunnel (N10.D.3.1½) Excavated & fitted 1 set of timber & covered 1½ sets with sheeting. 380 sandbags were filled & emptied. No 1 Dugout (N.11.C.0.5) Right-hand entrance excavated & one set of timber & sheeting fitted. 340 sandbags filled & emptied. Left entrance excavated & 2 sets of timber fitted & one of them covered with sheeting. 320 sandbags were filled & emptied. No 2 Dugout (N11.B4.6) Right Entrance excavated & one set of timber & sheeting fitted. Left [illegible] erected. A step was also [illegible] WORK ON BECQUINCOURT, HERBECOURT ROAD. Near DUMP at forest place water was drained off surface into a sump-pit which was dug. Mud was cleared off & part of road received a dressing of brick. Work at Coys Transport Lines, FONTAINE-LES-CAPPY. Harness-room partly erected. A start made with drain-cutting at stables & stagnant water run away into an old trench. Weather - Mild - Foggy.	WD

Instructions regarding War Diaries and Intelligence Summaries are contained in F. S. Regs., Part II. and the Staff Manual respectively. Title pages will be prepared in manuscript.

WAR DIARY
or
~~INTELLIGENCE SUMMARY.~~

(*Erase heading not required.*)

Army Form C. 2118.

Place	Date	Hour	Summary of Events and Information	Remarks and references to Appendices
2 Sections in Dugouts behind Supp Line. 2 Sections in Dugouts near BECQUINCOURT RE DUMP Transport Lines near FONTAINE LES-CAPPY	21/2/17		Contd work on Dugouts. (N.10.D.3.1½) Tunnel. Excavated for & erected one set of timber & covered with sheeting Filled & emptied 350 sandbags. (N.11.C.0.5) Not Dugout. The Left entrance erected 1 set & covered with sheeting Right " " filled & emptied 100 sandbags. (N.11.B.4.5) Not " Right entrance excavated & one set of timber erected Left " " " filled & emptied 200 sandbags. WORK ON BECQUINCOURT, HERBECOURT ROAD. Near the former place drains were cut at either side of road. At one point a box drain & conductor was made & the water led into an old cellar. Holes filled with brick etc. WORK at Transport Lines of Coy FONTAINE-LES-CAPPY. Work continued on drainage of stables. One of the main drains was half lined with brick & a bridge constructed for entrance to stables. A large sump-pit was dug: erected a new incinerator. One squad working with Land Scouts & engaged on the construction of O.P's. Weather - Wet - Foggy	WD

2353 Wt. W2544/1454 700,000 5/15 D. D. & L. A.D.S.S./Forms/C. 2118.

Instructions regarding War Diaries and Intelligence Summaries are contained in F. S. Regs., Part II. and the Staff Manual respectively. Title pages will be prepared in manuscript.

WAR DIARY
or
~~INTELLIGENCE~~ SUMMARY.
(Erase heading not required.)

Army Form C. 2118.

Place	Date	Hour	Summary of Events and Information	Remarks and references to Appendices
2 Sections on dugouts behind Supp line. 2 Sections on dugouts near BECQUINCOURT TRANSPORT LINES at FONTAINE LES-CAPPY	22/2/17.		Contd. work on forward Dugouts. (N.10.D.3.1½) Tunnel Excavated for & erected 1 set of timber & filled & emplaced 150 sandbags. (N.11.C.0.5.) No1 Dugout Right entrance excavated & a set of timber & sheeting fitted. Left " fitted. (N.11.B.4.6.) No 2 Dugout Left entrance excavated & a set of timber & sheeting fitted. Right " " " " " WORK ON BECQUINCOURT, HERBECOURT ROAD, near former place All existing drains were cleaned & deepened. A sump pit was dug Holes were filled with brick etc. WORK IN CAMP RE. DUMP, BECQUINCOURT. Work contd. on painting & printing of Notice Boards: making boxes for LEWIS GUN drums WORK AT TRANSPORT LINES of Coy. FONTAINE-LES-CAPPY. Continued work on the drainage of stables etc. & the clearing away of refuse from the lines. One squad working with Lovat Scouts on Observation Posts. Weather – Clear & Bright	WD

2353 Wt. W2544/1454 700,000 5/15 D. D. & L. A.D.S.S./Forms/C. 2118.

Instructions regarding War Diaries and Intelligence Summaries are contained in F. S. Regs., Part II. and the Staff Manual respectively. Title pages will be prepared in manuscript.

WAR DIARY
or
~~INTELLIGENCE SUMMARY.~~
(Erase heading not required.)

Army Form C. 2118.

Place	Date	Hour	Summary of Events and Information	Remarks and references to Appendices
2 Sections in dugouts behind Supp Line. 2 Sections in Dugouts near BECQUINCOURT RE DUMP TRANSPORT LINES near FONTAINE-LES-CAPPY	23/1/17		Work was continued on the Dugouts etc Tunnel at (N.10.D.3.1½). Excavated for & fitted one set of timber & covered this & previous set with sheeting. Steps fitted up to 4th set from face. Total Excavations Inclined shaft 100% Vertical 20% (N.1.C.0.5) No 1 Dugout. Right entrance excavated & 1 set of timber fitted Left Total % of excavations Right shaft 75.2% Left shaft 64.7%. (N.11.B.4.6) No 2 Dugout. In each of these entrances a set of timber was fitted. Total % of excavations in shaft = Left 60% & right 52% ROAD REPAIRING. BECQUINCOURT - HERBECOURT ROAD. Starting at control post at ASSEVILLERS ROAD, drains were cut on the North side at intervals: 50ʸ of surface cleared of mud: sump pits cleaned & deepened. New RE DUMP at BECQUINCOURT 3 wagon loads of brick & stone were filled into holes on road. 36ʸ of fascine road laid near MEUDON QUARRY (N.4.B.4.2) One Squad working at Bde Head Qrs carrying out repairs to dugouts. " " attached to Lovat Scouts & working on O.P's Two Sections & Drivers bathed at CHUIGNES & also had the anti-frost-bite foot treatment Weather - Clear & Bright	WD

2353 Wt. W2544/1454 700,000 5/15 D. D. & L. A.D.S.S./Forms/C. 2118.

Army Form C. 2118.

WAR DIARY
or
~~INTELLIGENCE SUMMARY.~~
(*Erase heading not required.*)

Instructions regarding War Diaries and Intelligence Summaries are contained in F. S. Regs., Part II. and the Staff Manual respectively. Title pages will be prepared in manuscript.

Place	Date	Hour	Summary of Events and Information	Remarks and references to Appendices
2 Sections on Dugouts. 2 Sections in Dugout at BECQUINCOURT & Transport Lines at FONTAINE LES CAPPY.	24/2/17		Work was continued on Dugouts.	
			(N.12 D 3.1½) Tunnel. Steps made & fitted over distance of 11'.	
			Total of excavations in shafts. Inclined 100% Vertical 20%	
			(N.11 C 0.5) Hd Qrs Dugout. Left Ent. excavated & fitted first lining frame. 71% of this shaft excavated.	
			Right " " " " " " 80% " "	
			(N.11 B 4.6) Hd Qrs Dugout. Excavated for & fitted 1 set of timber & covered two sets with sheeting in the left entrance. Right entrance excavated & fitted one set of timber. 71% of excavation done.	
			WORK AT LEFT BDE HEADQRS. Cleaned out trench & revetted a stretch of 15 yds.	
			Another 21 yds was revetted with stout wire-netting	
			WORK ON BECQUINCOURT, HERBECOURT ROAD. Near DUMP at former place the cleaning & deepening of two sump-pits was carried out.	
			About 2 wagon loads of brick was used in filling up holes.	
			Road near MEUDON QUARRY. (N4B42) × Preparatory to laying fascines a few holes filled up on road.	
			55 yds of fascines laid & firmly picketed down.	
			Coy Transport Lines. FONTAINE-LES-CAPPY. Completed the addition to stables.	
			1 NCO & 3 OR attached to Locat. Scouts & engaged on the making of O.Posts.	
			Weather – Wet & foggy	WD

Instructions regarding War Diaries and Intelligence Summaries are contained in F. S. Regs., Part II. and the Staff Manual respectively. Title pages will be prepared in manuscript.

WAR DIARY
or
~~INTELLIGENCE SUMMARY.~~
(Erase heading not required.)

Army Form C. 2118.

Place	Date	Hour	Summary of Events and Information	Remarks and references to Appendices
2 Sections billeted in Dugouts behind Support line. 2 Sections in Dugouts near R.E. DUMP BECQUINCOURT. TRANSPORT LINES at FONTAINE-LES-CAPPY.	25/2/17		Contd work on forward Dugouts etc. (N.10.D.3.1½) Tunnel. Excavated & fitted one set of timbers. About 150 sandbags filled & emptied. (N.11.C.0.5) No 1 Dugout. Right entrance excavated & fitted one set of timber. Total % of shaft excavated 84% Left 76% (N.11.B.4.6.) No 2 Dugout. Excavated & erected one set of timbers each entrance Total % excavated in Right Entrance 76% Left 66% WORK ON BECQUINCOURT, HERBECOURT ROAD. Near the DUMP at former place 300x of roadway was scraped clear of mud, road edges squared off & spoil thrown well clear. Holes filled with brickbats. Drains & sump-pits dug where necessary. (A working party of 6 Officers & 200 other ranks engaged on this work 2nd Roy. Sussex). On this road during night working N.E. towards HERBECOURT, 28 wagon loads of brick were loaded from ruined walls & dumped at intervals on roadsides. WORK AT LEFT BRIGADE HEADQRS. Officers Mess. Removed heavy runners & uprights supporting roof, & substituted two 6"x3" R.S. joists supported by 12"x8" timber sets at wall face. 1 NCO & 3 Sappers attached to Local Scouts & engaged on the constructing of O.Posts. Weather — Foggy	WD

2353 Wt. W2544/1454 700,000 5/15 D. D. & L. A.D.S.S./Forms/C. 2118.

Instructions regarding War Diaries and Intelligence Summaries are contained in F. S. Regs., Part II. and the Staff Manual respectively. Title pages will be prepared in manuscript.

WAR DIARY
or
~~INTELLIGENCE SUMMARY.~~

(Erase heading not required.)

Army Form C. 2118.

Place	Date	Hour	Summary of Events and Information	Remarks and references to Appendices
2 Sections in Dugouts behind Supp. Line 2 Sections in Dugouts near RE DUMP BECQUINCOURT TRANSPORT LINES at FONTAINE LES-CAPPY	30/2/17		Work was continued on Dugouts etc. (N11C0.5) No 1 Dugout. Left entrance excavated & fitted one set of timber. 85% of shaft excavated Right " " " " " 90% " " " (N11B4.6) No 2 Dugout. Left entrance excavated & one set of timber & sheeting fitted. 73% of the shaft excavated Right " " & about 200 sandbags filled & emptied. 80% of right entrance excavated. LEFT BRIGADE HEADQRS. Cut away earth around inside wall face of dugout to behind uprights supporting roof. Revetting put up on these faces & framing erected ready to receive T&G boarding. Revetted 5x of trench which had fallen in. WORK ON BECQUINCOURT, HERBECOURT ROAD (M6B2.0) Scraped mud off road for a distance of 50x & filled up holes with broken bricks. At (M6C2.0) built railing at side of road, 9x long, to prevent wagons going over bank into tunnel. Fitted 5' uprights in tunnel. Working on same road during night from RE DUMP, BECQUINCOURT to BDE HEADQRS. 22 wagon loads of brick were gathered & dumped at intervals between the two above mentioned points. 1 NCO & 3 sappers attached to Local [illegible] & engaged on the construction of Obsn. Posts Weather. — Bright & clear.	WD

2353 Wt. W2544/1454 700,000 5/15 D. D. & L. A.D.S.S./Forms/C. 2118.

Instructions regarding War Diaries and Intelligence Summaries are contained in F. S. Regs., Part II. and the Staff Manual respectively. Title pages will be prepared in manuscript.

WAR DIARY
or
~~INTELLIGENCE SUMMARY.~~
(Erase heading not required.)

Army Form C. 2118.

Place	Date	Hour	Summary of Events and Information	Remarks and references to Appendices
2 Sections in Dugouts behind Supp Line 2 Sections in Dugouts near DUMP at BECQUINCOURT TRANSPORT LINES at FONTAINE LES-CAPPY	27/2/17		Work was contd on Dugouts etc. (N11.C.9.5) No1 Dugout. Left shaft excavated & 1 set of timber erected. 87% of this shaft excavated. Right shaft excavated & 2 sets of timber & one of sheeting erected. 91% of this shaft has been excavated. (N11.B.4.6) No 2 Dugout Left Excavated & ready for erecting one set of timber. 75% of this shaft excavated. Right shaft " " erected 2 sets of timber 70% WORK AT LEFT BDE HEADQRS. Erected T & G boarding on walls of Officers mess & commenced the building of a brick fireplace. Revetted trench with sandbags & boarding for 15ft adjacent to G.O.C.'s office. WORK ON BECQUINCOURT, HERBECOURT ROAD. Made & fitted 12 uprights & sole-pieces, also two runners under top-sills of shaft. - Revetted 3 sq yds of roadside - all at tunnel under road at (M6 B ½ .0). Working on same road during night towards LEFT BDE HEADQRS. 80 loads of metal were dumped as required at roadside. WORK IN CAMP RE DUMP, BECQUINCOURT. Improving dugouts where men are billeted, these having fallen in, in parts. Made 6 Lewis Gun ammunition boxes. Made a ladder for entrance into trench at 1st BDE HEADQRS. 1 NCO & 3 sappers making O.Posts with Local Scouts. 1 NCO & 2 sappers working at stables for 2nd WELSH Weather Clear & Bright	WD

2353 Wt. W2544/1454 700,000 5/15 D. D. & L. A.D.S.S./Forms/C. 2118.

Instructions regarding War Diaries and Intelligence Summaries are contained in F. S. Regs., Part II. and the Staff Manual respectively. Title pages will be prepared in manuscript.

WAR DIARY

or

~~INTELLIGENCE SUMMARY.~~

(Erase heading not required.)

Army Form C. 2118.

Place	Date	Hour	Summary of Events and Information	Remarks and references to Appendices
2 Sections in Dugouts behind Supp. Line 2 Sections in Dugouts near RE DUMP BECQUINCOURT Transport lines near FONTAINE LES-CAPPY	28/2/17		Work was continued on the Dugouts etc. (N11C0.5) No1 Dugout. Left shaft excavated & erected 1 set of timber & covered two sets with sheeting. A total of 90% has been excavated in this shaft. Right shaft excavated & 1 set of timber fitted & 2 sets covered with sheeting (N11B4.6) No2 Dugout. Left entrance excavated & 150 sandbags filled & emptied. 76% of the shaft excavated Right " " " one set of timber erected 8% " LEFT BDE HEADQRS. Completed fireplace & also lining of dugout walls with T&G boarding. Revetted part of trench adjoining BRIGADE MAJOR'S OFFICE. WORK ON BECQUINCOURT – HERBECOURT RD. Mud cleared off road surface for 430y between (M6B2.0 & M6B5.7). 120y of this stretch had all holes etc filled with brick. 22 loads of brick were spread 575y of drain dug to an average depth of 2'. A sump-pit also dug An infantry working party of 6 Off & 190 OR were working on road WORK IN CAMP, RE DUMP, BECQUINCOURT. Made 4 Lewis gun ammunition boxes. Improved dugouts generally, where men are billeted. 1 NCO & 3 sappers attached to Lovat Scouts & engaged on the construction of Obsn. Posts 1 " & 2 " working at stables for 1st Div Train Weather – Bright – Mild	W. Downs. Major. R.E. O.C. 409th (Lowland) Fld Coy R.E. WD

2353 Wt. W2544/1454 700,000 5/15 D. D. & L. A.D.S.S./Forms/C. 2118.

WAR DIARY.

409th. Lowland Field Coy., R.E.

1st.DIVISION.

MARCH.1917.

Vol 27

CONFIDENTIAL

WAR DIARY

OF

409th LOWLAND FIELD Coy RE

FROM 1st MARCH 1917 to 31st MARCH 1917

VOLUME XXVII.

Army Form C. 2118.

WAR DIARY
or
~~INTELLIGENCE SUMMARY.~~
(Erase heading not required.)

Instructions regarding War Diaries and Intelligence Summaries are contained in F. S. Regs., Part II. and the Staff Manual respectively. Title pages will be prepared in manuscript.

Place	Date	Hour	Summary of Events and Information	Remarks and references to Appendices
2 Sections billeted behind Suff. Lines at N.16.A.7.3. 2 Sections billeted near RE DUMP BECQUINCOURT Transport-Lines near FONTAINE-LES-CAPPY	1/3/17.		Work was continued on the Dugouts in the forward area. (N.11.C.0.5.) No 1. Left entrance. Excavated for & erected 1 set of timber & covered 2 sets with sheeting. " Right " " " " " " " " " " " " " " . Total of excavated in left shaft is 90% & in right 92%. (N.11.B.1.6.) No 2. The digging has become very hard in both shafts of this dugout. Left shaft. Excavated & filled 150 sandbags which were emptied well away from working site. Right " " : erected 1 set of timber & filled & emptied about 200 sandbags. Total of excavations of shafts = Right 81% & Left 76%. WORK AT LEFT BDE HEADQRS. Completed the brick fire-place. Finished lining of dugout walls with T & G boarding. Continued the revetting of trench adjoining Brigade Major's Office. WORK ON BECQUINCOURT, HERBECOURT ROAD. Mud cleared off road surface for 430x between M.6.B.2.0. & M.6.B.5.7. 120x of this stretch had all holes filled with brick etc. On South-side of road a drain was dug 325x long & 2' deep & on North side 250x long by 1'-9" deep. A sump-pit was also dug. (Infantry working-party of 6 Off & 190 O.R. Lay. N. Lancs) WORK IN CAMP, BECQUINCOURT. 4 Lewis-gun ammunition boxes made. Half-Section working during night on BECQUINCOURT RD unloaded 22 wagon loads of brick at intervals by roadside. 1 NCO & 3 sappers attached to Divnl Scouts & engaged on the construction of Observation Posts. 1 NCO & 2 " working on stable-repairs for 1st DIVIS. TRAIN. Weather - Clear & Bright	WD

2353 Wt. W2544/1454 700,000 5/15 D. D. & L. A.D.S.S./Forms/C. 2118.

Instructions regarding War Diaries and Intelligence Summaries are contained in F. S. Regs., Part II. and the Staff Manual respectively. Title pages will be prepared in manuscript.

WAR DIARY
or
~~INTELLIGENCE SUMMARY.~~
(Erase heading not required.)

Army Form C. 2118.

Place	Date	Hour	Summary of Events and Information	Remarks and references to Appendices
2 Sections billeted in dugouts behind Supp Line at N.16.A.7.3. 2 Sections in Dugouts near RE DUMP BECQUINCOURT Transport Lines near FONTAINE-LES-CAPPY	2/3/17		Work continued on Dugouts in forward area.	
			(N.11.C.0.5) No 1 Dugout. Left shaft excavated & 1 set of timber & sheeting fitted. 95% of shaft excavated. Right " " " " " fitted 95% " "	
			(N.11.B.4.6) No 2 Dugout. Excavated 35 cubic ft & filled & carried 100 sandbags. 79% of the shaft (left) excavated. " 33 " " " " " 120 " 83% " " (right) "	
			(N.10.D.3.1½) Tunnel. Excavated, & erected one set of timbers & about 150 sandbags filled. Fitted one step	
			WORK AT LEFT BRIGADE HEADQRS. Fitted a door & a window. Fitted up a handrail at ladder entrance to Main Headqrs trench. Continued sand-bag revetting of trench.	
			WORK ON BECQUINCOURT – HERBECOURT RD. At (M.6.B.1½.2) a stretch of 100x cleared of mud & holes filled up. 5 small run-channels were cut.	
			ROAD NEAR MEUDON QUARRY. (N.9.D.). Fifty-yards of fascines laid & firmly picketed down.	
			GAS CHAMBER (NEAR BECQUINCOURT). Fitted corrugated sheeting over trench for roof. Fixed up wood framework for door at either end & arranged blanket for screen. Wired chamber all round.	
			1 NCO & 4 sappers attached to Local Scouts & engaged on the erection of Observation Post.	
			1 " " 2 sappers continued work on repairing stables for 1st DIV. TRAIN.	
			Weather Mild - Foggy	WD

2353 Wt. W2544/1454 700,000 5/15 D. D. & L. A.D.S.S./Forms/C. 2118.

Instructions regarding War Diaries and Intelligence Summaries are contained in F. S. Regs., Part II. and the Staff Manual respectively. Title pages will be prepared in manuscript.

WAR DIARY
or
INTELLIGENCE SUMMARY.
(Erase heading not required.)

Army Form C. 2118.

Place	Date	Hour	Summary of Events and Information	Remarks and references to Appendices
2 Sections billeted behind Supp Line at N16A7.3 2 Sections billeted near RE DUMP, BECQUINCOURT TRANSPORT LINES near FONTAINE-LES-CAPPY.	3/3/17		Work was continued on Dugouts in the forward area. (N.11.C.0.5) No1 Dugout. Continued the excavating of chambers & erected one frame at left entrance. About 250 sandbags filled & emptied. Chamber at right entrance excavated & 1 set of frames put in. 200 sandbags filled & emptied. (N.11.B.1.6) No 2 Dugouts. Continued the excavating of both shafts & removed six huge boulders & filled & emptied about 300 sandbags. No of excavated in each of these shafts is 9'5". (N.10.D.3.1½) Tunnel. Excavated for & erected 1 set of timber & filled & emptied 100 sandbags. WORK ON BECQUINCOURT, HERBECOURT ROAD. At (M6B3.2½) commenced clearing & deepening drain, which was done on a length of 100x. About 4 loads of brick were filled into holes. Roadsides were cut away & all spoil thrown well back. Half a dozen small drains were cut from road-edge to main drain. On same road during night near MEUDON QUARRY (N.9.D.) 30x of fascines were laid & firmly picketed down. Two large holes in roadway were filled up. WORK NEAR CAMP BECQUINCOURT: Improving dugouts generally, where men are billeted, these being now fairly habitable. 1 NCO & 3 sappers attached to Legal Scouts & engaged on the construction of Observation Posts. 1 " 2 " working on stable repairs for 1st DIV TRAIN. Weather Bright – Mild.	WD

2353 Wt. W2544/1454 700,000 5/15 D. D. & L. A.D.S.S./Forms/C. 2118.

Instructions regarding War Diaries and Intelligence Summaries are contained in F. S. Regs., Part II. and the Staff Manual respectively. Title pages will be prepared in manuscript.

WAR DIARY
or
~~INTELLIGENCE~~ SUMMARY.
(*Erase heading not required.*)

Army Form C. 2118.

Place	Date	Hour	Summary of Events and Information	Remarks and references to Appendices
2 Sectns billeted behind Supp Lines at N.16.A7.3. 2 Sections billeted near RE DUMP BECQUINCOURT. TRANSPORT LINES near FONTAINE LES-CAPPY	4/3/17		Work was continued on the Dugouts.	
			(N.10.D.3 1½) Excavated & erected 3 sets of timbers & filled & emptied 300 sandbags. 40% of tunnel excavated	
			(N.11.C.0.5) No1 Dugout. 400 sandbags filled & emptied between both ends of chamber. 30% of chamber excavated	
			(N.11.B.4.6) No2 Dugout. Excavated, & erected 1 set of frames in chamber at left & right entrances. 200 sandbags filled & emptied & many large boulders removed.	
			ROAD FROM FLAUCOURT TO MEUDON QUARRY. From (N.11.B.4.3) for a length of 50x all mud was cleared from surface & all holes filled up. Small drains cut from roadside to main drain.	
			During night 40x of fascine road was laid & firmly picketed down.	
			ROAD FROM BECQUINCOURT TO HERBECOURT. (M6B · to N1A). Cleared mud off surface & filled up holes for 200x Cut away road edges & threw all spoil well back. 460x of drain was cut, 2' deep, x 2' wide.	
			An infantry working party of 6 off & 144 OR engaged on this work.	
			1 NCO + 3 sappers attached to Lovat Scouts & engaged on the construction of Observation Post.	
			1 " - 2 " on stable repairs for 1st DIV TRAIN	
			Weather - Foggy - Mild	WD

2353 Wt. W2544/1454 700,000 5/15 D. D. & L. A.D.S.S./Forms/C. 2118.

Army Form C. 2118.

WAR DIARY
or
INTELLIGENCE SUMMARY.
(*Erase heading not required.*)

Instructions regarding War Diaries and Intelligence Summaries are contained in F. S. Regs., Part II. and the Staff Manual respectively. Title pages will be prepared in manuscript.

Place	Date	Hour	Summary of Events and Information	Remarks and references to Appendices
2 Sections billeted behind Supp. Line at N16A73 2 Sections at RE DUMP BECQUINCOURT Transport Lines near FONTAINE-LES-CAPPY.	5/3/17		Continued work on dugouts in the forward area. Tunnell at (N10.D3.1½) Excavated, & erected two sets of timber & filled & emptied 200 sandbags. (N11.C.0.5) No1 Dugout. In left side of chambers filled & emptied 250 sandbags & cleaned all the staircase " right " " " excavated & erected a temporary set of timber & 100 sandbags filled & emptied. Staircase cleaned on this side also. 32' of the chambers has been excavated (N11.B4.6) No 2 Dugout. In right shaft all steps were fitted & the staircase cleaned up. In left shaft filled 50 sandbags & placed runners for steps. WORK ON BECQUINCOURT, HERBECOURT ROAD (N1.A1.5 to N3.D1.1). Dug a drain 600x long x 2' deep x 2' wide Small drains cut at intervals of 15x leading from road into main drain. A working party of 3 Off & 136 OR (KRR") on this work 1 NCO & 3 Sappers attached to Lovat Scouts & engaged on the construction of Observation Post 1 " 2 " working on stable repairs for 1st DIV TRAIN Two Sections left for back billets at CHUIGNOLLES. Two " on forward dugouts were relieved by two sections of 23rd FIELD COY RE Weather - Foggy	WR

2353 Wt. W2544/1454 700,000 5/15 D. D. & L. A.D.S.S./Forms/C. 2118.

Army Form C. 2118.

Instructions regarding War Diaries and Intelligence Summaries are contained in F. S. Regs., Part II. and the Staff Manual respectively. Title pages will be prepared in manuscript.

WAR DIARY
or
~~INTELLIGENCE SUMMARY.~~
(Erase heading not required.)

Place	Date	Hour	Summary of Events and Information	Remarks and references to Appendices
2 Sections at BECQUINCOURT 2 Sections at CHUIGNOLLES Transport Lines at FONTAINE-LES-CAPPY	6/3/17		The remainder of Coy at BECQUINCOURT packed up & moved off at 11 AM. & marched to CHUIGNOLLES — less one Section which went into billets at CHUIGNES. WORK AT CHUIGNES. Made fascine road at CHUIGNES from ramp to watering trough, 61x in all. The fascines were firmly picketed down. WORK AT CHUIGNOLLES. Commenced work on workshop in RE DUMP. Levelling floor & digging drain. Started making Observation Boxes. Two Sections bathed at CHUIGNOLLES during day. Weather — Hazy – Breezy	WD

Instructions regarding War Diaries and Intelligence Summaries are contained in F. S. Regs., Part II. and the Staff Manual respectively. Title pages will be prepared in manuscript.

WAR DIARY
or
~~INTELLIGENCE~~ SUMMARY.
(Erase heading not required.)

Army Form C. 2118.

Place	Date	Hour	Summary of Events and Information	Remarks and references to Appendices
Whole Coy in Billets at CHUIGNOLLES RE. DUMP – less one Section billeted at CHUIGNES	7/3/17		WORK AT CHUIGNOLLES. Erected a fence 20x long at (R12B.37). Laid floor in Officers Hut (Black Watch) 14' x 13'. In RE DUMP work was continued on the Sawmill. Put 800' of purlins up & marked off centres for saw bench. Engine valves repaired One squad engaged on making fascines. Completed the making of two loophole boxes. Loading bricks & unloading same on road at stables Fitted 20 beds in one of the billets in camp. The Arms, Equipment, & Clothing of the whole Coy were inspected. Continued the fitting of the new Box Respirators. Half of Company bathed at CHUIGNOLLES during day Weather Clear & Bright. – Cold Winds	WD

2353 Wt. W2544/1454 700,000 5/15 D. D. & L. A.D.S.S./Forms/C. 2118.

Instructions regarding War Diaries and Intelligence Summaries are contained in F. S. Regs., Part II. and the Staff Manual respectively. Title pages will be prepared in manuscript.

WAR DIARY
or
~~INTELLIGENCE~~ SUMMARY.

(*Erase heading not required.*)

Army Form C. 2118.

Place	Date	Hour	Summary of Events and Information	Remarks and references to Appendices
Coy. billeted at RE DUMP CHUIGNOLLES - less 1 Section billeted at CHUIGNES	8/3/17		WORK AT CHUIGNES. Cleared & levelled off site for Church Army huts, connected up 11 trusses. Sorted out timber in DUMP at CHUIGNOLLES for the erection of Store & hut at CHUIGNES Rly. Stn. for ROD Continued the laying of raised footway in Camp at CHUIGNES; 40x completed except for ribands & 18x of piles & road-bearers laid. WORK AT CHUIGNOLLES. At C.R.A.'s Head Qrs one stove was fitted complete. Two doors were repaired & a chair made. Commenced making platform for engine at Water-tank near RE DUMP. WORK IN CAMP. 200 sq yds. of tarred felt roofing put on roof of sawmill. The wheels of the engine were wedged & secured. 2 loophole boxes made. 16 sq yds broken brick 6" deep laid on road at stables. Fitted 21 beds in one of the huts & also repaired the roof. Fitted up a guard-room. Weather - Clear & Bright	WD

2353 Wt. W2544/1454 700,000 5/15 D. D. & L. A.D.S.S./Forms/C. 2118.

Army Form C. 2118.

Instructions regarding War Diaries and Intelligence Summaries are contained in F. S. Regs., Part II. and the Staff Manual respectively. Title pages will be prepared in manuscript.

WAR DIARY
or
~~INTELLIGENCE SUMMARY~~.

(Erase heading not required.)

Place	Date	Hour	Summary of Events and Information	Remarks and references to Appendices
Coy. billeted at RE DUMP CHUIGNOLLES – less 1 Secn. billeted at CHUIGNES	9/3/17		The following work was carried out at CHUIGNES.	
			Church Army Hut. Erected one gable end & 5 trusses & fitted up another gable ready for erecting.	
			Store & Office for RTO at Rly. Stn. Cleared & laid off site. Erected both ends & inside of hut 40' x 15'.	
			A working party of 13 OR assisted with the above work	
			Ramp to Watering Trough. 46x of fascines were laid & a good dressing of rough chalk on top.	
			Two trestles were made & erected, & 45' of chalk shoot from Quarry towards road, to facilitate the loading of carts.	
			An Infantry working party of 20 OR assisted with this work	
			Brigade Headqrs.	
			The lining of the Generals' room was completed & the writing table covered with canvas	
			Raised Footway at Billets. A further 29x completed.	
			WORK AT CHUIGNOLLES R.E. DUMP.	
			Sawmill. Continued the making of heavy piles to support the saw-bench.	
			Put a further 80x of felt on the roof of the workshop & completed the roofing of the engine-shed.	
			Two loophole boxes made in the Coy's workshop.	
			Weather. Snow & Sleet – Very Cold Winds.	WD

2353 Wt. W2544/1454 700,000 5/15 D. D. & L. A.D.S.S./Forms/C. 2118.

* Instructions regarding War Diaries and Intelligence Summaries are contained in F. S. Regs., Part II. and the Staff Manual respectively. Title pages will be prepared in manuscript.

WAR DIARY
or
~~INTELLIGENCE SUMMARY.~~
(Erase heading not required.)

Army Form C. 2118.

Place	Date	Hour	Summary of Events and Information	Remarks and references to Appendices
Coy. billeted at R.E. DUMP CHUICNOLLES less 1 Section billeted at CHUIGNES	10/3/17		Work was continued on the following at CHUIGNES:– CHALK SHOOT AT QUARRY. Three trestles were made & erected & 22 ft of shoot & a further 30' lined with sheet iron BRIDGE (ROAD INTO CAMP). Made 3 trestle frames, & excavated ground ready for erecting CHURCH ARMY HUT. Completed the erection of framework & fitting of window frames & panels on both sides. STORE & OFFICE for R.O.O. at Rly Stn. Constructed & erected front wall of building & bolted together 5 trusses & erected these & also purlins. Excavated ground inside building to receive bearers & joists BATTALION HEADQRS. Three doors were hung & oiled linen fitted in 6 windows BRIGADE HEADQRS. Table made & sundry small jobs carried out. WORK AT CHUICNOLLES. Work was continued on the Sawmill in RE DUMP preparing piles & soleplates for saw. Piles cut & two soleplates fitted for counter shaft & concreting of same begun. The roofing of workshop adjoining sawmill was completed WORK AT COY. STABLES. Completed the concreting of one bay at stables 5x x 5x. Weather – Sleet – Breezy & fairly clear in afternoon.	WD

2353 Wt. W2544/1454 700,000 5/15 D. D. & L. A.D.S.S./Forms/C. 2118.

Army Form C. 2118.

Instructions regarding War Diaries and Intelligence Summaries are contained in F. S. Regs., Part II. and the Staff Manual respectively. Title pages will be prepared in manuscript.

WAR DIARY
or
~~INTELLIGENCE SUMMARY.~~
(*Erase heading not required.*)

Place	Date	Hour	Summary of Events and Information	Remarks and references to Appendices
Coy billeted at RE DUMP CHUIGNOLLES less 1 Section billeted at CHUIGNES	11/3/17		Work was continued on the following at CHUIGNES:-	
			<u>CHURCH ARMY HUT.</u> Completed the erection of this hut with the exception of 3 roof panels.	
			<u>LEAN-TO BUILDING.</u> Site cleared & the building half completed.	
			<u>STORE & OFFICE for ROO at Rly. Stn.</u> Completed the boarding of hut & fitted 5 windows.	
			<u>ROAD AT WATER POINT.</u> Laid 14 sq. yds of rough chalk on top of fascine road	
			<u>BRIDGE (ROAD INTO CAMP).</u> Made & erected 3 piers & laid bearers in position. 42' of framework complete	
			<u>BATHS AT CHUIGNES.</u> Erected 3 small partitions. Roofing over store commenced & 100 sq ft of CI roof laid with a zinc gutter.	
			No 3 geyser was substituted for No 2 which was leaking badly.	
			<u>BRIGADE HEADQUARTERS.</u> Oilcloth was fitted in three windows & floor of loft over the rooms was repaired.	
			<u>WORK ON SAWMILL AT CHUIGNOLLES RE DUMP.</u>	
			Continued the digging of foundation for counter-shafting & commenced the concreting of same.	
			<u>IN CAMP.</u> Two Sections had an inspection of kit, & all deficiencies noted.	
			Weather Dull & Cloudy - Raining during afternoon.	WD

2353 Wt. W2544/1454 700,000 5/15 D. D. & L. A.D.S.S./Forms/C. 2118.

Instructions regarding War Diaries and Intelligence Summaries are contained in F. S. Regs., Part II. and the Staff Manual respectively. Title pages will be prepared in manuscript.

WAR DIARY

or

~~INTELLIGENCE SUMMARY.~~

(Erase heading not required.)

Army Form C. 2118.

Place	Date	Hour	Summary of Events and Information	Remarks and references to Appendices
Whole Coy. billeted at CHUICNOLLES RE DUMP, - less 1 Sectn. billeted at CHUIGNES	12/3/17		The work was continued at CHUIGNES & the following progress made:-	
			BATHS. The roofing of store-room was completed & a roof 15' x 7' built over engine.	
			Drain was improved (ie), lined with brick etc.	
			FASCINE ROAD TO WATERPOINT. Laid 20x of this fascine road with a good dressing of chalk (a working party of 20 OR RFA on this work).	
			CHURCH ARMY HUT. Completed roofing of this hut & also erected a "lean-to".	
			Laid a footpath with brick. (12 OR assisted with this work - Infantry)	
			AT BILLETS. An ablution bench was erected.	
			WORK AT CHUICNOLLES RE DUMP.	
			Sawmill. Saw-bench was laid in position on the prepared foundation.	
			The counter-shaft was put in position & lined.	
			Boiler was filled & the engine tried & kept running for an hour, everything being satisfactory.	
			PONTOON BRIDGING. Two Sections were practising on this at FROISSY on the river SOMME.	
			REINFORCEMENTS. 12 Sappers joined this Company from BASE No 2.	
			Weather Clear & Dry - Breezy	

2353 Wt. W2544/1454 700,000 5/15 D. D. & L. A.D.S.S./Forms/C. 2118.

Army Form C. 2118.

WAR DIARY
or
~~INTELLIGENCE SUMMARY.~~
(Erase heading not required.)

Instructions regarding War Diaries and Intelligence Summaries are contained in F. S. Regs., Part II. and the Staff Manual respectively. Title pages will be prepared in manuscript.

Place	Date	Hour	Summary of Events and Information	Remarks and references to Appendices
Whole Coy in billets at RE DUMP CHUIGNOLLES – less 1 Sectn billeted at CHUIGNES	13/3/17		The following work carried out at CHUIGNES CHURCH ARMY HUT. Work was continued on this hut, tightening all nuts on roof + sides Completed the "lean to" + commenced to lay to lay flooring. FASCINE ROAD AT WATERPOINT. 20 OR. of RFA continued work on spreading chalk on this road which is now nearing completion. PONTOON BRIDGING. Two Sections practising this at FROISSY on the river SOMME. Two Sections marched to forward area to relieve two Sections of the 26th Field Coy, RE Weather Dull + Cloudy – Intermittent Showers.	

2353 Wt. W2544/1454 700,000 5/15 D. D. & L. A.D.S.S./Forms/C. 2118.

Instructions regarding War Diaries and Intelligence Summaries are contained in F. S. Regs., Part II. and the Staff Manual respectively. Title pages will be prepared in manuscript.

WAR DIARY
or
~~INTELLIGENCE SUMMARY.~~
(*Erase heading not required.*)

Army Form C. 2118.

Place	Date	Hour	Summary of Events and Information	Remarks and references to Appendices
2 Sections billeted in Dugouts behind Support Line. 2 Sections in Dugouts at (M.6.B.5.3) Trenches Lines near FONTAINE-LES-CAPPY.	14/3/17		Remainder of Company at CHUIGNOLLES packed up & marched to forward area & went into the various billets mentioned in the margin. Work was commenced on the forward dugouts. NORTHERN DUGOUT. This dugout when taken over was completely blocked in chambers & shafts with filled sandbags. These were all emptied - nearly 1400 - in shell holes well away from working site, so that no trace should be left of new work. Commenced excavating in chambers & a further 300 sandbags filled & emptied & roof shaling driven forward 2' further. (86% of chamber completed) SOUTHERN DUGOUT. A quantity of timber carried up to dugout & a quantity of sandbags emptied. WORK ON BECQUINCOURT, ASSEVILLERS ROAD. Mud scraped off surface & holes filled with metal & brick - 28 loads in all - between (M.6.D.1.1. & M.12.B.9.3). Sump-pits cleaned & deepened & numerous small drains cut. CASUALTY. One sapper wounded by shell-fire when working at NORTHERN DUGOUT referred to above. Weather - Dull - Showery	(?)

Army Form C. 2118.

Instructions regarding War Diaries and Intelligence Summaries are contained in F. S. Regs., Part II. and the Staff Manual respectively. Title pages will be prepared in manuscript.

WAR DIARY
or
~~INTELLIGENCE SUMMARY.~~
(Erase heading not required.)

Place	Date	Hour	Summary of Events and Information	Remarks and references to Appendices
2 Sections billeted behind Support Line. 2 Sections near BECQUINCOURT (M.6.D.5.3) Transport Lines near FONTAINE-LES-CAPPY.	15/3/17		Work continued on forward Dugouts.	
			NORTHERN DUGOUT. Excavated, & filled & emptied 400 sandbags. Erected 1 frame in chamber & fitted 9 lengths of sheeting on either side. Eleven lengths of sheeting driven in to support roof. 87½% of chamber completed.	
			SOUTHERN DUGOUT. Excavated & erected 1 frame in chamber & filled & emptied 450 sandbags. 61% of chamber completed.	
			WORK ON DOMPIERRE, ASSEVILLERS ROAD. Completed berm on both sides of road between M.6.D.1.1. for 250x towards ASSEVILLERS. High part of roadway cut away to a depth of 1'-6" & rebottomed with road-metal. Six sump-pits were dug with connecting drains to same, & some of the existing pits & drains cleaned & deepened.	
			From M.12.B.5.8. for 140x towards ASSEVILLERS a berm was constructed on both sides of road. 25 loads of metal & brick used on road.	
			Working parties totalling 133 on road work	
			WORK IN CAMP. (M.6.D.5.3.) Improving dugouts generally	CP
			Weather Clear & Bright	

Instructions regarding War Diaries and Intelligence Summaries are contained in F. S. Regs., Part II. and the Staff Manual respectively. Title pages will be prepared in manuscript.

WAR DIARY
or
~~INTELLIGENCE SUMMARY.~~
(Erase heading not required.)

Army Form C. 2118.

Place	Date	Hour	Summary of Events and Information	Remarks and references to Appendices
2 Sections billeted in dugouts behind Support Line 2 Sections in Dugouts near BECQUINCOURT (M 6 D 5.3) Transport Lines near FONTAINE-LES-CAPPY.	16/3/17		Work was continued on the dugouts in the forward area. In the Northern Dugout a set of timbers was fitted in the chambers & a quantity of sheeting fitted. In the Southern Dugout a set of timbers was also fitted & several hundred sandbags emptied. WORK ON DOMPIERRE, ASSEVILLERS ROAD continued & the following work carried out:- Cleared mud from surface from N14.B.3.5 to N15.A5.2 & filled up holes with brick & road-metal, 18 loads in all being spread. 11 sump-pits were dug 5'x5'x5' at parts of road where required & numerous sumps were cleaned & enlarged. 300x of berm cut on road banks up to point N17.B.1.9. A working party of 200 OR (Infantry) working on above road work under supervision of ½ section of Sappers. WATER TANK AT ASSEVILLERS. Work was commenced on foundation for this tank. The well near road in ASSEVILLERS was opened up (N13.B.8.7) Weather. Clear & Sunny.	C.D.

Army Form C. 2118.

Instructions regarding War Diaries and Intelligence Summaries are contained in F. S. Regs., Part II. and the Staff Manual respectively. Title pages will be prepared in manuscript.

WAR DIARY
or
~~INTELLIGENCE SUMMARY.~~
(*Erase heading not required.*)

Place	Date	Hour	Summary of Events and Information	Remarks and references to Appendices
2 Sections billeted in dugouts behind Support Line. 2 Sections in dugouts near BECQUINCOURT (M.6.D.5.3) Transport Lines near FONTAINE-LES-CAPPY.	17/3/17		Work on the forward dugouts continued.	
			SOUTHERN DUGOUT. Excavated, & filled & emptied 300 sandbags & erected some temporary timber	
			NORTHERN DUGOUT. Filled & emptied nearly 400 sandbags & repaired entrance to B shaft where damaged by shell-fire.	
			ROAD BRIDGES. Unloaded 15 Artillery Bridges at trees BOIS-de-BOULOGNE – BARLEUX ROAD near O.B.1 Support & laid 11 of these across trenches.	
			ROAD REPAIRING up to OLD GERMAN SUPPORT LINE.	
			Removed trees from off road, cut away wire entanglements & filled up numerous shell-holes	
			REPAIR OF DOMPIERRE – ASSEVILLERS ROAD.	
			Around M.12.B.5.8 the cleaning of sump-pits was continued & 3 new pits dug & 20x of berm cut on bank.	
			From N.15.B.0.1 to N.15.B.6.3 road was cleared of mud & 15 loads of brick spread.	
			15 new sump-pits 5'x5'x5' were dug between these points.	
			WORK ON WATER TANK AT ASSEVILLERS. Continued the forming of foundation for tank at N.13.B.8.7.	
			Filled up holes on site of water-troughs. Constructed 3 heavy trestles to support tank.	
			(M.6.D.5.3, near BECQUINCOURT). Erected NISSEN HUT for Divisional Head^qrs	
			Weather. Breezy – Clear	[initials]

2353 Wt. W2544/1454 700,000 5/15 D. D. & L. A.D.S.S./Forms/C. 2118.

Instructions regarding War Diaries and Intelligence Summaries are contained in F. S. Regs., Part II. and the Staff Manual respectively. Title pages will be prepared in manuscript.

WAR DIARY
or
~~INTELLIGENCE SUMMARY.~~
(Erase heading not required.)

Army Form C. 2118.

Place	Date	Hour	Summary of Events and Information	Remarks and references to Appendices
Head Q^rs & 2 Sections billeted near ASSEVILLERS (M.6.D.5.3) 2 Sections in Dugouts in forward area Transport Lines near FONTAINE-LES-CAPPY.	18/3/17		Continued the repair of BOIS-DE-BOULOGNE — BARLEUX ROAD filling up shell holes & clearing away wire entanglements & removing tree trunks which had fallen across roadway A small crater at forked road was wired round BECQUINCOURT DUMP. Commenced work there on constructing light boats for use in fording the river SOMME. WATER TANK AT ASSEVILLERS (N.13.B.8.7.) Work was continued on this during the day. The two sections in the forward area marched to the river SOMME & made footbridges across river at BRIE (O.26.D) The two back sections moved forward to the SOMME during the night ready to commence work on medium bridges WATER SAMPLE. The water sample taken from a well in BARLEUX (N.18.A) Sheet 62^c S.W. Edit 3A — was after being analysed, found to contain Metallic Arsenic. Weather — Clear & Sunny.	WD

2353 Wt. W2544/1454 700,000 5/15 D. D. & L. A.D.S.S./Forms/C. 2118.

Army Form C. 2118.

Instructions regarding War Diaries and Intelligence Summaries are contained in F. S. Regs., Part II. and the Staff Manual respectively. Title pages will be prepared in manuscript.

WAR DIARY
or
~~INTELLIGENCE SUMMARY.~~
(Erase heading not required.)

Place	Date	Hour	Summary of Events and Information	Remarks and references to Appendices
Headquarters at M6D53 near ASSEVILLERS Transport Lines near FONTAINE LES-CAPPY. 4 Sections in forward area near BRIE	19/3/17		BRIDGING of RIVER SOMME at BRIE (O.26.D.2.4) Materials were collected from surrounding district for making medium bridges & bridges over gaps No 1 2 3 4 & 5 were constructed, as well as a new footbridge at No 1 gap. Great trouble experienced at No 5 gap as the water was very deep, the bottom soft, & the stream flowing very fast. The Weldon Trestles were put in here & one of them sunk badly. All 5 gaps were bridged by 1-30 AM on 20th. BILLETS (BRIE). Commenced cleaning out debris from cellars & dugouts & making these habitable Weather. - Raining heavily & Cold Winds.	WD
"	20/3/17.		Work was continued on BRIDGING of RIVER SOMME at BRIE. (O.26.D.2.4) The handrails & ribands were improved on Bridge No 3 & a new transom put in on one of the trestles Work also continued on Weldon Trestle Bridge over gap No 5, same being completed. DEMOLITIONS A few walls & ruined buildings at BRIE MILL were blown down & the materials used for making up the bridge approaches & roads through them. Inf party of 200 men assisting Weather - Clear & Sunny	WD

Instructions regarding War Diaries and Intelligence Summaries are contained in F. S. Regs., Part II. and the Staff Manual respectively. Title pages will be prepared in manuscript.

WAR DIARY

or

~~INTELLIGENCE SUMMARY~~

(Erase heading not required.)

Army Form C. 2118.

Place	Date	Hour	Summary of Events and Information	Remarks and references to Appendices
Headqrs at M.6.D.5.3 near ASSEVILLERS Transport Lines near FONTAINE-LES-CAPPY	21/3/17		Work was continued on the bridges across RIVER SOMME at BRIE (O.26.D.4.4) A start was made on deviation bridges over gaps No 1 2 3 4 + 5 so that original bridges might be taken down to allow Heavy Bridges for all transport to be erected in their place. At No 1 gap two complete trestles were made + two bays of bridge completed At No 3 gap three trestles were made + erected + one bay completed. At No 4 gap three trestles were made + erected At No 4 gap the Weldon Trestle Bridge which was rather shaky owing to bad footings was repaired + two trestles for new bridge made. Work on the road through bridges + bridge approaches was continued A party of 400 Infantry assisted the work on roads + bridges. Head Qrs + Transport of Coy moved forward to BRIE from back area. Weather - Clear + Bright.	WD

2353 Wt. W2544/1454 700,000 5/15 D. D. & L. A.D.S.S./Forms/C. 2118.

Army Form C. 2118.

Instructions regarding War Diaries and Intelligence Summaries are contained in F. S. Regs., Part II. and the Staff Manual respectively. Title pages will be prepared in manuscript.

WAR DIARY

or

~~INTELLIGENCE SUMMARY.~~

(Erase heading not required.)

Place	Date	Hour	Summary of Events and Information	Remarks and references to Appendices
Whole Coy in billets at BRIE (O27.C) Sheet 62^c SW Edit 3A	22/3/17		Bridging of RIVER SOMME at BRIE (O26.D3.4) was continued. Work was completed on Deviation Bridges & commenced dismantling of original bridges. Started making bridges to carry a light railway across gaps No 1. 2. 3 & 4 The whole four Sections engaged on above work An Infantry working party of 175 assisted by unloading wagons & carrying materials for Heavy Bridges to working sites, & working on roads & bridge approaches. Weather Dull & Cloudy	WO

Instructions regarding War Diaries and Intelligence Summaries are contained in F. S. Regs., Part II. and the Staff Manual respectively. Title pages will be prepared in manuscript.

WAR DIARY
or
~~INTELLIGENCE SUMMARY.~~
(Erase heading not required.)

Army Form C. 2118.

Place	Date	Hour	Summary of Events and Information	Remarks and references to Appendices
Whole Coy in billets at BRIE (O27.c) Sheet 62c SW Edit 3 A.	23/3/17		The Bridging of the river SOMME at BRIE (O26.D 4.4.) was continued. One Section assisted by an Infantry working party of 25 O.R. completed dismantling of medium bridges No1 & 2. Commenced work on No 1 Heavy Bridge, A Type, preparing footings & bolting together the girders. 16 sappers of an Army Troops Coy. assisted with bolting One Section assisted by 25 OR Infantry completed No1. Decauville Bridge & laid light railway across. 2 Sections assisted by 50 OR Infantry dismantled No 3 medium bridge & completed No 3 Decauville bridge & also laid light railway from Bridges 2 to 4. Also commenced work on footings for No 2 Heavy Bridge. An Infantry working party of 150 unloading stores etc & taking them to DUMP or bridge sites as required. Weather - Clear & Bright - Showery	WD

2353 Wt. W2544/1454 700,000 5/15 D. D. & L. A.D.S.S./Forms/C. 2118.

Instructions regarding War Diaries and Intelligence Summaries are contained in F. S. Regs., Part II. and the Staff Manual respectively. Title pages will be prepared in manuscript.

WAR DIARY

or

~~INTELLIGENCE SUMMARY.~~

(Erase heading not required.)

Army Form C. 2118

Place	Date	Hour	Summary of Events and Information	Remarks and references to Appendices
Whole Coy in billets at BRIE (O27C) Sheet 62c SW Edit 3A.	24/3/17		BRIDGING of river SOMME at BRIE (O26.D3.4) was continued. One Section strutted No1 Decauville Bridge & completed No1 Heavy Bridge footings on West side of canal & continued work on footings on East side also. One section completed No2 Decauville Bridge & also the railway from store to No4 Bridge & worked on footings also for No1 Heavy Bridge Two sections worked on footings for No2 Heavy Bridge & also completed cribs An Inf. working party of 2 Off & 50 OR worked on footings for No3 Heavy Bridge A large quantity of debris was removed from the river at this point. Weather Showery – Mild.	WD
"	25/3/17		Bridging of SOMME at BRIE continued. Two sections completed footings & cribs & launched 4 girders into position & commenced bolting up on No1 Heavy Bridge. Two Sections working on No2 Heavy Bridge erected structional framework & laid decking curbs & fixed handrails. Shore ends were built up. (An Infantry working party of 50 assisting with this bridge) An Inf. party of 50 men engaged at No3 Heavy Bridge preparing footings & laying 9×4 rafts 125 Infantry engaged unloading stores & dumping where required Weather – Clear – Cold Wind.	WD

Instructions regarding War Diaries and Intelligence Summaries are contained in F. S. Regs., Part II. and the Staff Manual respectively. Title pages will be prepared in manuscript.

WAR DIARY

or

~~INTELLIGENCE SUMMARY.~~

(Erase heading not required.)

Army Form C. 2118.

Place	Date	Hour	Summary of Events and Information	Remarks and references to Appendices
Whole Coy. in billets at BRIE (O27 b) Sheet 62c SW Edit 3 A	26/3/17		Bridging of river SOMME at BRIE (O26D½.4) was continued Two Sections working on No1 Heavy Bridge laying cross joists & 9"x4" bearers for decking & also completed the whole of the decking Two Sections assisted by 50 OR Infantry, completed No2 Heavy Bridge & worked on No3 Bridge. Fixed two winches: bolted up derrick: built anchorages for derrick & also erected same: rove blocks: wound tackle on winches & launched first girder. A working party of 100 Infantry unloading stores from wagons & transporting to sites where required Weather – Wet & Cold.	WD
"	27/3/17		Bridging of SOMME continued. Two Sections on No1 Heavy Bridge. Completed curbs: erected handrails & made 2 heavy trestles for West side: fitted angle-iron supports on handrails & made wings at approaches to bridge. An Inf. working party of 50 men engaged on filling in roadway at both ends of bridge. This bridge was completed. Two Sections on No3 Heavy Bridge. Skidded No1 girder into position & also No2 for launching & then launched same & put in correct position. Fitted in steel & timber cross joists & bolted same down & laid decking A working party of 20 Infantry transporting stores to required points. Weather – Showery	WD

2353 Wt. W2544/1454 700,000 5/15 D. D. & L. A.D.S.S./Forms/C. 2118.

Instructions regarding War Diaries and Intelligence Summaries are contained in F. S. Regs., Part II. and the Staff Manual respectively. Title pages will be prepared in manuscript.

WAR DIARY
or
~~INTELLIGENCE SUMMARY.~~

(*Erase heading not required.*)

Army Form C. 2118.

Place	Date	Hour	Summary of Events and Information	Remarks and references to Appendices
Whole Coy in billets at BRIE (O27C) Sheet 62c S.W. Edit 3A	28/3/17		Bridging of RIVER SOMME at BRIE (O26.D½ ½) was continued Two Sections carried out the following work Fitted up wing rails at No2 Heavy Bridge & went over all bolts & nuts in Bridges 1 & 2 Made approaches to both these bridges & collected together all surplus stores Erected winches & anchorages ready to haul out wreckage from beneath No3 Bridge Two Sections assisted by 50 Infantry carried out the following on No3 Bridge Completed the whole of the decking & drilled holes in same & spiked decking down. Wing rails built at each side of bridge & improved the bridge approaches. Took down derrick & collected all surplus stores. An Infantry working party of 100 transporting all these stores to DUMP. Weather Wet & Blowy.	W.D.
"	29/3/17		Work at BRIE BRIDGES continued. All surplus stores lying at bridge sites were transported to DUMP & the various materials in DUMP sorted out ready for handing over. Two Sections commenced work on the erection of NISSEN HUTS for Advanced Army H.Qrs. near VILLERS-CARBONNEL Weather — Dull & Showery	W.D.

2353 Wt. W2544/1454 700,000 5/15 D. D. & L. A.D.S.S./Forms/C. 2118.

Instructions regarding War Diaries and Intelligence Summaries are contained in F. S. Regs., Part II. and the Staff Manual respectively. Title pages will be prepared in manuscript.

WAR DIARY
or
~~INTELLIGENCE SUMMARY.~~
(Erase heading not required.)

Army Form C. 2118.

Place	Date	Hour	Summary of Events and Information	Remarks and references to Appendices
Whole Coy. in billets at BRIE (O27b) Sheet 62° Ed. 3A.	30/3/17		Work was continued on the erection of NISSEN HUTS near VILLERS CARBONNEL for Advanced Army Headquarters. The ground was levelled off & the erection of 3 huts commenced. The framework of these 3 was completed. Weather – Clear – Showery.	W.D.
"	31/3/17		Two Sections left BRIE in marching order – accompanied by each section tool-cart – for LA-FLAQUE at 9-30 AM to work in III Corps Workshops making huts for new advanced Army HQrs. Two Sections continued work on NISSEN HUTS for Advanced Army Head Qrs near VILLERS CARBONNEL. Two of the huts had roofing completed & the lining of both also well in hand. The floor was laid in another hut. Weather – Showery.	W.D.

Wm Dow.... Maj RE(T)
Cmdg 409th (Lowl) Field Co RE(T)

2353 Wt. W2544/1454 700,000 5/15 D. D. & L. A.D.S.S./Forms/C. 2118.

WAR DIARY.

409th.(Lowland) Field Coy., R.E.,(T).

1st.DIVISION.

APRIL.1917.

Vol 28

CONFIDENTIAL

WAR DIARY

OF

409th (LOWLAND) FIELD COY. R.E. (T)

from 1st April 1917 to 30th April 1917

(VOLUME No XXVIII)

Army Form C. 2118.

Instructions regarding War Diaries and Intelligence Summaries are contained in F. S. Regs., Part II. and the Staff Manual respectively. Title pages will be prepared in manuscript.

WAR DIARY
or
~~INTELLIGENCE SUMMARY.~~

(Erase heading not required.)

Place	Date	Hour	Summary of Events and Information	Remarks and references to Appendices
Whole Coy. – less 2 Sections – billeted at BRIE (O27C). Two Sections at LA FLAQUE	1/4/17		Two Sections continued work on "NISSEN" HUTS for Advanced Army Headqrs near VILLERS CARBONNEL. The roofing of two huts was completed & good headway also made with the lining of both. The floor was laid in a third hut. Two Sections worked in III CORPS WORKSHOPS at LA FLAQUE making doors & panels & other parts of huts. In camp (O27C). All holes at horse standings were filled with broken brick & the standings improved generally. Weather. Wet & Stormy.	WD
"	2/4/17		Work continued on erection of huts for Advanced Army Headqrs near VILLERS CARBONNEL. Completed piled foundations for two "ARMSTRONG" HUTS & erected one of the huts. With the exception of foundation which was already laid, one NISSEN HUT was completely erected; all but a few yards of lining. Two Sections working in III CORPS WORKSHOPS at LA-FLAQUE made 18 doors; 42 small panels 3'-0" x 3'-0"; 104 floor panels 6'-6" x 4'-10" & 10 joiners benches. A quantity of stove-piping also made. Weather. Clear & Bright	WD

2353 Wt. W2544/1454 700,000 5/15 D. D. & L. A.D.S.S./Forms/C. 2118.

Instructions regarding War Diaries and Intelligence Summaries are contained in F. S. Regs., Part II. and the Staff Manual respectively. Title pages will be prepared in manuscript.

WAR DIARY
or
~~INTELLIGENCE SUMMARY.~~

(Erase heading not required.)

Army Form C. 2118.

Place	Date	Hour	Summary of Events and Information	Remarks and references to Appendices
Whole Coy billeted at BRIE (O27C) – less 2 Sects at LA-FLAQUE	3/4/17		Work continued on the erection of NISSEN HUTS etc for Advanced Army Head Qrs near VILLERS-CARBONNEL One hut had the bearers joists & flooring laid, & framework & gables erected. Roof fitted with the exception of 5 sheets & 70% of the lining completed. Another hut had joists, bearers & flooring laid, framework & gables erected, & the whole roof less two sheets fitted. 80% of the lining also completed. Two Sections working in III CORPS WORKSHOPS at LA FLAQUE made 104 roof panels 11' x 3" for special huts & continued work on the roof of a new workshop. Assisted at the construction of an engine for the workshop. Made 32 lengths of stove-piping. Weather. Clear – Showery	W.D.

2353 Wt. W2544/1454 700,000 5/15 D. D. & L. A.D.S.S./Forms/C. 2118.

Army Form C. 2118.

Instructions regarding War Diaries and Intelligence Summaries are contained in F. S. Regs., Part II. and the Staff Manual respectively. Title pages will be prepared in manuscript.

WAR DIARY
or
~~INTELLIGENCE SUMMARY.~~
(Erase heading not required.)

Place	Date	Hour	Summary of Events and Information	Remarks and references to Appendices
Whole Coy. at BRIE (O27C) less 2 Sections at LA-FLAQUE	4/4/17.		Two Sections continued work on Advanced Army Head^{qrs} near VILLERS CARBONNEL. Fifteen frames, as per design of 565th Army Troops Coy, were made from material salved locally & erected at Stables, making in all 72' run of framework (area 1300 sq.ft). 60' run of which was roofed with corrugated iron sheets The two Sections which were working in III CORPS WORKSHOPS at LA-FLAQUE packed up & rejoined Coy, in billets at BRIE (O27C) during forenoon. One squad of joiners from these sections carried out some repairs at 1st Divisional Engineers Head^{qrs} near BRIE during the afternoon. Weather Snowing heavily throughout the day	WD

Army Form C. 2118.

WAR DIARY
or
~~INTELLIGENCE SUMMARY.~~
(Erase heading not required.)

Instructions regarding War Diaries and Intelligence Summaries are contained in F. S. Regs., Part II. and the Staff Manual respectively. Title pages will be prepared in manuscript.

Place	Date	Hour	Summary of Events and Information	Remarks and references to Appendices
Whole Coy. billeted at BRIE (O27C)	5/4/17		Work was continued at the Advanced Army Head Qrs near VILLERS CARBONNEL Working on stables, 20 framed trusses were made & erected & 69x of roofing laid with corrugated iron sheets. Sixteen holes were dug for uprights ROAD WORK AT BRIE (O27C). Working on loop road in BRIE village 200x was cleared of debris & holes in road filled in & necessary repairs to road carried out. Weather – Clear & Sunny	WD
"	6/4/17		Work was continued at the Advanced Army Head Qrs near VILLERS CARBONNEL Working on stables, bales were fitted & a harness rack erected. Holes were made in the wall for the framing 910x of trench-board track was laid & ballasted. One "NISSEN" HUT erected. ROAD WORK AT BRIE (O27C). Working on a loop road, 150x of roadway was cleared of all debris, this debris being quite 18" deep in parts. A siding was made for transport wagons & 3 ruined walls close by were pulled down as they were unsafe. The Coy's Transport Lines were improved by laying a good quantity of broken brick etc. Weather. — Mild & Sunny	WD

2353 Wt. W2544/1454 700,000 5/15 D. D. & L. A.D.S.S./Forms/C. 2118.

Instructions regarding War Diaries and Intelligence Summaries are contained in F. S. Regs., Part II. and the Staff Manual respectively. Title pages will be prepared in manuscript.

WAR DIARY
or
~~INTELLIGENCE SUMMARY.~~
(Erase heading not required.)

Army Form C. 2118.

Place	Date	Hour	Summary of Events and Information	Remarks and references to Appendices
Whole Coy. in billets at BRIE (O27C)	7/4/17		Work was continued at the advanced Army Head^{qrs} near VILLERS CARBONNEL. Two cook-houses 15' x 10' were built with wood & corrugated iron sheeting, each having a wooden floor fitted. Two 15' ablution benches were made, & four stands made for other benches. 400^x of trench-board track laid & picketted down ROAD WORK. Working on loop road in BRIE village (O27C), the roadway was widened at several parts by cutting away road banks. Holes in roadway were filled up with broken brick. The road into the Coy's Transport Lines was laid with a good dressing of broken brick on a stretch of 20^x. Weather – Clear & Sunny.	WD

2353 Wt. W2544/1454 700,000 5/15 D. D. & L. A.D.S.S./Forms/C. 2118.

Army Form C. 2118.

Instructions regarding War Diaries and Intelligence Summaries are contained in F. S. Regs., Part II. and the Staff Manual respectively. Title pages will be prepared in manuscript.

WAR DIARY

or

~~INTELLIGENCE SUMMARY.~~

(Erase heading not required.)

Place	Date	Hour	Summary of Events and Information	Remarks and references to Appendices
Whole Coy, in billets at BRIE (O27.C)	8/4/17		Continued work at the Advanced Army Head Qrs near VILLERS CARBONNEL. Erected 4 "NISSEN" HUTS complete, the necessary timber for piles being salved & also most of the bolts. ROAD WORK Continued work on the loop road in BRIE village. (O27.C) The widening of roadway by cutting away banks was continued, & also the filling of holes in road surface with broken brick etc. A berm was constructed on a stretch of 15x. Weather – Warm & Sunny.	WD

Army Form C. 2118.

Instructions regarding War Diaries and Intelligence Summaries are contained in F. S. Regs., Part II. and the Staff Manual respectively. Title pages will be prepared in manuscript.

WAR DIARY

or

~~INTELLIGENCE SUMMARY.~~

(Erase heading not required.)

Place	Date	Hour	Summary of Events and Information	Remarks and references to Appendices
Whole Coy. in billets at BRIE (O27C) Sheet 62c S.W.	9/4/17.		Continued work on Advanced Army Head Qrs near VILLERS CARBONNEL. Salved sufficient timber for piled foundations for 2 "NISSEN" HUTS. Drove in the piles & erected the two huts complete, one of which was completed in 5½ hours. Erected two cookhouses, each 15'x10', with wood & corrugated iron sheeting, & fitted a wooden floor in each. WORK ON ROAD. Work was continued on the loop road in BRIE village (O27C) widening the roadway & filling up holes with brick etc. One Section in training. The day was spent in general smartening up, Section drill & rifle exercises etc. The Arms, Equipment & clothing etc of half of Coy was inspected Weather. – Heavy showers of hail & sleet all day.	WD

2353 Wt. W2544/1454 700,000 5/15 D. D. & L. A.D.S.S./Forms/C. 2118.

Instructions regarding War Diaries and Intelligence Summaries are contained in F. S. Regs., Part II. and the Staff Manual respectively. Title pages will be prepared in manuscript.

WAR DIARY
or
~~INTELLIGENCE SUMMARY.~~
(Erase heading not required.)

Army Form C. 2118.

Place	Date	Hour	Summary of Events and Information	Remarks and references to Appendices
Whole Coy in billets at BRIE (O.27.C).	10/4/17		Continued work on Advanced Army Head Qrs near VILLERS CARBONNEL. Sufficient timber was salved to serve as piles for foundations for two "NISSEN" HUTS Piles were driven in & the two huts completely erected, one of them being completed in 4½ hrs. One cook-house 15' x 10' was erected & a wooden floor fitted & another had all the framing put up & the floor laid. ROAD WORK Commenced work on mine-crater at PRUSLE cross roads P.25.C.1.4 Sheet 62c S.E. Edit 2A Completed the filling of the crater & commenced clearing away mud at corners of cross-roads. A quantity of brick was laid. Mine-crater at MONS-EN-CHAUSSÉE P.27.C.6.5. Sheet 62c S.E. Edit 2A. Tipped about 150 loads of brick into this crater. Cleared mud off deviation road & filled up holes & ruts with brick. TRAINING The Section in training continued with Section drill & rifle-exercises & general smartening up. Arms, Equipment & Clothing of remaining half of Coy, was inspected Weather - Snow & Sleet intermittently	WD

2353 Wt. W2544/1454 700,000 5/15 D. D. & L. A.D.S.S./Forms/C. 2118.

WAR DIARY
or
~~INTELLIGENCE SUMMARY.~~
(Erase heading not required.)

Instructions regarding War Diaries and Intelligence Summaries are contained in F. S. Regs., Part II. and the Staff Manual respectively. Title pages will be prepared in manuscript.

Place	Date	Hour	Summary of Events and Information	Remarks and references to Appendices
Whole Coy. in billets at BRIE (O27.C)	11/4/17.		Continued work at Advanced Army Head Qrs near VILLERS CARBONNEL Salved the necessary timber for piling for 5 "NISSEN" HUTS The piling was put in & the 5 huts completely erected. Laid part of piling for a Hospital "NISSEN" HUT. ROAD WORK. Mine-crater at PEUSLE cross roads P.25.C.1.4. Sheet 62c S.E. Edit. 2.A. 51 cart-loads of brick taken to site & spread in centre of crater & also on South side. Mine-crater at MONS-EN-CHAUSSEE. (P.27.C.6.5.) 260 cart-loads of bricks & debris dumped in this crater & the deviation roadway increased by 7'. The deviation roadway was improved & repaired A working party of 1 officer & 45 OR - Trench Mortar Bty. - assisted with this work, while 22 tip-carts were engaged transporting materials. TRAINING. The Section in training spent the forenoon with Section-drill & rifle exercises etc. In the afternoon this Section practised the speedy erecting & dismantling of the new Weldon Trestles Weather — Showery	WD

2353 Wt. W2544/1454 700,000 5/15 D. D. & L. A.D.S.S./Forms/C. 2118.

Instructions regarding War Diaries and Intelligence Summaries are contained in F. S. Regs., Part II. and the Staff Manual respectively. Title pages will be prepared in manuscript.

WAR DIARY

or

~~INTELLIGENCE SUMMARY.~~

(Erase heading not required.)

Army Form C. 2118.

Place	Date	Hour	Summary of Events and Information	Remarks and references to Appendices
Whole Coy. in billets at BRIE (O27C).	12/4/17		Continued work on Advanced Army Head Qrs near VILLERS CARBONNEL Erected 5 "NISSEN" HUTS complete on piles, the wood for piles being salved locally. Thirty piles were cut & pointed for a Hospital "NISSEN HUT" ROAD WORK. Mine-crater at MONS-EN-CHAUSSÉE P.27.C.6.5. Sheet 62c S.E. Edit.2.A 300 cart-loads of brick were tipped into crater & the deviation road widened at centre to a breadth of 33'. The mud was cleared away & 340 barrow loads of brick spread on roadway. Mine-crater at PRUSLE cross-roads P.25.C.1.4. Sheet 62c S.E. Edit.2.A 37 cart-loads of brick were broken & spread at cross-roads & the improvements of road corners continued. A working party of 52 OR - Trench Mortar Battery - assisted with this work & 23 tip-carts were engaged carting bricks. TRAINING The section on training continued with Section-drill & rifle exercises etc & in the afternoon continued practising the speedy erecting & dismantling of the New Weldon Trestles. Weather Rain & Sleet	WD

Instructions regarding War Diaries and Intelligence Summaries are contained in F. S. Regs., Part II. and the Staff Manual respectively. Title pages will be prepared in manuscript.

WAR DIARY
or
INTELLIGENCE SUMMARY.
(Erase heading not required.)

Army Form C. 2118.

Place	Date	Hour	Summary of Events and Information	Remarks and references to Appendices
Whole Coy. in billets at BRIE (O27C)	13/4/17		Work was continued at Advanced Army Head Qrs near VILLERS-CARBONNEL Two "NISSEN" HUTS were completely erected & half of a third hut Working on a Hospital "NISSEN" HUT, the framing was erected, the floor laid, 142 corrugated sheets & 4 roof windows fitted. ROAD-WORK. At PRUSLE cross-roads P.25.C.1.4, 40 loads of brick were laid Mine-crater at MONS-en-CHAUSSÉE, P.27.C.6.5., 301 carts & 300 barrow loads of brick were filled into this crater. At MONS-en-CHAUSSÉE a "NISSEN" HUT was completely erected with the exception of the lining. TRAINING Arms & Equipment of the Section in training were inspected after which they were given Squad & Section drill, Physical Training & also practice in Saluting In the afternoon this Section practised with the new Weldon Trestles erecting a bridge consisting of two trestles & shore bays Weather Clear & Dry.	WD

2353 Wt. W2544/1454 700,000 5/15 D. D. & L. A.D.S.S./Forms/C. 2118.

Instructions regarding War Diaries and Intelligence Summaries are contained in F. S. Regs., Part II. and the Staff Manual respectively. Title pages will be prepared in manuscript.

WAR DIARY

or

~~INTELLIGENCE SUMMARY.~~

(Erase heading not required.)

Army Form C. 2118.

Place	Date	Hour	Summary of Events and Information	Remarks and references to Appendices
Whole Coy. in billets at BRIE (O27C)	14/4/17		Continued work at Advanced Army HeadQrs near VILLERS CARBONNEL	
			Erected 1 "NISSEN" HUT complete on piles & completed the hut commenced on the previous day	
			Hospital NISSEN HUT. Finished off the lining: fitted 20 roof windows: nailed linen on windows: fitted 35 corrugated sheets on the roof: boarded under hut with weather boarding & put the fittings on the doors, thus completing this hut.	
			ROAD WORK. Mine-crater at PRUSLE cross roads P.25.C.1.4. Sheet 62°SE Edit. 2.A.	
			Thirty tip-carts of brick transported from MONS-EN-CHAUSSÉE to site, broken up, & the centre of the road made up. Two Sump-holes were cleaned out.	
			Mine-crater at MONS-EN-CHAUSSÉE P.27.C.6.5 Sheet 62°SE Edit. 2.A.	
			300 tip cart & 320 barrow loads of brick & debris dumped into crater & main road connected to road running South. The elevation road was made up with bricks.	
			A gable at ARTILLERY STABLES in MONS-EN-CHAUSSÉE was demolished as it was hanging dangerously over road.	
			The building of a "NISSEN" HUT at MONS-EN-CHAUSSÉE was completed.	
			On the road work 1 off & 50 O.R., French Mortar Bty, assisted, while 20 tip carts were engaged transporting material.	
			TRAINING. The section in training continued with Squad & Section drill & Rifle exercises etc.	WD
			Weather Clear & Dry.	

Instructions regarding War Diaries and Intelligence Summaries are contained in F. S. Regs., Part II. and the Staff Manual respectively. Title pages will be prepared in manuscript.

WAR DIARY

or

~~INTELLIGENCE SUMMARY.~~

(Erase heading not required.)

Army Form C. 2118.

Place	Date	Hour	Summary of Events and Information	Remarks and references to Appendices
Whole Coy in billets at BRIE, O27C	15/4/17		Work was continued at Advanced Army Head^{qrs} near VILLERS CARBONNEL. Two sections working in conjunction erected 5 NISSEN HUTS complete on piles. ROAD WORK. Mine-crater at PRUSLE cross roads P.25.C.1.4 Sheet 62c S.E. Edit 2.A. 24 loads of brick transported to site from MONS-EN-CHAUSSÉE, broken up, & the four corners of road made up. A sump-pit was deepened 3' Mine crater at MONS-EN-CHAUSSÉE. P.27 C.6.5 Sheet 62c S.E. Edit. 2.A. 305 loads of brick & debris dumped into crater which was filled in, in line with South side of main-road. The road running South from crater was cleared for 40^x x 5^x wide, & debris dumped in crater, as was also the earth around the crater. 1 Off + 52 OR, French Mortar Battery assisted, while 22 tip carts were engaged transporting materials. TRAINING. The section in training were given Squad & Section drill & rifle exercises. Weather – Dull & Cloudy – Showery.	WD

Army Form C. 2118.

Instructions regarding War Diaries and Intelligence Summaries are contained in F. S. Regs., Part II. and the Staff Manual respectively. Title pages will be prepared in manuscript.

WAR DIARY
or
INTELLIGENCE SUMMARY.
(Erase heading not required.)

Place	Date	Hour	Summary of Events and Information	Remarks and references to Appendices
Whole Coy in billets at BRIE (O27C)	16/4/17		Work was continued at Advanced Army Head Qrs near VILLERS CARBONNEL Sufficient timber for the erection of framing for stables for 42 horses was salved from VILLERS CARBONNEL. 11 frames were made & timber cut ready for other two. Two frames were erected at extreme ends of stable to act as guides in the erecting of the other frames. Canvas screens were fitted along the front & gable of the existing stable ROAD-WORK. The mine-crater at MONS-en-CHAUSSÉE P.27.C.6.5 Sheet 62c S.E. Edit 2 A, was again worked on. 206 cart loads of bricks & debris were emptied into crater. TRAINING The section in training continued with Section drill rifle exercises & physical training. Trestle & raft drill was also practised. Weather - Forenoon - Clear & Sunny - Afternoon - Wet.	WD

2353 Wt. W2544/1454 700,000 5/15 D. D. & L. A.D.S.S./Forms/C. 2118.

Instructions regarding War Diaries and Intelligence Summaries are contained in F. S. Regs., Part II. and the Staff Manual respectively. Title pages will be prepared in manuscript.

WAR DIARY

or

~~INTELLIGENCE SUMMARY.~~

(Erase heading not required.)

Army Form C. 2118.

Place	Date	Hour	Summary of Events and Information	Remarks and references to Appendices
Whole Coy. in billets at BRIE (O.27. b).	17/4/17		Work was proceeded with at Advanced Army Head^{qrs} near VILLERS CARBONNEL Working on Stables the following work was done:- 6 frames were erected & 2 more were prepared Timber was salved for purlins etc. Sheeted 3 bays with 10' sheeting & one bay with 6'. Garage. Made 8 trusses & erected 11, the timber for these being salved from VILLERS CARBONNEL Holes were dug for other 6 trusses & the Site laid off for the remainder of the building. In camp at BRIE (O.27.b). One Section improving billets etc. Weather – Clear - Showery.	WD

2353 Wt. W2544/1454 700,000 5/15 D. D. & L. A.D.S.S./Forms/C. 2118.

Army Form C. 2118.

WAR DIARY
or
~~INTELLIGENCE SUMMARY~~.

(*Erase heading not required.*)

Instructions regarding War Diaries and Intelligence Summaries are contained in F. S. Regs., Part II. and the Staff Manual respectively. Title pages will be prepared in manuscript.

Place	Date	Hour	Summary of Events and Information	Remarks and references to Appendices
Whole Coy. in billets at BRIE (O27.C)	15/4/17		Work was proceeded with at Advanced Army Head^qrs near VILLERS CARBONNEL. Working on stables, the following work was done:- Four trusses were made & erected & purlins fixed on eight bays Four frames were made & erected & two frames made the previous day were also erected 900 sq. ft. of corrugated iron roofing was laid. Canvas was fixed up on South side of stables on a length of 10 bays: 9 bays were fitted with harness racks. The timber used for the above work was salved from VILLERS CARBONNEL Working on a GARAGE 12 frames were made & erected & purlins put up on four bays, timber for this work also being salved from VILLERS CARBONNEL In Camp at BRIE (O27C). A squad was engaged on the erection of a Coy. Orderly Room & CQMS's store. Weather - Dull - Intermittent Showers	WD

Army Form C. 2118.

Instructions regarding War Diaries and Intelligence Summaries are contained in F. S. Regs., Part II. and the Staff Manual respectively. Title pages will be prepared in manuscript.

WAR DIARY
or
INTELLIGENCE SUMMARY.
(*Erase heading not required.*)

Place	Date	Hour	Summary of Events and Information	Remarks and references to Appendices
Whole Coy. in billets at BRIE (O.27C)	19/4/17		Work was continued at Advanced Army Head^qrs near VILLERS CARBONNEL. STABLES. 168 corrugated sheets were laid on roof: stable wall covered with canvas on a length of 9 bays & also on one gable end: fixed saddle rack on 9 bays. This work completed these stables. GARAGE. Work was completed on this with the exception of the flooring One "NISSEN" HUT was completely erected & another had the whole framework erected, the floor laid, & 3/4 of the roofing sheets fitted. In Camp at BRIE (O.27C). Completed the erection of Coy. Orderly Room & CQMS's store. 3 "ARMSTRONG" HUTS were completely erected. Weather – forenoon showery – afternoon clear & dry	WD

2353 Wt. W2544/1454 700,000 5/15 D. D. & L. A.D.S.S./Forms/C. 2118.

Instructions regarding War Diaries and Intelligence Summaries are contained in F. S. Regs., Part II. and the Staff Manual respectively. Title pages will be prepared in manuscript.

WAR DIARY
or
~~INTELLIGENCE SUMMARY.~~
(Erase heading not required.)

Army Form C. 2118.

Place	Date	Hour	Summary of Events and Information	Remarks and references to Appendices
Whole Coy. in billets at BRIE (O27C)	20/4/17		Work was continued at Advanced Army Head Qrs near VILLERS CARBONNEL. 2 "NISSEN" HUTS were fitted up complete & the hut which was commenced the previous day also completed. This hut required to finish 15 sheets & the whole of the lining A "NISSEN" Hospital hut was commenced. The framing was fitted up, the floor laid, 111 corrugated sheets fitted, & also 12 roof windows Repaired a number of damaged windows & packed floor seams in 24 huts. In Camp at BRIE (O27C). A number of the Coy. bathed in Coy. bath-house. Weather – Clear & Sunny	WD

2353 Wt. W2544/1454 700,000 5/15 D. D. & L. A.D.S.S./Forms/C. 2118.

Instructions regarding War Diaries and Intelligence Summaries are contained in F. S. Regs., Part II. and the Staff Manual respectively. Title pages will be prepared in manuscript.

WAR DIARY
or
INTELLIGENCE SUMMARY.

(Erase heading not required.)

Army Form C. 2118.

Place	Date	Hour	Summary of Events and Information	Remarks and references to Appendices
Whole Coy. in billets at BRIE (O27.C)	21/4/17		Continued work at Advanced Army Headqrs near VILLERS CARBONNEL The "NISSEN" Hospital hut commenced the previous day had the lining completed, 24 roof windows & 4 gable end windows fitted with linen & 64 roof sheets bolted. This completed this hut. Other two of these Hospital "NISSEN" huts were commenced Foundations levelled off & all bows put into position in one of these & the other had the piles, flooring, trusses, purlins & sheeting completed. One ordinary "NISSEN" hut was fully completed from foundations, with the exception of the lining Door latches were fitted on 21 "NISSEN" huts DMS Special Hut. The following work was done on this hut:- Piles & bearers laid: 9 trusses erected: purlins & ridges put on 6 bays: floored 4 bays & fitted 2 windows. A cookhouse was half erected. In Camp at BRIE (O27.C). A number of the Coy. bathed in Coy. bath-house during day Weather - Bright & Breezy	WD

2353 Wt. W2544/1454 700,000 5/15 D. D. & L. A.D.S.S./Forms/C. 2118.

Instructions regarding War Diaries and Intelligence Summaries are contained in F. S. Regs., Part II. and the Staff Manual respectively. Title pages will be prepared in manuscript.

WAR DIARY

or

~~INTELLIGENCE SUMMARY.~~

(*Erase heading not required.*)

Army Form C. 2118.

Place	Date	Hour	Summary of Events and Information	Remarks and references to Appendices
Whole Coy. in billets at BRIE (O27C).	22/4/17		Work was continued at Advanced Army Head^{qrs} near VILLERS CARBONNEL Two "NISSEN" Hospl. huts previously commenced were again worked on. One of these huts was completely finished & the other had the floor laid & the sheeting almost finished Another of these huts was commenced & the following progress made:- Erected foundations, flooring, framing & purlins, 2/3 of the sheeting & 12 roof windows complete, & also lined a half of the hut. D.M.S. Special Hut. Completed the framework & laid the flooring with the exception of 50 sq ft & sheeted completely round the walls. Fitted 7 window frames & 3 outside doors. The cookhouse commenced the previous day was again worked on & was completed so far as the materials available would allow. Weather Bright & Sunny	WD

Army Form C. 2118.

WAR DIARY
or
~~INTELLIGENCE SUMMARY.~~
(Erase heading not required.)

Instructions regarding War Diaries and Intelligence Summaries are contained in F. S. Regs., Part II. and the Staff Manual respectively. Title pages will be prepared in manuscript.

Place	Date	Hour	Summary of Events and Information	Remarks and references to Appendices
Coy in billets at BRIE (O27.b)	23/4/17		Work was continued at Advanced Army Headquarters near VILLERS CARBONNEL. Two Hospital "NISSEN" huts which had been half erected were again worked on. These two huts were entirely completed. The site for another Hospital NISSEN HUT was laid off & the following work done:- Piles driven, floor completed, trusses purlins & two gables & 3/4 of the iron sheeting & wood lining. Re-fixed interior cover plates at roof-lights in a previously completed hut & commenced fixing clips on windows. Work continued on the D.M.S. Special Hut. Completed all the sheeting & also the laying of the floor. A partition was erected with door. The lining was commenced of a partly erected NISSEN HUT & half of two bays completed. WORK AT CANAL BRIDGE AT BRIE (O26.D3.4) Commenced the removing of a quantity of debris from the canal at this point. Weather Bright & Sunny.	WD

2353 Wt. W2544/1454 700,000 5/15 D. D. & L. A.D.S.S./Forms/C. 2118.

Army Form C. 2118.

Instructions regarding War Diaries and Intelligence Summaries are contained in F. S. Regs., Part II. and the Staff Manual respectively. Title pages will be prepared in manuscript.

WAR DIARY
or
~~INTELLIGENCE SUMMARY~~.

(Erase heading not required.)

Place	Date	Hour	Summary of Events and Information	Remarks and references to Appendices
Coy. in billets at BRIE (O.27.C)	24/4/17		Work was proceeded with at Advanced Army Headquarters near VILLERS CARBONNEL. A partly erected Hospital "NISSEN" hut was again worked on & this was entirely finished off with the exception of 12 windows Three other Hospital "NISSEN" huts were commenced & the following progress made on these:- In one hut, laid foundations & floor & erected ribs & purlins complete: One gable end was erected & half of the other, sheeting was half finished & 3/8 of the hut lined. The other two huts had the foundations, part of floor & framework erected & the sheeting commenced. The lining of an ordinary "NISSEN" hut was completed & the lining continued of the DMS special hut. A number of windows were fitted with oiled linen in a previously erected hut WORK AT BRIE (O.26.D.3.4.) The removing of debris from under canal bridge was continued, this being entirely cleared away One re-inforcement rejoined this Coy. from Base Depot Weather Bright & Sunny.	WD

2353 Wt. W2544/1454 700,000 5/15 D. D. & L. A.D.S.S./Forms/C. 2118.

Army Form C. 2118.

Instructions regarding War Diaries and Intelligence Summaries are contained in F. S. Regs., Part II. and the Staff Manual respectively. Title pages will be prepared in manuscript.

WAR DIARY

or

~~INTELLIGENCE SUMMARY~~.

(Erase heading not required.)

Place	Date	Hour	Summary of Events and Information	Remarks and references to Appendices
Whole Coy. billeted at BRIE (O27C)	25/1/17		Work was continued at Advanced Army Head Qrs near VILLERS CARBONNEL. The three Hospital "NISSEN HUTS" commenced on the previous day were again worked on. No 1. Floor & framework was completed, one gable erected & half of the other, 2/3 of the sheeting finished & good headway made with the lining. No 2. Completed sheeting & lining & little remains now to be completed. No 3. Erected gables & good progress made with the sheeting & lining DMS. Special Hut The lining of this hut was completed. An ordinary NISSEN HUT was completely finished off from the foundations. Weather – Clear & Sunny	WD

2353 Wt. W2544/1454 700,000 5/15 D. D. & L. A.D.S.S./Forms/C. 2118.

Army Form C. 2118.

WAR DIARY

or

~~INTELLIGENCE SUMMARY.~~

(*Erase heading not required.*)

Instructions regarding War Diaries and Intelligence Summaries are contained in F. S. Regs., Part II. and the Staff Manual respectively. Title pages will be prepared in manuscript.

Place	Date	Hour	Summary of Events and Information	Remarks and references to Appendices
Whole Coy. in billets at BRIE (O27C)	26/4/17		Work was continued at Advanced Army Headquarters near VILLERS CARBONNEL. Continued the work on 3 Hospital "NISSEN" HUTS commenced 2 days ago. Two of these huts were almost finished off & the sheeting & lining of the 3rd hut was well advanced, & also the fitting of oiled linen in windows. Two other Hospital "NISSEN" HUTS were commenced & the following progress made on these:- No 1. Laid foundations & flooring, erected ribs & purlins, & completed one half of sheeting & 1/4 of the lining. Both gable ends were erected. No 2 Laid foundations & half of flooring & erected part of framework. The erecting of a Special Hut for a Printing Shop was commenced. Weather Clear & Sunny.	WD

Instructions regarding War Diaries and Intelligence Summaries are contained in F. S. Regs., Part II. and the Staff Manual respectively. Title pages will be prepared in manuscript.

WAR DIARY
or
~~INTELLIGENCE SUMMARY~~.
(Erase heading not required.)

Army Form C. 2118.

Place	Date	Hour	Summary of Events and Information	Remarks and references to Appendices
Whole Coy, in billets at BRIE (O.27.C)	27/4/17		Work was continued at Advanced Army Head Qrs near VILLERS CARBONNEL Continued the work on 5 Hospital "NISSEN" HUTS, the following progress being made:- The finishings of Nos 1 & 2 were continued No 3. Finished off the whole of the lining & sheeting & fitted linen in gable windows No 4. Finished the sheeting & lining & also the windows in roof & gables. No 5. Laid second half of flooring, erected both gables, completed bottom row of sheeting & 3/4 of the top row on each side. The lining of two bays was completed. Ordinary NISSEN HUT. Erected from piling up to side sheeting & lined half of two bays Work was much delayed on this hut owing to purlins breaking when putting on sheeting, which made it necessary to take down all sheeting & put in new purlins. Hut for Printing Shop. Work was continued on this hut & completed so far as materials available would allow. Weather Bright & Clear	WD

Instructions regarding War Diaries and Intelligence Summaries are contained in F. S. Regs., Part II. and the Staff Manual respectively. Title pages will be prepared in manuscript.

WAR DIARY

or

~~INTELLIGENCE SUMMARY.~~

(Erase heading not required.)

Army Form C. 2118.

Place	Date	Hour	Summary of Events and Information	Remarks and references to Appendices
Coy in Billets at BRIE (O27C).	28/4/17		Work was continued at Advanced Army Headquarters near VILLERS CARBONNEL	
			Working on four Hospital "NISSEN HUTS under construction, the following was the work done on these:-	
			No 1. This hut was completed: No 2. Also completed with the exception of a few facings	
			No 3. The top row of Sheeting fitted & the lining of hut completed. Only requiring a few facings to complete	
			No 4. Completed the Sheeting & lining & the fitting of roof windows & window facings, thus completing this hut.	
			Another Hospital "NISSEN" HUT was commenced. The foundations were laid & 4 bows erected	
			A partly erected ordinary "NISSEN" HUT was completed.	
			Other two of these huts were commenced & the following headway made with them:-	
			No 1. Floor was laid, trusses & purlins erected & also the two gable ends. Few roofing sheets fitted.	
			No 2 Laid the foundations, erected the framework & completed the whole of the Sheeting.	
			Two bays were lined & other two bays half so.	
			The Special Hut for a Printing Shop was completed with the exception of felt for roof.	
			SALVAGE.	
			38 rails of various lengths were salved from Quarry near VILLERS CARBONNEL & dumped at Bridging Store at river-side (O26.D)	
			Weather - Clear & Sunny	WD

Instructions regarding War Diaries and Intelligence Summaries are contained in F. S. Regs., Part II. and the Staff Manual respectively. Title pages will be prepared in manuscript.

WAR DIARY
or
~~INTELLIGENCE SUMMARY~~.
(Erase heading not required.)

Army Form C. 2118.

Place	Date	Hour	Summary of Events and Information	Remarks and references to Appendices
Coy in Billets at BRIE (O.27.C.)	29/4/17		Work was continued at Advanced Army Head Qrs near VILLERS CARBONNEL The work on 3 Hospital NISSEN HUTS under construction was continued Two of these were entirely finished off & the third had half of the floor, & the trusses & purlins erected The erection of another of these huts was commenced. Completed the laying of felt on roof of Special Hut for Printing Shops. The two ordinary NISSEN HUTS under erection were again worked on. No 1 Remainder of Sheeting & the whole of the lining was completed No 2 The lining was completed. These two huts were therefore entirely finished. 1 Pile-driver complete was transported from bridge at ETERPIGNY to Bridging Store near BRIE (O.26.D.) Two Sections left BRIE in cars at 1 pm & proceeded to billets at MERICOURT-SUR-SOMME Two Sections of the 26th Field Coy, RE relieved the above two sections on work at Army Head Qrs, VILLERS CARBONNEL. Weather Bright & Sunny	WD

2353 Wt. W2544/1454 700,000 5/15 D. D. & L. A.D.S.S./Forms/C. 2118.

Instructions regarding War Diaries and Intelligence Summaries are contained in F. S. Regs., Part II. and the Staff Manual respectively. Title pages will be prepared in manuscript.

WAR DIARY
or
INTELLIGENCE SUMMARY.

(Erase heading not required.)

Army Form C. 2118.

Place	Date	Hour	Summary of Events and Information	Remarks and references to Appendices
2 Sections in billets at MERICOURT-SUR-SOMME. Remainder of Coy in billets at BRIE (O.27.C.)	30/4/17.		The work was continued at Army Head Qrs near VILLERS CARBONNEL Working on two Hospital NISSEN HUTS the following work was done:- No1. Completed the floor, gables, 3/4ths of the sheeting & wood lining. No2. Flooring completed, one gable end erected & 1/4 of the corrugated iron sheeting. Three bays were lined up as far as the 2nd purlin. The two Sections at MERICOURT-SUR-SOMME were given 1/2 hrs Physical Drill in the morning, & the remainder of the day spent in cleaning up clothing & equipment & also in improving the billets. Weather - Clear & Sunny.	
			Wm Downs Major RE O.C. 409 (Lowland) Field Coy R.E.	WD

2353 Wt. W2544/1454 700,000 5/15 D. D. & L. A.D.S.S./Forms/C. 2118.

W A R   D I A R Y.

409th. (Lowland) Field Coy., R.E., (T).

1st. DIVISION.

MAY.1917.

Vol 29

CONFIDENTIAL

WAR DIARY

OF

409th (LOWLAND) FIELD COY R.E.(T.)

FROM 1st May 1917 to 31st May 1917

VOLUME No XXIX

Army Form C. 2118.

Instructions regarding War Diaries and Intelligence Summaries are contained in F. S. Regs., Part II. and the Staff Manual respectively. Title pages will be prepared in manuscript.

WAR DIARY
or
~~INTELLIGENCE SUMMARY.~~

(Erase heading not required.)

Place	Date	Hour	Summary of Events and Information	Remarks and references to Appendices
Two Sections at MERICOURT-SUR-SOMME. Remainder of Coy at BRIE (O27C)	1/5/17		The part of the Coy still remaining at BRIE worked on Hospl. NISSEN HUTS at Advanced Army Head Qrs near VILLERS CARBONNELT also packed transport ready for move. In the afternoon move took place & the whole Coy went into billets at MERICOURT-SUT-SOMME. The work on Advanced Army Head Qrs was handed over to 26th Field Coy RE. Weather - Bright & Warm	WD
Whole Coy in billets at MERICOURT-SUR-SOMME	2/5/17		During the morning the Coy paraded for Physical Exercises. All rifles in the Coy were inspected by an Armourer Sergt of the A.O.D. The afternoon was spent in the cleaning of all clothing & equipment Weather - Sunny	WD

2353 Wt. W2544/1454 700,000 5/15 D. D. & L. A.D.S.S./Forms/C. 2118.

Army Form C. 2118.

WAR DIARY
or
~~INTELLIGENCE SUMMARY.~~
(Erase heading not required.)

Instructions regarding War Diaries and Intelligence Summaries are contained in F. S. Regs., Part II. and the Staff Manual respectively. Title pages will be prepared in manuscript.

Place	Date	Hour	Summary of Events and Information	Remarks and references to Appendices
Coy. in billets at MERICOURT-SUR-SOMME.	3/5/17.		The Coy. paraded for Physical Exercises during the morning. The day was spent with squad & section drill etc. Weather - Very Warm.	WD
Coy in billets at MERICOURT-SUY-SOMME.	4/5/17.		The Coy paraded for Physical Exercises during the morning. The four sections continued training in Squad & Section drill, rifle exercises, guards & sentries & musketry instruction. Company & Ceremonial Drill during the afternoon. Weather - Very Warm.	WD
Coy. in billets at MERICOURT-SUY-SOMME.	5/5/17		The Coy. paraded for Physical Drill during the morning. The whole Coy. bathed during the day at baths in MERICOURT. Weather — Dull & Showery	WD

2353 Wt. W2544/1454 700,000 5/15 D. D. & L. A.D.S.S./Forms/C. 2118.

Army Form C. 2118.

Instructions regarding War Diaries and Intelligence Summaries are contained in F. S. Regs., Part II. and the Staff Manual respectively. Title pages will be prepared in manuscript.

WAR DIARY
or
~~INTELLIGENCE SUMMARY.~~
(*Erase heading not required.*)

Place	Date	Hour	Summary of Events and Information	Remarks and references to Appendices
Coy in billets at MERICOURT-SUR-SOMME	6/5/17		Church Services for Pres. & R.C's were held in the forenoon. The Coy was joined at the Pres. Service by the 216 Machine-Gun Coy. The Divisional Band was in attendance. Weather – Clear & Warm	WD
Coy in billets at MERICOURT-SUR-SOMME.	7/5/17.		One Section proceeded to CHUIGNOLLES & dismantled 6 "NISSEN" HUTS. The remainder of the Coy carried out Physical Training in the morning after which one Section was instructed in rowing drill, pontoon rafts, & bridging expedients. One Section went on a route march during which a lecture on demolitions was given. Practical demonstrations in laying charges were carried out. The remaining Section was under instruction for Musketry, range practice being included in the training. Weather – Bright & Warm	WD

2353 Wt. W2544/1454 700,000 5/15 D. D. & L. A.D.S.S./Forms/C. 2118.

Instructions regarding War Diaries and Intelligence Summaries are contained in F. S. Regs., Part II. and the Staff Manual respectively. Title pages will be prepared in manuscript.

WAR DIARY
or
~~INTELLIGENCE SUMMARY~~.
(Erase heading not required.)

Army Form C. 2118.

Place	Date	Hour	Summary of Events and Information	Remarks and references to Appendices
Coy in billets at MERICOURT-sur-SOMME	8/5/17		Owing to unfavourable weather the programme of training arranged had to be somewhat curtailed. One Section carried out training in bridging expedients & instruction was given on that subject to representatives of Batts & Coys of 2nd Inf Brigade. The remaining sections had kit inspections, lectures on demolitions, musketry & discipline, & also carried out training in knotting & lashing. The afternoon was dry & the Coy transport was washed & packed for inspection by G.O.C. Division on the following day. This inspection was, however, postponed. Weather - forenoon - raining heavily, afternoon - dull, dry.	WD
Coy in billets at MERICOURT-sur-SOMME	9/5/17		Physical training was carried out during the morning after which the various sections carried out training as follows:- 1 Section - Musketry & range practice. 1 Section - Bridging expedients & work in camp. 1 Section - Rowing, pontooning & rafting. 1 Section - Route march & lecture on demolitions with practical demonstrations. Weather - Bright & Warm.	WD

Instructions regarding War Diaries and Intelligence Summaries are contained in F. S. Regs., Part II. and the Staff Manual respectively. Title pages will be prepared in manuscript.

WAR DIARY
or
~~INTELLIGENCE SUMMARY.~~
(Erase heading not required.)

Army Form C. 2118.

Place	Date	Hour	Summary of Events and Information	Remarks and references to Appendices
Coy in billets at MERICOURT-SUR-SOMME.	10/5/17		Physical training carried out during the morning by the whole Coy after which the various sections carried out the following training 1 Section – Route march & lecture on demolitions with practical demonstrations 1 Section – Musketry & range practice. 1 Section – Practising bridging & bridging expedients. 1 Section – Practising rowing drill, pontooning & rafting. Weather – Close & Sultry.	WD
Coy in billets at MERICOURT-SUR-SOMME.	11/5/17		Physical training carried out in the morning by the whole Coy after which the four sections carried out the following programme:- 1 Section – Route march & lecture on demolitions with practical demonstrations 1 Section – Musketry & range practice. 1 Section – Practising Weldon trestle bridging & bridging expedients. 1 Section – Practising rowing, pontooning & rafting. The Coy. transport was cleaned up & overhauled in preparation for inspection by the G.O.C. Division – on the morrow. Weather – Very Warm.	WD

2353 Wt. W2544/1454 700,000 5/15 D. D. & L. A.D.S.S./Forms/C. 2118.

Army Form C. 2118.

Instructions regarding War Diaries and Intelligence Summaries are contained in F. S. Regs., Part II. and the Staff Manual respectively. Title pages will be prepared in manuscript.

WAR DIARY

or

~~INTELLIGENCE SUMMARY~~.

(*Erase heading not required.*)

Place	Date	Hour	Summary of Events and Information	Remarks and references to Appendices
Coy. in billets at MERICOURT-SUR-SOMME.	12/5/17		During the forenoon the Coy including the transport paraded & were inspected by the O/C. During the afternoon the Coy & transport in marching order were inspected by the G.O.C Division. Weather - Very Warm	WD
Coy. in billets at MERICOURT-SUR-SOMME.	13/5/17		Church Service in the forenoon with the Divisional Band in attendance. In the afternoon winter clothing was taken in & packed in bundles ready for transmission to the rail-head. Weather - Forenoon - showery. Afternoon - dull	WD

2353 Wt. W2544/1454 700,000 5/15 D. D. & L. A.D.S.S./Forms/C. 2118.

Instructions regarding War Diaries and Intelligence Summaries are contained in F. S. Regs., Part II. and the Staff Manual respectively. Title pages will be prepared in manuscript.

WAR DIARY

or

~~INTELLIGENCE SUMMARY.~~

(Erase heading not required.)

Army Form C. 2118.

Place	Date	Hour	Summary of Events and Information	Remarks and references to Appendices
Coy in billets at MERICOURT-SUT-SOMME	14/5/17		The whole Coy paraded for Physical Training during the morning after which the following was the programme:- 1 Section practising Weldon Trestle Bridging 1 Section proceeded to FROISSY & gave demonstration of bridging expedients to representatives of the 1st Brigade. Two Sections engaged part of the day in practising Standard wiring. The kit & equipment of these two Sections was inspected by the OC during the day. Weather - Forenoon - warm & sunny. Afternoon - showery	WD
Coy in billets at MERICOURT-SUT-SOMME	15/5/17		Two Sections & drivers paraded for Physical Drill during the morning & the following programme was afterwards carried out. 1 Section practising wiring. 1 Section practising Weldon Trestle Bridging 1 Section paraded complete in marching order with Section carts & were inspected by the CRE. 1 Section had an inspection of kit etc. One squad engaged on the making of Notice Boards. Weather - Clear & Sunny	WD

Instructions regarding War Diaries and Intelligence Summaries are contained in F. S. Regs., Part II. and the Staff Manual respectively. Title pages will be prepared in manuscript.

WAR DIARY

or

~~INTELLIGENCE SUMMARY.~~

(Erase heading not required.)

Army Form C. 2118.

Place	Date	Hour	Summary of Events and Information	Remarks and references to Appendices
Coy in billets at MERICOURT-SUR-SOMME	16/5/17		The whole Coy - less drivers - paraded for Physical Drill during the morning after which the following was the programme. Forenoon. - The Arms & Equipment of the four Sections were inspected after which Infantry Drill was engaged in Afternoon - The whole of the Coy transport was washed in preparation for inspection by the CE & CRE on the following day. One Squad continued work on the making of Notice Boards. Weather - Showery - Mild.	WD
Coy in billets at MERICOURT-SUR-SOMME	17/5/17		The whole Coy paraded complete in marching order with transport & were inspected by the CRE 1st Division Weather - Dull - Mild.	WD

2353 Wt. W2544/1454 700,000 5/15 D. D. & L. A.D.S.S./Forms/C. 2118.

Instructions regarding War Diaries and Intelligence Summaries are contained in F. S. Regs., Part II. and the Staff Manual respectively. Title pages will be prepared in manuscript.

WAR DIARY
or
~~INTELLIGENCE SUMMARY.~~
(Erase heading not required.)

Army Form C. 2118.

Place	Date	Hour	Summary of Events and Information	Remarks and references to Appendices
Coy. in billets at MERICOURT-SUR-SOMME	18/5/17		The whole Coy. paraded for Physical Drill in the morning One squad mounted on cycles proceeded to ESTREES for the purpose of testing experimental mobile charges for destroying dugouts. One squad worked on the making of Notice Boards. One squad of joiners worked on the making of special grenade stands. The remainder of Coy had a route march in full marching order the route covered being via, CHUIGNOLLES, FROISSY, BRAY, ETINEHEM, CHIPILLY & MORCOURT. Weather - Clear & Sunny.	WD
Coy in billets at MERICOURT-SUR-SOMME.	19/5/17		The whole Coy. packed up & moved off in marching order accompanied by transport at 2 PM from MERICOURT-SUR-SOMME, marched to VILLERS-BRETONNEUX arriving there at 5-45 pm marching with the 2nd Bde group. Wagons were all unloaded & the billets cleaned & improved generally before moving in. Weather - Warm & Sunny	WD

Army Form C. 2118.

Instructions regarding War Diaries and Intelligence Summaries are contained in F. S. Regs., Part II. and the Staff Manual respectively. Title pages will be prepared in manuscript.

WAR DIARY
or
~~INTELLIGENCE SUMMARY.~~

(*Erase heading not required.*)

Place	Date	Hour	Summary of Events and Information	Remarks and references to Appendices
Whole Coy. in billets at VILLERS-BRETONNEUX.	20/5/17		Billets & horse standings were cleaned up & improved Two Sections preparing sports ground for DE Sports on the morrow One section erecting a framework with tarpaulin covering for a harness & forage tent at piquet line Weather - Warm - Showery	WD
Whole Coy in billets at VILLERS BRETONNEUX	21/5/17		The whole Coy was paraded for physical drill during the morning. Forenoon. Two sections were marched to the outskirts of VILLERS BRETONNEUX & there lectured on the best possible way of placing the village in a state of defence, the main points receiving attention being, the materials required, the necessary working party & the time required to complete the work. Two sections continued the preparation of the ground for the DE Sports. Afternoon. The Divisional Engineers Sports were held Weather - forenoon, Showery Afternoon Clear & Sunny	WD

2353 Wt. W2544/1454 700,000 5/15 D. D. & L. A.D.S.S./Forms/C. 2118.

Instructions regarding War Diaries and Intelligence Summaries are contained in F. S. Regs., Part II. and the Staff Manual respectively. Title pages will be prepared in manuscript.

WAR DIARY
or
~~INTELLIGENCE SUMMARY~~.
(Erase heading not required.)

Army Form C. 2118.

Place	Date	Hour	Summary of Events and Information	Remarks and references to Appendices
Coy. in billets at VILLERS-BRETONNEUX	22/5/17		Two Sections cleared up the ground where the Divisional Engrs. Sports were held & commenced laying off the ground for the Divisional Sports. Two Sections lectured & instructed as to the best means of defending a cross-roads, the necessary materials required, the amount of working party & the time required to complete all being explained. One Squad making special boxes for grenade carrying for the 2nd Brigade. Weather – Warm & Sunny	WD /
Coy. in billets at VILLERS BRETONNEUX	23/5/17		The Coy. – less drivers – paraded for Physical Drill during the morning after which the four Sapper sections had a rifle inspection, gas respirator drill, & also practised guards & sentries. One section worked on the preparing of the ground for the Divisional Sports. One squad of joiners continued work on the making of boxes for carrying grenades for the 2nd Brigade. Weather – Warm & Sunny	WD /

Instructions regarding War Diaries and Intelligence Summaries are contained in F. S. Regs., Part II. and the Staff Manual respectively. Title pages will be prepared in manuscript.

WAR DIARY

or

~~INTELLIGENCE SUMMARY~~.

(Erase heading not required.)

Army Form C. 2118.

Place	Date	Hour	Summary of Events and Information	Remarks and references to Appendices
Coy in billets at VILLERS-BRETONNEUX	24/5/17		The Coy. paraded for physical training during the morning after which the rifles of the four dismounted sections were inspected. Two sections then continued the finishing of the sports ground for the Divisional Sports. One squad worked on the making of special grenade boxes The remainder of sappers worked at Coy. picquet line The Coy. was given the afternoon off for the Divisional Sports. Weather - Very Warm	WD
Coy in billets at VILLERS-BRETONNEUX.	25/5/17		The Coy paraded at 5-15 AM. Two sections proceeded to ground where Divisional Sports were held & dismantled bridging materials which had been in use there, & had same brought to picquet line. The other two sections pulled out & loaded up all wagons at the transport lines in preparation for inspection by the CRE. The Coy. again paraded at 9-45 AM in full marching order & accompanied by transport marched to selected inspection ground at WARFUSEE ABANCOURT & were there inspected by the CRE 1st DIVISION Part of the inspection included the hasty fitting on of the new box respirator & the trying of one section at work on Weldon Trestle Bridging. Contd. work in Camp of making special grenade boxes for the 2nd Brigade. Weather - Very Warm	WD

Army Form C. 2118.

WAR DIARY
or
~~INTELLIGENCE SUMMARY.~~
(Erase heading not required.)

Instructions regarding War Diaries and Intelligence Summaries are contained in F. S. Regs., Part II. and the Staff Manual respectively. Title pages will be prepared in manuscript.

Place	Date	Hour	Summary of Events and Information	Remarks and references to Appendices
Coy. in billets at VILLERS - BRETONNEUX	26/5/17		The Coy - less drivers - paraded for a rifle inspection etc during morning, after which practice in packing valises & fitting equipment was engaged in. The Coy. was given Gas helmet drill during the forenoon. A party was engaged during the day in preparing for the move on the morrow. Work was continued on the making of special grenade boxes for the 2nd Inf. Brigade An advanced party consisting of 1 Officer + 1 OR entrained at VILLERS BRETONNEUX for the new area for the purpose of fixing billets etc for the Coy. which moves on the following day. Weather - Very Warm.	WD
Coy. in billets at VILLERS - BRETONNEUX	27/5/17		The whole Coy engaged on the packing of wagons etc + the general preparation for the move during the afternoon. The whole Coy left VILLERS BRETONNEUX by train at 4-45 PM complete with transport for the new area. Weather - Warm	WD

2353 Wt. W2544/1454 700,000 5/15 D. D. & L. A.D.S.S./Forms/C. 2118.

Army Form C. 2118.

WAR DIARY
or
~~INTELLIGENCE SUMMARY~~.
(*Erase heading not required.*)

Instructions regarding War Diaries and Intelligence Summaries are contained in F. S. Regs., Part II. and the Staff Manual respectively. Title pages will be prepared in manuscript.

Place	Date	Hour	Summary of Events and Information	Remarks and references to Appendices
Coy billeted near BAILLEUL (X 10 P 4 8)	28/5/17		The Coy. de-trained at BAILLEUL at 4-0 AM & when unloading of transport had been completed were marched to billets at a farm on the outskirts of BAILLEUL at (X.10.P.4.8.). The remainder of the day was spent in the cleaning out of billets etc. Weather - Breezy - Warm	WD

2353 Wt. W2544/1454 700,000 5/15 D. D. & L. A.D.S.S./Forms/C. 2118.

Army Form C. 2118.

Instructions regarding War Diaries and Intelligence Summaries are contained in F. S. Regs., Part II. and the Staff Manual respectively. Title pages will be prepared in manuscript.

WAR DIARY

or

~~INTELLIGENCE SUMMARY~~.

(Erase heading not required.)

Place	Date	Hour	Summary of Events and Information	Remarks and references to Appendices
Coy. billeted near BAILLEUL (X10.P.4.8.)	29/5/17		During the forenoon the following programme was carried out. The Arms & Equipment of the whole Coy. were inspected All sections were drilled with the new box respirator. Rifle exercises, squad & section drill, & guards & sentries were all practised. One squad worked at Baths near METEREN During the afternoon the NCO's of the Coy carried out a reconnaissance of the village of METEREN & also the roads etc leading to same, each NCO afterwards rendering a written report Weather – Very Warm.	WD

Army Form C. 2118.

WAR DIARY

or

~~INTELLIGENCE SUMMARY.~~

(Erase heading not required.)

Instructions regarding War Diaries and Intelligence Summaries are contained in F. S. Regs., Part II. and the Staff Manual respectively. Title pages will be prepared in manuscript.

Place	Date	Hour	Summary of Events and Information	Remarks and references to Appendices
Coy billeted near BAILLEUL (X.10.b4.8.)	30/5/17		In the forenoon Physical Drill was carried out & afterwards the Coy marched to & bathed at Divisional Baths near METEREN. Afternoon. – One Section practising Weldon Trestle Bridging Remainder practising rifle exercises etc & Infantry drill open & close. One squad worked at baths near METEREN. The horses & harness of the Coy were inspected during the day Weather – Warm & Hazy	WR

2353 Wt. W2544/1454 700,000 5/15 D. D. & L. A.D.S.S./Forms/C. 2118.

Instructions regarding War Diaries and Intelligence Summaries are contained in F. S. Regs., Part II. and the Staff Manual respectively. Title pages will be prepared in manuscript.

WAR DIARY
or
~~INTELLIGENCE SUMMARY.~~
(Erase heading not required.)

Army Form C. 2118.

Place	Date	Hour	Summary of Events and Information	Remarks and references to Appendices
Coy billeted near BAILLEUL (X.10.P.43.)	31/5/17		The whole Coy with the exception of the drivers paraded for Physical Drill in the early morning, after which the following was the forenoon programme of training. Two Sections had a tactical route march included in which was practice in map reading. One Section practised Weldon Trestle Bridging One Section practised knotting & lashing, reaving of blocks & all work generally with regard to tackles. The afternoon programme was thus:- One Section practised wiring One Section lectured & also given practice on the packing of pontoon wagons Two Sections on a tactical route march the main point receiving attention being map-reading. 1 NCO + 2 sappers continued work on the making of filters at baths near METEREN Weather - Warm & Hazy	WD

Wm Downs. Major R.E.
O.C. 409th (Lowland) Field Coy. R.E.

2353 Wt. W2544/1454 700,000 5/15 D. D. & L. A.D.S.S./Forms/C. 2118.

WAR DIARY.

409th. (Lowland) Field Coy. R.E.,(T).

1st. DIVISION.

JUNE.1917.

DE.

Herewith War.

Diary complete

[illegible]

Vol 30

CONFIDENTIAL

WAR DIARY

OF

409th (LOWLAND) FIELD COY. R.E. (T)

FROM 1st JUNE 1917 TO 30th JUNE 1917

(VOLUME No. XXX)

Secret

Instructions regarding War Diaries and Intelligence Summaries are contained in F. S. Regs., Part II. and the Staff Manual respectively. Title pages will be prepared in manuscript.

WAR DIARY
or
~~INTELLIGENCE SUMMARY.~~
(Erase heading not required.)

409 Fd Coy

Army Form C. 2118.

Place	Date	Hour	Summary of Events and Information	Remarks and references to Appendices
Coy. billeted near BAILLEUL (X.10.P.4.5)	1/6/17		The whole Coy - less drivers - paraded for Physical Drill during the morning after which the following programme was carried out:- 1 Section - lecture on the use of cordage & practice in knotting & lashing. 1 Section - practising Weldon trestling 1 Section - practising Wiring 1 Section - Short tactical route march with instruction in map reading & reconnaissance. One squad of joiners, comprising two men from each section, proceeded to 2nd Army Workshops at HAZEBROUCK & commenced work on the making of special grenade carriers. Weather - Very Warm	WD

2353 Wt. W2544/1454 700,000 5/15 D. D. & L. A.D.S.S./Forms/C. 2118.

Instructions regarding War Diaries and Intelligence Summaries are contained in F. S. Regs., Part II. and the Staff Manual respectively. Title pages will be prepared in manuscript.

WAR DIARY
or
~~INTELLIGENCE SUMMARY.~~
(Erase heading not required.)

Army Form C. 2118.

Place	Date	Hour	Summary of Events and Information	Remarks and references to Appendices
Coy. billeted near BAILLEUL (X10P.4.8).	2/6/17		The Coy. - less drivers - paraded for Physical Exercises during the morning after which the Arms, Equipment & Box Respirators of the four sections were inspected, the four sections then being drilled with the respirators fitted. The following was the programme carried out during the remainder of the day:- 1 Section worked on Weldon trestle bridging 1 Section lectured on the various uses of cordage & tackle & given practice generally in knotting & lashing. 1 Section had a short tactical route march included in which was instruction in map reading. 1 Section had general practice in wiring The squad of joiners continued work at 2nd Army Workshops HAZEBROUCK on the making of special grenade carriers. Weather - Warm & Hazy.	WD

Instructions regarding War Diaries and Intelligence Summaries are contained in F. S. Regs., Part II. and the Staff Manual respectively. Title pages will be prepared in manuscript.

WAR DIARY
or
~~INTELLIGENCE SUMMARY.~~
(Erase heading not required.)

Army Form C. 2118.

Place	Date	Hour	Summary of Events and Information	Remarks and references to Appendices
Coy billeted near BAILLEUL (X.10.P.4.8.)	3/6/17		The Arms, Equipment & Box Respirators of the four sections were inspected & also the whole of the Coy. harness A Church Service was held during the afternoon Squad at 2nd Army Workshops HAZEBROUCK contd. work on making grenade boxes Weather - Warm, Breezy	WD
"	4/6/17		The four sapper sections paraded for Physical Exercises in the morning & during the rest of the forenoon the following was carried out :- An inspection of Arms & Equipment, drill with the Box Respirator fitted & afterwards a short route march at which simple tactical formations were practiced. During the afternoon the sappers were split into squads & lectured on machine guns, their mechanism & working, by NCOs of the No 2 MG Coy. The squad of joiners at 2nd Army Workshops HAZEBROUCK continued work on the making of Grenade Carriers Weather - Breezy - Warm	WD

2353 Wt. W2544/1454 700,000 5/15 D. D. & L. A.D.S.S./Forms/C. 2118.

Instructions regarding War Diaries and Intelligence Summaries are contained in F. S. Regs., Part II. and the Staff Manual respectively. Title pages will be prepared in manuscript.

WAR DIARY
or
~~INTELLIGENCE SUMMARY.~~
(Erase heading not required.)

Army Form C. 2118.

Place	Date	Hour	Summary of Events and Information	Remarks and references to Appendices
Coy. billeted near BAILLEUL (X10P7.8)	5/6/17		The sappers paraded for physical exercises in the morning & the following was the programme for the remainder of the day:- Inspection of Arms & Equipment: Gas Respirator drill: Infantry drill open & close. Lecture on tool-cart equipment & the packing of same One squad of joiners in Camp making ablution benches, box latrines, meat safes etc. One squad generally improving the sanitation of the camp. The squad of joiners at HAZEBROUCK contd. work on making special grenade carriers at 2nd Army Workshops. Weather - Very Warm	WD

2353 Wt. W2544/1454 700,000 5/15 D. D. & L. A.D.S.S./Forms/C. 2118.

Army Form C. 2118.

Instructions regarding War Diaries and Intelligence Summaries are contained in F. S. Regs., Part II. and the Staff Manual respectively. Title pages will be prepared in manuscript.

WAR DIARY
or
~~INTELLIGENCE SUMMARY~~.

(Erase heading not required.)

Place	Date	Hour	Summary of Events and Information	Remarks and references to Appendices
Coy. billeted near BAILLEUL at X.10.P.45	6/6/17		The Coy – less drivers – paraded for Physical Exercises in the morning & afterwards the Arms, Equipment & Kit of the whole Coy were inspected. The following programme was carried out during the day:– 1 Section lectured on construction & consolidation of strong points & afterwards were given practice in the tracing out of same. 1 Section lectured on the various explosives special attention being given to the laying of charges. 1 Section had a short tactical route march included in which instruction in map reading was given. The mounted section had instruction during the afternoon in the hasty fitting of the new Box Respirator, & were afterwards drilled with the Respirators fitted. One squad worked on the improvement generally of the Camp sanitation. The squad of joiners at 2nd Army Workshops HAZEBROUCK, continued work on the making of special grenade carriers. Weather – Very Warm	WD

2353 Wt. W2544/1454 700,000 5/15 D. D. & L. A.D.S.S./Forms/C. 2118.

Instructions regarding War Diaries and Intelligence Summaries are contained in F. S. Regs., Part II. and the Staff Manual respectively. Title pages will be prepared in manuscript.

WAR DIARY
or
~~INTELLIGENCE SUMMARY~~.
(*Erase heading not required.*)

Army Form C. 2118.

Place	Date	Hour	Summary of Events and Information	Remarks and references to Appendices
Coy. billeted near BAILLEUL at (X.10.P.4.6.)	7/6/17		The Coy - less drivers - paraded for Physical Exercises in the morning, after which, the Arms, Equipment & Box Respirators of the Coy. were inspected, drill being thus engaged as with the respirators fitted. The following was the training carried out during the remainder of the day - A short tactical route march by three sections, the other section receiving inoculation during the forenoon 1 Section had practice in Weldon trestling 1 Section practised wiring 1 Section lectured & given practice in tracing of strong points. The mounted section were given instruction on the fitting on of the new horse Gas Respirators. Squad of joiners at 2nd Army Workshops HAZEBROUCK continued work on the making of special grenade carriers. Weather - Warm throughout the day - Heavy rain in the evening	VOD

2353 Wt. W2544/1454 700,000 5/15 D. D. & L. A.D.S.S./Forms/C. 2118.

Instructions regarding War Diaries and Intelligence Summaries are contained in F. S. Regs., Part II. and the Staff Manual respectively. Title pages will be prepared in manuscript.

WAR DIARY
or
~~INTELLIGENCE~~ SUMMARY.
(Erase heading not required.)

Army Form C. 2118.

Place	Date	Hour	Summary of Events and Information	Remarks and references to Appendices
Coy. billeted at X10P.4.8. near BAILLEUL	8/6/17.		The Coy-less drivers - paraded for physical exercises in the morning after which the following was the training programme for the remainder of the day. An inspection of Arms & Equipment & Infantry drill open & close with the Box Respirator fitted. One section given instruction in map reading & visual training. One section lectured on demolitions & afterwards given practice in laying charges One section practiced the laying out of strong points & were lectured on the construction of same The remaining section was off duty having been inoculated. The squad of joiners at 2nd Army Workshops HAZEBROUCK continued work on the making of special grenade carriers. Weather - Very Warm	WD

2353 Wt. W2544/1454 700,000 5/15 D. D. & L. A.D.S.S./Forms/C. 2118.

Army Form C. 2118.

Instructions regarding War Diaries and Intelligence Summaries are contained in F. S. Regs., Part II. and the Staff Manual respectively. Title pages will be prepared in manuscript.

WAR DIARY
or
~~INTELLIGENCE SUMMARY.~~
(Erase heading not required.)

Place	Date	Hour	Summary of Events and Information	Remarks and references to Appendices
Coy. billeted at X.10.P.4.8. near BAILLEUL	9/6/17		Two Sections on physical drill in the early morning & afterwards drilled with the Box Respirator fitted. One of these sections was then given practice in map reading & the other section practiced the laying of charges & fuse jointing etc. The remaining two sections were inspected by the CRE at P.27.D.3.8. One section was inspected at work on rapid wiring & the other on Weldon Trestle Bridging The squad of joiners at 2nd Army Workshops HAZEBROUCK continued work on the making of special grenade carriers. Weather – Warm & Hazy.	WD
"	10/6/17		A Church Service was held during the forenoon after which the billets, Arms & Equipment of the Coy. were inspected Squad of joiners working at 2nd Army Workshops HAZEBROUCK continued work on the making of special grenade carriers. Weather – Very Warm.	WD

2353 Wt. W2544/1454 700,000 5/15 D. D. & L. A.D.S.S./Forms/C. 2118.

Instructions regarding War Diaries and Intelligence Summaries are contained in F. S. Regs., Part II. and the Staff Manual respectively. Title pages will be prepared in manuscript.

WAR DIARY
or
~~INTELLIGENCE~~ SUMMARY.
(Erase heading not required.)

Army Form C. 2118.

Place	Date	Hour	Summary of Events and Information	Remarks and references to Appendices
Coy. billeted near BAILLEUL at (X.10.P.4.8)	11/6/17		All stores were packed & wagons loaded ready for move. The Coy. in full marching order accompanied by transport left billets at X.10.P.4.8. & marched with 2nd Brigade VIA, METEREN - FLETRE & CAESTRE to billets at O.30. near QUEUE-d'-OXELAERE arriving there at 2-15 pm. A guard of 1 NCO & 3 sappers were left behind to guard area stores until handed over. The squad of joiners continued work at 2nd Army Workshops HAZEBROUCK making special grenade carriers. Weather - Dull during forenoon - Afternoon - Warm	WD
Coy. in billets at O.30 near QUEUE-d'-OXELAERE	12/6/17		A foot inspection was carried out in the morning after which the following work was done Billets cleaned out & improved. Wagons unloaded & cleaned up The remainder of the day was spent in the erecting of bivouacs. Squad of joiners at HAZEBROUCK continued work there on the making of special grenade carriers. Weather - Warm	WD

2353 Wt. W2544/1454 700,000 5/15 D. D. & L. A.D.S.S./Forms/C. 2118.

Instructions regarding War Diaries and Intelligence Summaries are contained in F. S. Regs., Part II. and the Staff Manual respectively. Title pages will be prepared in manuscript.

WAR DIARY
or
~~INTELLIGENCE~~ SUMMARY.
(Erase heading not required.)

Army Form C. 2118.

Place	Date	Hour	Summary of Events and Information	Remarks and references to Appendices
Coy. billeted at O30. QUEUE-D-OXELAERE	13/6/17		The Coy. - less drivers - paraded for physical exercises during the morning after which the following was the programme for the day. Inspection of Arms & Equipment: drill with the Box Respirator & after that a short route march. Work was continued on the washing & cleaning of wagons & wagon equipment in preparation for painting One squad of joiners working on the making of latrine boxes & ablution benches in Camp. The squad of joiners continued work at 2nd Army Workshops HAZEBROUCK on the making of special grenade carriers. Weather - Clear & Warm	WD

Army Form C. 2118.

Instructions regarding War Diaries and Intelligence Summaries are contained in F. S. Regs., Part II. and the Staff Manual respectively. Title pages will be prepared in manuscript.

WAR DIARY
or
~~INTELLIGENCE SUMMARY.~~
(Erase heading not required.)

Place	Date	Hour	Summary of Events and Information	Remarks and references to Appendices
Coy. in billets at O30. near QUEUE-d'-OXELAERE	14/6/17		The Coy - less drivers - were given physical drill during the morning after which the four sections were on the following work:- 1 Section on Weldon Trestle Bridging 1 Section given instruction in map reading & visual training, the section being afterwards tested on same. 1 Section practised knotting & lashing & uses of cordage & tackles generally. 1 Section had a lecture on demolitions after which practice was given in fuse jointing & the laying of charges etc. The squad of joiners at HAZEBROUCK continued work there in the 2nd Army Workshops on the making of special grenade carriers & also on meat safes. Weather - Clear & Sultry	WD

2353 Wt. W2544/1454 700,000 5/15 D. D. & L. A.D.S.S./Forms/C. 2118.

Army Form C. 2118.

Instructions regarding War Diaries and Intelligence Summaries are contained in F. S. Regs., Part II. and the Staff Manual respectively. Title pages will be prepared in manuscript.

WAR DIARY
or
~~INTELLIGENCE SUMMARY~~.

(Erase heading not required.)

Place	Date	Hour	Summary of Events and Information	Remarks and references to Appendices
Coy. in billets at O.30. near QUEUE-d'-OXELAERE	15/6/17.		The Coy. - less drivers - had physical exercises in the early morning. The four sections had instruction during the day in the tracing out & construction of Strong points points receiving Special attention being, the materials required, amount of working party & the time required to complete the work. Training was also given in map reading. The squad of joiners at 2nd Army Workshops HAZEBROUCK continued work on the making of Special grenade carriers etc. The whole Coy. bathed during the day at improvised baths in the vicinity. Weather - Very Warm	W.D.

2353 Wt. W2544/1454 700,000 5/15 D. D. & L. A.D.S.S./Forms/C. 2118.

Army Form C. 2118.

Instructions regarding War Diaries and Intelligence Summaries are contained in F. S. Regs., Part II. and the Staff Manual respectively. Title pages will be prepared in manuscript.

WAR DIARY
or
~~INTELLIGENCE~~ SUMMARY.

(*Erase heading not required.*)

Place	Date	Hour	Summary of Events and Information	Remarks and references to Appendices
Coy. in billets ~~at~~ O.30. near QUEUE-d'-OXELAERE	16/6/17		The four sections had physical drill in the morning followed by a route march in drill order. The squad of joiners at 2nd Army Workshops HAZEBROUCK continued work on the making of meat-safes & also on special grenade carriers. Squad in camp engaged on the cleaning & painting of pontoons etc Weather - Warm & Clear	WD
Coy. in billets at O30. near QUEUE-d'-OXELAERE	17/6/17		A Church Service was held during the morning after which the Arms & Equipment of the Coy. were inspected. The squad of joiners continued work in 2nd Army Workshops HAZEBROUCK on the making of special grenade carriers Weather - Very Warm	WD

Army Form C. 2118.

Instructions regarding War Diaries and Intelligence Summaries are contained in F. S. Regs., Part II. and the Staff Manual respectively. Title pages will be prepared in manuscript.

WAR DIARY
or
~~INTELLIGENCE SUMMARY.~~

(Erase heading not required.)

Place	Date	Hour	Summary of Events and Information	Remarks and references to Appendices
Coy billeted at O30.a near QUEUE-D'-OXELAERE	18/6/17		The four sections had a route march in full marching order, after which the whole Coy paraded & received instruction from the Divisional Gas Officer as to the fitting of the new extension piece to the Box Respirators. The four sapper sections then carried out the following training: 1 Section had practice in knotting & lashing & use of cordage generally. 2 Sections practiced the tracing out of strong points etc. 1 Section practiced Weldon Trestle Bridging The mounted NCO's had instruction in map-reading One Officer & a squad of NCO's proceeded to HAZEBROUCK & practiced barrel-piering The squad of joiners at 2nd Army Workshops HAZEBROUCK continued work on making meat-safes & also on special grenade carriers Weather - Warm. - Storms of wind & rain during afternoon.	MD

Secret

409 F. Coy

Army Form C. 2118.

Instructions regarding War Diaries and Intelligence Summaries are contained in F. S. Regs., Part II. and the Staff Manual respectively. Title pages will be prepared in manuscript.

WAR DIARY
or
~~INTELLIGENCE SUMMARY~~.

(*Erase heading not required.*)

Place	Date	Hour	Summary of Events and Information	Remarks and references to Appendices
Coy. billeted at O.30. near QUEUE-d-OXELAERE	19/6/17		All wagons were cleaned up & stores packed as far as possible in readiness for the move on the following day. The squad of joiners at 2nd Army Workshops HAZEBROUCK returned to the Company. Weather – Very Warm	
Coy. billeted at WORMHOUDT	20/6/17		The packing of wagons was completed & the Coy in marching order moved off at 5 a m & marched with 2nd Brigade to WORMHOUDT arriving there at 9-30 a m The remainder of the day was spent resting Weather – Wet & stormy during morning – Afternoon – dry & clear	

GH

Instructions regarding War Diaries and Intelligence Summaries are contained in F. S. Regs., Part II. and the Staff Manual respectively. Title pages will be prepared in manuscript.

WAR DIARY
or
~~INTELLIGENCE SUMMARY~~.
(Erase heading not required.)

409th Coy

Army Form C. 2118.

Place	Date	Hour	Summary of Events and Information	Remarks and references to Appendices
Coy. at WORMHOUDT.	21/6/17		The Coy paraded in full marching order at 4 am & marched with 2nd Brigade VIA. WYLDER & GALGHOECK to billets at I.S.D.9.1 near ROSENDAL arriving there at 10-30 am. Picquet lines were erected & all billets cleaned out, stores unloaded from wagons & all necessary camp duties carried out. Weather - Clear & Bright	
Coy. in billets at I.S.D.9.1. near ROSENDAL	22/6/17		A rifle & foot inspection was carried out during the morning, the Coy resting for the remainder of the day. Weather - Showery G.W.H.	

Army Form C. 2118. 3

4097 3

Instructions regarding War Diaries and Intelligence Summaries are contained in F. S. Regs., Part II. and the Staff Manual respectively. Title pages will be prepared in manuscript.

WAR DIARY
or
~~INTELLIGENCE SUMMARY.~~

(Erase heading not required.)

Place	Date	Hour	Summary of Events and Information	Remarks and references to Appendices
Coy. billeted near ROSENDAL at I.8.Dq.1.	23/6/17		The Coy moved off from billets at I.8.Dq.1. near ROSENDAL, entrained at LEFFRINCKHOUCKE at 9 a.m. & detrained near OOST-DUNKERKE marching from there to billets at R.32.B near COXYDE - BAINES. The transport was Brigaded & came by road leaving at 4.45 a.m. & arriving at new area at 2 p.m. Wagons were unloaded & picket lines erected. Weather - Bright & Breezy	
Coy. billeted at R.32.B. near COXYDE - BAINES	24/6/17		A Church Service was held during the morning A squad of joiners worked at Divisional Head^{qrs} erecting latrines etc. A squad of joiners worked at Head^{qrs} of Div. Eng^{rs} on the making of Notice Boards etc. During the afternoon a bathing parade was held. Weather - Bright & Warm.	G.W. [illegible] Major R.E.

2353 Wt. W2544/1454 700,000 5/15 D. D. & L. A.D.S.S./Forms/C. 2118.

Army Form C. 2118. 4

407 J.G.

Instructions regarding War Diaries and Intelligence Summaries are contained in F. S. Regs., Part II. and the Staff Manual respectively. Title pages will be prepared in manuscript.

WAR DIARY
or
~~INTELLIGENCE SUMMARY.~~
(Erase heading not required.)

Place	Date	Hour	Summary of Events and Information	Remarks and references to Appendices
Coy. billeted at R32B near COXYDE BAINES	25/6/17		The Coy moved from billets at R32B.5.5. to new billets at R27.C.4.0. (Sheet 11 NORT DUNKIRQUE) Two Sections then moved to billets in the forward area ready to commence work with 23rd Fld. Coy. RE One squad of joiners continued work at Div. Engrs. Head Qrs. One squad commenced work on the repairing of pumps at Northants' Camp near COXYDE - BAINES. The pumps at Field Ambulance also had attention. (W6A5.5.7. W6B9.0.) An examination was carried out of an O.P. in the forward area with a view to improvement. Weather - Bright & Sunny	G.W.H. Maj. ?

2353 Wt. W2544/1454 700,000 5/15 D. D. & L. A.D.S.S./Forms/C. 2118.

Army Form C. 2118.

5

409 Lowland Fd Coy

Instructions regarding War Diaries and Intelligence Summaries are contained in F. S. Regs., Part II. and the Staff Manual respectively. Title pages will be prepared in manuscript.

WAR DIARY
or
~~INTELLIGENCE SUMMARY.~~
(Erase heading not required.)

Place	Date	Hour	Summary of Events and Information	Remarks and references to Appendices
Coy. billeted in forward area. Hqrs at R27.C.4.0 near COXYDE-BAINES	26/6/17		Work was commenced on an OP in the forward area & work on this was half completed A reconnaissance was carried out on a light railway in the forward area. Work was commenced on the repair of pumps at Northawk camp, one of these being put in good working order. A squad of joiners continued work on the making of Notice Boards at Headqrs of 1st D.E. The two Sections at work in the forward area packed up & returned to Headqrs of Coy at R27.C.4.0. in preparation for the Coy moving on the morrow. Command of Company was handed over by Major Downes R.E. T. to Capt G. de C.E. Findlay R.E. authority (w) AG. GHQ A/26253 d 18/6/17 Weather - Bright & Clear ~~and AG GHQ A 26253 through 2 Army~~	
"	27/6/17		The Coy. packed up & moved off from billets at R27.C.4.0. at 7 am & marched to S.7.B.1.3. near ROSENDAL, approx. 16 miles, arriving 2 pm. Piquet lines were erected & billets cleaned out & all Stores necessary unloaded from wagons. Weather - Clear & Dry. G de C E Findlay Maj RE	

2353 Wt. W2544/1454 700,000 5/15 D. D. & L. A.D.S.S./Forms/C. 2118.

Instructions regarding War Diaries and Intelligence Summaries are contained in F. S. Regs., Part II. and the Staff Manual respectively. Title pages will be prepared in manuscript.

WAR DIARY
or
~~INTELLIGENCE SUMMARY~~.
(Erase heading not required.)

409 Fd Coy (Lowland)

Army Form C. 2118.

6

Place	Date	Hour	Summary of Events and Information	Remarks and references to Appendices
Coy. billeted near ROSENDAL I.7.B.1.3.	28/6/17		An inspection of rifles was carried out during the day, also gas drill and feet inspection. The billets & horse lines were cleaned up & improved generally. Remainder of day spent resting. Weather – Showery.	GelW
"	29/6/17		Two sections of the Coy in full marching order & accompanied by transport left the billets at I.7.B.1.3. & marched to camping ground near the CASINO, POINTE-de-GRAVELINES a distance of approx. 12 miles. Tents & piquet lines were erected & all necessary stores unloaded from wagons. Weather – Bright & Sunny	GelW
Two Sections at I.7.B.1.3. near ROSENDAL. Remainder of Coy. ~~at~~ camped near CASINO POINTE-de-GRAVELINES	30/6/17		The two sections billeted near ROSENDAL at I.7.B.1.3. moved with section transport to quarry at DUNKERQUE (near E.3. 2.50. 5.50 sheet 1/100,000). The two sections in new camp near the CASINO at POINTE-de-GRAVELINES commenced work on erection of cook-houses, harness sheds etc etc. Weather – Dull & Wet	

GelWhistley
Major R.E.,
o/c 409th Lowland Field Coy R.E.

2353 Wt. W2544/1454 700,000 5/15 D. D. & L. A.D.S.S./Forms/C. 2118.

W A R   D I A R Y.

409th. (Lowland) Field Coy., R.E., (T).

1st. DIVISION.

JULY.1917.

CONFIDENTIAL

Vol 31

WAR DIARY

of

409th (LOWLAND) FIELD COY R.E. (T)

from 1st July 1917 to 31st July 1917.

(VOLUME No XXXI).

Instructions regarding War Diaries and Intelligence Summaries are contained in F. S. Regs., Part II. and the Staff Manual respectively. Title pages will be prepared in manuscript.

WAR DIARY
or
INTELLIGENCE SUMMARY.
(Erase heading not required.)

409th (Lowland) Field Coy R.E. — Army Form C. 2118.

Place	Date	Hour	Summary of Events and Information	Remarks and references to Appendices
The Coy (less 2 sections) billeted near CASINO POINT-de-GRAVELINES Two Sections billeted at Quarry near DUNKERQUE	1/4/17		Unloading of stores carried out by two sections R.E. assisted by working parties of Pioneers. A Church Service was held during the morning. Two Sections at DUNKERQUE engaged on the quarrying of stone for the forward work at POINTE-de-GRAVELINES. Weather – Dry & Sunny	

G.R.H.

2353 Wt. W2544/1454 700,000 5/15 D. D. & L. A.D.S.S./Forms/C. 2118.

Instructions regarding War Diaries and Intelligence Summaries are contained in F. S. Regs., Part II. and the Staff Manual respectively. Title pages will be prepared in manuscript.

WAR DIARY
or
~~INTELLIGENCE SUMMARY.~~
(Erase heading not required.)

409th (Lowland) Field Coy R.E. Army Form C. 2118.

Place	Date	Hour	Summary of Events and Information	Remarks and references to Appendices
Coy - less two sections - billeted near CASINO POINT-de-GRAVELINES Two Sections billeted at Quarry near DUNKERQUE	2/4/17.		CANAL BANK. The work of excavating, filling & removing of sand was commenced & good headway made. Cross revetment was fixed. Drag scoops were made ready for use on the morrow, these to be used for the speedier removal of sand. A stretch of 280x of Decauville track was laid & levelled up from roadway to working site. WATER SUPPLY. A buried well East of the Casino was opened out & a reconnaissance also carried out of wells in the vicinity of the Camp. The two sections at DUNKERQUE were engaged on the quarrying of stone & the loading of same on lorries for transporting to near working site of Canal Bank referred to above. Twenty-six lorry loads were sent forward, these loads averaging 2 tons. Weather - Bright & Sunny	

Army Form C. 2118.

409th (Lowland) Field Coy, RE

Instructions regarding War Diaries and Intelligence Summaries are contained in F. S. Regs., Part II. and the Staff Manual respectively. Title pages will be prepared in manuscript.

WAR DIARY
or
~~INTELLIGENCE SUMMARY.~~
(Erase heading not required.)

Place	Date	Hour	Summary of Events and Information	Remarks and references to Appendices
The Coy - less 2 Sections - billeted near CASINO POINT - de - GRAVELINES. Two Sections billeted at Quarry near DUNKERQUE.	3/4/17.		<u>CANAL BANK</u>. Excavating & filling continued & with the assistance of the drag scoops about 1/4 of the excavating was completed. A screen was erected at the East end of working site to impede the view of the work from houses nearby. The shuttering was commenced & a mixing platform for the concrete was completed. A working party of 30 men engaged on the unloading of stone from lorries & breaking same from 1½" to 2" gauge. <u>WATER SUPPLY</u>. A well was located at the hotel BAMBOURG & samples from it were taken by the MO of the Div. Engrs. The two sections at DUNKERQUE continued work on the quarrying of stone & loading same on lorries for dispatch to forward work. Eleven loads were sent forward. Weather - Clear & Bright	GRS

2353 Wt. W2544/1454 700,000 5/15 D. D. & L. A.D.S.S./Forms/C. 2118.

Instructions regarding War Diaries and Intelligence Summaries are contained in F. S. Regs., Part II. and the Staff Manual respectively. Title pages will be prepared in manuscript.

WAR DIARY
or
~~INTELLIGENCE SUMMARY.~~
(Erase heading not required.)

Army Form C. 2118.

409th (Lowland) Field Coy. R.E.

Place	Date	Hour	Summary of Events and Information	Remarks and references to Appendices
Coy - less two sections - billeted near CASINO POINT-de-GRAVELINES Two Sections billeted at Quarry near DUNKERQUE	4/7/17		<u>CANAL BANK</u> Work was continued & 2/3 of the excavating completed. Screening at East end of working site was completed & poles for the West end prepared & a length of 30ft of screening erected. Shuttering for the concrete was prepared ready to be placed in position once the excavating is completed. A platform for the mixing of concrete was made & taken to site. A party continued work on the unloading & breaking of stone for the concrete work. Four Decauville trucks in use - horse drawn - moving stone from roadway to working site Two sections of RE's on the above work assisted by a pioneer working party of 120 men <u>WATER SUPPLY.</u> The well at Hotel BAMBOURG was opened as was also another nearly. The well in camp was deepened & a box fitted in, to prevent the pump from drawing sand. The yield of water in this well was at the rate of 200 gls. an hour The two sections near DUNKERQUE sent forward 14 lorry loads of stone. <u>CAMP WORK.</u> Ablution benches & latrines were made & erected. Grease traps for scullage water were also fixed. Weather - Bright & Breezy	GS

Instructions regarding War Diaries and Intelligence Summaries are contained in F. S. Regs., Part II. and the Staff Manual respectively. Title pages will be prepared in manuscript.

WAR DIARY
or
~~INTELLIGENCE SUMMARY.~~
(Erase heading not required.)

Army Form C. 2118.

409th (Lowland) Field Coy R.E.

Place	Date	Hour	Summary of Events and Information	Remarks and references to Appendices
The Coy - less 2 Sections - billeted near CASINO POINT-de-GRAVELINES Two Sections billeted near Quarry at DUNKERQUE.	5/4/17		<u>CANAL BANK</u> The excavations for actual work completed although a certain amount of work still remains to be done, preparing for foundations & clearing at bottom. Screening for West side was continued & good progress made A party continued work on the unloading of wagons & breaking up of stone. A sample concrete slab was made at the proposed proportion of 4. 2 & 1. Two sections of R.E.s assisted by a working party of 120 pioneers were engaged on the above work. These parties were arranged to work in two shifts so that the work should not be hampered by overcrowding, & that the best possible use should be got from trucks & barrows. <u>WATER SUPPLY.</u> Positions of camps were pointed out by staff & provisional position of wells selected. The two sections billeted near DUNKERQUE continued work on the quarrying & loading of stone, 17 lorry loads being sent to forward work. Weather - Clear & Sunny	

2353 Wt. W2544/1454 700,000 5/15 D. D. & L. A.D.S.S./Forms/C. 2118.

Army Form C. 2118.

WAR DIARY
or
~~INTELLIGENCE SUMMARY.~~
(*Erase heading not required.*)

409th (Lowland) Field Coy. R.E.

* Instructions regarding War Diaries and Intelligence Summaries are contained in F. S. Regs., Part II. and the Staff Manual respectively. Title pages will be prepared in manuscript.

Place	Date	Hour	Summary of Events and Information	Remarks and references to Appendices
Coy — less 2 Sections — billeted near CASINO POINT-de-GRAVELINES. 2 Sections camped near Quarry at DUNKERQUE	6/4/17.		CANAL BANK. Work on this was continued. Excavation & cleaning of bottom completed to enable foundation to be fixed. The slope was graded to the finished surface. The screening at East end of working site was extended an additional 50'. Party continued the unloading of stone & the breaking of same to the desired size. Notice boards were erected for the warning off of trespassers. Two Sections of RE's assisted by 120 Pioneers were engaged on the above work.	
			WATER SUPPLY. The sites were fixed for the first 6 wells & timbering prepared ready for work on these. Pumps & tanks were fitted to well at Hotel BAMBOURG for a supply of water for the concrete work at CANAL BANK	
			WORK IN CAMP. A quantity of Notice Boards for wells & latrines were prepared. The two sections billeted near DUNKERQUE continued work on the quarrying of stone & the loading of same on wagons for transporting to forward work	
			Weather — Dull - Dry	

2353 Wt. W2544/1454 700,000 5/15 D. D. & L. A.D.S.S./Forms/C. 2118.

Instructions regarding War Diaries and Intelligence Summaries are contained in F. S. Regs., Part II. and the Staff Manual respectively. Title pages will be prepared in manuscript.

WAR DIARY
or
~~INTELLIGENCE SUMMARY.~~
(Erase heading not required.)

Army Form C. 2118.

409th (Lowland) Field Coy, R.E.

Place	Date	Hour	Summary of Events and Information	Remarks and references to Appendices
Coy - less 2 Sections - billeted near CASINO at POINT-de-GRAVELINES 2 Sections billeted at Quarry near DUNKERQUE	7/7/17		CANAL BANK Work was continued on this Abutment at bottom - sheet piling was driven in, trench excavated & the trench filled up with concrete. A party continued work on the breaking of stone for concrete Work was also continued on the screening around working site The two back sections at DUNKERQUE worked on the quarrying of stone & loading same on wagons for concrete work referred to above. WATER SUPPLY. The sinking of 6 wells was commenced these being sunk to 6' or 8' into water. WORK IN CAMP Work on the preparation of Notice Boards for wells & latrines was continued One of the two back sections packed up & joined the forward part of Coy at CASINO near POINT-de-GRAVELINES Weather - Showery	

2353 Wt. W2544/1454 700,000 5/15. D. D. & L. A.D.S.S./Forms/C. 2118.

Instructions regarding War Diaries and Intelligence Summaries are contained in F. S. Regs., Part II. and the Staff Manual respectively. Title pages will be prepared in manuscript.

WAR DIARY
or
~~INTELLIGENCE SUMMARY.~~

(Erase heading not required.)

Army Form C. 2118.

409th (Lowland) Field Coy R.E.

Place	Date	Hour	Summary of Events and Information	Remarks and references to Appendices
Coy – less 1 Section – billeted near CASINO POINT-de-GRAVELINES 1 Section billeted at Quarry near DUNKERQUE	8/4/17		CANAL BANK. Work was continued on this. Apron was commenced & completed to height. Apron of 6' average Good progress was made with the screening of the working site. WATER SUPPLY Work on 6 wells was continued Three sections of RE" on the above work & 194 pioneers A Church Service was held during the afternoon The section camped near DUNKERQUE continued work on the quarrying & loading of stone. Weather – Wet & Cloudy.	

2353 Wt. W2544/1454 700,000 5/15 D. D. & L. A.D.S.S./Forms/C. 2118.

Instructions regarding War Diaries and Intelligence Summaries are contained in F. S. Regs., Part II. and the Staff Manual respectively. Title pages will be prepared in manuscript.

WAR DIARY
or
~~INTELLIGENCE SUMMARY.~~
(Erase heading not required.)

Army Form C. 2118.

409th (Lowland) Field Coy RE

Place	Date	Hour	Summary of Events and Information	Remarks and references to Appendices
Coy - less 1 section billeted near CASINO POINT-de-GRAVELINES 1 Section camped at Quarry near DUNKERQUE	9/9/17		CANAL BANK. Work was continued here & the concrete completed to within 10' of top. The surfacing of the lower half was completed Templates for coping were made The screening of the working site was continued the whole of the South side being completed All stone was brought in trucks from roadway to working site. WATER SUPPLY. Continued work on 6 wells & these now average 1'-6" of water. On the above work the following labour was employed:- 3 Sections of RE assisted by 198 Pioneers WORK IN CAMP. Two painters making & printing Notice Boards for wells & latrines. One squad building a large oven in the Coy. cookhouse. Weather - Clear & Sunny - Very Blowy	GR

2353 Wt. W2544/1454 700,000 5/15 D. D. & L. A.D.S.S./Forms/C. 2118.

Army Form C. 2118.

Instructions regarding War Diaries and Intelligence Summaries are contained in F. S. Regs., Part II. and the Staff Manual respectively. Title pages will be prepared in manuscript.

WAR DIARY
or
~~INTELLIGENCE SUMMARY.~~
(Erase heading not required.)

Place	Date	Hour	Summary of Events and Information	Remarks and references to Appendices
Whole Coy — less 1 Section — billeted near CASINO POINT - de - GRAVELINES 1 Section camped at Quarry near DUNKERQUE	10/7/17		<u>Work on CANAL BANK was continued</u> Concrete of coping over half section completed & carried back 6' on flat. The framing for the other half of the coping was fixed ready to commence work. The screening of the working site was practically completed with the exception of bridge screens, temporary bridge screens being erected to conceal coping work. The stone for concrete was transported from roadway dumps in Decauville horse drawn trucks. <u>WATER SUPPLY.</u> Six wells all sunk to final depth these wells now having a depth of water from 2'-9" to 3'-0". Three sections of RE" assisted by 170 Pioneers engaged on the above work, the men working in shifts so that the maximum amount of use should be got from both men & working gear. The section at DUNKERQUE continued work on the loading of stone etc for forward work. Weather — Clear & Sunny	

2353 Wt. W2544/1454 700,000 5/15 D. D. & L. A.D.S.S./Forms/C. 2118.

Army Form C. 2118.

WAR DIARY
or
~~INTELLIGENCE SUMMARY~~.
(Erase heading not required.)

Instructions regarding War Diaries and Intelligence Summaries are contained in F. S. Regs., Part II. and the Staff Manual respectively. Title pages will be prepared in manuscript.

Place	Date	Hour	Summary of Events and Information	Remarks and references to Appendices
Whole Coy. billeted near Casino Point-de-Gravelines less 1 Section billeted at Quarry near Dunkerque	11/7/17		Continued work on CANAL BANK at POINT-de-GRAVELINES The concrete of the coping was completed & also 30' back on flat The surfacing was completed to the foot of the coping. One bridge screen was made & is now in course of erection WATER SUPPLY The fences were completed round six wells, the lids fitted on four & pumps fitted on all six. Tanks & stands were transported to sites. Three sections of RE's assisted by 1/0 Pioneers were engaged on the above work. The section at Quarry near DUNKERQUE continued work on the quarrying of stone & loading same on wagons for the forward work WORK IN CAMP Continued work on the making & painting of Notice Boards for Wells, Latrines etc. Weather — Warm & Sunny	

2353 Wt. W2544/1454 700,000 5/15 D. D. & L. A.D.S.S./Forms/C. 2118.

Instructions regarding War Diaries and Intelligence Summaries are contained in F. S. Regs., Part II. and the Staff Manual respectively. Title pages will be prepared in manuscript.

WAR DIARY
or
~~INTELLIGENCE SUMMARY~~.
(Erase heading not required.)

Army Form C. 2118.

409th (LOWLAND) FIELD Coy R.E.

Place	Date	Hour	Summary of Events and Information	Remarks and references to Appendices
The Coy - less 1 Section - camped near CASINO near POINT-de-GRAVELINES 1 Section camped at Quarry near DUNKERQUE.	12/7/17		The work on the CANAL BANK was proceeded with & the concrete work practically finished with the exception of a small portion of the surfacing. The protecting apron of concrete at bottom was completed. One bridge screen was erected & another is fully made awaiting erection. WATER SUPPLY. Six wells are practically finished requiring only lids & Notice Boards, these latter being ready for erection. The yield of water was tested & in all six was found to be satisfactory. On the above work were engaged 3 Sections of REs assisted by 170 Pioneers. Section at DUNKERQUE continued work on the quarrying & loading of stone for the forward work. WORK etc IN FORWARD CAMP. Small squad of joiners & painters continued work on the making of the necessary Notice Boards for Wells & Latrines etc. The building of a large fireplace in the Coy Cookhouse was completed & is working satisfactorily. INSPECTION. Half the mounted section had an inspection of Harness during the day Weather - Clear & Sunny	

2353 Wt. W2544/1454 700,000 5/15 D. D. & L. A.D.S.S./Forms/C. 2118.

Instructions regarding War Diaries and Intelligence Summaries are contained in F. S. Regs., Part II. and the Staff Manual respectively. Title pages will be prepared in manuscript.

WAR DIARY
or
~~INTELLIGENCE SUMMARY~~.
(Erase heading not required.)

Army Form C. 2118.

409th (LOWLAND) FIELD COY R.E.

Place	Date	Hour	Summary of Events and Information	Remarks and references to Appendices
The Coy - less 1 Section - camped near CASINO near POINT-de-GRAVELINES 1 Section camped near Quarry at DUNKERQUE	13/7/17		Work on the concrete at the CANAL BANK was completed. The revetting of cutting at sides of apron was also finished off. The 2nd Bridge screen was erected. Commenced the levelling off, of hillocks within 300' of start of slope WATER SUPPLY. Six new wells started & good headway made with these " " Pipe System. A fair quantity of piping was laid out Levelling for tanks was commenced. Three sections assisted by working parties from 6th Welsh & Glosters pioneers engaged on the above work The section at DUNKERQUE continued work on the quarrying of stone etc. WORK IN FORWARD CAMP. Continued work on the making of Notice Boards & also on the making of small boxes for attaching to suction hose to prevent the pumps silting up with sand Weather - Close & Sultry.	[illegible]

2353 Wt. W2544/1454 700,000 5/15 D. D. & L. A.D.S.S./Forms/C. 2118.

Army Form C. 2118.

Instructions regarding War Diaries and Intelligence Summaries are contained in F. S. Regs., Part II. and the Staff Manual respectively. Title pages will be prepared in manuscript.

WAR DIARY
or
~~INTELLIGENCE SUMMARY.~~

(*Erase heading not required.*)

Place	Date	Hour	Summary of Events and Information	Remarks and references to Appendices
Coy-less 1 Section - billeted near CASINO near POINT-de-GRAVELINES. 1 Section camped near Quarry at DUNKERQUE	12/9/14		Completed the revetting at CANAL BANK & continued work on the levelling of ground to 100x back from start of slope A party continued work on the screening. WATER SUPPLY - WELLS. The six wells started yesterday were again worked on & good progress made. WATER SUPPLY. (Pipe System) A start was made on this new work (a) Engines & pump. - One of these in position & the bed for the 2nd prepared. (B) The timber framing for the tanks was erected. (C) About 200x of piping was jointed up Three sections of RE, & working parties of pioneers assisting, were engaged on the above work. SECTION AT DUNKERQUE. Continued work on stone quarrying & loading WORK IN FORWARD CAMP. Continued work on making Notice Boards etc. Weather - Close & Sultry	

2353 Wt. W2544/1454 700,000 5/15 D. D. & L. A.D.S.S./Forms/C. 2118.

Instructions regarding War Diaries and Intelligence Summaries are contained in F. S. Regs., Part II. and the Staff Manual respectively. Title pages will be prepared in manuscript.

WAR DIARY
or
~~INTELLIGENCE SUMMARY~~.
(Erase heading not required.)

~~[illegible]~~ 409th (Lowland) Field Coy. R.E. Army Form C. 2118.

Place	Date	Hour	Summary of Events and Information	Remarks and references to Appendices
Coy. billeted near CASINO near POINT-de-GRAVELINES – less 1 Sect. billeted near Quarry at DUNKERQUE	15/4/17		CANAL BANK. The damage done by gale was repaired & further screening prepared.	
			WATER SUPPLY. Working on an additional two wells these were entirely completed.	
			WATER SUPPLY (Pipe System). Both engines & pumps connected up: Delivery to spill tanks complete except cross tee: 10 lengths of pipe laid towards tank by railside: All four spill tanks complete: Total of 104 lengths of piping laid along the main road. Two sterilisers are in position.	
			LABOUR. On the above work were engaged 3 Sections of R.E.'s assisted by working parties from the Welsh & Gloster pioneers.	
			WORK IN FORWARD CAMP. Continued work on Notice Boards etc.	
			The Section at DUNKERQUE continued work on the quarrying & loading of stone.	
			Weather – Blowy – Dry & Clear	
			[initials]	

2353 Wt. W2544/1454 700,000 5/15 D. D. & L. A.D.S.S./Forms/C. 2118.

Instructions regarding War Diaries and Intelligence Summaries are contained in F. S. Regs., Part II. and the Staff Manual respectively. Title pages will be prepared in manuscript.

WAR DIARY of ~~INTELLIGENCE SUMMARY~~.

(Erase heading not required.)

409th (Lowland) Field Coy RE

Army Form C. 2118.

Place	Date	Hour	Summary of Events and Information	Remarks and references to Appendices
Coy — less 1 Section - billeted near CASINO near POINT-de GRAVELINES 1 Section at Quarry near DUNKERQUE	16/4/17		CANAL BANK. The camouflage work was completed as was also the fencing around work WATER SUPPLY. Another six wells commenced. " " (Pipe System). The system is now through to roadside tanks. Foul water system is complete. Engines satisfactory installed: Branch piping up to tanks at CASINO laid, less the connections to the tanks. Completed storage capacity for 16000 galls. near CASINO. Engine houses started in camp. 4" piping has now been laid out along the whole track ready for coupling & work commenced on the stand-pipes. The branch towards camp for battalions 1. 3 & 4 laid to railway. A small squad was engaged on the screwing & cutting of pipes for the work The section at DUNKERQUE packed up & marched to near the remainder of Coy. They were billeted at RAILHEAD where they will be employed on constructional work WORK IN CAMP. Contd work on Notice Boards etc	

Instructions regarding War Diaries and Intelligence Summaries are contained in F. S. Regs., Part II. and the Staff Manual respectively. Title pages will be prepared in manuscript.

WAR DIARY

or

~~INTELLIGENCE SUMMARY.~~

(Erase heading not required.)

Army Form C. 2118.

109th (Lowland) Field Coy RE

Place	Date	Hour	Summary of Events and Information	Remarks and references to Appendices
Coy-less 1 Sectn. billeted near CASINO POINT-de-GRAVELINES. 1 Section at Railhead near Coy.	17/7/17		WATER SUPPLY (WELLS) The progress of 6 wells was good & these will be completed on the morrow.	
			WATER SUPPLY (PIPE SYSTEM). Engine & pumps running by mid-day & ran most of the afternoon. One tank was filled.	
			All the main was laid less two connections.	
			Branch to DE & stand pipe will be fixed to-morrow	
			Section at Railhead continued work on platform & other constructing work.	
			In Camp. A squad continued work on making Notice Boards etc.	
			Weather - Very Warm	
			GP	

2353 Wt. W2544/1454 700,000 5/15 D. D. & L. A.D.S.S./Forms/C. 2118.

Instructions regarding War Diaries and Intelligence Summaries are contained in F. S. Regs., Part II. and the Staff Manual respectively. Title pages will be prepared in manuscript.

WAR DIARY

or

~~INTELLIGENCE SUMMARY.~~

(Erase heading not required.)

Army Form C. 2118.

409th (Lowland) Field Coy R.E.

Place	Date	Hour	Summary of Events and Information	Remarks and references to Appendices
Coy – less 1 Sectn – billeted near CASINO POINT-de-GRAVELINES. Section billeted at Railhead near the remainder of the Coy	18/4/17		CANAL BANK. A party continued work on the improving of the Camouflage at this work. WELLS. Extra three wells completed & as little extra work will finish off the remaining three. PIPE SUPPLY. All branches laid & standpipes fixed – less delivery hose. The tanks have been fixed. Main complete except connection to tank. One of the engine castings was repaired & fixed. Pond water level was found to be unsatisfactory. SECTION AT RAILHEAD. This section commenced work on the making of a platform etc. WORK IN CAMP. Squad of 2 joiners & 1 painter continued work on Notice Boards etc. Weather – Very Warm	

(97)

2353 Wt. W2544/1454 700,000 5/15 D. D. & L. A.D.S.S./Forms/C. 2118.

Army Form C. 2118.

WAR DIARY

or

~~INTELLIGENCE SUMMARY.~~

(Erase heading not required.)

Instructions regarding War Diaries and Intelligence Summaries are contained in F. S. Regs., Part II. and the Staff Manual respectively. Title pages will be prepared in manuscript.

Place	Date	Hour	Summary of Events and Information	Remarks and references to Appendices
Coy - less 1 Sect. billeted near CASINO at POINT-de-GRAVELINES. 1 Section billeted at Railhead near the remainder of Coy.	19/4/17		CANAL BANK. A party continued work on the screening, the 2nd series being completed & one side screen added & an extra one made WATER SUPPLY - WELLS. The last 3 wells were completed & another 3 cleaned & deepened WATER SUPPLY - PIPE SYSTEM. The roofing in of tanks was commenced. One engine shed was completed & the other is well in hand. Engine casting was repaired complete & after being tested was found satisfactory Works at pond. An irrigation channel was cut in marsh & sumps cleaned out Pipe line straightened & levelled out. The section working at Railhead continued work on the making of a platform etc In camp work was proceeded with on the making of small boxes for fitting on the ends of suction hose to prevent its silting up with sand Weather - Very Blowy - Dry	

2353 Wt. W2544/1454 700,000 5/15 D. D. & L. A.D.S.S./Forms/C. 2118.

Instructions regarding War Diaries and Intelligence Summaries are contained in F. S. Regs., Part II. and the Staff Manual respectively. Title pages will be prepared in manuscript.

WAR DIARY
or
~~INTELLIGENCE SUMMARY.~~
(Erase heading not required.)

Army Form C. 2118.

409th (Lowland) Field Coy RE.

Place	Date	Hour	Summary of Events and Information	Remarks and references to Appendices
Coy - less 1 Sect. at billeted near CASINO POINT-de-GRAVELINES. 1 Section at Railhead near the Coy	20/1/17		CANAL BANK. Side screens erected. WELLS (WATER SUPPLY.) Five wells for other units commenced & sunk to about 6'. PIPE SYSTEM (WATER SUPPLY). Connections were completed so far as fittings would allow. Water pumped & delivered to Hotel Sans Famille Stand Pipe Two irrigation channels put in & sump deepened The Section at Railhead continued work on platform & also on various other constructional work. Squad in Camp continued work on the making of Notice Boards etc. Weather - Warm - Breezy [signature]	

2353 Wt. W2544/1454 700,000 5/15 D. D. & L. A.D.S.S./Forms/C. 2118.

Instructions regarding War Diaries and Intelligence Summaries are contained in F. S. Regs., Part II. and the Staff Manual respectively. Title pages will be prepared in manuscript.

WAR DIARY
or
INTELLIGENCE SUMMARY.
(Erase heading not required.)

Army Form C. 2118.

Place	Date	Hour	Summary of Events and Information	Remarks and references to Appendices
Coy camped near CASINO near POINTE-de-GRAVELINES - less 1 Sectn	21/4/17		WORK at CANAL BANK. Erecting of Hangar to cover top of concrete work was commenced & fairly good headway made. Work was also continued on the camouflage a good quantity of new work being put up.	
1 Section at Railhead near remainder of Company.			WATER-SUPPLY - WELLS. Cleaned & deepened a further 3 wells	
			WATER-SUPPLY - PIPE SYSTEM. The roofing in of the tanks was continued	
			The section at Railhead near Coy continued work on the making of sidings etc	
			Squad of joiners in Camp continued work on Notice Boards etc.	
			Weather - Bright & Breezy	
			[initials in circle]	

2353 Wt. W2544/1454 700,000 5/15 D. D. & L. A.D.S.S./Forms/C. 2118.

Instructions regarding War Diaries and Intelligence Summaries are contained in F. S. Regs., Part II. and the Staff Manual respectively. Title pages will be prepared in manuscript.

WAR DIARY or ~~INTELLIGENCE SUMMARY~~.

(*Erase heading not required.*)

409th (Lowland) Field Coy. RE

Army Form C. 2118.

Place	Date	Hour	Summary of Events and Information	Remarks and references to Appendices
Coy. camped near CASINO near POINT-de-GRAVELINES less one Section 1 Section at RAILHEAD near remainder of Company.	22/7/17.		WORK ON CANAL BANK. Commenced work on preparation of screens & guys & uprights: An aeroplane ~~The~~ Hangar was erected & guyed. Poles for guys were found to be too light so 4" piping was substituted in their stead. (site on exposed Hill) 1½ Sections of RE's assisted by 100 Pioneers were engaged on the above work. The other two sections less 12 men on above work were engaged on the following:– Rifle Inspection: Instruction in the fitting of the New Box Respirator & drill with the same fitted. One Officer & 10 OR proceeded to the Central Repair Shops, Heavy Branch MGC. ERIN to work on Special Work. A Coy. Church Service was held during the afternoon. One Section – less one squad – working at Railhead near Coy. Camp on constructional work etc. Weather – Very Warm.	

2353 Wt. W2544/1454 700,000 5/15 D. D. & L. A.D.S.S./Forms/C. 2118.

Instructions regarding War Diaries and Intelligence Summaries are contained in F. S. Regs., Part II. and the Staff Manual respectively. Title pages will be prepared in manuscript.

WAR DIARY ~~or INTELLIGENCE SUMMARY~~. 409th (Lowland) Field Coy, RE.

(Erase heading not required.)

Army Form C. 2118.

Place	Date	Hour	Summary of Events and Information	Remarks and references to Appendices
Whole Coy - less 1 section - Camped near the CASINO at POINT-de GRAVELINES. 1 Section at Railhead near the Coy.	23/7/17		CANAL BANK. Continued work on the erection of screening etc, adjusting same to allow for windage. WATER SUPPLY (Pipe System) One tarpaulin was changed at storage tank owing to leakage. Irrigation channels were further deepened at water point. WELLS. One section completed work on camp wells. Section working at Railhead continued on constructional work etc. 1 Officer & 10 OR at ERIN. (Central Repair Shops, Heavy MGC) working on special work. WORK IN CAMP near CASINO. A small squad continued work on the making of Notice Boards etc. for Wells & Latrines. Weather - Very Blowy - Dry [initials]	

2353 Wt. W2544/1454 700,000 5/15 D. D. & L. A.D.S.S./Forms/C. 2118.

Instructions regarding War Diaries and Intelligence Summaries are contained in F. S. Regs., Part II. and the Staff Manual respectively. Title pages will be prepared in manuscript.

WAR DIARY
or
~~INTELLIGENCE SUMMARY.~~
(Erase heading not required.)

109th (Lowland) Field Coy. R.E.

Army Form C. 2118.

Place	Date	Hour	Summary of Events and Information	Remarks and references to Appendices
Coy – less 1 Sect:– Camped near CASINO near POINT-de-GRAVELINES. 1 Section at Railhead near remainder of Company	24/7/17		CANAL BANK. Continued work on the adjusting of roof screens & connecting to Hangar. WATER SUPPLY. (Pipe System). Continued work on deepening & cleaning of pond & a connecting trench made between two ponds. The branch to the DE* was completed. (* Divisional Headquarters & 1 battalion branch pipe 700 x long) An Iron Well was started at 2nd source of supply for the Pipe System & the Well is 3 Cassions down. All Tanks shifted to desired sites. The section at Railhead continued on constructional work. One Section in training in Camp: Squad drill: Rifle exercises etc. This section had an inspection of Rifles kit books etc. & all deficiencies noted. 1 Officer & 10 OR on Special Work at ERIN. (Central Repair Shops, Heavy MGC) CASUALTIES. One sapper drowned while bathing & another admitted to Hospl. Weather — Very Warm G.E.H.	

2353 Wt. W2544/1454 700,000 5/15 D. D. & L. A.D.S.S./Forms/C. 2118.

Instructions regarding War Diaries and Intelligence Summaries are contained in F. S. Regs., Part II. and the Staff Manual respectively. Title pages will be prepared in manuscript.

WAR DIARY
or
~~INTELLIGENCE SUMMARY~~.
(Erase heading not required.)

Army Form C. 2118.

Place	Date	Hour	Summary of Events and Information	Remarks and references to Appendices
Coy. camped near CASINO at POINTE-de-GRAVELINES – less 1 Sect. working at Railhead near Coy.	25/7/17		CANAL BANK. The screening over of both slopes & Marquee is now complete WATER SUPPLY. The sinking of Iron Well was continued & excellent progress made A Patrol inspects all Wells & gear each day to see that all is correct. Section at Railhead – less one squad – continued work on the making of sidings & also on sundry other work. 1 Off & 10 OR working on Special Work at ERIN (Central Repair Shops, Heavy MGC.) 1 Section ~~&~~ part of another in training the following being the Programme for the day:- Physical drill: Communicating drill: Section drill with rifles: Kit inspection & Bathing parade Weather – Very Warm GLW	

Army Form C. 2118.

Instructions regarding War Diaries and Intelligence Summaries are contained in F. S. Regs., Part II. and the Staff Manual respectively. Title pages will be prepared in manuscript.

WAR DIARY
or
~~INTELLIGENCE SUMMARY~~.
(Erase heading not required.)

Place	Date	Hour	Summary of Events and Information	Remarks and references to Appendices
Coy – less ½ Section – at CAMP near POINT-de-GRAVELINES – ½ Section at Railhead near the Coy. One Squad at ERIN	26/7/17		WATER SUPPLY. The sinking of the well near the Railhead was continued & this well is now 60% completed. The remainder of the Coy carried out the following training during the forenoon:– Instruction in the packing of toolcarts: Giving the best mode of arranging Fighting Order Equipment: Training on the CANAL BANK. The kit etc of two sections was inspected & all deficiencies etc noted. The Coy. attended the Burial Service at (MARDICK D.3.3.0. Sheet DUNKERQUE 1A 1/100,000) of Sapper Thomson who was drowned while bathing. ½ Section at Railhead constructing sidings etc. 1 Officer & 10 OR working on Special Work at Central Repair Shops Heavy MGC ERIN. Weather – Cloudy – Dry GWH	

2353 Wt. W2544/1454 700,000 5/15 D. D. & L. A.D.S.S./Forms/C. 2118.

Instructions regarding War Diaries and Intelligence Summaries are contained in F. S. Regs., Part II. and the Staff Manual respectively. Title pages will be prepared in manuscript.

WAR DIARY

or

~~INTELLIGENCE SUMMARY~~.

(Erase heading not required.)

409th (Lowland) Field Coy R.E. (T.) — Army Form C. 2118.

Place	Date	Hour	Summary of Events and Information	Remarks and references to Appendices
Coy - less 1 Sectn - camp at CASINO near POINTE-de-GRAVELINES. ½ Section at Railhead near Coy. 1 Squad at ERIN.	27/7/17		WATER SUPPLY. Continued work on Well sinking & 7 rings sunk approx 10' of water. CANAL BANK. Work was continued on the thickening of the camouflage screening. TRAINING. Physical Drill & Communicating Drill followed by experimental drill in the fitting of kits & carts. During the afternoon open order work was practiced on the dunes - dress - fighting order. ½ Section at Railhead working on the making of sidings 1 Officer & 10 OR working on Special Work at Central Repair Shops, Heavy, MGC, ERIN Weather - Showery (initials, circled)	

2353 Wt. W2544/1454 700,000 5/15 D. D. & L. A.D.S.S./Forms/C. 2118.

Instructions regarding War Diaries and Intelligence Summaries are contained in F. S. Regs., Part II. and the Staff Manual respectively. Title pages will be prepared in manuscript.

WAR DIARY
or
INTELLIGENCE SUMMARY.
(Erase heading not required.)

409th (Lowland) Field Coy RE

Army Form C. 2118.

Place	Date	Hour	Summary of Events and Information	Remarks and references to Appendices
Coy - less 1 Section - encamped near CASINO at POINTE-de-GRAVELINES. ½ Section at Railhead & 1 squad at ERIN.	28/4/17		WATER SUPPLY. Work was continued on the sinking of Well at Snipers Bog (near Railhead) ½ Section at Railhead working on the making of sidings etc. TRAINING. Physical Training followed by practice in Bayonet Fighting during the forenoon. Afternoon. Lectures on Wiring & Bangalore Torpedoes followed by practical demonstration. 1 Officer & 10 OR at Central Repair Shops Heavy MGC ERIN working on Special Work. Weather - Dull & Blowy [illegible]	
"	29/4/17		Tents were struck & moved to clean ground. A Church Service was held during the forenoon. ½ Section at Railhead continued work on sidings etc. 1 Officer & 10 OR at Central Repair Shops Heavy MGC ERIN working on Special Work Weather - Clear & Dry - Breezy [illegible]	

Instructions regarding War Diaries and Intelligence Summaries are contained in F. S. Regs., Part II. and the Staff Manual respectively. Title pages will be prepared in manuscript.

WAR DIARY
or
~~INTELLIGENCE SUMMARY.~~
(Erase heading not required.)

409 (Lowland) Field Coy R.E. Army Form C. 2118.

Place	Date	Hour	Summary of Events and Information	Remarks and references to Appendices
Coy - less 1 Section - camped near CASINO at POINT-de-GRAVELINES. ½ Section at Railhead near Coy. Squad at ERIN.	30/4/17		The following was the training programme for the day:- Forenoon: Physical Exercises: Bayonet Fighting. Musketry:- aiming - trigger pressing - positions etc. Afternoon: Practice in taking up wire entanglement & relaying in new positions. ½ Section at Railhead continued work on making sidings etc. Squad at Central Repair Shops Heavy MGC ERIN working on Special Work. Weather - Showery. G.W.H.	

2353 Wt. W2544/1454 700,000 5/15 D. D. & L. A.D.S.S./Forms/C. 2118.

Instructions regarding War Diaries and Intelligence Summaries are contained in F. S. Regs., Part II. and the Staff Manual respectively. Title pages will be prepared in manuscript.

WAR DIARY
or
~~INTELLIGENCE~~ SUMMARY.
(Erase heading not required.)

409th (Lowland) Field Coy. R.E. Army Form C. 2118.

Place	Date	Hour	Summary of Events and Information	Remarks and references to Appendices
Coy - less 1 Sectn - at CASINO near POINTE de GRAVELINES. ½ Section at Railhead near Coy. 1 Squad at ERIN.	3/7/17		The following was the training programme for the day:- Physical Exercises etc in the early morning. Forenoon. Instruction in Bayonet Fighting & Musketry generally. Afternoon. Dismantling a belt of wire: Constructing two strong points & wiring same special attention being given to working conditions when under observation. Instruction also given as to the placing of covering parties.	
			½ Section working at Railhead - near the Coy - on the making of sidings & sundry other work.	
			1 Officer & 10 OR at Central Repair Shops, Heavy MGC ERIN.	
			Weather - Showery - Breezy	

[signature]
Major. R.E.
O.C. 409th (Lowland) Field Coy R.E. (T)

W A R   D I A R Y.

409th (Lowland) Field Coy., R.E.,(T).

1st. DIVISION.

AUGUST.1917.

WAR DIARY.

409th.(Lowland) Field Coy., R.E.(T).

1st.Division.

SEPTEMBER.1917.

CONFIDENTIAL

VII 33

WAR DIARY

OF

409th (LOWLAND) FIELD COY R.E. (T)

from 1st August 1917 to 31st August 1917

(Volume No. XXXII)

Instructions regarding War Diaries and Intelligence Summaries are contained in F. S. Regs., Part II. and the Staff Manual respectively. Title pages will be prepared in manuscript.

WAR DIARY of 409th (LOWLAND) FIELD COY RE.

Army Form C. 2118.

~~or~~

~~INTELLIGENCE SUMMARY.~~

(*Erase heading not required.*)

Place	Date	Hour	Summary of Events and Information	Remarks and references to Appendices
Coy camped near CASINO C.3.57.38 Sheet 1A DUNKERQUE 1/100,000.	1/8/17		The Coy continued work on Training etc The forenoon programme of training was as follows:- Bayonet Exercises & instruction in bayonet fighting generally. Instruction in musketry, snapshooting etc followed by practice in knotting & lashing Afternoon:- Senior NCO's lectured by O/c on Demolitions ~~after~~ after the various sections were given practice in the joining of fuzes, detonators, leads etc. Detached Parties Squad of 4 OR at Railhead near Coy assisting with work generally there. 1 Officer & 10 OR at ERIN working on Special Work Weather - Wet & Stormy. [signature]	attached Appendix A 3 pages & plan A.B.C.

2353 Wt. W2544/1454 700,000 5/15 D. D. & L. A.D.S.S./Forms/C. 2118.

Instructions regarding War Diaries and Intelligence Summaries are contained in F. S. Regs., Part II. and the Staff Manual respectively. Title pages will be prepared in manuscript.

WAR DIARY of 409th (LOW) FD. Co. R.E.

or

~~INTELLIGENCE SUMMARY.~~

(Erase heading not required.)

Army Form C. 2118.

Place	Date	Hour	Summary of Events and Information	Remarks and references to Appendices
Coy camped near CASINO 63.51.38 Sheet 1A DUNKERQUE 1/100,000.	2/8/17		The following work was carried out during the day:- One Section engaged on the construction of an Obstacle Course for the 3rd Bde. WATER SUPPLY. Connections for 4" valves commenced. CAMOUFLAGE Extra camouflage was erected at "SEA WALL" near Coy. TRAINING. Three sections carried out the following training during the day:- Musketry drill followed by firing practice at which the worst shots were given special instruction with a view to effecting their improvement. Experiments were carried out on SEA-WALL near camp (i.e.) the scaling of Wall with cycles. (Cycles were shouldered by each individual man & the Slope negotiated quite successfully). The kits of three sections were examined during the day & all deficiency noted. Detached Parties. 4 OR at Railhead assisting with work 1 Off & 10 OR at ERIN working on Special Work Weather - Blowy - Showery [illegible]	

Instructions regarding War Diaries and Intelligence Summaries are contained in F. S. Regs., Part II. and the Staff Manual respectively. Title pages will be prepared in manuscript.

WAR DIARY of 409th (LOW) FD. CO. R.E.
or
INTELLIGENCE SUMMARY.
(Erase heading not required.)

Army Form C. 2118.

Place	Date	Hour	Summary of Events and Information	Remarks and references to Appendices
Coy camped near CASINO C.3.57.38. Sheet 11A. DUNKERQUE 1/100,000.	3/11/		One Section continued work on making of Obstacle Course for the 3rd Brigade. A party engaged fixing up additional camouflage at SEA-WALL. TRAINING. One Section on Musketry – firing practice on foreshore. One Section on practice at bomb-throwing & also instructed in the use of Bangalore Torpedoes. One Section practised the construction of Strong Points. Detached Parties. 1 Officer & 10 OR at ERIN working on Special Work 1 small squad at Railhead assisting with work there. Weather – Clear & Bright	

2353 Wt. W2544/1454 700,000 5/15 D. D. & L. A.D.S.S./Forms/C. 2118.

Instructions regarding War Diaries and Intelligence Summaries are contained in F. S. Regs., Part II. and the Staff Manual respectively. Title pages will be prepared in manuscript.

WAR DIARY of 409th (LOW) FD. CO. R.E.
or
~~INTELLIGENCE SUMMARY.~~
(*Erase heading not required.*)

Army Form C. 2118.

Place	Date	Hour	Summary of Events and Information	Remarks and references to Appendices
Coy camped near CASINO C.3.51.38 Sheet 1 A DUNKERQUE 1/100,000	4/8/17		WORKS: Work was proceeded with on Obstacle Course at 3rd Bde although work was hampered through lack of materials One Section engaged on the reerection of a screen blown down by gale near SEA-WALL. WATER-SUPPLY. A patrol examines each day the whole of the wells furnishing the Camps Water Supply. All broken gear is repaired or replaced & a record also taken of the yield of water in each well. TRAINING. One Section on Musketry, Bombing & Bangalores these latter receiving special attention, their construction & methods of firing all being explained. One Section received instruction & also carried out practical work on the construction of strong points & their wiring. Detached Parties. 4 OR at Railhead near Coy engaged on work there. 1 Officer & 10 OR at ERIN working on special work. Weather - Blowy - Dry	

[signature]

2353 Wt. W2544/1454 700,000 5/15 D. D. & L. A.D.S.S./Forms/C. 2118.

Instructions regarding War Diaries and Intelligence Summaries are contained in F. S. Regs., Part II. and the Staff Manual respectively. Title pages will be prepared in manuscript.

WAR DIARY of 409th (LOWLAND) FIELD Coy RE ~~or~~ ~~INTELLIGENCE SUMMARY.~~

(Erase heading not required.)

Army Form C. 2118.

Place	Date	Hour	Summary of Events and Information	Remarks and references to Appendices
Coy camped near CASINO 6.3 51. 38. Sheet 1A DUNKERQUE 1/100,000.	5/8/14		A Church Service was held during the morning followed by a bathing parade at which non-swimmers were given instruction. WORKS. A party of 7 OR working on Special Work at 1st DE. 1 Officer & 10 OR at ERIN working on Special work. A Small squad at Railhead near Coy assisting with work there. WATER SUPPLY. Repairs were carried out on gear at various wells. SPECIAL PARADE. The Coy - less drivers - turned out at midnight & practised the scaling of the sample SEA-WALL. The night was foggy & the Coy were lectured by O/C on the need for absolute silence throughout the whole of the practice. Weather — Warm throughout the day	

[signature]

Instructions regarding War Diaries and Intelligence Summaries are contained in F. S. Regs., Part II. and the Staff Manual respectively. Title pages will be prepared in manuscript.

WAR DIARY of 409th (LOWLAND) FIELD COY RE
or
INTELLIGENCE SUMMARY.
(*Erase heading not required.*)

Army Form C. 2118.

Place	Date	Hour	Summary of Events and Information	Remarks and references to Appendices
Coy camped near CASINO C3.57.38. Sheet 1A DUNKERQUE 1/100,000.	6/8/17		The following training was carried out during the day:- 1 Section – Drill & Lecture on Bangalores. 2 Sections – Bombing: Lecture & instruction on the defence of houses Officers & senior NCOs were given a lecture by the O/c on a Defensive System, included in which was the construction of Strong Points & siting of wire etc. The rifles kits & cycles of 3 Sections were inspected & all deficiencies noted. 1 Section continued work on 3rd Bde Obstacle Course. WATER SUPPLY. A water patrol examines each day all wells in the Camps. The yield of water in each well is checked daily & all gear out of order repaired. Detached Parties. 1 Officer & 10 OR at ERIN working on special work Inoculation. A Section & ½ half of the Coy were inoculated TAB. Weather – Showery – Clear	GCS

2353 Wt. W2544/1454 700,000 5/15 D. D. & L. A.D.S.S./Forms/C. 2118.

Instructions regarding War Diaries and Intelligence Summaries are contained in F. S. Regs., Part II. and the Staff Manual respectively. Title pages will be prepared in manuscript.

WAR DIARY of 409th (LOWLAND) FIELD COY RE

or

~~INTELLIGENCE SUMMARY.~~

(*Erase heading not required.*)

Army Form C. 2118.

Place	Date	Hour	Summary of Events and Information	Remarks and references to Appendices
Coy. camped near CASINO C.3.57.38. Sheet 1A DUNKERQUE 1/100000.	4/8/17		A squad continued work at Divisional Head Qrs on erecting a Hangar to join up with the one already up. This work was almost completed.	
			Forenoon { 1 Section received training in knots & lashings & also instruction in loopholing. 1 Section on firing practice	
			Afternoon. – The above 2 sections practiced wiring of Strong Points.	
			Detached Parties. A party of 1 Officer & 10 OR at ERNY working on Special Work. Small squad at Railhead near the Coy assisting generally ~~work~~ work there	
			Weather Showery	

Instructions regarding War Diaries and Intelligence Summaries are contained in F. S. Regs., Part II. and the Staff Manual respectively. Title pages will be prepared in manuscript.

WAR DIARY of 409th (LOW) FD. COY. R.E. or ~~INTELLIGENCE SUMMARY~~.

(*Erase heading not required.*)

Army Form C. 2118.

Place	Date	Hour	Summary of Events and Information	Remarks and references to Appendices
Coy. camp at near CASINO C.351.38 Sheet 1A DUNKERQUE 1/100,000	1/1/17		The Coy less drivers paraded for Physical Training during the morning followed by a forenoon's training thus:- Packing contents of tool-cart. * Practice on slope with Carts Cycles & Bangalore Torpedoes. Passage of Orders etc. Afternoon. The four sections marched to near Div. Head Qrs & there practised the off loading of the sample Pontoons under Bde. arrangements. A squad continued work on Hangar at 1st Div. H.Q. & ~~little~~ now remains to complete. Detached Parties. 1 Officer & 10 OR at ERIN working on special work. A small squad at Head Qrs Dumps (Railhead) assisting with general work there. * A handcart with 250 lbs weight was taken up slope by 15 men devoid of any assistance from above. Cycles were carried up slope on shoulders - one man per cycle - & no difficulty experienced. Numerous ways were tried with Bangalores - still undecided which is the best. Weather	

2353 Wt. W2544/1454 700,000 5/15 D. D. & L. A.D.S.S./Forms/C. 2118.

Instructions regarding War Diaries and Intelligence Summaries are contained in F. S. Regs., Part II. and the Staff Manual respectively. Title pages will be prepared in manuscript.

WAR DIARY of 409th (LOW) Fd. Coy. R.E. ~~or~~ ~~INTELLIGENCE~~ ~~SUMMARY~~.

Army Form C. 2118.

(Erase heading not required.)

Place	Date	Hour	Summary of Events and Information	Remarks and references to Appendices
Coy camped near CASINO C3.51.38. Sheet 1A DUNKERQUE 1/100,000	9/8/17		The whole Coy - less drivers - paraded for Physical Exercises in the morning - followed by Demolitions - Lecture & practice. The following were the main points covered: - Firing precautions: Placing charges: Demonstration of placing & firing of charges: Results of bad contact in laying charges: Effects of charges not being continuous: Bangalores used as land mine (using 2" water-pipe) WORKS. 6 men engaged on the strengthening of the guys on old Hangar near Div. Head Qrs. 4 men engaged on the repair of pipe line tanks & wells. 4 men " " screening at SEA WALL. Hangar was also repaired where damaged. Detached Parties. 1 Officer & 10 OR at ERIN working on special work there. Small squad at Railhead near Coy working on general work. Weather - Blowy - Dry [initials]	

WAR DIARY of 409th (LOW) FD COY. R.E. Army Form C. 2118.

~~**INTELLIGENCE SUMMARY.**~~

(Erase heading not required.)

Instructions regarding War Diaries and Intelligence Summaries are contained in F. S. Regs., Part II. and the Staff Manual respectively. Title pages will be prepared in manuscript.

Place	Date	Hour	Summary of Events and Information	Remarks and references to Appendices
Coy camped near CASINO C.3.51.38. Sheet 19 DUNKERQUE 1/100,000.	Night of 9/10 Aug 17.		Night Operations. All sections & attached Infantry working on Strong Point which was dug to 3' deep & wired practically all round. Afternoon of 10th/8/17 Inspection of Gas Helmets. Preparation of Bangalores & Wiring etc for night operations following night. Detached Parties. 1 Officer & 10 OR at ERIN working on special work there. 1 Small party at Railhead near Coy assisting with work generally. Weather – Wet & stormy during night Dry & clear throughout the day.	

Instructions regarding War Diaries and Intelligence Summaries are contained in F. S. Regs., Part II. and the Staff Manual respectively. Title pages will be prepared in manuscript.

WAR DIARY 7. 409th (LOW). FD. COY. R.E.
or
~~INTELLIGENCE SUMMARY.~~
(*Erase heading not required.*)

Army Form C. 2118.

Place	Date	Hour	Summary of Events and Information	Remarks and references to Appendices
Coy. Camped near CASINO C.3.57.38 Sheet 1A DUNKERQUE 1/100,000	Night of 10/11 Aug 1917		Night Operations. – No. 1 + 4 Sections and attached infantry Strong Point siting, selection + construction with covering portions. No. 2 + 3 Sections Night marching across Dunes by Compass attacking Strong Points under construction by 1 + 4.	
			Afternoon + evening 11/8/17 – Demonstration in firing of Bangalore Torpedoes attended by whole Coy, attached Infantry + Special Party from 2nd Brigade – Practice on + off Pontoon loading + unloading stores etc on same.	
			Weather – Dry + fine –	
			Note on Bangalores.	
			Four Torpedoes were fired as under:	
Time 2" pipe slightly quicker.			20' wire – Jointed Tube 4/6ft lengths under wire – complete gap.	
			20' wire 2" pipe 18' long " " – complete gap except last few strands owing to torpedo being too short.	
2" pipe very quick – Jointed pipe awkward + not recommended over wire			18 wire 2" " 18' long over wire – complete gap	
			18 – Jointed Tube 4/6ft length " " – complete gap	
			Average gap 10 yards.	

(stamp: [illegible])

2353 Wt. W2544/1454 700,000 5/15 D. D. & L. A.D.S.S./Forms/C. 2118.

Instructions regarding War Diaries and Intelligence Summaries are contained in F. S. Regs., Part II. and the Staff Manual respectively. Title pages will be prepared in manuscript.

WAR DIARY of 409th (LOW) FD. COY. R.E.

~~or~~

~~INTELLIGENCE SUMMARY.~~

(*Erase heading not required.*)

Army Form C. 2118.

Place	Date	Hour	Summary of Events and Information	Remarks and references to Appendices
Coy Camped near CASINO C.3.51.38 Sheet 19 DUNKERQUE 1/100,000	12/8/17		Forenoon. – Church Parade Afternoon. – Free. Weather – Dry & fine.	

2353 Wt. W2544/1454 700,000 5/15 D. D. & L. A.D.S.S./Forms/C. 2118.

Instructions regarding War Diaries and Intelligence Summaries are contained in F. S. Regs., Part II. and the Staff Manual respectively. Title pages will be prepared in manuscript.

WAR DIARY of 409th (LOW) FD. COY. R.E.
or
~~INTELLIGENCE SUMMARY.~~
(*Erase heading not required.*)

Army Form C. 2118.

Place	Date	Hour	Summary of Events and Information	Remarks and references to Appendices
Coy. Campbell near CASINO C. 3. 51. 38 Sheet 1A DUNKERQUE 1/100,000	13/8/17		Morning – Coy paraded for Physical Exercises & Bathing	
			Forenoon – Sections under Section Officers visited Strong Points made previous evenings, officers pointing out lessons of each.	
			Afternoon – Sections under 2nd Offs wiring & lifting wire – Officers and N. C. Os. notes on Village Defence by O.C. followed by Sections defending LE CLIPON VILLAGE.	
			Weather – Fine occasional showers.	

[initials, circled]

Instructions regarding War Diaries and Intelligence Summaries are contained in F. S. Regs., Part II. and the Staff Manual respectively. Title pages will be prepared in manuscript.

WAR DIARY of 409th (LOW) FD. COY. RE.

or

~~INTELLIGENCE SUMMARY.~~

(Erase heading not required.)

Army Form C. 2118.

Place	Date	Hour	Summary of Events and Information	Remarks and references to Appendices
Coy. Camp at near CASINO C. 3. 51. 38 Sheet 1A DUNKERQUE 1/100,000	14/8/17		Morning. – Physical Exercises for whole Coy. Attached Infantry on Slope.	
			Forenoon – Sections engaged under Section Officers Squad & Rifle Drill, followed by Drill Inspection in turn by O.C. finishing with Coy Drill & Bathe.	
			Attached Infantry – Demonstration on wall slope before O.C.	
			Afternoon. – 2 Sections Rifle firing (10 rds)	
			2 Sections Bombing practice (Live bombs)	
		9-30 A.M.	Harness Inspection	
			Working Parties 6 men of No. 3 Section commenced work on Cinema Plant	
			Weather – Dry windy.	

[signature]

2353 Wt. W2544/1454 700,000 5/15 D. D. & L. A.D.S.S./Forms/C. 2118.

Instructions regarding War Diaries and Intelligence Summaries are contained in F. S. Regs., Part II. and the Staff Manual respectively. Title pages will be prepared in manuscript.

WAR DIARY of 409th (LOW) FD. COY. R.E.
or
~~INTELLIGENCE~~ SUMMARY.
(*Erase heading not required.*)

Army Form C. 2118.

Place	Date	Hour	Summary of Events and Information	Remarks and references to Appendices
Coy. Camped near CASINO C.3. 51. 38. Sheet 19 DUNKERQUE 1/100,000	15/8/17		The whole Coy paraded at 8.15 A.M. for practice on Pontoons, returning to Camp 2 P.M. Remainder of day free. — Working Party — The 6 men at Cinema plant, completed bedding of engine, screen in side, exhaust pipe prepared ready for fitting & engine base built. Weather — wet showers on & off all day.	

Instructions regarding War Diaries and Intelligence Summaries are contained in F. S. Regs., Part II. and the Staff Manual respectively. Title pages will be prepared in manuscript.

WAR DIARY of 409th (LOW) FD. COY. R.E.

Army Form C. 2118.

~~or INTELLIGENCE SUMMARY.~~

(Erase heading not required.)

Place	Date	Hour	Summary of Events and Information	Remarks and references to Appendices
Coy. Camped near CASINO C.3.51.38. Sheet 1A DUNKERQUE 1/100,000	16/8/17		Morning. – The whole Coy including attached Infantry Physical Exercises Forenoon. – No 2 + 3 Sections engaged in firing 10 rds " 1 + 4 " Live bombing + visual training. – Rifle Inspection at 1.30 P.M. Afternoon. – Experiments in Slope followed by Kit Inspection	

2353 Wt. W2544/1454 700,000 5/15 D. D. & L. A.D.S.S./Forms/C. 2118.

Instructions regarding War Diaries and Intelligence Summaries are contained in F. S. Regs., Part II. and the Staff Manual respectively. Title pages will be prepared in manuscript.

WAR DIARY of 404th (Low) Fd. Coy. R.E.

~~or~~

~~INTELLIGENCE SUMMARY.~~

(*Erase heading not required.*)

Army Form C. 2118.

Place	Date	Hour	Summary of Events and Information	Remarks and references to Appendices
Coy. Camped near CASINO C.3.51.38 Sheet 1A DUNKERQUE 1/100,000	17/8/17		Morning — Physical Exercises & Inf. Drill. whole Coy including attached Infantry. Forenoon — Nos 1,4 Sections — Musketry. Nos 2 & 3 " — Live Bombing followed by Rifle Inspection for all. Afternoon — Free in view of night operations. —	
Ditto	17/18 8/17		Night Operations — Disembarkation and practice up SEAWALL was indulged in. It was found considerably more difficult in the dark with loose sand. It is regarded as essential that the leading men take up a rope. The Unit should not dump equipment at bottom if called on to assist in off loading. Arrangements for orderlies as guides to lead section to Coy Dump when ready to move, was practised. Practice in marching across Dunes, taking & landing own tools, including practice with orderlies messages & Reports was carried out.	
	18/8/17	Day	Rifle & Kit Inspection of whole Coy including attached Infy. Weather — Dull & Stormy throughout.	G.W.

Instructions regarding War Diaries and Intelligence Summaries are contained in F. S. Regs., Part II. and the Staff Manual respectively. Title pages will be prepared in manuscript.

WAR DIARY of 2/1 09th (LOW) FD. COY. R.E.

Army Form C. 2118.

~~INTELLIGENCE SUMMARY.~~

(*Erase heading not required.*)

Place	Date	Hour	Summary of Events and Information	Remarks and references to Appendices
Coy Camped nr CASINO C.3.51.85 Sheet 1A DUNKERQUE 1/100,000	19/8/17		Forenoon – Church Parade Afternoon – Recreational training. Weather – fine & dry.	

2353 Wt. W2544/1454 700,000 5/15 D. D. & L. A.D.S.S./Forms/C. 2118.

Instructions regarding War Diaries and Intelligence Summaries are contained in F. S. Regs., Part II. and the Staff Manual respectively. Title pages will be prepared in manuscript.

WAR DIARY
or
INTELLIGENCE SUMMARY.
(Erase heading not required.)

409th (LOWLAND) FIELD COY R.E.

Army Form C. 2118.

Place	Date	Hour	Summary of Events and Information	Remarks and references to Appendices
Coy camped near CASINO C3.51.38. Sheet 19 DUNKERQUE 1/100,000.	20/8/17.		The five sections formed for future operations marched to Brigade Headquarters & there practiced the embarkation scheme on the supposed monitor. The afternoon was free in view of night operations which are given below.	
	20/21/8/17		Night Operations. The scheme was the practice (under cover of darkness) in embarking on monitor & disembarking at landing point, unloading stores etc. The five Sections therefore with cycles & handcarts complete carried out the scheme, included in which was the Scaling of the SEA-WALL, the fixing of a site for a proposed Bde Dump a Coy Headqrs etc etc. A short lecture on the nights work was given on completion of the operation after which the Coy returned to billets. Weather – Clear & Warm during day – Night – Dry & not too dark to impede operations.	GWS

2353 Wt. W2544/1454 700,000 5/15 D. D. & L. A.D.S.S./Forms/C. 2118.

Instructions regarding War Diaries and Intelligence Summaries are contained in F. S. Regs., Part II. and the Staff Manual respectively. Title pages will be prepared in manuscript.

WAR DIARY
or
~~INTELLIGENCE~~ SUMMARY.
(*Erase heading not required.*)

409th (LOWLAND) FIELD Coy R.E. (T)

Army Form C. 2118.

Place	Date	Hour	Summary of Events and Information	Remarks and references to Appendices
Coy. camped at CASINO C.3.51.38 Sheet 1a DUNKERQUE 1/100,000.	21/8/17		The following training was carried out during the day:- FORENOON:- All sections were lectured on the packing of handcarts & pack animals after which each squad packed & unpacked section's cart. Practice was also carried out in the speedy moving of carts when loaded. AFTERNOON:- The Coy paraded in fighting order (i.e) the usual marching order less greatcoat haversack shirt & a little small kit but with the following extras:- 70 rounds SAA: 2 Mills' Bombs: 1 spare iron ration: 5 sandbags & 10 lbs of tools etc. Instruction was given in the packing of Yukon Carriers & also in the packing in as small a compass as possible the kit each man would leave behind should the intended operation be carried out. Weather - Breezy - Clear & Sunny	(initials)

2353 Wt. W2544/1454 700,000 5/15 D. D. & L. A.D.S.S./Forms/C. 2118.

Instructions regarding War Diaries and Intelligence Summaries are contained in F. S. Regs., Part II. and the Staff Manual respectively. Title pages will be prepared in manuscript.

WAR DIARY
or
INTELLIGENCE SUMMARY.
(Erase heading not required.)

409th (LOWLAND) FIELD Coy R.E. (T)

Army Form C. 2118.

Place	Date	Hour	Summary of Events and Information	Remarks and references to Appendices
Coy camped at CASINO C3. 57.38 Sheet 1A DUNKERQUE 1/100,000	22/8/17		The training was proceeded with as follows:- FORENOON. Whole Coy less drivers paraded for Physical Exercises in the morning 6.30 to 7-15 included in which was the scaling of the SEA-WALL Two Sections for the forenoon on the following:- Filling a quantity of Bangalores & repairing a part of the Decauville track near the camp. One section of cyclists carried out practice in general reconnaissance which practice also included instruction in map-reading. One section & those inefficient from other sections carried out a forenoon's practice on firing & musketry generally. Much improvement was noticed in the case of the worst shots AFTERNOON. Whole Coy on Ceremonial Drill on fore-shore followed by an inspection of rifles. Detached Party. 1 Officer & 10 OR. at ERIN engaged on Special Work. Weather - Breezy - Dry & Clear	[initials]

2353 Wt. W2544/1454 700,000 5/15 D. D. & L. A.D.S.S./Forms/C. 2118.

Army Form C. 2118.

Instructions regarding War Diaries and Intelligence Summaries are contained in F. S. Regs., Part II. and the Staff Manual respectively. Title pages will be prepared in manuscript.

WAR DIARY
or
INTELLIGENCE SUMMARY.
(*Erase heading not required.*)

409th (LOWLAND) FIELD COY R.E.

Place	Date	Hour	Summary of Events and Information	Remarks and references to Appendices
Coy camped near CASINO C3.51.38. Sheet 12 DUNKERQUE 1/100,000.	23/8/17		A wire obstacle was erected at the SEA-WALL & a few repairs carried out to camouflage etc. The Coy - less drivers - paraded at 2-0 pm & marched to selected ground on foreshore & were inspected by CRE 1st Div (Troops drenched during march) 1 Off & 10 OR at ERIN working on special work. Weather - Heavy Rainstorm just previous to inspection	[initials]
ditto	24/8/17		The Coy paraded at 8-45 am & marched to selected ground on foreshore & were inspected by Div General (Major Gen Strickland G.O.C. 1st Div.) TRAINING . A short practice was carried out on the scaling of the SEA-WALL during the afternoon. A section turned out at 8-0 pm to repair Hangar which was badly rent by gale Weather - Very strong winds.	[initials]

2353 Wt. W2544/1454 700,000 5/15 D. D. & L. A.D.S.S./Forms/C. 2118.

Instructions regarding War Diaries and Intelligence Summaries are contained in F. S. Regs., Part II. and the Staff Manual respectively. Title pages will be prepared in manuscript.

WAR DIARY
or
~~INTELLIGENCE~~ SUMMARY.
(Erase heading not required.)

409th (LOWLAND) FIELD COY R.E. — Army Form C. 2118.

Place	Date	Hour	Summary of Events and Information	Remarks and references to Appendices
Coy. Camp at near CASINO C3.51.38. Sheet 1A DUNKERQUE 1/100,000.	25/8/17		The Coy paraded at 9-30 AM & marched to selected ground on foreshore & were inspected – along with the whole of the Divisional troops – by the Army Commander. WORKS. A party of 16 OR were engaged in the early morning tracing out the inspection ground. The whole Coy were engaged during the afternoon on the making & erecting of camouflage on SEA-WALL. This camouflage is to take the place of the Aeroplane Hangar which owing to the gale was practically torn to ribbons & had to be dismantled. 1 Officer & 10 OR returned from Special Work at ERIN. Weather – Very Boisterous. [initials]	
ditto.	26/8/17		A Church Service was held during the forenoon & all hands available were on the camouflage at SEA-WALL for the remainder of the day. Good headway was made with this work, despite the very strong wind. [initials]	

2353 Wt. W2544/1454 700,000 5/15 D. D. & L. A.D.S.S./Forms/C. 2118.

Army Form C. 2118.

WAR DIARY
or
~~INTELLIGENCE SUMMARY~~.

(*Erase heading not required.*)

409th (LOWLAND) FIELD Coy R.E.

Instructions regarding War Diaries and Intelligence Summaries are contained in F. S. Regs., Part II. and the Staff Manual respectively. Title pages will be prepared in manuscript.

Place	Date	Hour	Summary of Events and Information	Remarks and references to Appendices
Coy-camped near CASINO C.3.57.38. Sheet 1A DUNKERQUE 1/100000.	24/8/17		Two Sections carried out a Tactical Scheme with the 2nd Brigade Two Sections continued work on camouflage at SEA-WALL & good progress made WATER SUPPLY. Repairs were carried out to various wells in the Camps. Weather - Very Wet & Stormy	
ditto.	28/8/17		The whole Coy on Physical Exercises during the morning. 1 Section Carried on the re-erection of camouflage at SEA-WALL The remainder of the Coy received instruction in Signalling & also on Knotting & Lashing Repairs & improvements were carried out to Camp. Weather - Stormy.	

2353 Wt. W2544/1454 700,000 5/15 D. D. & L. A.D.S.S./Forms/C. 2118.

Instructions regarding War Diaries and Intelligence Summaries are contained in F. S. Regs., Part II. and the Staff Manual respectively. Title pages will be prepared in manuscript.

WAR DIARY of 409th (LOWLAND) FIELD COY RE
or
INTELLIGENCE SUMMARY.

(Erase heading not required.)

Army Form C. 2118.

Place	Date	Hour	Summary of Events and Information	Remarks and references to Appendices
Coy camped near CASINO C3.57.38. Sheet 1A DUNKERQUE 1/100,000.	29/8/17		Two Sections with attached Infantry carried on re-erection of camouflage at SEA-WALL. This work was extremely difficult owing to the very high wind. Some of the Camp structures were badly damaged by storm these therefore were repaired & improved. Two Sections instructed in rope-splicing & knotting & lashing. These two sections also received some instruction in signalling. Weather - Very Cold & Wet with accompanying cold winds.	

Instructions regarding War Diaries and Intelligence Summaries are contained in F. S. Regs., Part II. and the Staff Manual respectively. Title pages will be prepared in manuscript.

WAR DIARY of 409th (LOWLAND) FIELD Coy R.E. (T) or ~~INTELLIGENCE SUMMARY.~~

(*Erase heading not required.*)

Army Form C. 2118.

Place	Date	Hour	Summary of Events and Information	Remarks and references to Appendices
Coy camped near CASINO C.3.57.38 Sheet 1A DUNKERQUE 1/100,000.	30/8/17		Two sections & attached Infantry worked all day on the making & erecting of camouflage at SEA-WALL good progress being made with this work. A squad in Camp repairing & improving generally various Camp Structures. Remainder of Coy received instruction in Signalling & also engaged on Rifle Exercises etc for a short time. A squad of joiners working at 1st Div. Engr Headqrs making good the damage done by storm. Weather - Dull & Showery	

2353 Wt. W2544/1454 700,000 5/15 D. D. & L. A.D.S.S./Forms/C. 2118.

Instructions regarding War Diaries and Intelligence Summaries are contained in F. S. Regs., Part II. and the Staff Manual respectively. Title pages will be prepared in manuscript.

WAR DIARY of 409th (LOW) Fd. Coy. R.E.

~~or~~

~~INTELLIGENCE SUMMARY.~~

(*Erase heading not required.*)

Army Form C. 2118.

Place	Date	Hour	Summary of Events and Information	Remarks and references to Appendices
Coy Camped Nr CASINO C.3.51.38 Sheet 1A DUNKERQUE 1/40,000	31/8/17		Two Sections out on Bde manoeuvres.	
			Two Sections & attached Infantry repairing camouflage on SEA WALL	
			WORKING PARTY. Squad working at D.E. Head Qrs.	
			Weather. – Very stormy.	
			[illegible]	

A5834 Wt. W4973/M687 750,000 8/16 D. D. & L. Ltd. Forms/C.2118/13.

Appendix A to August War Diary.

Instructions regarding War Diaries and Intelligence Summaries are contained in F. S. Regs., Part II. and the Staff Manual respectively. Title pages will be prepared in manuscript.

WAR DIARY
or
INTELLIGENCE SUMMARY.
(Erase heading not required.)

Page 1

Army Form C. 2118.

Place	Date	Hour	Summary of Events and Information	Remarks and references to Appendices
Work.			Replica of SEAWALL for training Purposes constructed by 409 Lowland Field Coy — at Casino	Point de GRAVELINES
			The above work was reported under heading CANAL BANK in July Diary and the following is a summary	
			Attached are plans marked A, B, C. (A = Original Section B & C Section. 20 ft. width of each section on big map)	
Work Involved			(a) Selection of site, supply of material and transport to site	
			(b) Cut & fill to obtain correct slope for concrete & anchoring pickets	
			(c) Laying concrete	
			(d) Screening.	
A. Selection of Site etc.			The site was selected and approved by CRE — The service pocket Clinometer was most useful in obtaining approximate slopes.	
			Tools and materials required for the work were demanded and arrived throughout in time to avoid delaying the work —	
			All materials were dumped by lorry about 250 yards from the work and were run up on a 9 lb Decauville Track with trace horses to the site of work.	

2353 Wt. W2544/1454 700,000 5/15 D. D. & L. A.D.S.S./Forms/C. 2118.

Appendix to August War Diary
SEAWALL.

Instructions regarding War Diaries and Intelligence Summaries are contained in F. S. Regs., Part II. and the Staff Manual respectively. Title pages will be prepared in manuscript.

WAR DIARY
or
INTELLIGENCE SUMMARY.
(Erase heading not required.)

Page 2

Second

Army Form C. 2118.

Place	Date	Hour	Summary of Events and Information	Remarks and references to Appendices
B.			Preparation of Formation	
			(1) A provisional profile was erected above ground and section taken. – This was plotted and the final line selected which was 6 ft. below this provisional profile – Work on excavation of main part had meanwhile been commenced –	Sketch A attached shewing original slope
Cut.			The sand was shovelled to foot of slope and removed from there by drag scoops drawn by horses (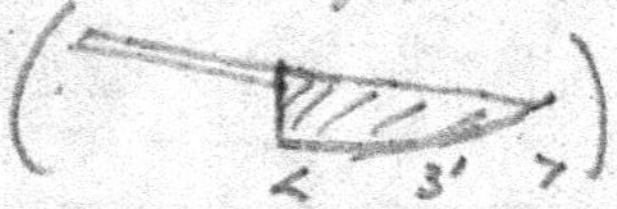). These scoops had to be improvised and were made of wood causing increased friction in haulage. It was found best to work horses singly with ¼ hour reliefs	
Fill.			The surface to be filled was revetted at intervals with stakes & wire netting anchored back – The first portion was done by hand shovelling but on arrival of Tip trucks on 2nd day the remainder was completed by Tip Truck.	
Revetting.			The sides were revetted and strutted back where above original sand dune level, in addition revetment was placed across the slope every 6 ft. and anchored back. The heads of the pickets being arranged to project into the concrete a few inches	
Work Involved			Approx. 500 yards cube of sand to Remove. 250 — — — — – Fill } Note owing to steepness of slope it was found quicker to fill with sand drawn from above —	

2353 Wt. W2544/1454 700,000 5/15 D. D. & L. A.D.S.S./Forms/C. 2118.

Sea Wall

Instructions regarding War Diaries and Intelligence Summaries are contained in F. S. Regs., Part II. and the Staff Manual respectively. Title pages will be prepared in manuscript.

WAR DIARY
or
INTELLIGENCE SUMMARY.
(Erase heading not required.)

Page (3)

Army Form C. 2118.

Place	Date	Hour	Summary of Events and Information	Remarks and references to Appendices

C Laying Concrete

The labour was organised by O.C. Work in five gangs. (1) Bringing material to site (2) Stone Breaking (3) Mixing Gangs (4) Laying party including reinforcing (5) Finishing Gang who followed close behind with surfacing.

Approx Quantity.	
Concrete	300 tons
(Cement	40 tons)

All mixing was done at the top & work commenced with bottom abutment & then the apron – The junction of each days work was left thicker and reinforcement left as a key – The concrete was put direct from mixing platforms into shoots of corrugated iron (portable). The slope of 1/2 was just sufficient to allow it to slide down at a rate at which the laying gang could deal with it – An anticipated difficulty of cement separating from aggregate was NOT found to be serious —

(d) Screening. The whole work & assembly ground had to be screened. Wire netting interwoven with strips of canvas was found most suitable — In all about 2000 sq yds of screening was erected.

(e) Time & Labour. For first 3 days 2 Sections RE. This was then increased by 1 Coy Pioneers working strength 120. Also unloading parties of from 30 – 70 Infantry daily —

The estimated time required was 14 days – The concrete work was complete in 12 days more labour being available than was anticipated —

5/8/17

G. [illegible] Major RE
OC 409 Fd Coy

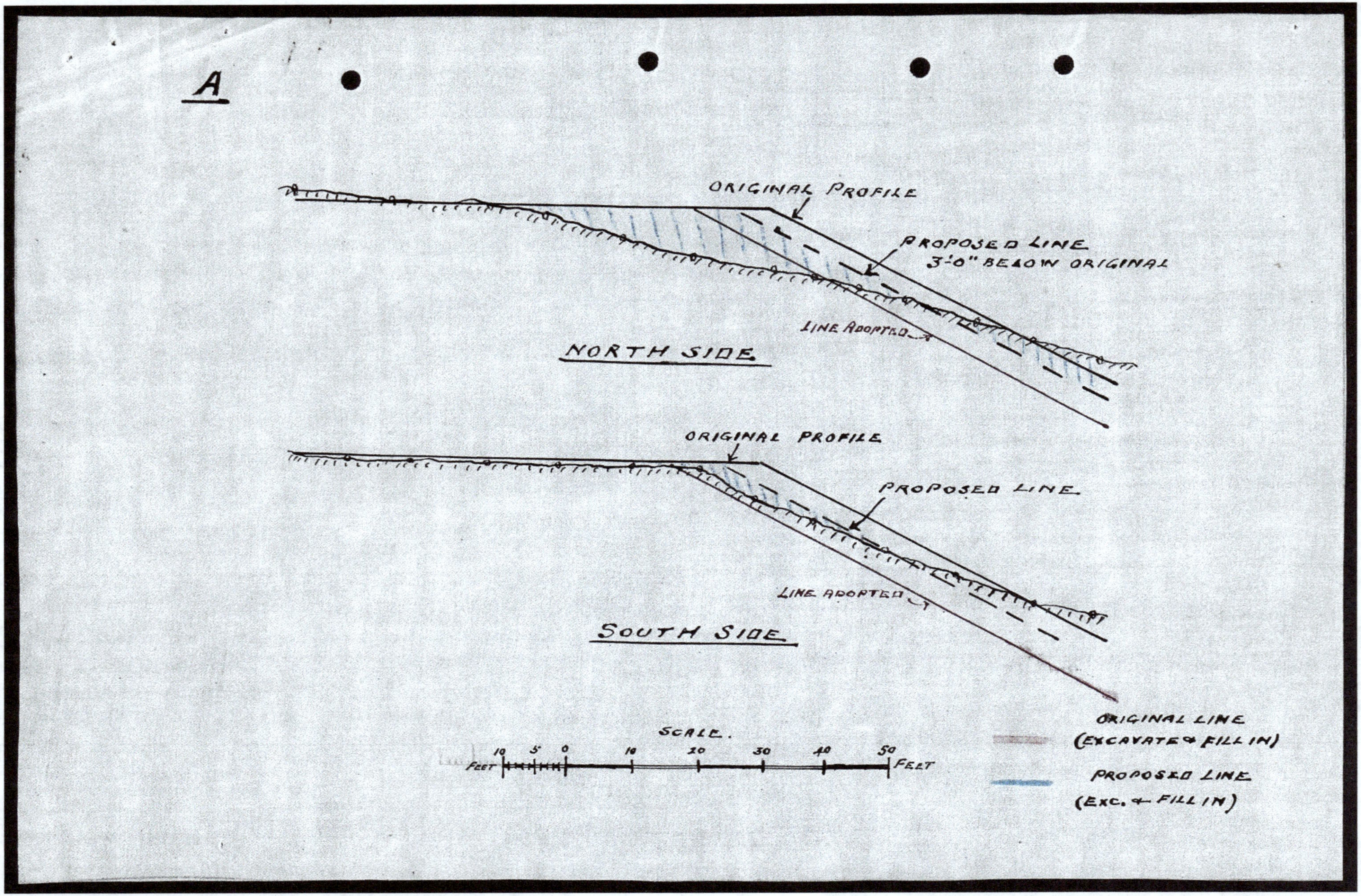
A
ORIGINAL PROFILE
PROPOSED LINE
3'-0" BELOW ORIGINAL
LINE ADOPTED
NORTH SIDE
ORIGINAL PROFILE
PROPOSED LINE
LINE ADOPTED
SOUTH SIDE
SCALE.
10 5 0 10 20 30 40 50
FEET
FEET
ORIGINAL LINE
(EXCAVATE & FILL IN)
PROPOSED LINE
(EXC. & FILL IN)

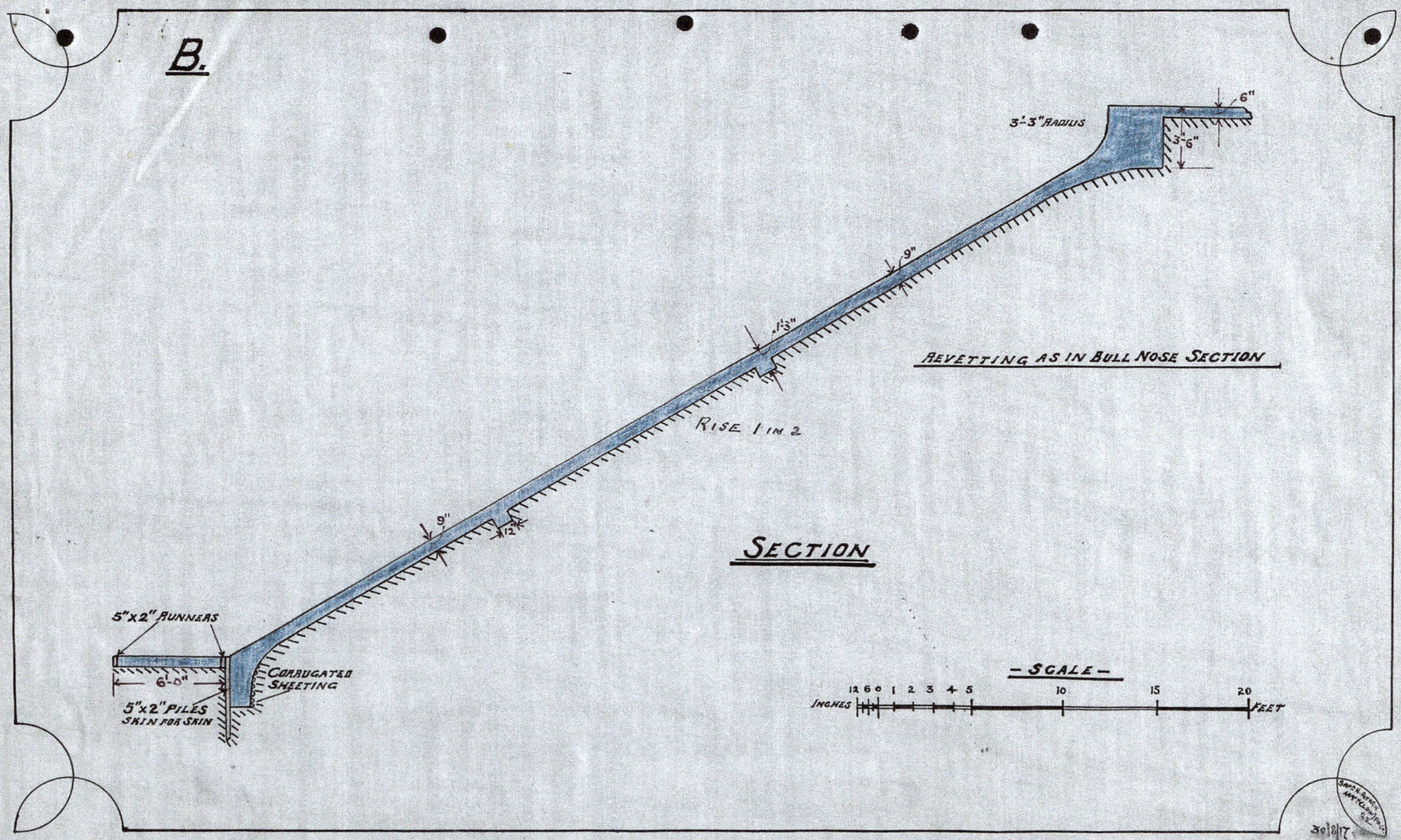
B.
3'-3" RADIUS
6"
3'-6"
9"
1'3"
REVETTING AS IN BULL NOSE SECTION
RISE 1 IN 2
9"
12
SECTION
5"x2" RUNNERS
6'-0"
5"x2" PILES
SKIN FOR SKIN
CORRUGATED
SHEETING
- SCALE -
12 6 0 1 2 3 4 5 10 15 20
INCHES
FEET
30/8/17

CONFIDENTIAL

VR 34

WAR DIARY

OF

409th (LOWLAND) FIELD COY. R.E. (T)

from 1st SEPT 1917 to 30th SEPT 1917

(VOLUME No XXXIII)

Instructions regarding War Diaries and Intelligence Summaries are contained in F. S. Regs., Part II. and the Staff Manual respectively. Title pages will be prepared in manuscript.

WAR DIARY of 409th (Lowland) Fd. Coy. R.E. ~~or INTELLIGENCE SUMMARY.~~

Army Form C. 2118.

(Erase heading not required.)

Place	Date	Hour	Summary of Events and Information	Remarks and references to Appendices
Coy. Campbell near CASINO	1/9/17		Two sections engaged repairing screen round SEA WALL " " " making wire entanglements on SLOPE, attached Infantry assisted at these works. Weather - Stormy but dry. GWS [initials, circled]	

Instructions regarding War Diaries and Intelligence Summaries are contained in F. S. Regs., Part II. and the Staff Manual respectively. Title pages will be prepared in manuscript.

WAR DIARY of 400th (Low) Fd. Coy. R.E.

~~or~~

~~INTELLIGENCE SUMMARY.~~

(Erase heading not required.)

Army Form C. 2118.

Place	Date	Hour	Summary of Events and Information	Remarks and references to Appendices
Coy. Camped near CASINO C.3.57.38. Sheet 1.A DUNKERQUE 1/100,000	2/9/17		Forenoon — Church Parade Afternoon — Company Sports. Weather — Dry but windy.	

G.R.B.

A5834 Wt. W4973/M687 750,000 8/16 D. D. & L. Ltd. Forms/C.2118/13.

Instructions regarding War Diaries and Intelligence Summaries are contained in F. S. Regs., Part II. and the Staff Manual respectively. Title pages will be prepared in manuscript.

WAR DIARY of 400th (Low) Fd. Coy. R.E. ~~or INTELLIGENCE SUMMARY.~~

Army Form C. 2118.

(*Erase heading not required.*)

Place	Date	Hour	Summary of Events and Information	Remarks and references to Appendices
Coy Camped near CASINO C.3.57.38 Sheet 1A DUNKERQUE 1/100,000	3/9/17		Morning – Coy & Attached Infantry in Physical Exercises.	
			Forenoon – Two sections repairing Camouflage in SEA WALL	
			" " Rifle Exercises followed by Coy Drill when the two sections in finishing Camouflage work joined in.	
			Afternoon – Free.	
			Weather – Mild	
			[illegible]	

A5834 Wt. W4973/M687 750,000 8/16 D. D. & L. Ltd. Forms/C.2118/13.

Instructions regarding War Diaries and Intelligence Summaries are contained in F. S. Regs., Part II. and the Staff Manual respectively. Title pages will be prepared in manuscript.

WAR DIARY of 409th (Lowland) Fd: Coy. R.E. ~~or INTELLIGENCE SUMMARY.~~

Army Form C. 2118.

(Erase heading not required.)

Place	Date	Hour	Summary of Events and Information	Remarks and references to Appendices
Coy. Camped near CASINO C.3.51.38 Sheet 1A DUNKERQUE 1/100,000	4/9/17		Morning. Coy and Attached Infantry on Physical Exercises – a squad of R.E.s finished wiring on SEA WALL.	
			Forenoon. Nos 1, 2 + 4 Sections were engaged making wire obstacles. – No 3 Section + Attached Infantry were employed repairing Camouflage Screen round SEA WALL.	
			Afternoon. One Section prepared Pontoon wagons + Bridging material for Bde. manoeuvres to be held following day. Two Sections busy making wire obstacles – One Section + Attached Infantry repairing Screen round SEA WALL.	
			Weather – Dry but windy.	
			(initials, circled)	

A5834 Wt. W4973/M687 750,000 8/16 D. D. & L. Ltd. Forms/C.2118/13.

Instructions regarding War Diaries and Intelligence Summaries are contained in F. S. Regs., Part II. and the Staff Manual respectively. Title pages will be prepared in manuscript.

WAR DIARY of 409th (Lowland) Field Company R.E.

~~or~~

~~INTELLIGENCE SUMMARY.~~

(Erase heading not required.)

Army Form C. 2118.

Place	Date	Hour	Summary of Events and Information	Remarks and references to Appendices
Coy Camped near CASINO C.3.51.38 Sheet 1A DUNKERQUE 1/100,000	5/9/17		The whole Coy paraded at 7-15 AM & marched to Canal some distance away, where they were engaged all day in Bde Scheme returning to Camp 6-30 P.M. – The attached Infantry accompanied The Scheme was Forcing Passage of Canal – A footbridge for Infantry – pile 62'0" long was made in branch of Canal & floated down to position in main Canal, and had to be formed several times to allow barges to pass. The attached Infantry formed covering parties while this work was being carried out – Two sections prepared for improvised crossing, situation did not allow of work commencing till just before confin one raft was made & crossed, time 6 minutes from arrival. Main Lessons learnt Hd. Fog of War, necessity for R.E. officer with Advd Guard and importance of Reports being sent back Section. Rapid reorganisation of parties for work after being opened out by rapid advance under fire – Quickness & ease of making improvised raft with tarpaulin filled with grass or G.S. Wagon body meant. Weather. – Dull but dry. [signature]	

2353 Wt. W2544/1454 700,000 5/15 D. D. & L. A.D.S.S./Forms/C. 2118.

Instructions regarding War Diaries and Intelligence Summaries are contained in F. S. Regs., Part II. and the Staff Manual respectively. Title pages will be prepared in manuscript.

WAR DIARY of 409th (Lowland) Fd. Coy. R.E. ~~or INTELLIGENCE SUMMARY.~~

(Erase heading not required.)

Army Form C. 2118.

Place	Date	Hour	Summary of Events and Information	Remarks and references to Appendices
Coy Camped near CASINO C.3.51.38 Sheet 1A DUNKERQUE 1/100,000	6/9/17		The Coy had practice in signalling, followed accustoming themselves to passage of obstacles, two sections and attached Infantry were working on camouflage + wiring on SLOPE. One Section overhauled all the cycles.	
			Results of Passage of obstacle reported on 15/9/17.	
			Weather – Dull & showery.	
			~~Passage of Wire Entanglement.~~	
			~~Methods tried. (a) Rolling out canvas. too soft under~~	
			~~(b) Wire netting covered with canvas – Successful ... [illegible]~~	
			over	
			[signature] Maj RE OC 409	

A5834 Wt. W4973/M687 750,000 8/16 D. D. & L. Ltd. Forms/C.2118/13.

Instructions regarding War Diaries and Intelligence Summaries are contained in F. S. Regs., Part II. and the Staff Manual respectively. Title pages will be prepared in manuscript.

Army Form C. 2118.

WAR DIARY of 404th (Low) Fd. Coy. R.E ~~OR~~ INTELLIGENCE SUMMARY.

(*Erase heading not required.*)

Place	Date	Hour	Summary of Events and Information	Remarks and references to Appendices
Coy Camped near CASINO C.3.51.38. Sheet 1a DUNKERQUE 1/100,000	4/9/17		The Coy. and Attached Infantry were out in Bde. Scheme all day, leaving camp at 7.15 a.m. returning 6 P.M. The Scheme was - Forcing Passage of Canal de Bourbourg - During operations 2 Rafts, and a Bridge for Infantry in Single file had to be made, these were made and thrown across Canal satisfactorily.	
			Lessons.	
			1o. Value of good reports from officers with Adv. G. helping to keep in touch with action. Necessity for good orderly work. Value of cyclists for this.	
			Weather. Showery in the morning Clearing up later.	
			[illegible signature]	

A5834 Wt. W4973/M687 750,000 8/16 D. D. & L. Ltd. Forms/C.2118/13.

Instructions regarding War Diaries and Intelligence Summaries are contained in F. S. Regs., Part II. and the Staff Manual respectively. Title pages will be prepared in manuscript.

WAR DIARY of 409th (Lowland) Fd: Coy. R.E.

~~INTELLIGENCE SUMMARY.~~

(Erase heading not required.)

Army Form C. 2118.

Place	Date	Hour	Summary of Events and Information	Remarks and references to Appendices
Coy Camped near CASINO C.3.51.38. Sheet 1A DUNKERQUE 1/100,000	8/9/17		Forenoon. The Coy & attached Infantry paraded for a Rifle Inspection, followed by Gas Drill including wearing of Helmets for one hour. The Coys Tool Carts & Tools were also inspected by OC	
			Afternoon. Practice in Passage of Obstacles was carried out, Afterwards Kit Inspection.—	
			Weather.—	
			[signature]	

A5834 Wt. W4973/M687 750,000 8/16 D. D. & L. Ltd. Forms/C.2118/13.

Instructions regarding War Diaries and Intelligence Summaries are contained in F. S. Regs., Part II. and the Staff Manual respectively. Title pages will be prepared in manuscript.

WAR DIARY of 409th (Lowland) Fd: Coy. R.E. ~~or INTELLIGENCE SUMMARY.~~

(*Erase heading not required.*)

Army Form C. 2118.

Place	Date	Hour	Summary of Events and Information	Remarks and references to Appendices
Coy Camped near CASINO C.3.51.38. Sheet 1A DUNKERQUE 1/100,000	9/9/17		Forenoon — Church Parade Afternoon — Sports. G.E.B. Weather — Dull, showery.	

2353 Wt. W2544/1454 700,000 5/15 D. D. & L. A.D.S.S./Forms/C. 2118.

Instructions regarding War Diaries and Intelligence Summaries are contained in F. S. Regs., Part II. and the Staff Manual respectively. Title pages will be prepared in manuscript.

WAR DIARY ~~or INTELLIGENCE SUMMARY.~~ of 408th Lowland Field Coy. R.E.

Army Form C. 2118.

(Erase heading not required.)

Place	Date	Hour	Summary of Events and Information	Remarks and references to Appendices
Coy Camped near CASINO C.3.51.38. Sheet 1A DUNKERQUE 1/100,000	10/9/17		Forenoon. The Coy had Section Drill followed by practice in Signalling finishing with Coy Drill.	
			Afternoon – No. 4 Section gave demonstration of Gun Demolition at Div. H.Q.	
			Nos. 1-2 + 3 were working on Strong points.	
			Result of Gun Demolition 9.2 How. (separate report submitted through CRE)	
			Charges in Breech. 1 lb, 2 lb, 2 lbs. against screw thread. damage pronounced repairable by I.O.M.	
			Weather – Dull but fair.	
			Charge in Muzzle. 4 lbs placed in muzzle + tamped bulged the inner tube + split the outer tube permanently destroying the gun beyond repair even in an Arsenal –	
			Charge on Buffer. 2 lbs used but 1 lb w^d have been sufficient (in my opinion) Blew Buffer completely away + damaged cradle – I.O.M. verdict Gun temporarily out of action. both buffer + cradle can however be replaced in the field.	

A5834 Wt. W4973/M687 750,000 8/16 D. D. & L. Ltd. Forms/C.2118/13.

Instructions regarding War Diaries and Intelligence Summaries are contained in F. S. Regs., Part II. and the Staff Manual respectively. Title pages will be prepared in manuscript.

WAR DIARY of 409th (Lowland) Fd. Coy. R.E.

~~or~~

~~INTELLIGENCE SUMMARY.~~

(*Erase heading not required.*)

Army Form C. 2118.

Place	Date	Hour	Summary of Events and Information	Remarks and references to Appendices
Coy. Camped near CASINO C.3.51.38 Sheet 1A DUNKERQUE 1/100,000	11/9/17		Two Sections were withdrawing bridging equipment which had been used in the erection of Bde Obstacle Courses Two Sections spent the forenoon at Pontoon & Trestle Exercises Afternoon Four sections completed withdrawal of bridging equipment and overhauled transport equipment. [illegible] Weather — Bright & fair.	

2353 Wt. W2544/1454 700,000 5/15 D. D. & L. A.D.S.S./Forms/C. 2118.

Instructions regarding War Diaries and Intelligence Summaries are contained in F. S. Regs., Part II. and the Staff Manual respectively. Title pages will be prepared in manuscript.

WAR DIARY of 409th (Lowland) Fd: Coy, R.E.

~~or INTELLIGENCE SUMMARY.~~

(*Erase heading not required.*)

Army Form C. 2118.

Place	Date	Hour	Summary of Events and Information	Remarks and references to Appendices
Coy Camped near CASINO C.3.51.38 Sheet 1A DUNKERQUE 1/100,000	12/9/17		Morning – Physical Exercises for whole Coy & attached Infantry.	
			Forenoon – The Coy had practice in Gas Helmet Drill, followed by Rifle Inspection –	
			Afternoon – One Section on Camp duties remainder free. –	
			[signature]	
			Weather – Morning fair Afternoon wet.	

A5834 Wt. W4973/M687 750,000 8/16 D. D. & L. Ltd. Forms/C.2118/13.

Instructions regarding War Diaries and Intelligence Summaries are contained in F. S. Regs., Part II. and the Staff Manual respectively. Title pages will be prepared in manuscript.

WAR DIARY ~~or~~ ~~INTELLIGENCE SUMMARY.~~ of 409th (Lowland) Field Coy. R.E.

(Erase heading not required.)

Army Form C. 2118.

Place	Date	Hour	Summary of Events and Information	Remarks and references to Appendices
Coy. Camped near CASINO C.3.51.38. Sheet 1A DUNKERQUE 1/100,000	13/9/17		The Coy. paraded at 7.45 a.m. & marched to site by Canal Bourbourg, where they were inspected by C.R.E., including Kit inspection. – Practice in Bridging was carried out, Pontoon Rafts* being formed & thrown across Canal, also Launching of Weldon Trestles – notes of time required to do this was taken showing very satisfactory results. The Coy marched back Home by Sections reaching Camp 5.30 – 7 P.M. Weather – Dull but fair. * Forming raft including unpacking of wagon & 30 x carry with party of 17 time 14 mins. (initialled)	

Instructions regarding War Diaries and Intelligence Summaries are contained in F. S. Regs., Part II. and the Staff Manual respectively. Title pages will be prepared in manuscript.

WAR DIARY of 409th (Lowland) Field Coy. R.E.

~~or~~

~~INTELLIGENCE SUMMARY.~~

(Erase heading not required.)

Army Form C. 2118.

Place	Date	Hour	Summary of Events and Information	Remarks and references to Appendices
Coy Camped near CASINO C.3.51.38. Sheet 1A DUNKERQUE 1/100,000	14/9/17.		Sections Nos 3 & 4 paraded at 5 a.m & marched to Canal where a Bridge had to be put across by 8 a.m - This was done & during the day ~~the~~ Bridge was swung six times to allow barges to pass - Best time 1½ mins - The Bridge was used by troops on Field manoeuvres. All equipment was packed up & party returned to camp about six P.M.	
			No 2 Section started work on Divl Bath house	
			No 1 " made obstacle for 2nd Bde to replace material taken used by Nos 3 & 4 Sections.	
			Attached Infantry were engaged, loading, unloading & carrying materials.	
			Weather - Bright & warm	
			[illegible signature]	

A5834 Wt. W4973/M687 750,000 8/16 D. D. & L. Ltd. Forms/C.2118/13.

Instructions regarding War Diaries and Intelligence Summaries are contained in F. S. Regs., Part II. and the Staff Manual respectively. Title pages will be prepared in manuscript.

WAR DIARY of 409th (Lowland) Fd. Coy. R.E.

~~or~~

~~INTELLIGENCE SUMMARY.~~

(Erase heading not required.)

Army Form C. 2118.

Place	Date	Hour	Summary of Events and Information	Remarks and references to Appendices
Coy Camped near CASINO	15/9/17		All the Coy, less No 2 Section & party of attached Infantry, practised crossing obstacles of barbed wire – Following methods were demonstrated over irregular thick entanglements about 30'0" wide (I) Canvas thrown over found useless (II) " on wire netting satisfactory but heavy, time to place 1st man across 1¾ min (III) Wire netting 6'0" wide – 2 Sections crossing times 1st Section 1st man over 1 min, 2nd Section 1st man over 1¼ mins. – Attached Infantry believed under 1 min. (IV) Ladders made of 3"x1" timber about 14'0" long & 18" wide – 1st man over ¾ min; last of 10 men 1¾ mins, this method was found to be rather unsteady. (V) Trenchboards – 1st man over 1¼ min, last of 10 men 2 mins, this method was found to be very useful when tramped down and a few tight strands cut. (VI) Cutting through with folding wire cutters & hooks, best time 5½ mins other 6½ mins for clear lane 6'0" wide – Another party against a tangle mass of Knife Rests was not through in 17 mins. About 50 men were passed over the wire netting tracks & proved satisfactory. From these trials it is considered that a double width roll of wire netting is a very valuable assistance, rolled out as the men cross. Casualties would not stop this, 2 men are sufficient. The ladders in time are better than they look as they appear uncertain. Trench boards require 6 men, found difficult to lay straight but enable a pathway through to be made quicker than cutting. When cutting through Grapnels (better a plain hook) is useful for dragging out wire after being cut clear from posts – This has also been found on the SEA WALL experiments. No 1 Section & party attached Infantry were engaged drawing in wagons, fencing in the Camp & at Infantry Drill No 2 " erected framework of Divn. bath house made connection & laid 2" pipe from main weather. – Showery	GCHt

2353 Wt. W2544/1454 700,000 5/15 D. D. & L. A.D.S.S./Forms/C. 2118.

Army Form C. 2118.

Instructions regarding War Diaries and Intelligence Summaries are contained in F. S. Regs., Part II. and the Staff Manual respectively. Title pages will be prepared in manuscript.

WAR DIARY of 409th (Lowland) Fd. Coy. R.E.

~~or~~

~~INTELLIGENCE SUMMARY.~~

(*Erase heading not required.*)

Place	Date	Hour	Summary of Events and Information	Remarks and references to Appendices
Coy Camped near CASINO C.3.51.38. Sheet 1A DUNKERQUE 1/100,000	16/9/17		Forenoon – Church Parade Afternoon – Free Weather – Fair & bright [signature]	

2353 Wt. W2544/1454 700,000 5/15 D. D. & L. A.D.S.S./Forms/C. 2118.

Instructions regarding War Diaries and Intelligence Summaries are contained in F. S. Regs., Part II. and the Staff Manual respectively. Title pages will be prepared in manuscript.

WAR DIARY of 409th (Low) Fd: Coy. R.E.

~~or~~

~~INTELLIGENCE SUMMARY.~~

(Erase heading not required.)

Army Form C. 2118.

Place	Date	Hour	Summary of Events and Information	Remarks and references to Appendices
Coy Camped near CASINO C.3.51.38	17/9/17		The Officers & Senior N.C.O's of the Coy carried out practice in wiring during the day. Remainder had Rifle exercises + section drill – The Coy afterwards had practice in dismantling camp structures, loading same with all other kit & stores, on Coy transport ready for moving. Weather Sunny + warm G.R.W.F.	

Instructions regarding War Diaries and Intelligence Summaries are contained in F. S. Regs., Part II. and the Staff Manual respectively. Title pages will be prepared in manuscript.

WAR DIARY of 409th (Lowland) Fd. Coy R.E.

~~or~~

~~INTELLIGENCE SUMMARY.~~

(*Erase heading not required.*)

Army Form C. 2118.

Place	Date	Hour	Summary of Events and Information	Remarks and references to Appendices
Coy Camped near CASINO C.3.51.38 Sheet 1A DUNKERQUE 1/100,000	18/9/17		No 1 Section was employed restretching tarpaulins in Camps an Sheds etc.—	
			No 2 " finished work at Div Bath-house including water supply.—	
			" 3 & 4 were engaged saling wire, attached Infantry had Squad drill & Rifle Exercises.	
			Evening Nos 3 & 4 Sections erected wire entanglements in SEA WALL working from 6-9 P.M	
			Weather – Showery & Windy	
			[signature]	

A5834 Wt. W4973/M687 750,000 8/16 D. D. & L. Ltd. Forms/C.2118/13.

Instructions regarding War Diaries and Intelligence Summaries are contained in F. S. Regs., Part II. and the Staff Manual respectively. Title pages will be prepared in manuscript.

WAR DIARY of 409th (Lowland) Fd. Coy. R.E.

~~or~~

~~INTELLIGENCE SUMMARY.~~

(Erase heading not required.)

Army Form C. 2118.

Place	Date	Hour	Summary of Events and Information	Remarks and references to Appendices
Coy Camped near CASINO C.3.51.38. Sheet 1A DUNKERQUE 1/100,000	19/9/17		Two Sections paraded at 5-30 A.M. & cycled to Canal about 8 miles away, where a Bridge had to be rushed across Canal ready for traffic by 8-45 a.m. – The Bridge was made including forming Cut 3 times for barges passing during construction, time taken 3/4 hour. – One Section engaged repairing Camouflage round SEAWALL The remaining section & attached Infantry carried out Guard & Sentries Drill followed by Knotting & Lashing. In the afternoon No. 3 & 4 Sections along with attached Infantry did S. H. Q. System of Wiring. 7-45 – 8-45 a.m. A party of 10 men cut their way through the wire on top of Slope in 2 min 5 secs, another party took 3 mins, cutting through same by Infantry took 9 mins – R.E's watching & noting points. Weather – Dry & Windy. [illegible]	

A5834 Wt. W4973/M687 750,000 8/16 D. D. & L. Ltd. Forms/C.2118/13.

Instructions regarding War Diaries and Intelligence Summaries are contained in F. S. Regs., Part II. and the Staff Manual respectively. Title pages will be prepared in manuscript.

Army Form C. 2118.

WAR DIARY of 409th (Lws) Fd. Coy. R.E.
~~or~~
~~INTELLIGENCE SUMMARY.~~

(Erase heading not required.)

Place	Date	Hour	Summary of Events and Information	Remarks and references to Appendices
Coy Camped near CASINO C.3.51.38 Sheet 1A DUNKERQUE 1/100,000	20/9/17		Two Sections + party of attached Infantry did G.H.Q. wiring followed by cycle cleaning also a Transport One Section + party of Infantry working on Div H.Q. Stables, the remaining section completed work on Div Bath house, (with exception of roofing of passage) water was laid on + in use, a second marquee is to be erected to-morrow. – [signature] Weather. – Dull + showery.	

A5834 Wt. W4973/M687 750,000 8/16 D. D. & L. Ltd. Forms/C.2118/13.

Army Form C. 2118.

Instructions regarding War Diaries and Intelligence Summaries are contained in F. S. Regs., Part II. and the Staff Manual respectively. Title pages will be prepared in manuscript.

WAR DIARY of 409th (Lowland) Fd. Coy. R.E.

~~INTELLIGENCE SUMMARY.~~

(*Erase heading not required.*)

Place	Date	Hour	Summary of Events and Information	Remarks and references to Appendices
Coy. Camped near CASINO C.3.51.38 Sheet 1A DUNKERQUE 1/100,000	21/9/17		The Div. Bathhouse was completed ready for use, 2 marquees were erected the seating to be completed to-morrow. The Stables at Divn. H.Q. were completed – Nos. 1 & 4 Sections, carried on with wiring different systems including wiring to Drill Attached Infantry engaged wiring G.H.Q. method followed by Drill Experiments laying out Expanded Metal Roadways* were done proving quite satisfactory. * for passage of vehicles over sand. In the evening 2 Sections wired the slope, SEAWALL. Weather – Bright & warm Gillett	

A5834 Wt. W4973/M687 750,000 8/16 D. D. & L. Ltd. Forms/C.2118/13.

Instructions regarding War Diaries and Intelligence Summaries are contained in F. S. Regs., Part II. and the Staff Manual respectively. Title pages will be prepared in manuscript.

WAR DIARY of 409th (Lowland) Fd. Coy. R.E.

or

~~INTELLIGENCE SUMMARY.~~

(Erase heading not required.)

Army Form C. 2118.

Place	Date	Hour	Summary of Events and Information	Remarks and references to Appendices
Coy Camped near CASINO C.3.51.38. Sheet 19 DUNKERQUE 1/100,000	22/9/17		The Divn Bath-house was completed to-day and used – The engine shed was moved & reconnected & running on new site. One Section continued with G.H.Q. wiring, another was engaged on camp duties – Attached Infantry were employed salving stores & levelling sand. –	
			Weather – Bright & fair	
			[signature]	

A5834 Wt. W4973/M687 750,000 8/16 D. D. & L. Ltd. Forms/C.2118/13.

Army Form C. 2118.

Instructions regarding War Diaries and Intelligence Summaries are contained in F. S. Regs., Part II. and the Staff Manual respectively. Title pages will be prepared in manuscript.

WAR DIARY ~~of 408~~th (Lowland) Fd. Coy. R.E.

or

~~INTELLIGENCE SUMMARY.~~

(Erase heading not required.)

Place	Date	Hour	Summary of Events and Information	Remarks and references to Appendices
Coy Camped near CASINO C.3.51.38. Sheet 1A DUNKERQUE 1/100,000	23/9/17		Forenoon – Church Parade Afternoon – Do. (initialled) Gp Weather – Dull & windy.	

2353 Wt. W2544/1454 700,000 5/15 D. D. & L. A.D.S.S./Forms/C. 2118.

Instructions regarding War Diaries and Intelligence Summaries are contained in F. S. Regs., Part II. and the Staff Manual respectively. Title pages will be prepared in manuscript.

WAR DIARY of 409th (Low) Fd: Coy. R.E. Army Form C. 2118.

~~or~~

~~**INTELLIGENCE SUMMARY.**~~

(Erase heading not required.)

Place	Date	Hour	Summary of Events and Information	Remarks and references to Appendices
Coy Camped near CASINO C.3.51.38. Sheet 1A DUNKERQUE 1/100,000	24/9/17		Morning – Coy & Attached Infantry paraded & had Physical Exercises. Forenoon – One Section & party of attached Infantry had firing practice, one Section in Camp Duties, remaining two Sections & A.I. G.H.Q. wiring.– Afternoon – Two Sections practising signalling A.I. salving wire & other materials. Weather.– Bright & fair. [signature]	

Instructions regarding War Diaries and Intelligence Summaries are contained in F. S. Regs., Part II. and the Staff Manual respectively. Title pages will be prepared in manuscript.

WAR DIARY of 409th (Low) Fd. Coy. R.E. Army Form C. 2118.

~~or~~

~~INTELLIGENCE SUMMARY.~~

(Erase heading not required.)

Place	Date	Hour	Summary of Events and Information	Remarks and references to Appendices
Coy Camped near CASINO	25/9/17		One Section and attached Infantry spent the forenoon practising firing.	
C.3.51.38.			One " " " " engaged making sand muzzles for horses also repairing water trough.	
Sheet 19 DUNKERQUE 1/100,000			" " " " " wiring	
			" " " " " salving wire	
			In the afternoon	
			One Section went on with firing practice	
			" " erected wire entanglement in SEA WALL	
			" " Duty Section in Camp also made sand muzzles for horses.	
			" " went for Cycle Run a tactical scheme being set.	
			Weather – Bright & warm	

2353 Wt. W2544/1454 700,000 5/15 D. D. & L. A.D.S.S./Forms/C. 2118.

Instructions regarding War Diaries and Intelligence Summaries are contained in F. S. Regs., Part II. and the Staff Manual respectively. Title pages will be prepared in manuscript.

WAR DIARY of 409th (Lowland) Fd. Coy. R.E.

~~or~~ ~~INTELLIGENCE SUMMARY.~~

(Erase heading not required.)

Army Form C. 2118.

Place	Date	Hour	Summary of Events and Information	Remarks and references to Appendices
Coy Camped near CASINO C.3.51.38. Sheet 1A DUNKERQUE 1/100,000	26/9/17		The whole Coy paraded in the morning continuing with Physical training, later 2 sections on G.H.Q. wiring, 1/2 section working on Erection near Div. H.Q., 1/2 section making muzzles, the remaining section overhauling cycles.	
			The afternoon was spent in Bathing, Football match & Rounders	
			[signature]	
			Weather – Dull but fair	

A5834 Wt. W4973/M687 750,000 8/16 D. D. & L. Ltd. Forms/C.2118/13.

Instructions regarding War Diaries and Intelligence Summaries are contained in F. S. Regs., Part II. and the Staff Manual respectively. Title pages will be prepared in manuscript.

WAR DIARY of 409th (Lowland) Fd. Coy R.E.

~~or~~

~~INTELLIGENCE SUMMARY.~~

(Erase heading not required.)

Army Form C. 2118.

Place	Date	Hour	Summary of Events and Information	Remarks and references to Appendices
Coy Camped near CASINO C.3.51.38 Sheet 1A DUNKERQUE 1/100,000	27/9/17		Three Sections + Attached Infantry marched to Div. H. Qr. where a lecture an explanation of demolition carried out on 9.2 Howitzer was given, a short route march was made in the return journey to camp..	
			One Section was employed making fascines + muzzles.	
			In the Afternoon the whole Company paraded and attended lecture given by C. R. E on 'Duties of Field Coys' this lecture was attended by the two other Fd. Coys.	
			The attached Infantry were engaged salving wire, timber & Rails.	
			Weather – Bright + warm	
			[signature]	

A5834 Wt. W4973/M687 750,000 8/16 D. D. & L. Ltd. Forms/C.2118/13.

Instructions regarding War Diaries and Intelligence Summaries are contained in F. S. Regs., Part II, and the Staff Manual respectively. Title pages will be prepared in manuscript.

WAR DIARY of 409th (Lowland) Fd: Coy R.E

~~or~~

~~INTELLIGENCE SUMMARY.~~

(*Erase heading not required.*)

Army Form C. 2118.

Place	Date	Hour	Summary of Events and Information	Remarks and references to Appendices
Coy Camped near CASINO C.3.51.38	28/9/17		The Coy was engaged loading up transport, toolcart equipment inspected, dismantling bridging equipment used temporarily for Coy sheds, also C.Q.M.S. Store, overhauling transport + cycles all preparatory for moving tomorrow.	
			GRCHardy	
			Weather Bright + warm	

Instructions regarding War Diaries and Intelligence Summaries are contained in F. S. Regs., Part II. and the Staff Manual respectively. Title pages will be prepared in manuscript.

WAR DIARY of 409th (Lowland) Field Coy R.E.

~~or INTELLIGENCE SUMMARY.~~

(Erase heading not required.)

Army Form C. 2118.

Place	Date	Hour	Summary of Events and Information	Remarks and references to Appendices
Coy Camped near CASINO C.3.51.38 Sheet 1A DUNKERQUE 1/100,000	29/9/17		The Coy paraded at 6-45 AM & marched along with transport to new camp in forward area map reference 1/40000 Sheet FORMES. X 9 a. The Coy reached their new Quarters 6 P.M. & went into billets. Wagons were unloaded so far as necessary, & billets generally improved. Transport 24 miles by road, no casualties, one slightly rubbed shoulder with Breast Collar. Camp shelled no casualties, in our Company Gillett Weather – Bright & Warm	

Instructions regarding War Diaries and Intelligence Summaries are contained in F. S. Regs., Part II. and the Staff Manual respectively. Title pages will be prepared in manuscript.

WAR DIARY of 409th (Lowland) Fd: Coy. R.E.

~~or~~ ~~INTELLIGENCE SUMMARY~~.

(Erase heading not required.)

Army Form C. 2118.

Place	Date	Hour	Summary of Events and Information	Remarks and references to Appendices
Coy Camped at W.G. B. 26 Sheet FURNES 1/40,000	30/9/17		During night of 29/30/17 the new Quarters were heavily shelled. In the morning it was thought necessary to move the Horse Lines and later in the day the Coy moved to other billets in COXYDE BAINS. O.C. visited Machine Gun emplacements being taken over with O.C. 289 A.T. Coy.	
			[illegible] Coy Major R.E. O.C. 409 Fd. Coy.	
			Weather — Bright & Warm	

2353 Wt. W2544/1454 700,000 5/15 D. D. & L. A.D.S.S./Forms/C. 2118.

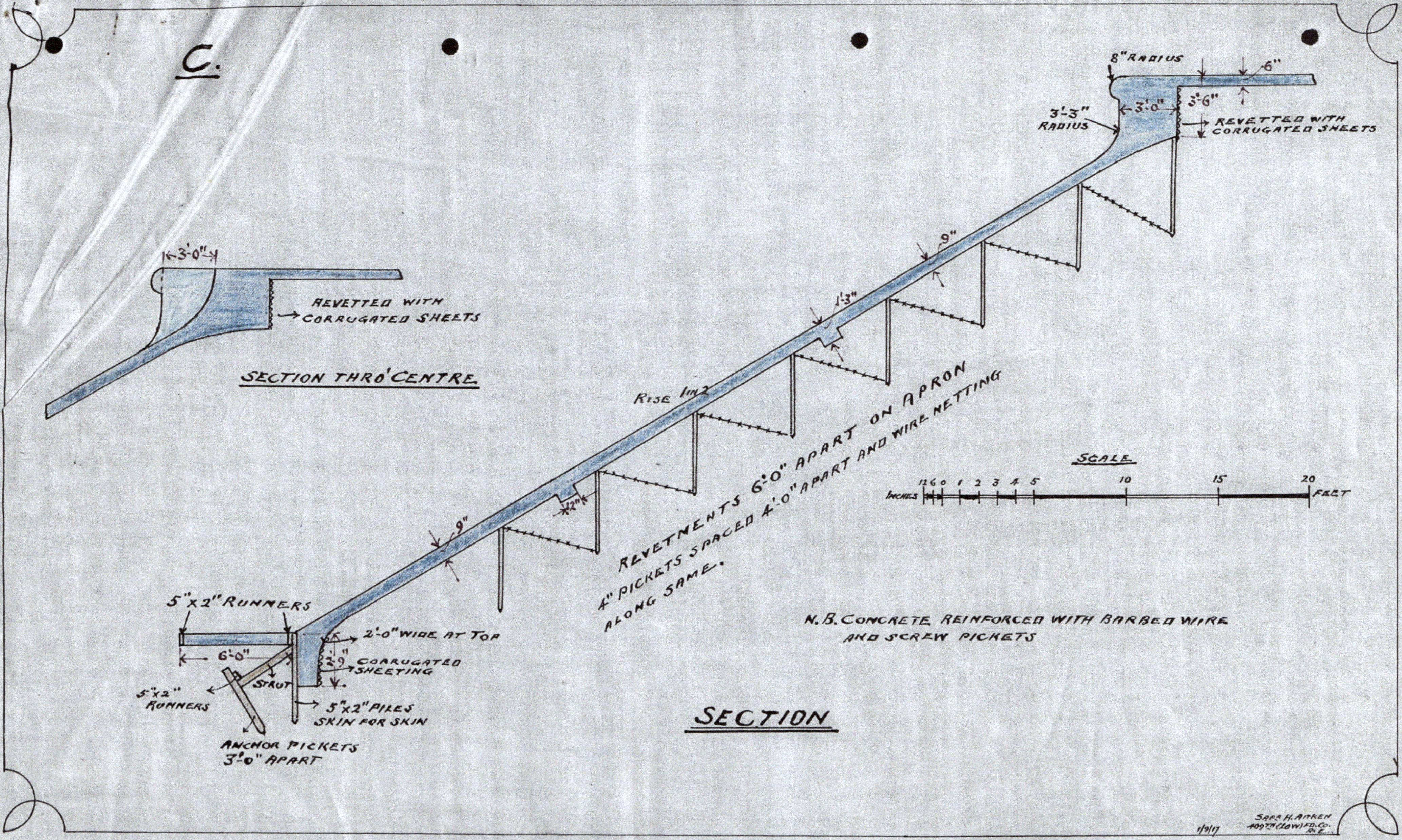
C.
8" RADIUS
6"
3'-3" RADIUS
3'-0"
3'-6"
REVETTED WITH CORRUGATED SHEETS
3'-0"
REVETTED WITH CORRUGATED SHEETS
SECTION THRO' CENTRE.
9"
1'-3"
RISE 1 IN 2
REVETMENTS 6'-0" APART ON APRON
4" PICKETS SPACED 4'-0" APART AND WIRE NETTING ALONG SAME.
SCALE.
INCHES 12 6 0 1 2 3 4 5 10 15 20 FEET
12"
9"
5"x2" RUNNERS
6'-0"
2'-0" WIRE AT TOP
2'-9"
CORRUGATED SHEETING
5"x2" RUNNERS
STRUT
5"x2" PILES SKIN FOR SKIN
ANCHOR PICKETS 3'-0" APART
N. B. CONCRETE REINFORCED WITH BARBED WIRE AND SCREW PICKETS
SECTION
1/9/17
SAPR H. AITKEN
409TH (LOW) FD. CO. R.E.

W A R D I A R Y.

(With Appendices.)

409th. (Lowland) Field Coy., R.E., (T).

1st. DIVISION.

OCTOBER & ~~NOVEMBER~~. 1917.

Vol 34

CONFIDENTIAL

WAR DIARY

OF

409th (LOWLAND) FIELD COY. R.E. (T.)

from 1st OCTOBER 1917 to 31st OCTOBER 1917

(VOLUME No XXXIV)

409th LOWLAND. Fd Coy. Secret P.1

Army Form C. 2118.

WAR DIARY for October 1917.
or
INTELLIGENCE SUMMARY.

(Erase heading not required.)

Instructions regarding War Diaries and Intelligence Summaries are contained in F. S. Regs., Part II. and the Staff Manual respectively. Title pages will be prepared in manuscript.

Place	Date	Hour	Summary of Events and Information	Remarks and references to Appendices
COXYDE BAINS [Sheet 1/40000 FURNES ref. W 6 b 2.6]	1/10/17	—	a.m.: Gas Drill & Inspection of Box Respirators — Rifle Inspection — Bathing Parade — Weather fine. p.m. free except for billet repairs — party standing by for night work, 1/2/10/17. — Arrangements for taking over work from 289 A.T. Coy R.E. completed in accordance with orders recd from C.R.E. Corps troops XV Corps.	
	2/10/17	—	2.15 am — Working party paraded to work concurrently with 289 A.T. Coy & take over work — detailed organisation of work & progress is given in Appendix A attached — Return by lorry 10.30 am. Meals. Breakfast 11 am on return from work — Dinners 5 pm — Teas 1.30 am.	
	3/10/17.	—	Handing over by 289 A.T. Coy Completed and work on 9 M.G. Emplacements in full swing — Minor delays caused through insufficient supply of material being available on site. — Infantry working party of 140 O.R. furnished by 10th Manchesters taken over with job output of work very poor and strength of parties variable — O.C. detail written to and called on. Stables in billets repaired — and sandbagging round cellars of billets commenced. Enemy shelled lightly on an average every 2nd night no damage done — many shells came from Sea.	
	4/10/17	—	Work carried on as above — Warning that infantry would not be available for work on night 4/5th	
	5/10/17	—	No infantry available — New party from Royal Fusiliers arrived in COXYDE 2 pm. O.C. Detail Lt Hobday — Detail of parties required given him and whole party paraded and spoken to re work to be done. Strength of party 160 O.R. 4 off. weak in NCO's. Extra Officer & NCO's asked for. Owing to non arrival of stores train Nos 1 & 2 Section were kept in camp and cellars of billets were strengthened.	
	6/10/17		Work as on 4/10/17 Hours altered from 2.15 am to 4.15 am returning 12.15 p.m. — This alteration allowed 1 hour for daylight to adjust or move materials and the full shift in daylight. — Carrying parties reorganised so that materials were delivered in emplacements during dark. Visited all Emplacements with Inf. Officer and told him what was required of Carrying parties.	
	7/10/17		Work as above — Work of Infantry Party very satisfactory and O.C. Lt HOBDAY was of great assistance.	[signature] Major RE

A5834 Wt. W4973/M687 750,000 8/16 D. D. & L. Ltd. Forms/C.2118/13.

SECRET LOWLAND F^d Coy

(P3)

Army Form C. 2118.

Instructions regarding War Diaries and Intelligence Summaries are contained in F. S. Regs., Part II. and the Staff Manual respectively. Title pages will be prepared in manuscript.

WAR DIARY Oct 1917.
or
INTELLIGENCE SUMMARY.
(*Erase heading not required.*)

Place	Date	Hour	Summary of Events and Information	Remarks and references to Appendices
Coxyde les BAINS. [Map Ref 1/40,000 sheet FURNES W.6.b.2.6.]	8/10/17		Work continued as usual — Met Col Clarke Corps M.G officer 6.30am and visited all old M.G. Emplacements & 2 new ones and fired lines of fire — also fixed some other M.G. Emplacements on outskirts of NIEUPORT.	
	9/10/17.		Inspection of Barrack Rooms — Works as usual whole coy employed.	
	10/10/17		Went out with party at 4.15 am and shewed new M.G. emplacements to Lt Kelly and went into arrangements required for putting them in hand on 12/10/17 — Work to be done by No 4 Sectn under Lt Kelly —	
	11/10/17		Inspection of Barrack Rooms satisfactory condition — Works as usual — Enemy shelling battery positions in vicinity of M.G. Emplacements daily generally between 9 & 11 am — Work occasionally delayed. Capt POWELL R.E. & Lt GALLOWAY R.E. returned from leave — Lt BOST R.E. went on leave.	
	12/10/17.		Went through Store arrangements with Capt Powell — Spoke CRE re cement shortage causing delay to work — Works as usual. — Parties reduced by 1 dop [illegible] increased 1 [illegible] to allow of starting 2 new Emplacements.	
	13/10/17		Visited all M.G. emplacements with Lt Galloway starting 4.15 am — called up Adjt CRE Corps Troops re supply of Cement & Shingle. No 4 Sect. Gas & Rifle inspection. Night 7.45pm Work on forward emplacements arranged — Railway line cut in 3 places so materials were stopped	
	14/10/17.		Works as usual — Gen BUCKLAND CE 1st Army visited works and expressed satisfaction. — Saw CRE Corps Troops re increasing supply of shingle & cement which was insufficient to keep a reserve. [all attached Infantry BATHS] Work on Forward M.G. Emplacements started 7 tons of materials & decauville track taken up	
	15/10/17	—	Lt Kelly going on leave 16/10/17 — visited two new emplacements with Lt Neave also all the back 6 under him progress satisfactory	
	16/10/17	—	Visited all M.G. Emplacements — Work as usual — orders recd to hand over to 289 A.T. Coy on 17/10/17 preparatory to move. — Lt Kelly proceeded on leave.	
	17/10/17	—	Orders recd. dated 18th inst. Handing over notes prepared & work handed over to 289 A T Coy visited all Emplacements with O/C. Transport overhauled & packed ready for move on 18/10/17	[illegible] Major R.E. O.C. 409 Lowland Fd Coy

A5834 Wt. W4973/M687 750,000 8/16 D. D. & L. Ltd. Forms/C.2118/13.

409 LOWLAND F^d Coy RE   SECRET   3

Army Form C. 2118.

Instructions regarding War Diaries and Intelligence Summaries are contained in F. S. Regs., Part II. and the Staff Manual respectively. Title pages will be prepared in manuscript.

WAR DIARY OCT 1917
or
INTELLIGENCE SUMMARY.
(Erase heading not required.)

Place	Date	Hour	Summary of Events and Information	Remarks and references to Appendices
Poupe Bain	18/10/17	7.45 am	Marching out Parade. Coy moved by march route a distance of 14 miles to billets in Ferme St Pierre 3 miles S. of GHEVELDE [Ref. Sheet FURNES 1/40000. J15c 8.10] — Arrived about 7.30 pm. — Horses picketed men in barns. — Farmer very obliging	
	19/10/17		Gas Helmet & Rifle Inspection — Baths for whole Company & Drivers. ~~at~~ GHEVELDE.	
	20/10/17	8 am	Marching out Parade. Coy vacated billets and proceeded ~~by bus~~ to billets 1½ miles NE of LEGGARSCAPPEL. [Ref. Sheet 5A 1/100,000] 2E. 7. 8. Dismounted men by Bus transport by road distance 15 miles approx. — Billets close but good in farms — the farmer very obliging.	
	21/10/17		Church Service & Football match.	
	22/10/17		Rifle & Gas Inspection followed by Signalling ½ hour & Drill ½ hour. — ~~pm Packing Transport~~. assisted farmer in bringing in crops.	
	23/10/17		Rifle Inspection by OC. generally condition of rifles ~~bad~~ compared with remarks made 3 months previously. pm. Packed Transport — OC. rode over to DE HQ. 12 miles to receive orders re future movements.	
	24/10/17		Moved with 2nd Bde Group (starting point 10.29 am). to new billets near HERZEELE Sheet 27 1/40000 D15 a 5.8. Billeted in 3 farms. — Farmer (of large farm) very obliging & all out to help the men. —	
	25/10/17	8.45	Marching out Parade moved to new billets 1½ miles E of POPERINGHE Ref Sheet 27 1/40,000 L3 b 8.8.	
	26/10/17		1½ section in camp making habitable & overhaul transport. — 2½ section erecting NISSEN HUTS for HQ of Bde —	

G. W. Haird Maj RE
OC 409 Lowland F^d Coy

A5834 Wt. W4973/M687 750,000 8/16 D. D. & L. Ltd. Forms/C.2118/13.

409th Lowland Fd. Coy. R.E.

Instructions regarding War Diaries and Intelligence Summaries are contained in F. S. Regs., Part II. and the Staff Manual respectively. Title pages will be prepared in manuscript.

WAR DIARY for Oct. 1917
or
INTELLIGENCE SUMMARY.
(Erase heading not required.)

Army Form C. 2118.

Place	Date	Hour	Summary of Events and Information	Remarks and references to Appendices
EAST of POPERINGHE Sheet 27 1/40,000 L.3.6.8.8.	27/10/17		2 Sections continued work on erection of Nissen Huts for Inf. Bde. – Party of 12 men under Lt. Neave employed on Camp repairs at School Camp adjoining our own – remainder of men working in Camp under Capt. Powell.	
Ditto	28/10/17	3.P.M.	The Company paraded and attended Church Service – Transport overhauled ready for movement on 29/10/17.	
NE. of YPRES Sheet 28 N.W. 1/10,000 C.26.d.Y.Y.	29/10/17	8a.m.	Transport hooked in and moved to site near St. Jean (map ref) Sheet 28 N.W. 1/10,000 C.26.d.Y.Y.	
		9-45 am.	marching out Parade, Dismounted men proceeded by Motor Lorries to site near St. Jean arriving about 1 P.M. – men billeted in tents & bivouacs. Camp bombed & shelled at night – Evacuated billets were inspected by O.C. before leaving.	
NE of Ypres Sheet 28 NW 1/20,000 C26d 7.7	30/10/17	6–11	2 section work in vicinity of St. Julien doubling Duckboard track – Guided to work by officer of 249 Fd Coy 63rd Div –	
		1.30–6.30	1 Section work as above and maintenance of tracks. Both parties shelled before end of shift & withdrawn. Bombing at night of surrounding camps but none in immediate vicinity.	
"	31/10/17	A–11	2 section work as above – no interference by shelling till 9.45 am.	
		1.30–7.30	1 — — — — — Shelling ALBERTA Track 2.30 – 3.30 heavily – shelled other tracks after 5 pm	

Enemy aeroplane dropped bombs in vicinity of camp about 2 pm and again during night commencing 10 pm – full moon. – nearest about 1/2 mile majority in back area

[illegible] Major RE OC 409 RE
1/11/17

A5834 Wt. W4973/M687 750,000 8/16 D. D. & L. Ltd. Forms/C.2118/13.

409th Lowland Fd Coy

Appendix A

SECRET.

Army Form C. 2118.

Instructions regarding War Diaries and Intelligence Summaries are contained in F. S. Regs., Part II. and the Staff Manual respectively. Title pages will be prepared in manuscript.

WAR DIARY
or
INTELLIGENCE SUMMARY.
(Erase heading not required.)

Place	Date	Hour	Summary of Events and Information	Remarks and references to Appendices
COXYDE BAINS	1st – 17th Oct		Work on Machine Gun Emplacements in Reserve & Corps Line General. Work was taken over from 289 A T Coy on 2/10/17, work directly under Corps CE thro CRE Corps Troops. 1 Double machine Gun emplacement in a cottage was taken over well in hand and 8 shelters for detachments – These shelters were designed to be Shell Proof against 8" & consisted of Baby Elephant shelter with 4 ft of concrete on roof & 2'6" thick in walls the whole reinforced with 3 grillages of iron rods one inside two outside – Entrances also were shellproof – Each shelter required about 3000 c.f. of concrete & 3000 ft. of iron rods. All work had to be carried on under Camouflage as some emplacements were under direct observation from enemy dunes and all under observation from Balloons which were up most days – One new emplacement for 2 guns in a cottage and one Double Shelter for 2 detachments was sited & decauville track laid to one and about 70 tons of material delivered in dump near job. Below is report on state of work on taking over and vacating. Organisation of Work (a) Supplies. (1) Material for 3 emplacements on canal bank was sent up by barge from FURNES. barges were offloaded and carried to work at night by infantry carrying party. (2) Cement & Sundries to above by Lorry daily. (3) All supplies to Northern group of em by light Railway to a siding thence by horse transport & carrying parties to job – A forward dump was started & stocked as railway & supply of material was not sufficiently certain to allow of unimpeded organised work – ~~Stuff~~ Materials for this were demanded at following rates: (over)	

A5834. Wt. W4973/M687. 750,000. 8/16. D. D. & L. Ltd. Forms/C.2118/13.

Appendix A (p 2).

Army Form C. 2118.

Instructions regarding War Diaries and Intelligence Summaries are contained in F. S. Regs., Part II. and the Staff Manual respectively. Title pages will be prepared in manuscript.

WAR DIARY
or
INTELLIGENCE SUMMARY.

(*Erase heading not required.*)

Place	Date	Hour	Summary of Events and Information	Remarks and references to Appendices
Rate. Perwick.			Shingle 100 tons Sand 50 tons Cement 30 tons - other materials special indent.	
			(4) Two new Emplacements. Materials & carrying party by light railway to within 300 x of site. Thence by Decauville under camouflage at time of handing over this was being completed.	
			(5) Sand & Cement required bagging (in camp & at wharf) prior to being sent on job - Iron Reinforcing rods were bent (to shape) & sent out to job in bundles.	
			B. Labour. Hours. Available Company less Detmt. with Div. & men on leave Attached Infantry 150 Working Strength.	
			(1) On taking over work on Canal Bank was in single party from 2.30 - 10.30 am. — Total Strength 24 RE + 27 Inf. - As work outside camouflage was impracticable after daylight the parties were split up and rearranged as ~~[illegible]~~ in table below.	
			(2) On Northern Group existing arrangements continued except that numbers in each emplacement were reduced to allow of freeer work.	
			(3) ~~[illegible]~~ To enable new jobs to start on 12/10/17 each party was reduced by one sapper to enable two new parties to be formed the Infantry for them being found from parties formerly bagging sand.	
			(4) Reliefs Works was continuous, men being relieved singly in rotation to give each man one night in camp in seven. 3 officers took relief 2 out & 1 in - Carrying parties supervised by Inf officers	
			(5) Hours on Work 4.15 am - 12.15 pm. Carrying parties Canal 10 pm - 4 am (approx), Northern 6 pm - 1 am.	
			Table of Working parties & progress on p. 3.	

A5834 Wt. W4973/M687 750,000 8/16 D. D. & L. Ltd. Forms/C.2118/13.

Appendix A. (3)

Army Form C. 2118.

Instructions regarding War Diaries and Intelligence. Summaries are contained in F. S. Regs., Part II. and the Staff Manual respectively. Title pages will be prepared in manuscript.

WAR DIARY
or
INTELLIGENCE SUMMARY.

(Erase heading not required.)

Place Nature of Work	~~Date~~ Labour RE No.	RE Sh	Inf No.	Inf Ptes	~~Hour~~ Location	Name	Decimal of Progress 2/10/17	Decimal of Progress 16/10/17	Summary of Events and Information Remarks.	Remarks and references to Appendices
Construction of Shelters.	1	5	1	6	S4a 3.5	R1 R2.	·65	1.00	parading 4.15 am and proceeding by lorry returning by lorry 12.15pm	
"	1	5	1	6	S3b 95.25	R3 R4	·07	·32		
"	1	5	1	6	S8b 2.4	A1 & A2.	·08	·33		
	2		1	22	Carrying Party parading nightly at 10pm and proceeding by lorry with cement supply for next days work.					
	1		1	10	Party at FURNES bagging sand & shingle & loading barge.					
	½		½		Officers Superintending.					
Construction of Shelters.	1	5	1	6	S2a 71	Nos A3 & 4	·06	·25	Double Emplacement.	
	1	5	1	6	M32b 2.5.	A5	·13	·49	Shelling in vicinity of these about daily. Parade 4.15am returning 12.15pm. Road near assembly point frequently shelled about 9 to 11 am.	
"	1	5	1	6	M32b 25	A6	·16	·49		
"	1	5	1	6	M32a 3.5	A7	·15	·46		
"	1	5	1	6	Coolgardie (a)	M32d 4.3.	·12	·37		
"	1	5	1	6	Coolgardie (b)	— 5.2.	·12	·37		
	1		3	21	Carrying party for 6 emplacements parade 6pm proceed with 3 limbers to site (about 4 miles) & return on completion about 1am to 2 am.					
	1				i/c Stores & Dispatch & loading of trains					
			1	8	Sand bag & Cement Bagging Party & loading of same.					
1	15	1	17.		Party commencing two new forward emplacements unloading trucks near NIEUPORT & laying Decauville to emplacement.					

Galt Anderson
Major
OC 409 Coy (Lowland)

A5834 Wt. W4973/M687 750,000 8/16 D. D. & L. Ltd. Forms/C.2118/13.

W A R D I A R Y.

(With Appendices).

409th. (Lowland) Field Coy., R.E.,(T).

1st.DIVISION.

NOVEMBER. 1917.

ORIGINAL.

409 LOWLAND Fd Co RE

WAR DIARY for Nov 1917 409 Fd Coy
or
INTELLIGENCE SUMMARY.

(Erase heading not required.)

Army Form C. 2118.

Instructions regarding War Diaries and Intelligence Summaries are contained in F. S. Regs., Part II. and the Staff Manual respectively. Title pages will be prepared in manuscript.

Vol 35

Place	Date	Hour	Summary of Events and Information	Remarks and references to Appendices
NE of YPRES	1/11/17		In Camp at IRISH FARM Resting Section Working in Camp making Splinter proof Shelters for men and Sandbagging of NISSEN HUTS – Line work on laying duckboards shown – Separate appendix A	Appendix A 4 pages + 1 map attd
			Casualty 1 Sapper slightly wounded by shell fire	
	2/11/17		Continued above	
			Casualty 1 Driver slightly wounded in camp by shell fire	
	3/11/17 4/11/17		as above	
	5/11/17		as above Rifle & Kit Inspection No 1.	
			Casualty 1 Sapper dangerously wounded by shell fire admitted to hospital while on works.	
	6/11/17		(as above).	
			Casualty one Sapper slightly wounded shellfire	
	~~7/11/17~~		Reconnaissance Reconnaissance of proposed track & [illegible] road and general alignment fixed	
			as above During above period Coy was employed on maintenance and improvement of tracks in area round the Field Guns and found [illegible] carrying parties at their disposal.	
			Summary of work Duckboards carried from dump.	
			laid in New Track.	
			Repaired	
			No of men days	
				[signature] Capt RE Comdg 1/12/17

A5834 Wt. W4973/M687 750,000 8/16 D. D. & L. Ltd. Forms/C.2118/13.

409 Lowland Fd Coy RE

WAR DIARY for Nov 1917.
or
INTELLIGENCE SUMMARY.

(Erase heading not required.)

P2

Army Form C. 2118.

Instructions regarding War Diaries and Intelligence Summaries are contained in F. S. Regs., Part II. and the Staff Manual respectively. Title pages will be prepared in manuscript.

Place	Date	Hour	Summary of Events and Information	Remarks and references to Appendices
NE of YPRES IRISH FARM Camp	7/11/17		Casualty 1 Sapper wounded Shell fire (admitted to Hospital)	
			Work Commenced work on forward portion of duckboard tracks for extending new track — all four sections on works.	
			Lt Macleod RE & Sergt Rennie noted for excellent work under fire	
	8/11/17		Ditto above	
	9/11/17		Casualty Lieut GALLOWAY RE. slightly wounded Shell fire —	
			2 guides from Coy; {Sapr CLOTHIER, " " } guided up MUNSTER FUSILIERS over new track to SOURCE FARM successfully — No 2 Section acting as pilot gang one hour in advance	
	10/11/17		Sappers to keep track in repair —	
			Combined attack by Canadians & 1st Div. objective ~~PASSCHENDAELE~~ the crest of the ridge in front of PASSCHENDAELE for Canadians — A spur running approx West from main ridge on N. side of PADDEBEEK for 1st Div —	
			RE officer Reconnaissance possibilities of extension of new track forward of SOURCE FARM	
			extension of No 6 track to SOURCE FARM — both above extensions taped out — reconnoitred also Position round SOURCE FARM was very obscure. Troops holding same did NOT know their location and had wrongly reported the same — Correct information given as above and verbal report to Division on condition forward.	
	11/11/17		Casualty 1 Sapper Killed 2 wounded in camp by Shrapnel fire	
	12/11/17		No 4 Section from IRISH FARM to billets in CANAL BANK for 3 days rest — No remain at IRISH FARM Camp.	

GCL

A5834 Wt. W4973/M687 750,000 8/16 D. D. & L. Ltd. Forms/C.2118/13.

Instructions regarding War Diaries and Intelligence Summaries are contained in F. S. Regs., Part II. and the Staff Manual respectively. Title pages will be prepared in manuscript.

409 Lowland F

WAR DIARY
or
INTELLIGENCE SUMMARY.
(*Erase heading not required.*)

Nov 1917. P. 3

Army Form C. 2118.

Place	Date	Hour	Summary of Events and Information	Remarks and references to Appendices
NE of YPRES	13/11/17		Movement. No 1 Section moved from IRISH FARM to Dugouts in Canal Bank. No 2 & 3 Sections from same place to forward billets approx 1 mile in rear of St JULIEN. & 3 Sgts Attached Infantry.	
	14/11/17		Works as Appendix att; No 1 & 4 improving accomodation in Canal Bank & guides for Carrying party.	
	15/11/17		ditto.	
	16/11/17.		Movement. Nos 1 & 4 Sections from CANAL BANK to Forward billets, No 2 & 3 from forward billets to CANAL BANK.	
			Inspection. Gas helmet & rifle inspection for Nos 1 & 4	
	17/11/17 18/11/17		work as Appendix A. back Section work on accomodation. Inspection of Rifles & Gas helmets & Baths.	
	19/11/17		Movement. No 1 Section from Forward to back billets. No 2 & 3 from Back to forward Billets. H.Q. from Irish Farm to Canal Bank. Transport remain at Irish Farm.	
	20/11/17		Baths Drivers & No 1 Section.	
			Works for back section preparing back new horse lines.	
	21/11/17		Military Medal awarded to No 412108 Cpl W Johnston 409 F Coy RE & No 412577 L/Cpl R.S. MLaughlin.	
	22/11/17		Handing over to O.C. 206 F Coy. & visit to line & forward work – Capts arranging re transfer of billets.	
	23/11/17.		Completed handing over to 206 F Coy, ready for move on 24/11/17. Responsibility for work ceases at midnight 23/24. Movement – No 4 Section & 1st Att. Infantry from forward billet to HOSPITAL FARM Camp. 2 miles N.W. of VLAMERTINGHE	

A5834 Wt. W4973/M687 750,000 8/16 D. D. & L. Ltd. Forms/C.2118/13.

Army Form C. 2118.

Instructions regarding War Diaries and Intelligence Summaries are contained in F. S. Regs., Part II. and the Staff Manual respectively. Title pages will be prepared in manuscript.

409th Lowland Fd. Coy.

WAR DIARY or INTELLIGENCE SUMMARY.

Nov 1917.

(Erase heading not required.)

P. (5)

Place	Date	Hour	Summary of Events and Information	Remarks and references to Appendices
YPRES AREA.	24/11/17.		Movement Coy (less No 4 Section) moved from forward area to back area to billets in HOSPITAL FARM — Placed at disposal of CE II Corps for work.	
	25/11/17		Rest & Clean up / Officers shewn work.	
	26/11/17.		9.30am. Gas Drill & Inspection. 10.45am. Rifle Inspection. 11.30am. Feet & Kit Inspection —	
	27/11/17		Works on Stables & Rest Camp till 1.30pm Standing by to move to PROVEN. Billeting Party sent forward orders for move cancelled.	
	28/11/17		Baths whole Coy. pm. Football. Visited site for Div H.Q. work laid out by Lt R Hood	
	29/11/17.		Commenced work on Div H.Q. materials arrived 10 am.	
			Work consists of I Road of brick 120x. II/ 900x Trenchboards III/ 30 NISSEN HUTS + 4 Armstrong Huts IV./ 7 Cookhouses; 6 Latrines; Officers Servants Quarters. V/ Internal fittings of above VI/ Camouflage of whole camp, work being carried out underneath same.	
	30/11/17		Work on D.H.Q. Contd good progress. Wkg Party 100 Inf. Black Watch. contd Fair. Movement 4 sects + 40 Attd Inf moved from HOSPITAL FARM to WORSTEN.	
			G.A.C. Findlay Major RE OC. 409 Lowland Fd Coy RE	

A5834 Wt. W4973/M687 750,000 8/16 D. D. & L. Ltd. Forms/C.2118/13.

409 Lowland Fd Coy — November — Appendix A (b)

Army Form C. 2118.

Instructions regarding War Diaries and Intelligence Summaries are contained in F. S. Regs., Part II. and the Staff Manual respectively. Title pages will be prepared in manuscript.

WAR DIARY or INTELLIGENCE SUMMARY.

(Erase heading not required.)

Place	Date	Hour	Boards taken from St Julien Dump	Boards taken from Forward Dumps	Boards laid in repairs	Boards laid on new tracks	No of Men.	Summary of SECTION.	Events and Information — REMARKS.	Remarks and references to Appendices
N.E. of YPRES.	Oct. 30th	6.30. a.m. – 4.30. p.m.	270	NIL.	8.	220.	71.	1. & 4. / 2.	Commenced doubling the St. JULIEN SWITCH TRACK from ST. JULIEN DUMP forward. Repaired breaks in the original track. (Track doubled for use of stretcher bearers).	See tracing attached!
"	31st	4.0. a.m.	200	NIL.	20	180	48.	1. & 4.	Continued doubling track – ST. JULIEN SWITCH. Repaired the original track and also MOUSETRAP AVENUE. 20 boards were dumped at ALBERTA FARM for the next shift to repair ALBERTA TRACK forward of ALBERTA FARM.	Ref. 1/20,000 Sheets.
		1.30 p.m.	60	NIL.	7.	33.	20.	3.		
"	Nov. 1st	4.0. a.m.	60	14	14	60	44	2. & 4.	Continued doubling St. JULIEN SWITCH. up to C.12.d.6.8. Repaired ALBERTA TRACK from ALBERTA FARM to C.11, b, 6.4.	20 S.W. 20 S.E. 28 N.W. 28 NE
		12 noon	140	NIL.	46	100	23	3.	Also repaired breaks in MOUSETRAP AV. and St. JULIEN SWITCH.	
"	2nd	4.0. a.m.	80	6	6	80	44.	1. & 2.	Continued doubling St. J. SWITCH. up to road at C.12, b, 7.2. Repaired ALBERTA TK. to 150x beyond the STEENBECK.	
		12.n. p.m.	80+40 at Alberta.		28.	52	23.	3.	Repaired MOUSETRAP AV. and St. J. SWITCH all the way to HUBNER FM. 40 boards carried to ALBERTA FM. for use of next shift.	
"	3rd.	4.0. a.m.	40	NIL.	40	20.	41.	1. & 2.	40x double track laid N.E. of road at C.12, b, 7.2.	
		12 n. p.m.	20.	NIL.	10.	NIL	22.	4	Repairs:– ALBERTA TK. 40x relaid N. of STEENBECK. MOUSETRAP AV. 3 gaps mended. St. JULIEN SWITCH. 28 breaks repaired.	
"	4th.	4.0. a.m.		NIL.	45.	55.	43.	2. & 3.	Double tracked St. J. SWITCH. – 75 boards to C.12, b, 4, 1½.	
		12 n. p.m.	75 (20 at Alberta)		4	20	23.	4.	Repairs:– ALBERTA TK. up to C, 12, a, 3.7. ALBERTA – St. J. DUMP (SWITCH) 4 breaks repaired. St. J. SWITCH. 4 breaks mended.	
"	5th.	4.0. a.m.	50	NIL.	6	44	43.	2. & 3.	88x double track laid on St. J. SWITCH.	
		12 n. p.m.	20	NIL.	NIL.	NIL	23.	4.	Repairs:– ALBERTA TK. up to St. J. – POEL CPLE ROAD. MOUSETRAP AV. 3 gaps. St. J. SWITCH. large stretch damaged by convoy of mules had to be repaired in afternoon.	
"	6th.	4.0. a.m.	60.	NIL.	13.	56	46.	2. & 3.	Double track on new alignment – 56 boards to C.12, b, 9.3.	
		12 n. p.m.	15.	NIL.	NIL	NIL	19.	1	Repairs:– ALBERTA TK. – 5 gaps. ALBERTA – St. J. SWITCH – 6 gaps. MOUSETRAP AV. – 3 gaps. St. J. SWITCH. – 15 gaps.	
			1230	20	246	910	533			

Upkeep of ALBERTA, MOUSETRAP, and St. JULIEN SWITCH TRACKS from St. JULIEN to HUBNER Farm. (see sketch)

A5834 Wt. W4973/M687 750,000 8/16 D. D. & L. Ltd. Forms/C.2118/13.

Instructions regarding War Diaries and Intelligence Summaries are contained in F. S. Regs., Part II. and the Staff Manual respectively. Title pages will be prepared in manuscript.

WAR DIARY
or
INTELLIGENCE SUMMARY.

(Erase heading not required.)

Appendix A (p 2)

Army Form C. 2118.

Place	Date	Hour	Boards taken from St Julien Dump	Boards taken from Forward Dumps	Boards laid in repairs.	Boards laid on New Tracks	No. of Men	Summary of Section.	Events and Information REMARKS.	Remarks and references to Appendices
N.E of YPRES.	Nov. 7th	4.0. a.m.	50	100. ~~Nil~~	10	130	45	2. & 4.	Laid new SWITCH TRACK from MOUSETRAP AV. to meet No 6 TRACK at KRONPRINZ FM. – 268x. 100 boards had been previously dumped at ALBATROSS FM. by carrying party. Repaired from STROPP FM to INCH HOUSES. 300 boards carried by carrying party of 14th Worcesters (Pioneers) to WALLEMOLEN for night party.	Ref 1/20000 Sheets 20 S.W. 20 S.E. 28 N.W. 28 N.E.
			300				10	+10 A.I.		
	7th/8th	8 p.m. to 4.30 a.m.	50	60	NIL	110	62.	1 & 3 + A.I.		
		10 p.m. to 6 a.m.	90	NIL	NIL	50	40	2 Sections 26 Fd. Coy.	Laid 320x new track from N.E. end of WALLEMOLEN ROAD towards SOURCE FM.	
	8th	4.0. a.m.	55	NIL	50	NIL	60	1 & 3 + A.I.	Relaid part of new switch from about D.3.C.3.7 to No.6. TRACK (this part had been lifted and removed).	60 pioneers carried up 120 boards to WALLEMOLEN.
			120	NIL	NIL	NIL	60	" "	Repairs – MOUSETRAP AV. as far as D.3.b.8.8. No.6 TRACK – in vicinity of CEMETRY	
		5.30 p.m.	20	80	NIL	~~Nil~~ 150	60	No 2 & 2 Sects 26th Fd Coy	Continued new track across PADDEBEK to within 30x of SOURCE FM. BOARDS laid on worst parts of WALLEMOLEN ROAD	
	9th	4.0. a.m.	36	NIL	NIL	NIL	52	1 & 3 + A.I.	Repaired MOUSETRAP AV. up to WALLEMOLEN, and No6. up to CEMETRY. also SWITCH to KRONPRINZ. 110 pioneers carried up 220 boards to WALLEMOLEN.	
			220	"	"	"	110			
		3.0 p.m.	75	"	"	"	200	No 2 + A.I. + 150 H.L.I.	Repaired MOUSETRAP AV. up to WALLEMOLEN and new track to SOURCE FM. H.L.I. carried up boards, cleaned mud off the WALLEMOLEN RD. and laid boards in worst places.	
	10th	4.0. a.m.	25	5	30	"	29.	1 + A.I.	Repaired No 6 track from KRONPRINZ FM. back to KANSAS. HO. as this specially reqd. repair.	
		3.0. p.m.	114.	NIL	NIL	"	134		Pioneers carried boards up to ALBATROSS FM.	
		(NIGHT)	45	"	45	"	53	3 & 4 + A.I.	Repaired new track (SOURCE FM) up to PADDEBEKE.	
	11th	4.0. a.m.	17	"	17	"	39	1 Sect 26 Coy.	Drained marshy ground and relaid MOUSETRAP AV. round ALBATROSS FM. Doubled track to BATT. HDQRS. near ALBATROSS FM.	
			36	"	8	78	41	247 249 1 & 2		
		3.0. p.m.	25	"	25	NIL.	43	4 & 2 + A.I.	Repaired KRONPRINZ SWITCH.	
		Night	25	"	"	"		1 Sect 26 Coy	Pioneers carried 130 boards to WALLEMOLEN and 129 to ALBATROSS FM.	
		4.0. a.m.	{130	"	"	"	130	–	Night-Shift:– Carried up a board each to SOURCE FM. and laid raised track over the swollen PADDEBEKE.	
			129.	"	"	"	129	–		
	12th	p.m.	25	"	25	"	28	1 + A.I.	Repaired No6 TRACK forward of the CEMETRY.	
			30	"	30	"	56	2 & 3 + A.I.	" track from WALLEMOLEN to SOURCE FARM.	
			90	"	90	"	53	26 Coy.	Repaired MOUSETRAP AV. up to D.3.b.7.6. No6. TRACK up to D.4.a.5.3	
			208	"	NIL	"	107	"	Pioneers carried up to WALLEMOLEN.	
			1915	245	320	468	1541		Many boards used by Infantry & our men for immediate repairs owing to breakages of track	

CONSTRUCTION AND UPKEEP OF TRACKS in forward area from HUBNER FARM to SOURCE FARM.

A5834 Wt. W4973/M687 750,000 8/16 D. D. & L. Ltd. Forms/C.2118/13.

Instructions regarding War Diaries and Intelligence Summaries are contained in F. S. Regs., Part II. and the Staff Manual respectively. Title pages will be prepared in manuscript.

WAR DIARY
or
INTELLIGENCE SUMMARY.
(Erase heading not required.)

Appendix A (p 3)

Army Form C. 2118.

Place	Date	Hour	Boards taken from St Julien Dump	Boards taken from Forward Dump	Boards used in repairs.	Boards used in New tracks	No. of Men.	Summary of Section.	Events and Information — Remarks.	Remarks and references to Appendices
N.E. of	Nov. 13th		Change	of	Shifts.					Ref. 1/20.000
YPRES.	14th	4.0 a.m.	–	NIL	NIL	142	47	2&3&A.I.	Laid 284x of new track from No 6 TRACK near YETTA Hos. to join No 5 track. (PETER PAN)	Sheets
			72.	"	"	NIL	72	"	Black Watch carried 72 boards to YETTA Hos.	20 S.W.
			123.	"	"	"	62	"	Pioneers carried 123 boards, of which 61 were left at ALBATROSS.	20 S.E.
	15th	4.0. a.m.	46	"	"[illegible] Repairs done daily" employing 1 section.	156	50	2&3&A.I.	Continued PETER PAN TRACK – End of track at D.4, c. 1.4. Track taped out as far as D.4, d, 6. 1½.	28 N.W. 28 N.E.
			200	"		NIL	~~106~~ 106.	"	2 Companies of Pioneers carrying.	
	16th	4.0. a.m.	31	100		130	40.	2&3&A.I.	Completed new track as far as PETER PAN. D.4,C, 2½.2. Fixed notice boards at junctions, etc.	
			95.	NIL.		NIL	48.	"	Company of Black Watch carrying.	
	17th	4.0. a.m.	37	"		101	37	1&4&A.I.	Laid 101 new boards, and relaid and improved about 200x of old loop round PETER PAN.	
			150	"		NIL	150	"	3 Coys. of Infantry carried up to PETER PAN.	
	18th	a.m.	NIL	"		325	38	1&4&A.I.	Completed PETER PAN SWITCH as far as BELLEVUE FM.	
			340	"		NIL	340	"	Infantry carried up to PETER PAN.	
			1094	100	NIL	854	990			

Construction and Upkeep of Tracks in Forward Areas from KRONPRINZ FM. to BELLEVUE and VANITY FM.

A5834 Wt. W4973/M687 750,000 8/16 D. D. & L. Ltd. Forms/C.2118/13.

Appendix A (P. 4)

Army Form C. 2118.

WAR DIARY
or
INTELLIGENCE SUMMARY.
(Erase heading not required.)

Instructions regarding War Diaries and Intelligence Summaries are contained in F. S. Regs., Part II. and the Staff Manual respectively. Title pages will be prepared in manuscript.

Place	Date	Hour	Boards taken from St.Julien Dump	Boards taken from Forward Dump	Boards Used in Repairs	Boards Used in New Tracks	No. of Men	Summary of Section	Events and Information REMARKS	Remarks and references to Appendices
N.E. of YPRES.	Nov. 19th	am.	NIL	75	NIL	75	29	1 & A.1.	As carrying party did not arrive at proper meeting place, no boards were carried up. 75 boards were laid on new track, Ending at D.4.C.5.3. Minor repairs were done to No 6 TRACK and PETER PAN SWITCH	Ref 1/20.000 Sheets
	20th	am.	—	230.	—	230	40.	2 & 4.	Laid 460x new track from near PETER PAN to D.4.d.2.6. (up to daylight limit)	20 S.W.
			—	40	40	—	20	3.	Repaired No 6 TRACK between YETTA HOUSES and CEMETRY. and between PETER PAN and BELLEVUE FARM	20 S.E. 28 N.W. 28 N.E.
			390.	—	—	—	—	—	4 Coys. from III.rd Bde. as carrying party.	
									Track taped out continuously to VANITY FARM with a branch to VINE COTTAGE. ~~[illegible]~~	
	21st	am	350	50	20	30	20	3	New track extended 60x towards Vine Cottage — small party went ahead and worked on Drainage in Woodland Plantation	
		pm					40	2 & 4	84 boards carried from intermediate to forward dump 150x forward of PETER PAN — Heavy shelling on end of track — Carrying party on	
	22/11/17	am.	350	46	16	30	20	3	Maintenance | The 1st shift delayed 1 hour on way up by heavy retaliation barrage dropped at 4.15 pm at KRONPRINZ — party arrived on job 6.15 and had absolute quiet till 8.30 pm when shelling commenced and continued throughout night.	
		3rd — mn		190	~~190~~	190	14 / 47	2 Sect / 2 Welsh	2nd Shift laid 100 boards in quiet intervals — and extra carrying party of 125 from Northumberland carried 150 boards well forward and formed a dump ~~[illegible]~~	
				100	~~100~~	100	25 / 125	2 Welsh / Northumb		
	23/11/17	am / pm	Maintenance No 3 Section with pilot party for Relief — 350 / 1440	731	366	365	10. 409/791	No 1 63 Div	~~Maint~~ Carrying party of 400 or 2 Coys dumped boards at forward dump of KRONPRINZ 1000x in front of PETER PAN. 2 Coys dumped boards. Balance of 300 boards left in forward dump.	

CONSTRUCTION AND UPKEEP of TRACKS in Forward Area from KRONPRINZ to BELLEVUE and VANITY FARM.

[illegible signature]

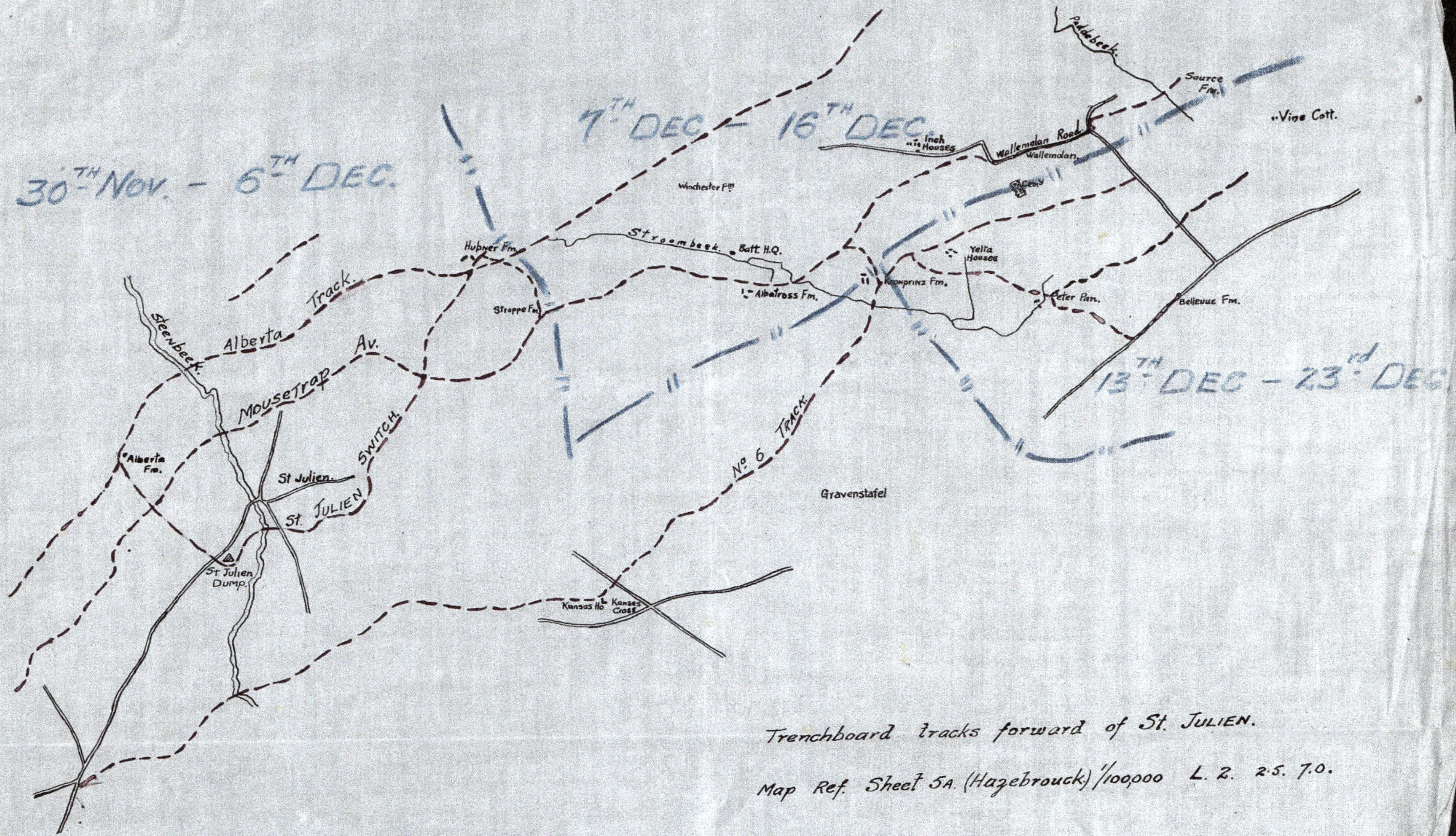

Trenchboard tracks forward of St. JULIEN.

Map Ref. Sheet 5A. (Hazebrouck) 1/100,000 L. 2. 25. 7.0.

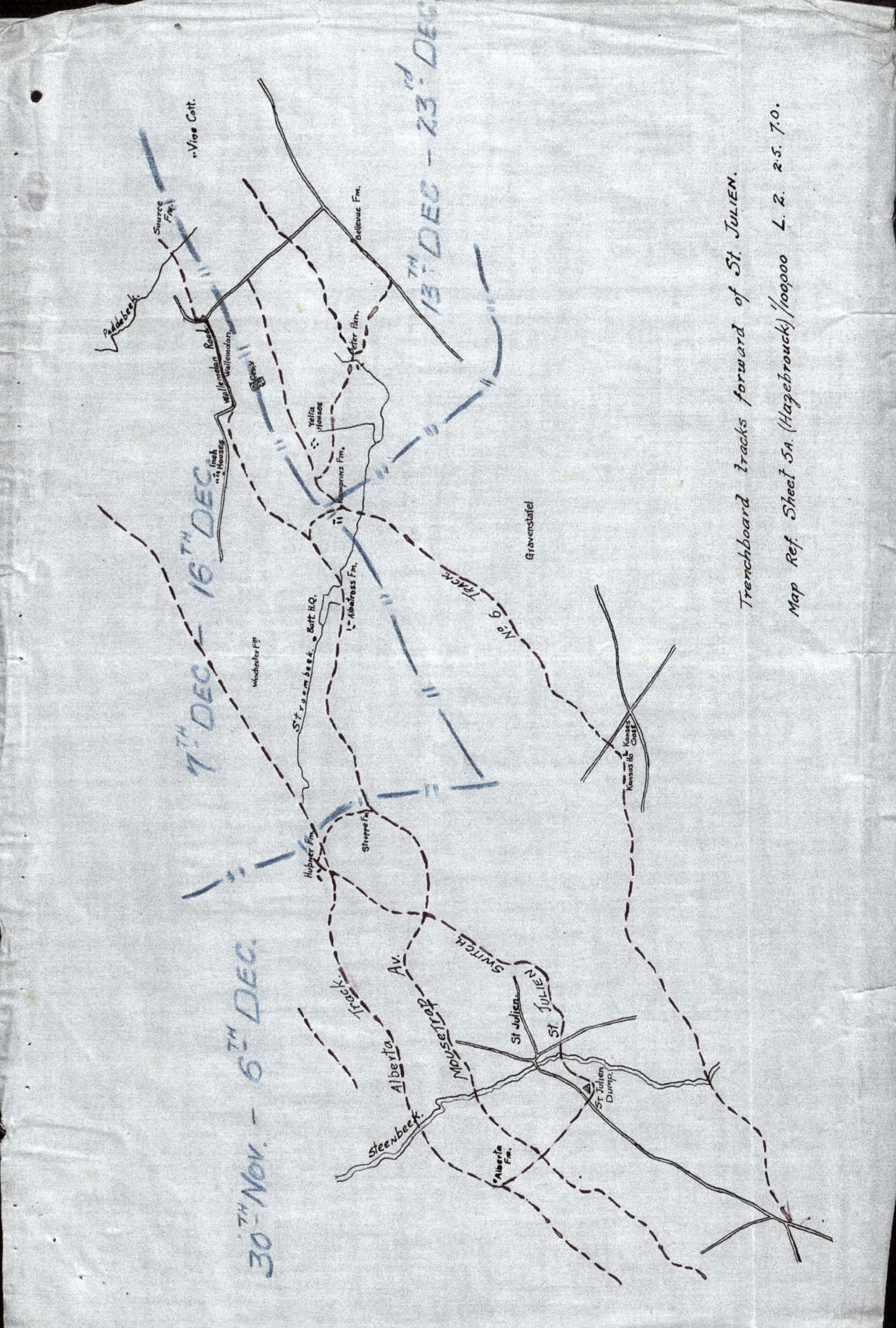

WAR DIARY.

409th. (Lowland) Field Coy., R.E., (T).

1st. DIVISION.

DECEMBER. 1917.

Vol 36

CONFIDENTIAL

WAR DIARY

OF

409th (LOWLAND) FIELD COY. R.E. (T)

from 1st Dec. 1917 to 31st Dec. 1917

(VOLUME. No. XXXVI)

Army Form C. 2118.

Instructions regarding War Diaries and Intelligence Summaries are contained in F. S. Regs., Part II. and the Staff Manual respectively. Title pages will be prepared in manuscript.

WAR DIARY
or
~~INTELLIGENCE SUMMARY.~~

(Erase heading not required.)

Place	Date	Hour	Summary of Events and Information	Remarks and references to Appendices
WOESTEN	1-12-17		Commenced erection of Nissen Huts for 1st Divisional Headquarters. Four sections with 140 attached Infantry employed on this work. Infantry detailed to construct roads and entrances to camp under R.E. supervision.	
	2-12-17		Continued erection of Divisional Headquarters, and construction of roads etc.	
	3-12-17		do do do do do.	
	4-12-17		do do do do do.	
	5-12-17		do do do do do.	
	6-12-17		do do do do do.	
	7-12-17		Huts completed and ready for occupation on morning of 7th. Twenty-two Nissen Huts erected, also six cookhouses, one hut (Armstrong) for C.R.E. and one shelter for Officers servants.	

A5834 Wt. W4973/M687 750,000 8/16 D. D. & L. Ltd. Forms/C.2118/13.

Instructions regarding War Diaries and Intelligence Summaries are contained in F. S. Regs., Part II. and the Staff Manual respectively. Title pages will be prepared in manuscript.

Army Form C. 2118.

WAR DIARY
or
~~INTELLIGENCE SUMMARY.~~
(Erase heading not required.)

Place	Date	Hour	Summary of Events and Information	Remarks and references to Appendices
WOESTEN.	8-12-17		Two sections commenced erection of Divisional Baths, one and a half miles north of Woesten. Twenty attached Infantry assisting this section.	
			Two sections employed finishing Divisional Headquarters, and commencing the erection of earth walls round huts.	
			One hundred attached Infantry continue work on roads and entrances at D.H.Q.	
	9-12-17		Two sections and attached Infantry continue work at D.H.Q as on previous day.	
			Two sections and attached Infantry continue work at Baths as on previous day.	
	10-12-17		One section and attached Infantry continue work at D.H.Q.	
			One section and ten attached Infantry detailed to construct road and entrance to Divisional Baths.	
			Two sections and attached Infantry continue the erection of baths as on previous day.	

CP

A5834 Wt. W4973/M687 750,000 8/16 D. D. & L. Ltd. Forms/C.2118/13.

Instructions regarding War Diaries and Intelligence Summaries are contained in F. S. Regs., Part II. and the Staff Manual respectively. Title pages will be prepared in manuscript.

WAR DIARY
or
~~INTELLIGENCE SUMMARY.~~
(Erase heading not required.)

Army Form C. 2118.

Place	Date	Hour	Summary of Events and Information	Remarks and references to Appendices
WOESTEN	11-12-17		One section and attached Infantry continue work on D.H.Q	
			Divisional Baths:- Six Nissen Huts and one clothes store hut completed.	
			One section and attached Infantry continue road and entrance to Baths.	
	12-12-17		One section and attached Infantry continue work on D.H.Q.	
			Three sections and attached Infantry continue work on Baths.	
	13-12-17		Work continued as on day previous.	
	14-12-17		do do do do.	
	15-12-17		Six men detailed for work on Divisional Concert Hall	
			One section, less above 6 men continue work on D.H.Q assisted by attached Infantry as before. This work was completed on this date	
			Three sections continue work at Baths as on previous day.	
	16-12-17		Church Parade.	
	17-12-17		One section and ten attached Infantry work on Company Billets and stables.	
			Three sections continue work at Baths.	

A5834 Wt. W4973/M687 750,000 8/16 D. D. & L. Ltd. Forms/C.2118/13.

eG

Army Form C. 2118.

Instructions regarding War Diaries and Intelligence Summaries are contained in F. S. Regs., Part II. and the Staff Manual respectively. Title pages will be prepared in manuscript.

WAR DIARY
or
~~INTELLIGENCE SUMMARY.~~
(Erase heading not required.)

Place	Date	Hour	Summary of Events and Information	Remarks and references to Appendices
WOESTEN	18-12-17		Three sections continue work at Baths	
			One section working in Billets and Stables as on previous day.	
			Attached Infantry party of one hundred men completed road into D.H.Q.	
	19-12-17		Three sections continue work at Baths.	
			One section working in Billets and Stables.	
	20-12-17		Two sections continue work at Baths	
			One section detailed for work on Divisional Concert Hall.	
			One section working in Billets and stables.	
	21-12-17		Work continued as on previous day.	
	22-12-17		do do do do.	
	23-12-17		One section continues work at Baths.	
			One section continues work at Concert Hall.	
			One section detailed to construct Nissen Hut.	
			One section working in Billets and Stables.	
	24-12-17		Work continued as on previous day.	
	25-12-17		Nil.	
	26-12-17		One section moved to Rousbrugge to commence work on Divisional Laundry	
			Three sections work as on 23rd.	

A5834 Wt. W4973/M687 750,000 8/16 D. D. & L. Ltd. Forms/C.2118/13.

Army Form C. 2118.

Instructions regarding War Diaries and Intelligence Summaries are contained in F. S. Regs., Part II. and the Staff Manual respectively. Title pages will be prepared in manuscript.

WAR DIARY
or
~~INTELLIGENCE SUMMARY.~~
(Erase heading not required.)

Place	Date	Hour	Summary of Events and Information	Remarks and references to Appendices
WOESTEN	27-12-17		One section commenced work on Divisional Laundry at ROUSBRUGGE.	
			Three sections work as on 23rd. Two N.C.O's and 6 O.R. superintend erection of	
	28-12-17		7 Nissen Huts, at R.F.A. transport lines, 500 yds N.E. of Woesten.	
	28-12-17		One section continued work at Laundry.	
			One section continued work at Baths.	
			One section moved ~~to~~ Moyan Camp to erect Divisional Spray Baths.	
			Party continues work on huts at R.F.A. transport lines.	
			Party working in Church Army hut in Woesten.	
			Party erecting Nissen Hospital Hut at KRUISDOORN.	
	29-12-17		Work continued as on previous day.	
	30-12-17		do. do. do. do.	
	31-12-17		do do do do.	
			All work completed except at Divisional Baths.	

Chas Powell Capt R.E.
O/C 409th (Lowland) Fld ~~Coy RE~~ Coy

2353 Wt. W2544/1454 700,000 5/15 D. D. & L. A.D.S.S./Forms/C. 2118.

1ST DIVISION
ROY. ENGINEERS

409TH (LOWLAND) FIELD COY. R.E.

~~JAN - DEC 1918~~

1918 JAN – 1919 SEP

Vol 37

CONFIDENTIAL

WAR DIARY

OF

409th (LOWLAND) FIELD COY R.E. (T)

from 1st JANY 1918 to 31st JANY 1918

(VOLUME No. XXXVII)

409th (LOWLAND) Fd. Coy R.E.

P.1

Army Form C. 2118.

Instructions regarding War Diaries and Intelligence Summaries are contained in F. S. Regs., Part II. and the Staff Manual respectively. Title pages will be prepared in manuscript.

WAR DIARY for JANUARY 1918.
or
INTELLIGENCE SUMMARY.
(Erase heading not required.)

Place	Date	Hour	Summary of Events and Information	Remarks and references to Appendices
Moulin à Vent WOESTON	1/1/18		Officers: On leave O.C. / on Course at Army Inf School. Lt Macleod RE / Sick Leave Lt Galloway.	Attached to Company from Infantry 1 Off. & 40 O.R. drawn 10 from each of four Btns
			Works in hand – (1) DIVISIONAL BATHS. (2) HUT ERECTION at ~~Div Bath~~ D.A.C. Wagon Lines (3) Ablution & Baths at NOYON and CHAUNY Camps.	
			1. Div Baths erection of sock Drying Fireplace and chamber.	
			2. HUT ERECTION at D.A.C. Wagon Lines Dismantling Adrian hut transporting and re-erecting same.	
			3/ Noyon Camp. Ablution Room dismantled & seats fitted in for use as a Dressing Room for Baths.	
			4/ CHAUNEY Camp. Partitions in building altered for use as Bathhouse.	
	2/1/18.		Inspection of Rifles, Equipment and Gas Helmets —	
			Works. Continued works in hand 1/1/18.	
	3/1/18.		Continued above works and commenced alterations to baths	
			No 4 Section. Erected one Nissen Hut Complete for accomodation for Staff of Pigeon Loft.	
	4/1/18		Above Work Continued — New organisation started for control of RE Work in Back Area — one officer 2 NCO's & 11 Sappers detached from Coy and distributed among Camps for control of material & continuity of policy the whole under the Officer who was appointed DOAE and worked direct under CRE.	
	5/1/18.		Continued Work on above — Survey of old Cellars at Div HQ made and plans prepared for strengthening same for Battle HQ for Divn.	[signature] Major

D. D. & L., London, E.C. (A8001) Wt. W1771/M2031 750,000 5/17 Sch. 52 Forms/C2118/14

409th (LOWLAND) FIELD Coy RE

WAR DIARY Jan. 1918.
or
INTELLIGENCE SUMMARY.
(Erase heading not required.)

Army Form C. 2118. P3

Instructions regarding War Diaries and Intelligence Summaries are contained in F. S. Regs., Part II. and the Staff Manual respectively. Title pages will be prepared in manuscript.

Place	Date	Hour	Summary of Events and Information	Remarks and references to Appendices
(Same).	6/1/18.		Works as above Continued – Work at DAC Wagon Lines Completed. Div HQ. erection of two Armstrong Huts. / Church Service held at Billets after work.	•
	7/1/18.		Continue Work as above –	
	8/1/18.		ditto. add. Materials delivered at Div HQ. for commencing erection of Battle Station.	
	9/1/18.		ditto add. Work Commenced on Div HQ.	
	10/1/18.		Work now in hand: 1 Alteration to baths. 2 sections (less special men for items 3 & 4)	
			2 Battle Station Div HQ. 2 sections (" " " " ")	
			3 New Water Point for Brigade Transport at S24 c.0.0.	
			4 Sundry odd repairs & maintenance jobs in Camps & Div HQ.	
			Fire. Special Orders re fire precautions issued.	
	11/1/18.		Works Contd on above.	
			INSPECTION for Drivers & HQ. Rifles –	
	12/1/18.		(1) Works as above + fitting Stoves in Church Army Hut EIKHOEK. + Erection of 2nd Hut at DAC Wagon Lines Commenced. + Fireplace in Office at Div HQ.	
			(2) Painting of Transport Commenced. / Note. Maj Findlay rejoined from leave to U.K.	
	13/1/18.		contd above + small jobs on Canteen at Baths (Forward) + Laying Stable floor at No 2 M.V.S. with Concrete Slabs.	

D. D. & L., London, E.C. (A8001) Wt. W1771/M2031 750,000 5/17 Sch. 52 Forms/C2118/14

404? LOWLAND FD. Coy RE.

WAR DIARY Jan 1918
or
INTELLIGENCE SUMMARY.
(Erase heading not required.)

Army Form C. 2118. No 3

Instructions regarding War Diaries and Intelligence Summaries are contained in F. S. Regs., Part II. and the Staff Manual respectively. Title pages will be prepared in manuscript.

Place	Date	Hour	Summary of Events and Information	Remarks and references to Appendices
(Same)	14/1/18.		Div HQ. Battle Station 3 section. (less detail) Div Baths 1 section (less detail) Work as on 13/1/18 Contd.	
	15/1/18.		Officers. Leave to U.K. Capt. C. Powell M.C. RE. Work as above Contd + Repairs to Boiler of Forward Baths. Very heavy rain at night.	
	16/1/18.		Work as above (Contd) — till 10 am. Whole Company standing by ready to undertake any work required forward. Heavy floods caused by rain completely flooding road at TROIS CHEMINS and submerging bridges over BROUENBEEK & STEENBEEK. — At first reports were received that bridges were washed away, reconnaissance proved this report false, and normal work.	
	17/1/18.		Contd as above — Work on Billets in CANAL BANK carried out preparatory to 2 sections moving forward on 18th & 19th inst — ~~Resume of Work during Past Week ending 17/1/18.~~ ~~Divisional Baths~~ ~~Reconstruction of baths on improved design carried out and baths ready for use 16/1/18. Minor Finishings still reqd. Reconstruction involved dismantling Bath & 6 Nissen Huts & reerecting so as to reduce passageway —~~ (next sheet) Div HQ Battle Station G. Offices to be made by strengthening old cellars. G. Wl?? Major RE.	

D. D. & L., London, E.C.
(A8004) Wt. W1771/M2031 750,000 5/17 Sch. 52 Forms/C2118/14

409th (LOWLAND) Fd. Coy R.E.

Instructions regarding War Diaries and Intelligence Summaries are contained in F. S. Regs., Part II. and the Staff Manual respectively. Title pages will be prepared in manuscript.

WAR DIARY Jan 1918.
or
INTELLIGENCE SUMMARY.
(Erase heading not required.)

Army Form C. 2118.

p(4)

Place	Date	Hour	Summary of Events and Information	Remarks and references to Appendices
Same	11th–17th Jan		Summary of Work Done	
			A. DIVISIONAL BATHS – Reconstruction. Dismantling bath & 6 NISSEN HUTS & reconstructing so as to reduce passage ways as a precaution agst colds and also to increase efficiency. Continuing finishing of Sock Washing & Drying Plant – Consisting of Wash House & two sock Drying apparatus each capable of drying 1000 prs per day.	revised plan attached. marked A.
			B. Div. H.Q. Battle Station. G Office – (i) Strutted & completed timbering of Old Cellars & made new entrance to connect with existing dugout. (ii) Laid 1 ft Reinforced Concrete over whole roof. (iii) " 3 ft earth over half roof.	
			Burster. / Earth 3' / [illegible] / rails touching. / Earth 3'. / Reinforced Concrete 1 ft / Old 18" Cellar Arches. / Section through Roof of G Office	
			G Office (etc) 5 English Shelters with 2'6" Concrete end walls & traversed entrances. Work done. Erected 5 Shelters & Timbering for roof. Concreted 4 floors. Protected Back Wall.	
			Roof. Concrete Arch 1' / Earth 1' / Rails & Steel Troughs on Timber Frame / Earth 2'6" / Rails Touching. / Earth 3' / Burster.	
			C. WATER POINT S 24 a 00. 120 yds Corduroy road way completed. 120 ft troughing erected.	
			D. CHURCH ARMY HUT. Repairs & improvements. E. DAC LINES dismantling French ADRIAN HUT & re-erection of same.	
			F. No 2 MVS 280 ft. Concrete Slabs laid on stable floor. G. Forward Baths – Repairs & Maintenance	

G.C.W.H. [illegible] Maj RE

Instructions regarding War Diaries and Intelligence Summaries are contained in F. S. Regs., Part II. and the Staff Manual respectively. Title pages will be prepared in manuscript.

WAR DIARY
or
INTELLIGENCE SUMMARY.
(Erase heading not required.)

Army Form C. 2118.

p 4

Place	Date	Hour	Summary of Events and Information	Remarks and references to Appendices
Same	18/1/18.		One Section preparing accommodation in CANAL BANK for moving two Sections forward	
			~~One " finishing off baths~~	
			Two " on Div HQ.	
	~~19/1/18~~	–	Work on DHQ Cont^d. & work on CANAL BANK BILLETS (Cont^d)	
			No 1 Section parade Marching Order 8·30 am — Inspection of Gas Equipment & Efficiency moved into Shelter in CANAL BANK for work on Corps Line Shelters with 26th Fd Coy RE	
	19/1/18.		No 1 Section under 26th Fd Coy RE.	
			No 2 Section parade Marching Order Inspection of Gas Equipment proceeding to forward billets.	
	20/1/18.		No 3·4 & HQ. Inspection of Rifles & Equipment & Handling of Arms.	
			Baths for Drivers No 3·4 & HQ. Cars employing.	
			Baths & Inspection for those employed on works on 20/1/18.	
	21/1/18.		forward Work Cont^d	
	22/1/18	}	Work Cont^d	
	23/1/18			
	24/1/18		Continued Work.	
			Inspection Gas Helmets on horses ——	
			Summary of Weeks Work b. s.	

[signature]

D. D. & L., London, E.C.
(A8001) Wt. W1771/M2031 750,000 5/17 Sch. 52 Forms C2118/14

p 5.

409th (LOWLAND) F Coy RE

Instructions regarding War Diaries and Intelligence Summaries are contained in F. S. Regs., Part II. and the Staff Manual respectively. Title pages will be prepared in manuscript.

WAR DIARY Jan 1918
or
INTELLIGENCE SUMMARY.
(Erase heading not required.)

Army Form C. 2118.

Place	Date	Hour	Summary of Events and Information	Remarks and references to Appendices
WOESTON (Same place)	17/1/18. 24/1/18.		Summary of Weeks Work.	
			I. Div. HQ. Battle Station.	Labour. DHQ. 100 Inf daily. Canal. 60 " "
			G. Offices. Completed covering cellar with 3' earth added layer of rails added 3' earth. Fixed Sound Proof walls round G.O.C.'s room.	
			A Mess. Completed Excavation for same erected timber framing to carry Splinter proof roof. Excavation of passage connecting this with G Offices.	
			Q Offices. Laid 1st arch ring on roof of 4 Shelters & finished floors of all five. Prepared Sheltering front wall.	
			II Water Point at S24 a.o.o. Completed fixing of Pump tank & draw off also Blinding of Corduroy Road with brick rubble. COMPLETED and handed over for use	
			III DIVISIONAL BATHS. COMPLETED all outstanding jobs and withdrew party.	
			IV DAC Wagon Lines. Erection of 2nd Adrian hut in hand.	
			V No 2 M.V.S. One sapper laid 690 F.S concrete blocks including draining of subsoil & filling up same.	
			VI CANAL BANK (1) Made & fixed 120 bunks. (2) Drained frontage & Shelters. (3) 104 x of Double Duckboard track laid along face (4) Covering Shelters with 1'6" earth — Splinterproof. (5) Salvage of RE Material.	
			Galt	

D. D. & L., London, E.C. (A8004) Wt. W1771/M2031 750,000 5/17 Sch. 52 Forms/C2118/14

ADQ^rs LOWLAND F^d Coy RE.

Instructions regarding War Diaries and Intelligence Summaries are contained in F. S. Regs., Part II. and the Staff Manual respectively. Title pages will be prepared in manuscript.

WAR DIARY Jan 1918.
or
INTELLIGENCE SUMMARY.
(Erase heading not required.)

Army Form C. 2118.
p. 6.

Place	Date	Hour	Summary of Events and Information	Remarks and references to Appendices
			No 1 Section work on Corps line dugouts.	
(Same)	25/1/18.		DHQ. CANAL BANK. DAC. (cont^d) + Div Baths extras Cookhouse Dirty Clothes Store and Delousing Emporium.	
	26/1/18.		NO2 MVS.	
	27/1/18.		HQ. & No 3 & 4 Section Cleaning Equipment & Church Parade. Nos 1 & 2 cont^d work.	
	28/1/18		Cont^d works as above + Preparations for work at ROUGE BRUGGE Laundry.	
	29/1/18.		ditto.	
	30/1/18.		ditto. Lt Bort proceeded on leave to U.K. 2nd Lieut T.G. Mitchell RE joined Coy.	
	31/1/18		ditto. Capt C. Powell rejoined from leave to U.K.	
			Weekly Summary of work completed attached (p 7)	
			Gold (signature)	

D. D. & L., London, E.C. (A8004) Wt. W1771/M2031 750,000 5/17 Sch. 52 Forms C2118/14

409th (Lowland) Fd Coy RE

p7.

Army Form C. 2118.

Instructions regarding War Diaries and Intelligence Summaries are contained in F. S. Regs., Part II. and the Staff Manual respectively. Title pages will be prepared in manuscript.

WAR DIARY Jan 1918.
or
INTELLIGENCE SUMMARY.
(Erase heading not required.)

Place	Date	Hour	Summary of Events and Information	Remarks and references to Appendices
	25/1/18 to 31/1/18.		Weekly Summary of Work	
			I Div HQ Battle Station.	
			G office Complete except burster & internal fittings	
			Annex Timbering completed & roof covering fixed. & Floor & heating arrangements completed.	
			Connecting passage to G office Completed	
			Q Offices (1) 2 End Wall & traverse complete 3rd one started	
			(2) On roof about 100 sq yds covered with rails, trenching, & 3' earth.	
			II CANAL BANK. (1) Made & fixed 280 double bunks making total of 302	
			(2) Laid 536 yds duckboard track along front.	
			(3) Drainage of Shelters and & track in front completed	
			(4) Plan prepared & all Shelters numbered 1–150	
			III DAC Wagon lines 2nd Hut (Adrian) completed.	
			IV No 2 MVS floor completed.	
			(V) Rousbrugge Laundry work put in hand to improve drying capacity	
			VI No 1 Section completed its work on Dugouts in Corps Line	
			G. W. Findlay Capt RE OC 409th Lowland Fd Coy RE 31/1/18.	

D. D. & L., London, E.C. (A8001) Wt. W1771/M2031 750,000 5/17 Sch. 52 Forms C2118/14

Divn[l] Baths.

Scale 1/20" = 1 Foot.

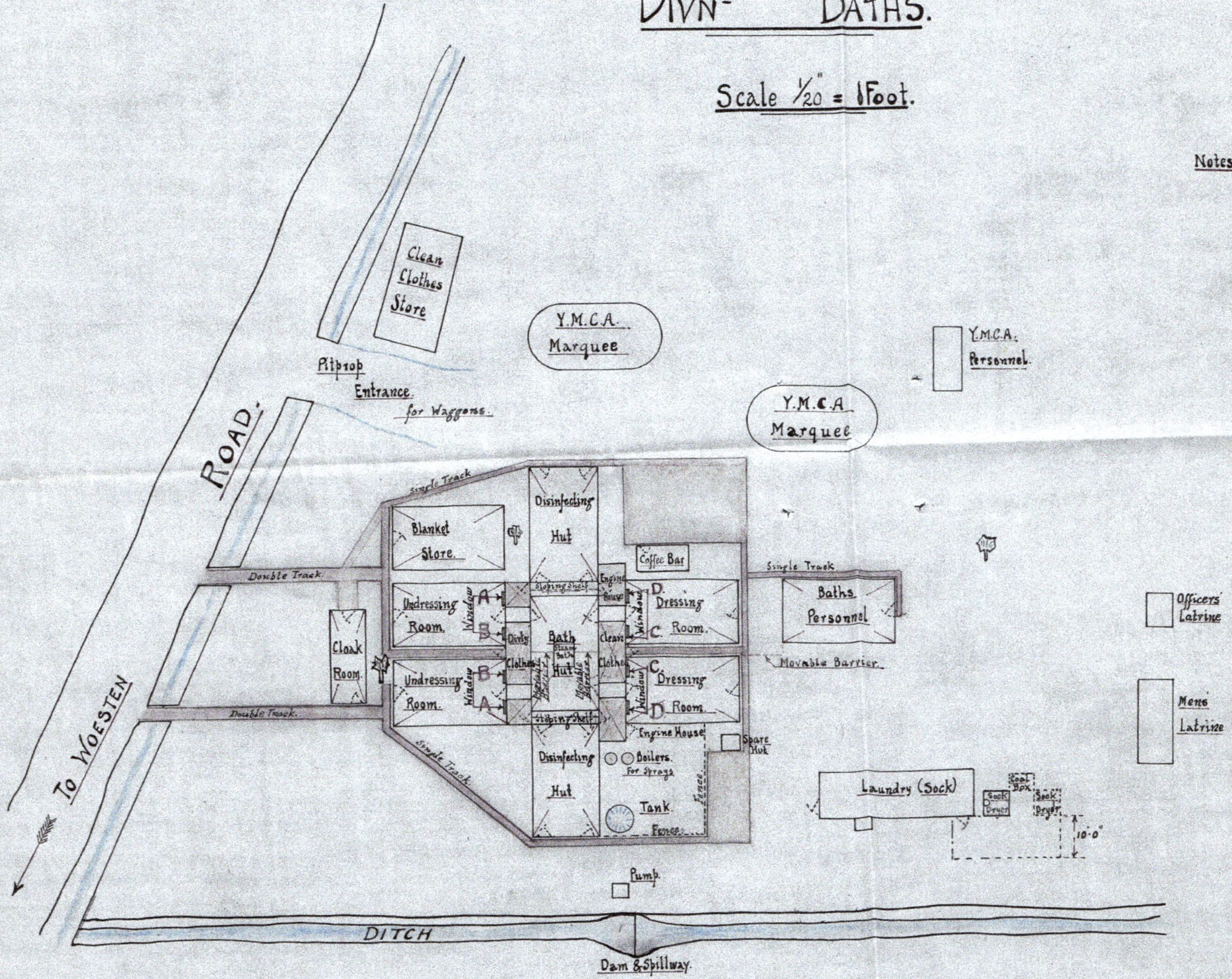

Notes.-

Each man to leave Great Coat & Valuables at Cloakroom & draw Sandbag & 3 numbers, and proceed to Undressing Room.

Khaki to be passed through "A" Window, also Cap & Boots in sandbag.

Dirty clothing to be passed through "B" Window.

Man will then proceed to Bathhouse for Steam & Spray Bath. On leaving this he will enter Dressing Room, where he will draw Clean Clothing at Window "C".

Khaki, Cap & Boots to be drawn at Window "D".

He will leave Dressing Room at Rear Door & return to Cloak Room with Sandbag, and draw Great Coat and Valuables, passing by way of Coffee Bar.

Men with Blankets to be disinfected will hand these in with Khaki.

It is suggested that Spare Hut be used as additional Coffee Bar.

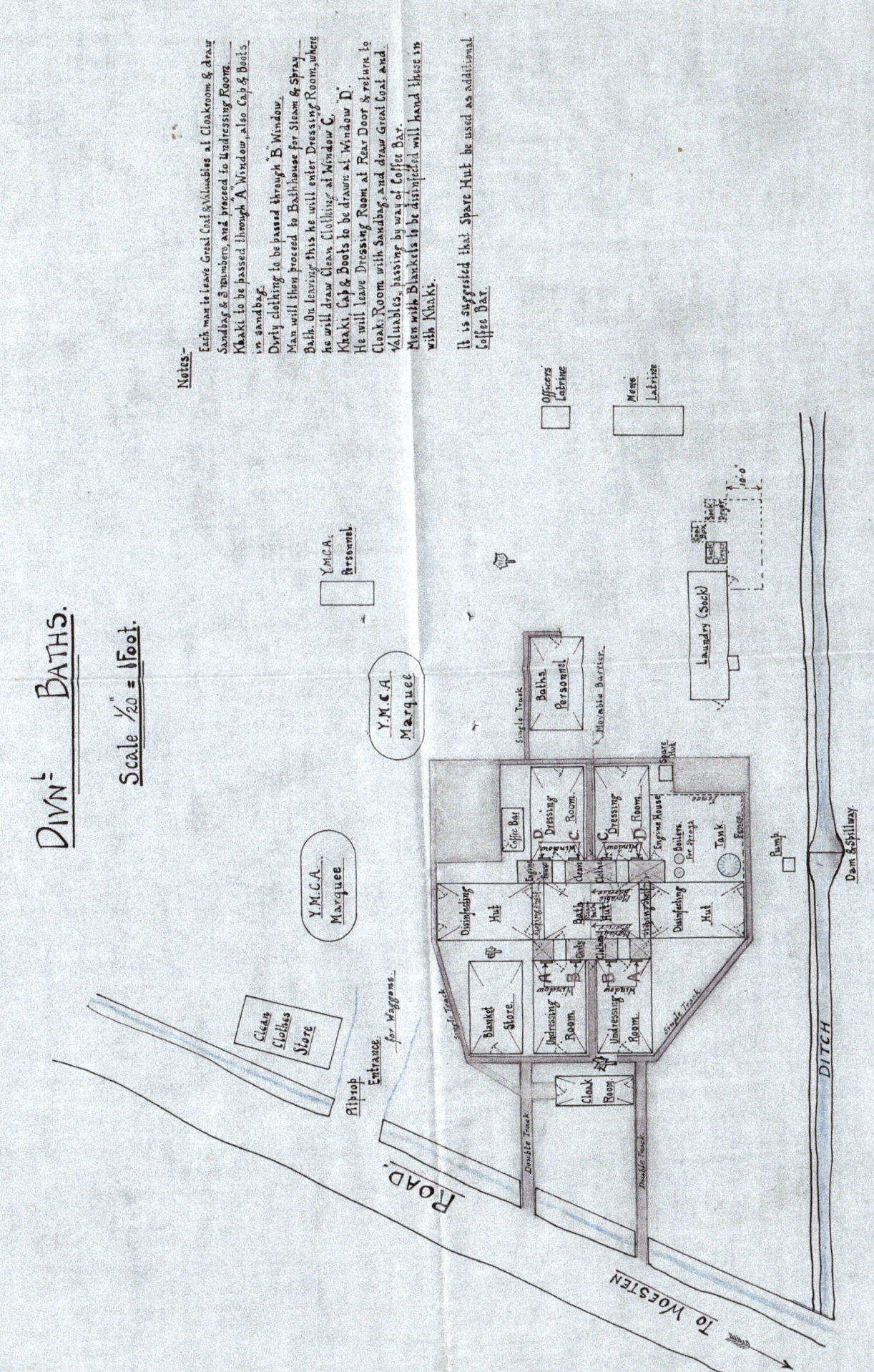

SECRET.

Feb 1918

WAR DIARY
or
~~INTELLIGENCE SUMMARY.~~
(Erase heading not required.)

409th (Lowland) Fd Coy RE

Army Form C. 2118.

Instructions regarding War Diaries and Intelligence Summaries are contained in F. S. Regs., Part II. and the Staff Manual respectively. Title pages will be prepared in manuscript.

Vol 38

Place	Date	Hour	Summary of Events and Information	Remarks and references to Appendices
H.Q. WOESTEN. 2 Secs in shelter in CANAL BANK near BOESINGHE. J.1 Bridge.	1/2/18.		DISTRIBUTION & EMPLOYMENT – (a) 1 Off + 12 OR. permanent Camp Improvement party – allotted one or two men to each camp and responsible for supply of materials, economy in use of same and superintending and assisting occupants with technical work, and ensuring continuity of the policy laid down by Q and worked out by Area Cmdt advised by RE officer.	
			(b) two sections [illegible] above Battle HQ for Div and odd jobs on maintenance & improvement of baths, laundry etc.	
			(c) one section, work on Corps line detailed for work under 26th Coy RE.	
			(d) one section, bunking draining and improving conditions of accomodation in CANAL BANK. between J.1 & J.4 Bridges.	
	2/2/18		Ditto. two forward sections completed work and returned to HQ. at WOESTEN.	
			Summary of Work.	
	3/2/18.		No 1 Section. in Corps line excavated drained erected & covered 5 shelters leaving a clean finished job	Sheet 28 NW B56 6.1
			No 2 – (1) Numbered & organised accomodation between J.1 & J.2 bridges & provided Area Cmdt. with plans (Ref 1/10000 to	Sheet 20 SW T23c92.)
			(2) Drained whole frontage from J.1 Bridge to Lock Gates (Sheet 28 NW B5b61) to (Sheet 20 SW. T29b05)	
			(3) Duckboard track along whole frontage (Inf Working Party of 60 daily)	
			(4) Prepared & fixed between 26/1/18 & 2/2/18, 300 bunks.	
	3/2/18.	am	Church Parade & Baths.	
		pm.	Inspection parade by CRE. followed by a lecture to officers NCO's & 30% of men.	

Gill Hindley
O.C. 409th (Lowland) Fd. Coy. R.E.

D. D. & L., London, E.C. (A8004) Wt. W1771/M2031 750,000 5/17 Sch. 52 Forms C2118/14

SECRET

Instructions regarding War Diaries and Intelligence Summaries are contained in F. S. Regs., Part II. and the Staff Manual respectively. Title pages will be prepared in manuscript.

P2

Army Form C. 2118.

O.C. 409th (Lowland) Fd. Coy. R.E. WAR DIARY for Feb 1917
or
INTELLIGENCE SUMMARY.

(Erase heading not required.)

Place	Date	Hour	Summary of Events and Information	Remarks and references to Appendices
WOESTEN	4/2/18		Nos 1 & 2 Section + 2 Squads A1 Training (Kit Inspection, Rifle Inspection Gas Drill & Drill).	
			No 3 & 4 Section Continue work on Battle HQ.	
	5/2/18		1.2.3 Sects + 2 Squads A1. Training. (No 1 & 2 as above + Practise with WELDON TRESTLES. No 3. as above new GHQ Gas Drill practised).	
			No 4 Contd Work at Div HQ.	
	6/2/18.		1.2.3 Sects + 3 Squads A1 Training as above & drill pm. Football.	
			No 1 Sect. Felling trees by hand & using explosives.	
			No 4. Contd at DHQ.	
	7/2/18.		Whole Coy General Training 8am. Company Parade followed by Section Training.	
			Passing of all company blankets through Delousing Plant completed.	
			Also all company had bath.	
			Bridging Equipment handed in to 4th Army for Parking	
	8/2/18.		1st Parade 8am. Physical Training.	
			9am Rifle Inspection. inspection of Gas Helmets, Identity Discs & Field Dressings.	

G. Ll. Lindsay Maj. R.E.
O.C. 409th (Lowland) Fd. Coy. R.E.

D. D. & L., London, E.C. (A8001) Wt. W1771/M2031 750,000 5/17 Sch. 52 Forms C2118/14

SECRET. 409th (Lowland) Fd Coy RE

P 3

Army Form C. 2118.

Instructions regarding War Diaries and Intelligence Summaries are contained in F. S. Regs., Part II. and the Staff Manual respectively. Title pages will be prepared in manuscript.

WAR DIARY for Feb 1918
or
INTELLIGENCE SUMMARY.
(Erase heading not required.)

Place	Date	Hour	Summary of Events and Information	Remarks and references to Appendices
WOESTEN to IRISH FARM Camp.	9/2/18		Coy vacated billets at WOESTEN and proceeded by route march to Huts at Irish Farm Camp (Ref. Sheet 28 NW 1/20,000. C 27 a 2.6.)	
			New Sector. Reconnoitered by O.C. with 203rd Fd Coy 35 Div.	
			~~Two subalterns~~ Lt Galloway reconnoitred work on left front with officer of 203rd Fd Coy } on night 9/10th. Lt Kelly " " Right " " " "205th Fd Coy }	
	10/2/18		No 3 Section. Coy on repair of Duckboard Tracks by day.	
			No 2 & 4 Section parade 12 mn 10/11th & Continued work in Sector taken over.	
			No 1 Sect. in camp.	
	〃		SECTOR. POELCAPELLE Sector. Right Boundary. Inch Houses (D 3 6 0 8) exclusive to COMPROMISE Fm (V 13 b 1.2)	
			Right Bn Sector. TRACAS Fm (V 20 d 6 4) exclusive GLOSTER Fm (V 20 c 4.3) ~~exclusive~~ inclusive)	
			Work in hand (a) Provision of splinter proof shelter for garrisons of posts in main line of resistance & Drainage of trenches & revetment at VACHER Fm, BURNS Ho, & TERRIER Fm.	
			(b) Back Entrances to 2 Pillboxes. OXFORD Ho	
			Left Bn Sector (a) Provision of Shelter for garrison of posts in Outposts & Main Line of Resistance & outposts.	
			(b) Back entrance to Coy HQ & Bn HQ. & traverses to entrances to other pillboxes.	
			(c) DEFENCE SCHEME for POELCAPELLE required.	
			(d) Upkeep of Forward Duckboards.	
			(e) Reclaiming flooded pillboxes in POELCAPELLE.	

D. D. & L., London, E.C.
(A8001) Wt. W1771/M2031 750,000 5/17 Sch. 52 Forms/C2118/14

409th (Lowland) **WAR DIARY** for Feb

or

INTELLIGENCE SUMMARY.

(Erase heading not required.)

Army Form C. 2118.

Instructions regarding War Diaries and Intelligence Summaries are contained in F. S. Regs., Part II. and the Staff Manual respectively. Title pages will be prepared in manuscript.

Place	Date	Hour	Summary of Events and Information	Remarks and references to Appendices
IRISH FARM Camp. N. of Ypres.	11/2/18		No 2 & 4 Section contd. work. No 3. Work on WINCHESTER SWITCH LINE	
			No 1 in camp. O.C. visited posts in right sector with G.O.C. 2nd Bde and settled works programme.	
	12/2/18.		Work as above	
			Company moved from Irish Farm to Kempton Park Camp C 15 c. (Sheet 28 NW)	
			Visited left sector with G.O.C. 2nd Bde. Reconnaissance of Poelcapelle made and defence scheme prepared and submitted to division.	
	13/2/18.		Visited POELCAPELLE with Lt RHIND and fixed detailed sites for fire trenches.	
	14/2/18.		Visited POELCAPELLE at dawn with G.O.C. 2nd Bde, GSO1, CRE, — Scheme approved & trenches taped out.	
	15/2/18.		No1 Section commenced work, carrying party 120 Inf. No3 Section closed down work on WINCHESTER Ridge. } Work done. Dug posts for 16 sections & [illegible] & [illegible] same.	A. Summary of work by No 2 & 4 Sects. from 11/2/18 – 17/2/18.
	16/2/18.		No 1 & 3 Sections work on POELCAPELLE. No 2 & 4 in line — in morning went round proposed wire & emplacements with Lt BOST & 2 NCO's of No 3	
	17/2/18		ditto.	
	18/2/18		ditto. went round with Col SANKEY CRE & D.M.G.O.	
	19/2/18		No 1 & 3 Sections in camp. No 2 & 4 as usual	

D. D. & L., London, E.C.
(A8001) Wt. W1771/M2031 750,000 5/17 Sch. 52 Forms/C2118/14

6

409th (Lowland) Fd Coy

Army Form C. 2118.

Instructions regarding War Diaries and Intelligence Summaries are contained in F. S. Regs., Part II. and the Staff Manual respectively. Title pages will be prepared in manuscript.

WAR DIARY Feb. or INTELLIGENCE SUMMARY.

(*Erase heading not required.*)

Place	Date	Hour	Summary of Events and Information	Remarks and references to Appendices
KEMPTON Park (C15a 11)	20/2/18	8.30pm.	No 1 & 3 Sections on POELCAPELLE; Nos 2 & 4 continue work in front Sectors. 30 Attached Infantry mainly loading and carrying. — Brigade Relief.	
	21/2/18	8.30pm	Continued above	
	22/2/18	8.30pm	ditto.	
	23/2/18	8.30pm	Nos 1 & 3 in camp. Footbaths in afternoon.	
	24/2/18	8.30pm	Nos 1 & 3 Rifle Inspection. Nos 2 & 4. continue work Reliefs running within the Section. Nos 1 & 3 Wiring POELCAPELLE.	
	25/2/18	8.30pm	Wiring in POELCAPELLE No 2 & 4 continue.	
	26/2/18	8.30pm	ditto.	
	27/2/18	8.30pm	~~ditto~~ Nos 1 & 3 & 2 & 4 footwashing Nos 2 & 4 Continue night work.	
	28/2/18	8.30pm	Nos 1 & 3 Sect. Wiring Poelcappelle. No 2 & 4 continue night work.	
			Summary of work executed is attached ~~also Plan of defences~~. ~~on which work was done.~~	
			4/3/18	
			G. Hindley Major R.E. OC Lowland Fd Coy R.E.	

Instructions regarding War Diaries and Intelligence Summaries are contained in F. S. Regs., Part II. and the Staff Manual respectively. Title pages will be prepared in manuscript.

WAR DIARY *Feb 1918.*
or
~~INTELLIGENCE SUMMARY.~~
(*Erase heading not required.*)

Appendix A. Army Form C. 2118.

Place	Date	Hour	Summary of ~~Events and Information~~ Work on POELCAPELLE DEFENCES.	Remarks and references to Appendices
			(1) Reconnaissance & plan.	
			(2) Digging, draining, revetting and camouflage of 18 Section posts each with about 40 to 50 ft fire bay.	Comd. 15/2/18.
			(3) Erecting an inner belt of wire encircling new posts & joining ~~them~~ the posts together with wire — Pattern employed G.H.Q double Apron. Total length about 4000x ~~Sited~~ for fire effect.	to
			(4) Finishing off item 2	1.3.18.
			(5) Erection of B type Shelter for each garrison.	
			(6) Provision of guides for & organisation of ~~large~~ carrying parties of from 100 to 200 men daily.	daily.
			(7) Supply of material at rate of 5 wagons a day & later other ~~four~~	
			(8) Erecting Outer Belt of wire total length about 6000x.	
			Between 15/3/18 – 28/3/18 with 2 Sections items 1, 2, 3 were completed and the defences in a state fit for defence. Item 7 all materials delivered without any delay to work to within 1500x of outposts.	
			[signature]	

D. D. & L., London, E.C.
(A8004) Wt. W1771/M2031 750,000 5/17 Sch. 52 Forms/C2118/14

Instructions regarding War Diaries and Intelligence Summaries are contained in F. S. Regs., Part II. and the Staff Manual respectively. Title pages will be prepared in manuscript.

Appendix B.

Army Form C. 2118.

WAR DIARY
or
INTELLIGENCE SUMMARY.
(Erase heading not required.)

Place	Date	Hour	Summary of ~~Events and Information~~ Work on Right Bn. Front 10th – 28th March.	Remarks and references to Appendices
Main Line of Resistance			Ref Map 1/10,000 Sheet	
Oxford Houses. (V26 b 4.4.)			Existing strongpoint linked up by revetted trench. Drainage of whole point organised. New fire bay constructed for 1 section firing to North & linked to main defences by fire trench firing East. — Increased accomodation from 1 platoon to Coy HQ + 2 platoon by erecting 9 B type shelters.	
Terrier Fm. (V 26 a 5 4)			(Garrison 1 platoon) Completed fire trench for 1 section & arranged for drainage of same. Dug revetted & drained & camouflaged a second trench for 1 section. Erected B type shelters sufficient for whole garrison also for Trench Mortar Detachment.	
Vachea Farm. (1 platoon) (V26 d 80)			Revetted fire trench and drained same and increased accomodation to 1 platoon by addition of 4 B type shelters.	
Duckboards			Maintenance of forward tracks.	
Burns House			Construction of rear entrance to pillbox commenced } ~~Method~~ Cold chisel, Jumping bar, small charges ammonal; & reinforcement cut with Hacksaws.	
Nameless Pillbox (V26 c 8.0)			" " " " " " "	
Winchester Fm. Ridge. (D2 A 4.4)			2 Platoon Posts drained & accomodation for garrison erected. Coy HQ at York Farm (D2 A 1 4) damaged Pillbox strutted.	

Gollett

D. D. & L., London, E.C.
(A8004) Wt. W1771/M2031 750,000 5/17 Sch. 52 Forms/C2118/14

Instructions regarding War Diaries and Intelligence Summaries are contained in F. S. Regs., Part II. and the Staff Manual respectively. Title pages will be prepared in manuscript.

WAR DIARY *or* INTELLIGENCE SUMMARY. Appendix C.

(*Erase heading not required.*)

Army Form C. 2118.

Place	Date	Hour	Summary of ~~Events and Information~~ Work in Left Bn. Sector. Ref 1/10,000 map.	Remarks and references to Appendices
N. & S. of POELCAPELLE.			GLOSTER FARM (V20 c 3.3). 2 Gas Curtains fitted & ~~one~~ steel shelter erected. Strutted roof of Coy H.Q. Dugout.	
			FERDAN Ho (V19 a 6.4) Completed back entrance to pill box & closed up front entrance with reinforced concrete wall – Bunked interior – Erected one shelter outside for H.Q personnel.	
			TRACAS FARM (V20 d 6.5) Erected 2 B type shelters completing accomodation for garrison.	
			Brewery (POELCAPELLE) Partitioned off Coy H.Q. & bunked pillbox – Traverse to entrance in hand.	
			String Houses (V13 d 5.4) Increased accomodation from nil to 2 platoons by erection of 6 5 bay B type shelters including drainage.	
			Compromise Fm. V.13 b 1.1 Increased accomodation up to 1 platoon by erection of 5 B type shelters.	
			Duckboards. Upkeep, relaying of portions forward of Bn. H.Q.	
			DELTA Hos. ~~Drained~~ Cleaned & reclaimed old shelters to accomodate 2 platoons.	
			POELCAPELLE PILLBOXES. Drained cleaned out and made fit for occupation 7 Pillboxes & fitted Gas Curtains, resulting increase in Shellproof accomodation by 50 – Some pillboxes in use were made more habitable. Assistance in some cases was obtained from Garrison.	
			[illegible signature]	

D. D. & L., London, E.C.
(A8004) Wt. W1771/M2031 750,000 5/17 Sch. 52 Forms/C2118/14

VA 39

CONFIDENTIAL

WAR DIARY

OF

409th (LOWLAND) FIELD COY. R.E. (T.)

from 1st MARCH 1918 to 31st MARCH 1918

(VOLUME. No XXXIX)

Secret

409th Lowland Fd Coy RE

WAR DIARY March 1918
or
INTELLIGENCE SUMMARY.
(*Erase heading not required.*)

Army Form C. 2118.

Instructions regarding War Diaries and Intelligence Summaries are contained in F. S. Regs., Part II. and the Staff Manual respectively. Title pages will be prepared in manuscript.

Place	Date	Hour	Summary of Events and Information	Remarks and references to Appendices
KEMPTON Park Sheet 28NW. 1/20000	1/3/18	8.30pm	No 1.2.3.4 Section also 25th A.I. } parade for forward work No 4 Section Right Battalion Sector, No 2 Section Left Bn Sector, No 3 & 1 Defence of Poelcapelle.	
			Remaining Squad Attached Infantry in camp loading and forward loading party —	
	2/3/18	9pm.	ditto. Time altered to suit moonlight	
	3/3/18.	8.30pm	Works Parade ~~Nos 1 & 3 continue also~~ No 2 & 4 closing down work, Attached Inf. total 20 as for 2/3/18	
			No 1. 3 & balance of 204 & 25th A.I. in camp making barbed wire concertinas.	
	4/3/18	9am 12m.	No 1, 2, 3, 4 } Sects. 25th A.I. making Barbed Wire Concertinas & Camp Improvements.	
			1st A.I. loading	
	5/3/18	12.30am	No 1, 2, 3, 4, & 25th A.I. Wiring Defences of Poelcapelle. Very dark night - work badly delayed	
	6/3/18.	1.30 am	ditto. Light very fair.	
	7/3/18	4.30pm.	No 1234 Section + 25th A.I. parade for same work. Light fair (no moon)	
			1st A.I. loading & transport.	
	8/3/18.	4.30pm.	No 1.2.3.4. Sects + 25th A.I. Complete outer Belt of Wire round POELCAPELLE light fair No moon.	
			1st A.I. Loading	
			Handed over all work to 23rd Fd Coy RE. and took over work from 26th Fd Coy RE & 204th Fd Coy RE.	
	~~9/3/18~~		Move of Camp cancelled — Coy parades 9am for work in camp. — Rifle & Gas Inspection.	
	9/3/18.		HQ. & Sapper moved from KEMPTON PARK to ENGLISH FARM Camp relieving 26th Fd Coy RE.	
	10/3/18		Baths for whole Coy on way —	
			Capt. Powell placed in charge of all forward work.	
	11/3/18	6am. 8am.	Nos 2 & 4 Sects. Works Wiring Support System.	
			— 1 & 3 — In camp revetting huts. NCO's rub up in musketry 1.45 - 2.45 1.3 Section Musketry Positions & Trigger Pressing.	
	12/3/18	6 am. 8 am	ditto.	

Secret

409th Lowland Fd Coy RE

Instructions regarding War Diaries and Intelligence Summaries are contained in F. S. Regs., Part II. and the Staff Manual respectively. Title pages will be prepared in manuscript.

WAR DIARY March 1918
or
INTELLIGENCE SUMMARY.
(Erase heading not required.)

Army Form C. 2118.

Place	Date	Hour	Summary of Events and Information — Map. 1/10000 (Sheet B1 round POELCAPELLE)	Remarks and references to Appendices
NE of Ypres.	13.3.18	6 am	2 Sections wiring Support line from Btrack V24 d 0.5 to V24 d 5.3 approx 350x and round Mouths of dugout 150x.	
			Party on Gas frames for Dugouts & repair of concrete Pillbox	
		8 am.	2 Section in camp revetting huts and 1 hour musketry training.	
			Repairs carried out to trestle Bridge at LANGEMARCK which had been damaged by shell fire	
	14/3/18.	8 am	2 Section Wiring completed 350x Double Apron fence in V24 work on Gas frames contd	
			2 Sections. Revetting huts in Camp & musketry training	
	15/3/18	8 am	2, 3, 4 Sects Erecting Shelters & amn recesses for T.M. battery & completed 600x of wire portion previously half done	
			1 Sect. in camp Revetting & training	
	16/3/18		as above contd wiring	
			Started work on Double Cotts Pill Box converting same into O.P.	
	17/3/18.	8 am.	2 sections Wiring completed 380x in V24	
			1 Section. Continued other work — as above.	
		8.30 am	No 3 Section. Taking over inspection by new section officer	
	18/3/18.	6 am	1 Section work on Posts [illegible] in Defended localities.	
		12 nn	1 — ditto relieved above	
		6 am	1 — Work on T.M. Emplacements	
		8.30 am	No 3 Section — Rifle Inspection & Inspection of results of Musketry training - satisfactory	

A5834 Wt. W4973/M687 750,000 8/16 D. D. & L. Ltd. Forms/C.2118/13.

Secret

409th (Lowland) Fd Coy RE

Instructions regarding War Diaries and Intelligence Summaries are contained in F. S. Regs., Part II. and the Staff Manual respectively. Title pages will be prepared in manuscript.

WAR DIARY March 1918
or
INTELLIGENCE SUMMARY.
(Erase heading not required.)

Army Form C. 2118.

Place	Date	Hour	Summary ~~of Events and Information~~ of Work 1 - 9th March.	Remarks and references to Appendices
NE of Ypres. chiefly in vicinity of Poelcappelle.	1/3/18		All work carried out by the Coy was in the Front System Forward Zone — Ref to map sheet 1/10,000	
			Odd Jobs with Infantry Assistance.	
			POELCAPELLE. Brewery Pill box — Traverse made to protect entrance.	
			Centre Post " " — fitted with 2 gas curtains.	
			Norfolk Ham " " — Completed rear entrance & Gas Protection.	
			6, 9, 22 Pillboxes — Work on reclamation 6-22 left fit for occupation.	
			MEUNIER Ho post — completed erection of 3 B type shelters delivered Concrete slabs for bursters & partly laid some structures to be 4.2 proof.	
			GLOSTER Fm. — Strutted roof of Coy HQ and improved firebays.	
			Notice Boards. — Erected 35 Notice Boards.	
			DELTA Houses. — Completed accomodation for 2 platoons	
			Trenchboard Tracks. — Relaid bad places on Branch Track to Regt Aid Post.	
			POELCAPELLE DEFENCES. 2 section 1-3. 4 Section 4-9th. Completed Inner Belt wire 520 yds & erected 9 shelters in posts for garrison. Wiring outer Belt of Wire round front end and two flanks both Belt drawn back to link in with switch wire to neighbouring posts.	
			Work Done approx 3500 x wire — Organisation & guiding of a carrying party of 200 men nightly delivering of approx 2000 men loads of material for the above work.	
			G.L.E. Findlay Maj RE OC 409th Lowland Fd Coy RE	

A5834 Wt. W4973/M687 750,000 8/16 D. D. & L. Ltd. Forms/C.2118/13.

SECRET

409th Lowland Fd Coy RE.

Instructions regarding War Diaries and Intelligence Summaries are contained in F. S. Regs., Part II. and the Staff Manual respectively. Title pages will be prepared in manuscript.

WAR DIARY for March 1918 or INTELLIGENCE SUMMARY.

(Erase heading not required.)

Army Form C. 2118.

Place	Date	Hour	Summary of Events and Information	Remarks and references to Appendices
NE. of Ypres.	19/3/18.	5.30am – 1pm	1 Sect. Forward work. + 1st A.I. Awards: Sergt RANKIN (Bar to M.M)	
		6pm	1 Sect. " " + 1st A.I. 2nd Cpl McWatt (MM)	
		6 am.	1 Sect " " 2 Cpl Fox (MM)	
		8.30am	1 Sect Revetting in Camp also 1st A.I.	
	20/3/18	5am	1 Sect. + 1st A.I. Work on Posts. 1 Sect in Camp protection ~~[illegible]~~ & Internal traverses in huts.	
		6 pm.	1 " + 1st A.I. " "	
		6 am	1 "	
	21/3/18	5am	1 Sect + 1st A.I. Casualty Capt POWELL, C, RE(T). wounded on works and died of wounds.	
		6 pm	1 " + 1st A.I.	
		6 pm.	1 " + 1st A.I. loading	
			1 " Camp.	
			Summary of Work for week ending 21/3/18.	
			1) 5 Shelters for garrison of T.M.B. erected complete covered & camouflaged (each B Type shelter 4 bays)	
			Ammunition Recesses for " " " "	
			2) SPRINGFIELD GUNNER O.P. 99% Completed – Concreting on roof.	
			Double Cotts " O.P. Reinforced Concrete Work Strengthening and extending same 7%	
			Whitemill Defensive Locality 80%.	
			Eagle Post " " 80%.	
			Bear Post " " 30%.	
			3) Work on Gas Protection continued.	
			4) 1290 yds Wire obstacle completed on general line U 24 c & d. 5) Section in Camp. Training & Revetting huts – training camp.	

[Signature] Lt Col, OC 409th Fd Coy RE

A5834 Wt. W4973/M687 750,000 8/16 D. D. & L. Ltd. Forms/C.2118/13.

Instructions regarding War Diaries and Intelligence Summaries are contained in F. S. Regs., Part II. and the Staff Manual respectively. Title pages will be prepared in manuscript.

WAR DIARY *of March 1918.*
or
INTELLIGENCE SUMMARY.
(Erase heading not required.)

Army Form C. 2118.

Place	Date	Hour	Summary of Events and Information	Remarks and references to Appendices
NE of YPRES	22/3/18	5am	No 2 Sect. 7 S! A1. Work on Posts in Support System.	Appendix (A) Summary of Work done for week will be attached. (PP)
ILMINSTER Camp		[illegible]	No 3 Sects + 1 S! A1. Work on Posts	
nr ENGLISH FARM.		8.30am	No 4 Sect & 1 S! A1. Camp Work, Revetting etc. pm. Musketry and inspection of kit & equipment.	
			Capt Powell was buried at 6pm in cemetery West of CANAL.	
	23/3/18.	~~5am~~	~~Sect~~ as above. No 1 Sect in Camp.	
	24/3/18.	7.30am	No 4 Sect + Details of No 2. Work on Dimple Mines. PROMOTIONS. 3 NCO's to ?rank to fill vacancies by casualties.	
		5am	No 2, 1 S! A1. less carpenters work on Posts as above.	
		6pm.	No 3 + 1 S! A1. " " " " "	
	25/3/18.		Ditto.	
	26/3/18.	5am.	Two Sections work on. DIMPLE MINES and 19 METAL HILL Bunking & Double Cotts. & Work on Gas Curtains.	
			MOVEMENT. (1) Coy was relieved by 23rd Fd Coy RE. and took over work of 26th Fd Coy RE.	
			(2) Coy. moved into billets in dugouts in CANAL BANK N of Ypres	

G. [illegible] Coy
Maj RE
O.C. 409th Lowland Fd Coy RE

A5834 Wt. W4973/M687 750,000 8/16 D. D. & L. Ltd. Forms/C.2118/13.

Secret

409th Lowland Fd Coy RE

Instructions regarding War Diaries and Intelligence Summaries are contained in F. S. Regs., Part II. and the Staff Manual respectively. Title pages will be prepared in manuscript.

WAR DIARY for March
or
INTELLIGENCE SUMMARY.

(Erase heading not required.)

Army Form C. 2118.

Place	Date	Hour	Summary of Events and Information	Remarks and references to Appendices
CANAL BANK Nth of Ypres.	27/3/18.		General Distribution 2 Sections on Forward Tramline 1 section back Area Work 1 section. Overhaul Kit & Training.	
			Camp Section in 2 days programme Overhaul of Equipment & Inspection & Gas Drill & Rapid Loading — & Baths.	
		6.30 am.	2 Sections Work on Tramline in Forward Area & Finish Foot Track between rails.	
			1 Section. Strengthening & Repairing dugouts in Canal bank. & fixing Gas Curtains.	
			25% A.T. with each of the forward sections.	
	28th		work — Inspection of Technical Wagon & Ponton Equipment	
	29th		as for 27th Inspection of Toolcarts Nos 3 & 4.	
	30th			
	31st			
			Summary of Work Attached. 1/4/18	
			Capt. [illegible] Maj RE. O.C. 409th Lowland Fd Coy RE.	

SECRET.

409th (Lowland) Field Coy RE.

Instructions regarding War Diaries and Intelligence Summaries are contained in F. S. Regs., Part II. and the Staff Manual respectively. Title pages will be prepared in manuscript.

WAR DIARY
or
INTELLIGENCE SUMMARY.
(Erase heading not required.)

Appendix "A"

Army Form C. 2118.

Place	Date	Hour	Summary of Events and Information	Remarks and references to Appendices
			Summary of Work from 22nd to 31st March 1918.	
N. of Ypres.	22nd to 26th		1) Company continued work on posts for Infantry and M.G's in Support System of Forward Zone. – Bear, Eagle, White Mill	
			2) Bunking deep dugouts at DIMPLE MINES and 19 METRE HILL.	
			3) Continued construction of reinforced Concrete O.P. at DOUBLE COTTS.	
			4) " gas protection for pill-boxes in Support System	
			5) Camp Section employed draining Camp and revetting huts; also practice in musketry.	
	26th March		Company was relieved in S.S.F.Z. by 23rd Field Coy. RE. and took over work and Billets of 26th Field Coy. RE.	
	24th to 31st		1) Improvement and Extension of Divisional Tramway. – 185x new track laid in Forward Area. 542x of mule grid substituted for trench boards on tram line.	
			2) Improvement of gas protection to dugouts at D.W. Hdqrs.	
			3) Strengthened dugouts for 1st D.A. Hdqrs.	
			4) Resting Section – Baths. Cleaning Equipment and overhauling kit. Practice in Gas drill and Musketry.	

R. Angus Galloway Lt RE(T)
for O.C. 409th (Lowland) Fd Coy RE.

D. D. & L., London, E.C.
(A8004) Wt. W1771/M2031 750,000 5/17 Sch. 52 Forms/C2118/14

1st Divisional Engineers

<u>409th (Lowland) FIELD COMPANY R. E.</u>

<u>APRIL 1918.</u>

Secret. 409th Lowland Fd Coy RE.

Instructions regarding War Diaries and Intelligence Summaries are contained in F. S. Regs., Part II. and the Staff Manual respectively. Title pages will be prepared in manuscript.

WAR DIARY for APRIL 1918
or
INTELLIGENCE SUMMARY.
(Erase heading not required.)

Army Form C. 2118.

Vol 40

Place	Date	Hour	Summary of Events and Information	Remarks and references to Appendices
CANAL BANK immediately North of YPRES	1/4/18		General Distribution: 2 Section + Attached Infantry laying TRAMLINE. 1 Section + A. " Gas curtains & Back Area. 1 Section Inspection, Drill & Musketry.	
POELCAPPELLE SECTOR		6.30am	2 Section for Tramway. Laid 50x New Track including erection of 9 trestles, packed 330x & 2 culverts.	
		8am	1 — Back Area Work	
		10am	No 4 Section Inspection of Rifles, Equipment & Gas Protective measures, Gas Drill & Drill. Inspection of Tool Carts by O.C.	
	2/4/18	ditto	as for 1/4/18 for No 4 read No 1.	
	3/4/18	ditto	for No 1 read No 3. — Cooks & All Coy Employ — Gas Drill, Rifle Inspection & Kit Inspection.	
	4/4/18		for No 3 read No 1	
	5/4/18		Work as usual [Squad of 20 Carpenters detached for work under 23rd Fd Coy RE.]	
	6/4/18		ditto [Work handed over to 121st Fd Coy RE.]	
	7/4		Summary of Work for Week 1–7th	
			Tramlines (a) Formation Prepared 108x including 45 trestles. (b) New track laid 270x (c) Packing 1445x (d) Culverts 5 [N.B. Country mass of shell holes.]	
			GAS PROTECTION Squad working on repairs & refitting	
			Mule Grids on Tramlines 250x laid & 700x duckboards salved.	
			CANAL BATHS — repairs & refitting & Repairs to Dugouts	[signature] Capt. RE for Major Commanding 409 Lowland Fd Coy RE

A5834 Wt. W4973/M687 750,000 8/16 D. D. & L. Ltd. Forms/C.2118/13.

Secret

Instructions regarding War Diaries and Intelligence Summaries are contained in F. S. Regs., Part II. and the Staff Manual respectively. Title pages will be prepared in manuscript.

April

WAR DIARY
or
INTELLIGENCE SUMMARY.
(Erase heading not required.)

Army Form C. 2118.

Place	Date	Hour	Summary of Events and Information	Remarks and references to Appendices
CANAL BANK	7/4/18	11.45am	(a) Moved out to camp behind WOESTEN arriving at 3pm.	
			(b) Transport & Cyclists less Water Cart & 2 Limbers & Cooks Cart hooked in at 5pm & proceeded under Capt RHIND R.E.(T) to billets between FLETRE & CAESTRE arriving midnight en route for unknown destination.	
	8/4/18.		(a) Coy less above detachment by rail paraded and entrained at PESELHOEK	
			Transport paraded 5am. Dinner 4am. — Arrived CHOCQUES 2pm and marched via BETHUNE to LE QUESNOY where billets were found.	
			(b) Transport proceeded by road arriving 6pm. and unhooked at Stables on hill N.W. of LE QUESNOY.	
	9.4.18.		Heavy bombardment started on LE QUESNOY at 4am. all telephone wires cut — thick fog	
			All men were ordered out of billets and took up defensible position in broken ground on hill —	
			Horses were got away and later harnessed up as shelling in vicinity was very heavy —	
			Transport and Bde Transport hooked in at 1pm and moved farther back; dismounted part of company remaining for tactical action if required —	
			Taking over from 422nd Coy was interfered with as their office in GORRE had been destroyed and no records available —	
			Move to new billets. Situation cleared about 4pm and orders issued for move to forward billets after touch had been found with Bde — Arrived forward billets 10pm.	
ANNEQUIN.	10.4.18		Disposition — HQ & 4 Sections at ANNEQUIN F23 d 3 5	
			transport at FOUQUEREIL	

Army Form C. 2118.

Instructions regarding War Diaries and Intelligence Summaries are contained in F. S. Regs., Part II. and the Staff Manual respectively. Title pages will be prepared in manuscript.

WAR DIARY APRIL
or
INTELLIGENCE SUMMARY.
(Erase heading not required.)

Place	Date	Hour	Summary of Events and Information	Remarks and references to Appendices
CAMBRIN Sector billets as above	11/4/18	5am	Reconnaissance made of left sector & camouflaged trench sites selected in front of VILLAGE LINE & new platoon post at CAMBRIN.	
		8am – 12 noon	1 section forward & completed about 50%. 1 sect + 30 Inf reclaiming & revetting trenches. 1 section forward & 70% completed new platoon post CAMBRIN LOCALITY.	
		8am	1 section concrete Battery Command Posts taken over about 60% continued also alteration & strengthening of Signal cellars	
	12/4/18	8am	all sections continue as above – Gas curtain repairs started on right front	
	13/4/18	4 45 am	Nos 2 & 4 sections continue work on camouflaged trenches.	
		8am	Nos 1 continue back work No 3 continue maintenance of Gas Curtain work in Right Sector in Village line	
	14/4/18		Work as above continued No 3 sect commenced repairs to trench line. **Left Sector** Scheme for Defence of Lock in Canal fixed and arrangements for night work made also scheme for defence of PONT FIXE made. 2 Sections of 25th Fd Coy attached for work and officers taken round work.	
	15/4/18		(1) Defence of Lock fire position 50%. (2) Right Sector reclaiming & Gas Curtain continued (3) CAMBRIN LOCALITY wire round new post inner belt completed outer belt 50% – Reclaiming old works damaged in bombardment (4) Defences of PONT FIXE commenced	

A5834 Wt. W4973/M687 750,000 8/16 D. D. & L. Ltd. Forms/C.2118/13.

Instructions regarding War Diaries and Intelligence Summaries are contained in F. S. Regs., Part II. and the Staff Manual respectively. Title pages will be prepared in manuscript.

WAR DIARY ~~or~~ APRIL
or
INTELLIGENCE SUMMARY.
(Erase heading not required.)

Army Form C. 2118.

Place	Date	Hour	Summary of Events and Information	Remarks and references to Appendices
ANNEZIN F23 c 3.6	16/4/18	8.15am	No 3 Section Maintenance Gas Curtain & Reclaiming in Right Sector. 1 platoon working party	
		8.15am	½ No 2 Sect Gas Curtain Left Sector	
		6pm	½ No 2 Sect Lock Defences. 2 platoons working party	
		8.15am	No 1 ~~sect~~ Continue back work	
			No 4 Sect Gas curtain Wire & Posts CAMBRIN Locality up to 4 platoons Working party.	
		8.15	2 sections 23rd on PONT FIXE Defences — 42 Inf Garrison ~~working~~ with them Fin. position 60%.	
	17/4/18		2 Section 23rd withdrawn, relieved on work by ½ Sect No 4.	
	18/4/18	4am	Heavy Bombardment started North of Canal and on left Bde accompanied by Gas Shells. Company less HQ. details paraded 4.30am in Gas Helmets and proceeded to Battle Stations and stood to all day standing down at 9pm. 6 men placed in charge of bridges over canal. — Continuous shifts started at 8pm on reopening blown in tunnel.	
	19/4/18		CAMBRIN Locality. Wiring round posts — digging 2 new concealed platoon post. PONT FIXE Defences continued about 70%. Gas Curtain 37 completed to date. Continuous shifts of 4 men on tunnel reopening.	
	20/4/18		ditto	
	21/4/18		Work continued as above. Divine Service for men in Camp 6pm.	

A5834 Wt. W4973/M687 750,000 8/16 D. D. & L. Ltd. Forms/C.2118/13.

Instructions regarding War Diaries and Intelligence Summaries are contained in F. S. Regs., Part II. and the Staff Manual respectively. Title pages will be prepared in manuscript.

WAR DIARY ~~or~~ INTELLIGENCE SUMMARY. APRIL

(*Erase heading not required.*)

Army Form C. 2118.

Place	Date	Hour	Summary of Events and Information	Remarks and references to Appendices
Fte AMMEQUIN	22/4/18		<u>Distribution</u>:	
			No 1 Section: Repairing Slip in Tunnel working 4 shifts.	
			18. 7.30pm LOCK DEFENCES. (Rock sheet GORRE 1/20000 A15c 3.8.)	
			No 2 Section: Back Section — (i) Work on two ~~[illegible]~~ reinforced concrete shelters (ii) Connecting tunnel between two dugouts. (iii) Notice Boards. } withdrawn midday 22nd.	
			No 3 Section: Repairs to ~~[illegible]~~ Tramway & maintenance of Trenches & Gas Curtains	
			No 4 Section: Normally Defences PONT FIXE & CAMBRIN — withdrawn on 22nd	
			<u>Bridging</u>: (1) Orders for Bridge over canal span 50ft recd 11.30 am. Trestle Bridge erected and completed by 2.30pm all materials salved from Houses on spot. DETAILED REPORT attached.	
			(2) Barrel Pier Bridge one span too short was assembled & used to form infantry single file bridge.	
	23/4/18		Extra Barrel Pier obtained bridge dismantled & reassembled with 6ft roadway & hand rail. Details as per Sketch & Notes attached.	
			Work as per Normal distribution continued also recovering OP laid bare by shell fire also repaired trestled portion of Infantry track damaged by fire	
	24/4/18		as above & Strutting cellars at PONT FIXE	
	25/4/18		Reinforced Concrete Artillery Posts completed.	
	-31/4/18		~~Continued~~ as above Connecting tunnel between dugouts completed 29/4/18	
			[signature illegible]	

A5834 Wt. W4973/M687 750,000 8/16 D. D. & L. Ltd. Forms/C.2118/13.

Instructions regarding War Diaries and Intelligence Summaries are contained in F. S. Regs., Part II. and the Staff Manual respectively. Title pages will be prepared in manuscript.

WAR DIARY
or
INTELLIGENCE SUMMARY.
(Erase heading not required.)

Army Form C. 2118.

Place	Date	Hour	Summary of Events and Information	Remarks and references to Appendices
			General Summary of Work done in period 11/4/18 – 3/4/18 by or under supervision of Coy	
			Bridging (1) Trestle Bridge for Infantry in file 50 ft long – all material salved erected by night	
			(2) Barrel Pier Bridge Infantry in file 84 ft span – all super[illegible] salved	
			Rear Defences. Constructed 14 section posts camouflaged & wire for same (3000 x)	
			New loophole for protected MG emplacement.	
			Flank Defences. Constructed 8 section posts – Inserted 2 Bligh Shelters for same. Strutted 2 cellars each for 1 Platoon. Wired approx 1800 x.	
			Forward Defences. Repair Shelters on Platoon post. Repair Shelters for approx 2 platoons. Dug & camouflaged & concealed section posts in front of village line.	
			Repaired tram line between CAMBRIN & PONT FIXE. Worked 2 days clearing slip in tunnel. Continuous shifts.	
			Gas Curtains. Refitted or supplied frames for about 120 curtains	
			Bath Area – Laid approx 15 tons reinforced concrete – Erected 5 large shelters – 2 [illegible] connecting channel 18 ft long 6 x 3' — Strutted cellar.	

G. W. Hindley [signature]
Maj. R.E.
O.C. 409th (Lowland) Fd. Coy. R.E.

A5834 Wt. W4973/M687 750,000 8/16 D. D. & L. Ltd. Forms/C.2118/13.

Report on Bridge Construction at
[illegible] 28/4/18 by 409th Lowland Fd. Coy RE.

General. Existing Bridge was blown in, order was given on ground about 11.30pm to replace it by trestle bridge alongside — materials to be salved from Houses

Preliminary Arrangements. On return [illegible] 12 noon:

(a) one section just moving off to other work was stopped, an other section was ordered to stop work on which it had been engaged in morning & stand by.

(b) a preliminary list of timber reqd. was made out in duplicate and a Salvage party strength 14 dispatched at 12.30 pm.; The spare section was dispatched at 1pm immediately dinners were finished to assist in this.

(c) Section Officer, Sergt & Surveyor left 1pm to take out section & prepare draft plan with due regard to material being found

(d) No construction was possible till dusk so following arrangements were made for work

(1) Balance of Section Teas 4pm parade 4.30pm. Make trestles under cover ready for launching at dusk — This party was reinforced by 6 Carpenters from Section on [illegible] Work

(2) Spare Section return for teas after salving & stand by for ~~construction~~ assembly of barrel Bridge at dusk.

(3) a 3rd section returning to billets 4.30pm was warned to be prepared to relieve section on bridge about 1am [illegible] unforseen delays make it necessary.

This was not required in practice so the work of this & the 4th Section [6 carpenters] remained NORMAL except for

__Design.__ as per attached sketch was approved about 3pm & working plan given to carpenters to commence work.

__Execution.__

(a) Material including sufficient for one spare trestle & bay of superstructure was collected by 6pm.

(b) 5 trestles were ~~collected~~ constructed by 6.30pm – Materials laid out by 7.30pm. behind large building 150x from bridge site. Observation balloons necessitated this choice of assembly site.

(c) Work on erection commenced 8 pm. First trestle in position 8.15 pm. 2nd, 3rd & far span trestle required adjustment. as a longitudinal bump probably a barge was struck midway between the section lines for the legs.

(d) All trestles were placed and bridge completed & spare trestle & bay stacked at Bridgehead at 2.30 am. [illegible]

(e) Barrel Bridge was meanwhile assembled by the other Section ~~[illegible]~~

Times & Strength table attached.

TIMES & STRENGTHS.

TRESTLE BRIDGE 50 ft span infantry in ~~single~~ file 6' roadway.

SALVEING PARTY.

		Billets Parade.	On Job.
(a) 7 Saps + 7 Att. Inf.	= 14	12.45 pm	1.15 – 6.15 pm.
(b) No 4 Sect. No 2 Sect.	= 24	1 pm	1.45 – 6.15 pm.

Men Hours. = 178

Assembly Party.

(a) No 4 Sect less party (a) above + 1 NCO + 6 Saps of No 1 Sect.
parade 4.30 on job 5.15 to 6.30. Strength 18.
Made 6 trestles then adjusted material till 7.30 then
½ hour rest waiting for dusk & balloons.
Sorting Materials 18 men hours Construction 22 men hours.

(b) Erection.

No 4 Section including Salveing party (a) above rejoined after tea.
+ 7 men of No 1 Sect = 25
Time 8 – 2.30' = 6½ hours.
Total men hours 162 men hours.
Including carrying the 150x the party was found just about correct.

Summary. (a) Salveing Material & Laying out in dump
150 yds from site 178 + 18 = 196 men hours.
(b) Construction
Preparatory 22 Erection 162 = 182 men hours.
75 men hours per foot run.

26/4/18

Geo E Hindley
Maj RE
OC 409 Fld Coy RE
(LOWLAND)

Design

Gap 50 ft. 4 trestles spaced about 9'6"

Service Stretchers & Infantry in file

TRESTLE

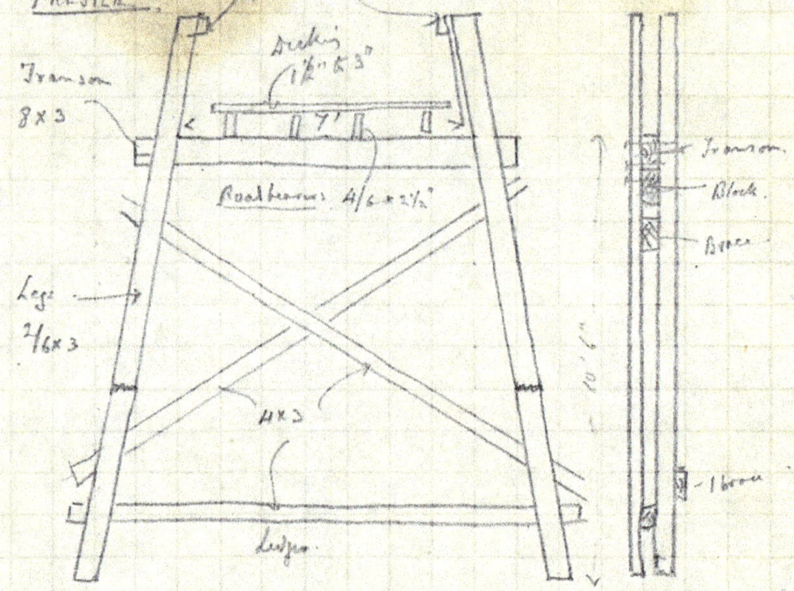

NB. Transom lightly lashed till in position then levelled up or down & nailed.

Section of Gap.

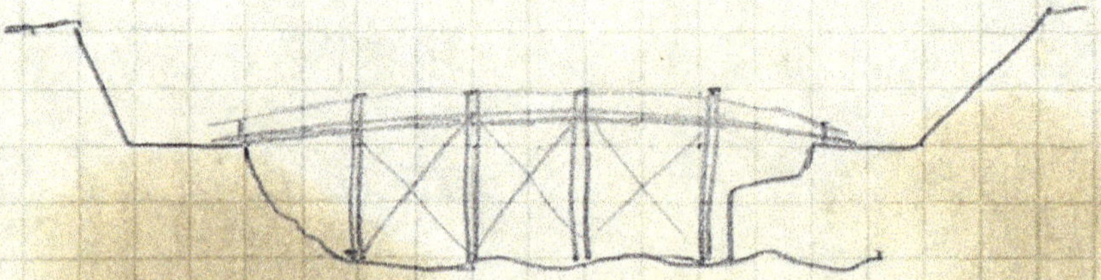

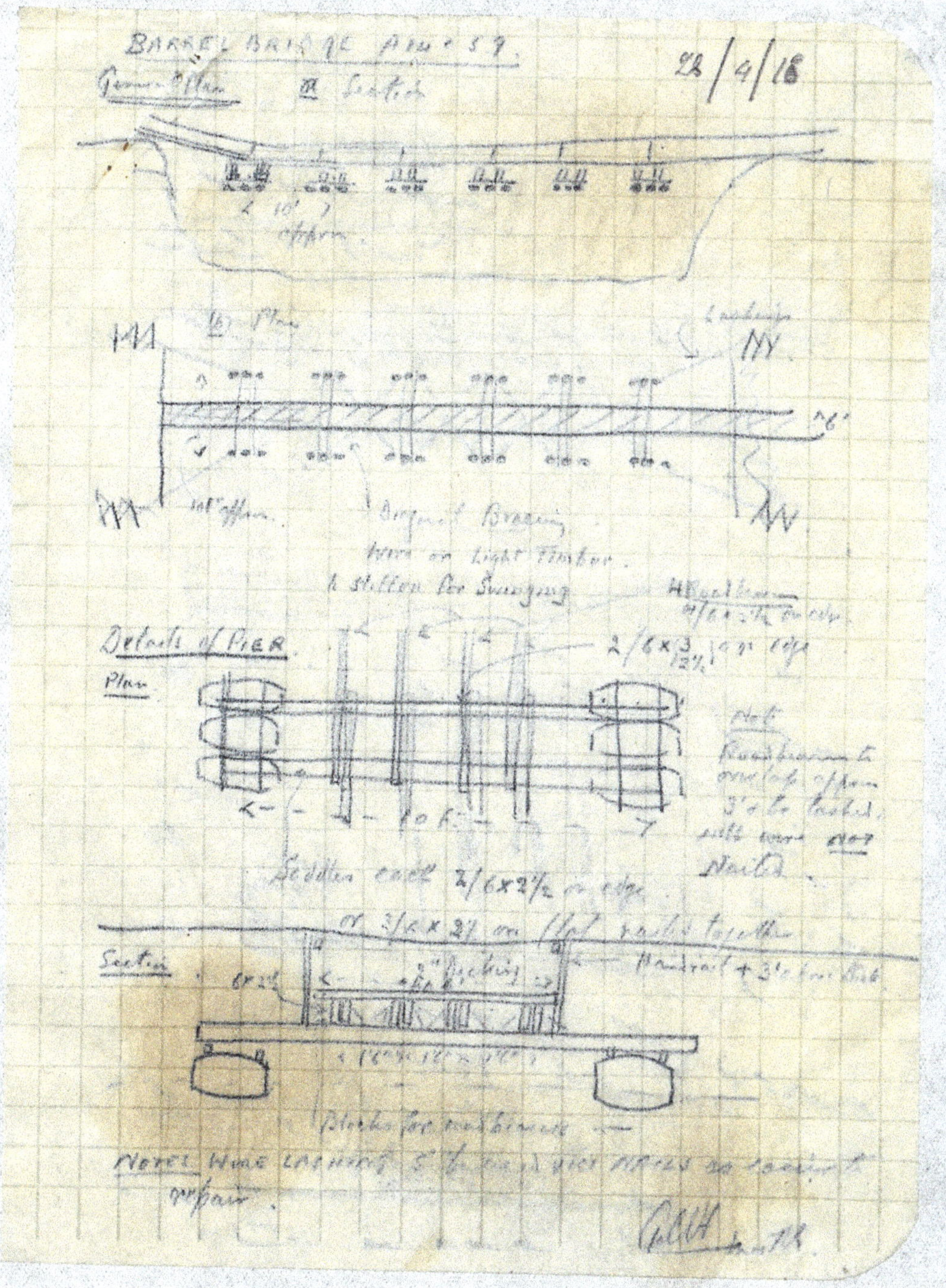

22/4/18
Details of PIER
Plan
Section
Wire on Light Timber
2/6×3
Handrail

Lists of Materials Req'

1) Decking for 70 ft Bridge 2" Stuff.
Stringers tightly nailed – Planks spaced 1½"
requires say 100 pieces at 6' long
or 70 pieces at 10' long.

2) Roadbearers total 7×4 = 28 14' lengths
6 × 2½. (including Shore logs)

3) Hand Rails 4×2" etc. 14 @ 12 ft long.
Uprights for " 14 " 3'

4) Ribbons 4×3 14 @ 10 ft long.

5) Swoozes total 24 @ 13'
(6 × 2½")

6) Wire for 150 ft of Diagonal Bracing.

7) Shore lashings & Swinging ropes —

Collett
24/4/18

available approx 30 pieces 6×3

Notes on Construction

1) All superstructure to be put on with a view to rapid replacement in case of damage and stiffness in swinging.

Work to be done (a) Collect material
(b) Dismantle Bridge
(c) Form up bridge swing downstream on N. Bank. Collett

SECRET

Instructions regarding War Diaries and Intelligence Summaries are contained in F. S. Regs., Part II. and the Staff Manual respectively. Title pages will be prepared in manuscript.

WAR DIARY or INTELLIGENCE SUMMARY.

MAY 1918

(Erase heading not required.)

409 Fd Coy

Vol 41

Army Form C. 2118.

Place	Date	Hour	Summary of Events and Information	Remarks and references to Appendices
ANNEQUIN Nr.	1/5/18 & 2/5/18	11.30 pm 8.15 am	No 1 Section + A.1. — Work on Defences of Loch & KINGSCLERE	
			No 2 — + A1 — Work in Right Sector of Bde front	
			No 4 — — One Squad Gas Curtain Left Sector remainder Defences of CAMBRIN LOCALITY	
			No 3 — — Belt of Wire joining CAMBRIN & ANNEQUIN DEFENCES & clearing field of fire & making splinter proof shelter in Coy Billets.	
			A.1. — Loading & Packing of stores to Forward Dump	
	3/5/18	8.15 am	Nos 2.3.4 Sections on [illegible] — 1 NCO & 5 Sap [illegible] to form Special Wiring Party with 1 Squad of Attached Infantry the Squad [illegible] training back wiring in morning & [illegible] work forward.	
	4/5/18 & 5/5/18	7.15 am 1.15 pm 1.15 am	No 1 Sect & A1 } working — Shifts on same work.	
	6/5/18	1 am	Northants A1 Strength 18 + Sap supervision wiring round KINGSCLERE.	
	7/5/18 8/5/18		No 1 Sect + K.R.R.s + Northants). } Rifle Inspection & Gas Drill — also Coy employ.	
			<u>Work Done During Period 1st — 8th May</u>	
			(a) <u>Right Bde Section</u>. — Revetting damaged portion of C.T.s & making firebays in same. [illegible] Loch line & GAS CURTAINS	
			(b) <u>Left Bde Section</u> (a) Revetting & repairing C.T's	
			(b) Provision of GAS CURTAINS.	
			(c) Loch & KINGSCLERE Defences. 500x wire [illegible] — completed — 2 Splinter proof [illegible] at [illegible] & [illegible] proof culvert for accommodation of Section [illegible] firebays for same — completed digging & [illegible] of [illegible] Posts round KINGSCLERE.	

A5834 Wt. W4973/M687 750,000 8/16 D. D. & L. Ltd. Forms/C.2118/13.

SECRET. 409th Lowland Fd. Coy RE

MAY — WAR DIARY or INTELLIGENCE SUMMARY.

(Erase heading not required.)

Army Form C. 2118.

Instructions regarding War Diaries and Intelligence Summaries are contained in F. S. Regs., Part II. and the Staff Manual respectively. Title pages will be prepared in manuscript.

(P2)

Place	Date	Hour	Summary of Events and Information	Remarks and references to Appendices
HQ & 4 Sects	Period 1-8th		Summary of work	
ANNEQUIN			CAMBRIN SECTOR Erection of 18 Shelters B Type & Concrete [illegible] in PLATOON POSTS	
N.			Wiring round MG [illegible] emplacements & new Posts	
Transport Lines			Rear Section Wiring 1000x between CAMBRIN & ANNEQUIN DEFENCES —	
MESNIL-RUITZ				
about 600 Trench Book			Accommodation strutting Cellars & erecting shelters sufficient for [illegible] + 60 A1 [illegible] 1 Sect.	
	9/5/18		News of Impending Enemy Attack Received — Labour on Maintenance work after Consultation	
			will be Switched on to Wiring & Contact Mine	
			No 1 Sect + A1 continue work in Shelters as previous days.	
			No 3 Sect + A1 ½ Sect Cont. work as before, ½ Sect detailed for laying CONTACT MINE	(Appendix A)
			No 4 — Continue work on Shelters in Posts in CAMBRIN locality	
		8pm	No 2 Sect + A1 From Maintenance of Trenches to Wiring round MG Emplacement	
			Movement 2 Sects RE + A1 detailed for Garrison duty at CAMBRIN moved into Shelters & [illegible]	
			vicinity of the posts on evening of 9th remaining there all 11th midday — Cooks [illegible] moved forward with them.	
			Special Mine [illegible] in garrison of Posts — [illegible] of Section on night work by [illegible]	
	10/5/18	7.45pm	No 1 Sectn + A1 Repairing Damage to Posts & Wiring	
	11/5/18		No 2 & 4 as for 10/5/18	
			No 3 [illegible]	
	[illegible]			

(A9175) Wt W2358/P360 600,000 12/17 D. D. & L. Sch 52a. Forms/C2118/15

Secret

Instructions regarding War Diaries and Intelligence Summaries are contained in F. S. Regs., Part II. and the Staff Manual respectively. Title pages will be prepared in manuscript.

MAY WAR DIARY
or
INTELLIGENCE SUMMARY.
(Erase heading not required.)

Army Form C. 2118.

P 3

Place	Date	Hour	Summary of Events and Information	Remarks and references to Appendices
ANVREUIN	12/5/18	3.15pm	No 1&2 Sect + 2nd A.I. Wiring [illegible]	
			No 3 Sect — Revetting Trenches & [illegible] with [illegible] at [illegible]	
			No 4 Sect ½ Sect [illegible] Shelters ½ Sect Billet [illegible]	
	13/5/18		Ditto — Fired CONTACT mine [illegible] for [illegible]	
			Summary of Work 9th to 14th	
			Light for night work during the period was very bad & owing [illegible] till [illegible] got up again, conditions necessitated [illegible]	
			Right Sector (1) INSTALLED & FIRED MINE in front line trench [illegible] (2)	
			crossing at — (2) 450x wire round MG Emplacement in front of Village line (3) Blocks in CT	
			Left Sector (1) 2 Blocks in CT's made. (2) [illegible] 800x Wire, completed repair of [illegible]	
			over railway Bridge — (3) Revetted portion of [illegible]	
			Completed Wiring at [illegible] (4) [illegible] material for [illegible] Emplacements.	
			CAMBRIN (1) Completed erection & Camouflaging of 24 Shelters in Post	
			(2) [illegible] Rifle Post	
	14/5/18		am Work till [illegible] for No 3 Sect & ½ No 4 as usual — Relieved midday by 20th [illegible]	

(A9175) Wt W2358/P360 600,000 12/17 D. D. & L. Sch 52a. Forms/C2118/15

Secret

Instructions regarding War Diaries and Intelligence Summaries are contained in F. S. Regs., Part II. and the Staff Manual respectively. Title pages will be prepared in manuscript.

MAY

WAR DIARY
or
INTELLIGENCE SUMMARY.
(Erase heading not required.)

409 Lowland F Coy RE

Army Form C. 2118.

P.4.

Place	Date	Hour	Summary of Events and Information	Remarks and references to Appendices
SAILLY LA BOURSE	14/5/18		Movement. The Coy + 3 Squads A.I. moved into billets in SAILLY LA BOURSE vacated by 26th Field Coy RE. Move completed by 6 pm. All movement done by small parties.	
	15/5/18		All Coy in billets resting & cleaning up — Work & Defence Position Reconnoitred by Officers & NCO's — Visited New work with CRE.	
	16/5/18		Work Commenced in New Area	
			General Distribution (1) 1 Sect — Concrete Shell Proof Cover for [illegible] — [illegible]	
			PRES (2) 2 Sections + 1½ A.I. (+ ½ S.1 A.I.) on ANNEQUIN Defences	
			(3) 1 Section + 1 Sd A.I. Training (Complete programme carried through given separately)	
			TACTICAL ROLE In event of ATTACK the company comes under orders of [illegible] and acts as reserve for Northern half of SAILLY LA BOURSE LOCALITY — Company [illegible] [illegible] & ANTI AIRCRAFT [illegible]	
			TRANSPORT LINES at MESNIL RUITZ about 7 miles back on [illegible] line.	
	17/5/18		INSPECTION by Div GAS OFFICER of Gas Training & Equipment	
	18-23/5		Normal work except Sunday ½ day	
	24/5/18		Squad of NCO's & Sappers sent to transport lines for instruction in use of LEWIS GUN.	
	22-24 / 25/5/18		Normal all Area work. 33 OR inoculated being all men 12 months since last inoculation	

Second

MAY

WAR DIARY
or
INTELLIGENCE SUMMARY.
(Erase heading not required.)

409 Lowland Fd Coy RE

Army Form C. 2118.

R.5

Instructions regarding War Diaries and Intelligence Summaries are contained in F. S. Regs., Part II. and the Staff Manual respectively. Title pages will be prepared in manuscript.

Place	Date	Hour	Summary of Events and Information	Remarks and references to Appendices
SAILLY LA BOURSE	26/5/18		Sunday Divine Service 6pm — Pay 11am	
	27/5/18	28/5/18	Normal	
	29/5/18		Normal except works parade [illegible] by ½ hour Company drill	
	30/5/18		ditto	
	31/5/18		ditto	

31/5/18

[illegible signature]
Major RE
OC 409 Lowland Fd Coy RE

(A9175) Wt W2358/P360 600,000 12/17 D. D. & L. Sch. 52a. Forms/C2118/15

Secret

MAY 409th Lowland F^d Co RE — Appendix A

Army Form C. 2118.

Instructions regarding War Diaries and Intelligence Summaries are contained in F. S. Regs., Part II, and the Staff Manual respectively. Title pages will be prepared in manuscript.

WAR DIARY
or
INTELLIGENCE SUMMARY.
(*Erase heading not required.*)

Place	Date	Hour	Summary of Events and Information	Remarks and references to Appendices
CONTACT MINE			An ANTI TANK CONTACT MINE was required – The following was improvised as no ready made contact system was available	
			Ground. 3 boxes 5 ft long each with two lighters stretched across the road [illegible] so to ensure a tank passing over at least [illegible]	[illegible]
			DESIGN 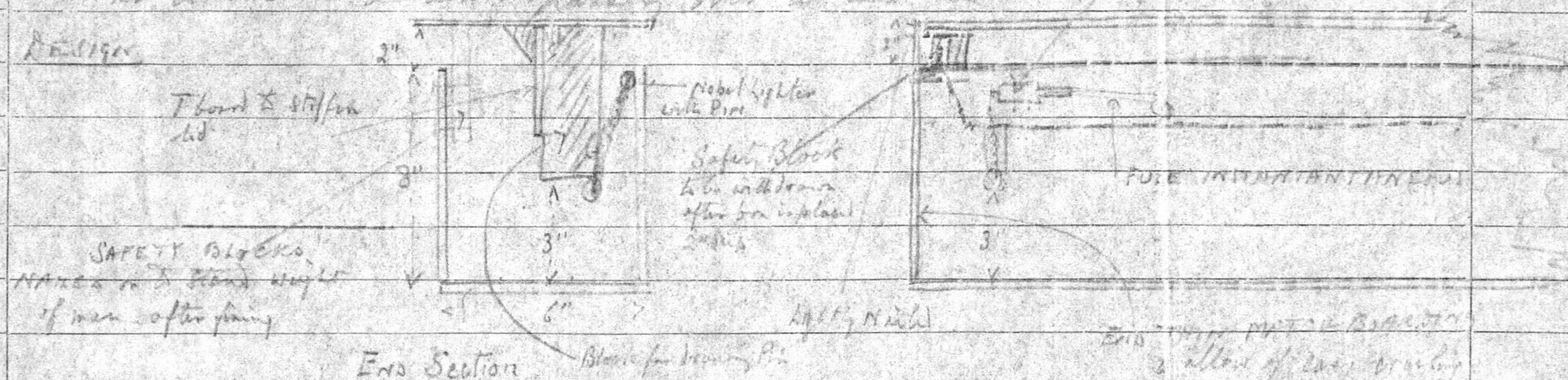	
			NOTES (1) The only action required on ground is place box connect up [illegible] Fuze [illegible] then withdraw Safety Blocks from under lid [illegible]	
			(2) SAFETY (a) 2 Safety Blocks [illegible] (b) [illegible]	
			(3) Firing [illegible] required when setting the Block for Drawing Pin (a) Clearance [illegible] must be greater than drop of lid (b) [illegible] more than 1" – [illegible] 2 blocks [illegible] in place of Safety Blocks and Firing Block [illegible]	

(A9475) Wt W2358/P360 600,000 12/17 D. D. & L. Sch. 52a. Forms/C2118/15

[illegible] 409th Lowland F^d Co RE

SECRET

Appendix B

Instructions regarding War Diaries and Intelligence Summaries are contained in F. S. Regs., Part II. and the Staff Manual respectively. Title pages will be prepared in manuscript.

May

WAR DIARY
or
INTELLIGENCE SUMMARY.
(Erase heading not required.)

409 [illegible]

Army Form C. 2118.

Place	Date	Hour	Summary of Events and Information	Remarks and references to Appendices
			Summary of Work when in Reserve 14th — 31st May	
			ARMENTIERES DEFENCES	
			(1) Erected 35 Shelters in Posts for garrison	
			(2) Erected 1000x double Apron Fence	
			(3) Constructed 3 C.T. Blocks	
			(4) Strutted 10 Cellars (completing same) + [illegible]	
			(5) Levelled off approx 50x wall + 200x hedges to open field of fire	
			CHATEAU [illegible]	
			(1) Completed one concrete pillbox in cellar taken over at 50%	
			(2) Completed 2nd — — — all reinforced	
			Concrete [illegible] 1600 ft. including cutting + fixing reinforcement —	
			all work had to be worked — from [illegible] under floor [illegible]	
			ODD JOBS. Repairs to Baths + Water Supply [illegible]	
			Work in the Dumps (brick work) average of 7 men per day	
			Stretchers for Blankets, Billet [illegible]	
			Supervision for [illegible] depot	
			Solder Burning [illegible] 50%	

[illegible signature]

[illegible signature] OC 409 [illegible] RE

(A9175) Wt W2358/P560 600,000 11/17 D. D. & L. Sch. 52a. Forms/C2118/15

Secret

Instructions regarding War Diaries and Intelligence Summaries are contained in F. S. Regs., Part II. and the Staff Manual respectively. Title pages will be prepared in manuscript.

May

WAR DIARY
or
INTELLIGENCE SUMMARY.
(*Erase heading not required.*)

409 F Cy RE

Army Form C. 2118.

Append C

Place	Date	Hour	Summary of Events and Information	Remarks and references to Appendices
SAILLY			TRAINING & OVERHAUL OF Equipment	
			Training was confined mainly to [illegible]	
			(1) All Sappers in the Coy & Attached Infantry fired an average of 20 to 25 rounds per man, in some cases with gas masks on.	
			Working details under NCOs on Living [illegible] [illegible]	[illegible]
			(2) Each section had 3 hours drill under section officers	
			also coy drill & one section [illegible] bayonet fighting	
			(3) [illegible]	
			Company training	
			(1) 3 mornings ½ hour Company drill including 10 minutes — Gas Masks	
			(2) Field Day Programme as under all transport taken out	
			March 3 miles Dinner [illegible] Sappers 8 am — 8 pm	
			Inspection by CRE Transport [illegible] — 7.30 [illegible]	
			March 7 miles including 1½ hours [illegible]	
			Bridging Gap 81 ft [illegible] all transport [illegible]	
			Dismantling Bridge	
			March Home 3 miles	
			LEWIS GUN	
			18 men trained in use of LEWIS GUN	

(A9175) Wt. W2358/P360 600,000 12/17 D. D. & L. Sch. 52a. Forms/C2118/15

Vol 42

CONFIDENTIAL

WAR DIARY

OF

409th (LOWLAND) FIELD COY R.E. (T)

from 1st JUNE 1918. to 30th JUNE 1918.

(VOLUME No XLII.)

SECRET

Instructions regarding War Diaries and Intelligence Summaries are contained in F. S. Regs., Part II. and the Staff Manual respectively. Title pages will be prepared in manuscript.

June WAR DIARY or INTELLIGENCE SUMMARY. 409 (Home) Field Co R.E. (T)

(*Erase heading not required.*)

Army Form C. 2118.

(1)

Place	Date	Hour	Summary of Events and Information	Remarks and references to Appendices
SAILLY-LA	1		Coy inspected by C.R.E. at NOEUX-LES-MINES. Route march, & S. Trestle bridge erected	
BOVESE.	2		Church Parade	
"	3		Coy moved forward to ANNEQUIN.N. & took over work in R. Sector from 23rd Fd Co	
ANNEQUIN.N	4		Usual bridge & water patrols. ANNEQUIN DEFENCE SCHEME. Dug out for 40th Bde, R.F.A. Improvements to Coy Billets	
"	5		28 beds completed at L Bde HQrs. Dug outs for 40th & 46th Bde R.F.A. ANNEQUIN Defences. Bridge & water patrols & improvements to Coy billets	
"	6		ANNEQUIN Defences, including strutting of cellars. R.F.A. dug outs & improvements to Bde Hd Qrs.	
	7		as above	
"	8		Bunking M.G. Dug out A.36.d.35.40. ANNEQUIN Defences R.F.A. dug outs	
"	9		6 notice boards (contaminated water) completed & as above	
"	10		ANNEQUIN Defences R.F.A. Dug Outs. Erection of bunks in GLOSTER POST. Commenced work on Dug out G.3.D.8.6. C.T. floors at Right boundary & between BAETS ALLEY & LEFT BOYAU. Clearing LEWIS ALLEY now in passable condition.	

(A9475) Wt W2358/P360 600,000 12/17 D. D. & L. Sch 52a. Forms/C2118/15

SECRET

Instructions regarding War Diaries and Intelligence Summaries are contained in F. S. Regs., Part II. and the Staff Manual respectively. Title pages will be prepared in manuscript.

June **WAR DIARY** 409(?) (How) Field Coy R.E.(?)

or

INTELLIGENCE SUMMARY.

(Erase heading not required.)

Army Form C. 2118.

Place	Date	Hour	Summary of Events and Information	Remarks and references to Appendices
ANNEQUIN N	11.		Dug out at G.3.d.8.6. 9 trenches completed GLOSTER POST. C.T. Blocks in DUNDEE WALK RICHMOND POST. S. of SAVILLE ROW. [illegible] ALLEY. Shelters at Baths ANNEQUIN N.	
"	12		As above	
"	13		" " Completion and set of [illegible] AT SAILLY DUMP	
"	14		C.T. Block at HENLEY POST, ANNEQUIN DEFENCES. R.F.A. dug outs. Completed shelters at ANNEQUIN Baths	
"	15		Dug out G.3.d.8.6, Completion C.T. block in RESERVE LINE near RICHMOND POST. Continued on C.T. block at HENLEY POST. ANNEQUIN DEFENCES. R.F.A. dug outs. Work at SAVILLE ROW & dug out 38. Coy Billets & preparing BANGALORE	
"	17		Continued as above. Training for Bangalores	
"	18		Erecting tanks in dug out at G3d8.6. C.T. blocks ANNEQUIN DEFENCES. R.F.A. dug outs	
"	19		Continued as above	
"	20		" " Coy took over EAST FOSSE TUNNEL (ANNEQUIN) commenced	
"	21		As above.	

SECRET

Instructions regarding War Diaries and Intelligence Summaries are contained in F. S. Regs., Part II. and the Staff Manual respectively. Title pages will be prepared in manuscript.

June **WAR DIARY** 409 (Low) Field Coy R.E. (T) Army Form C. 2118.

or

INTELLIGENCE SUMMARY.

(Erase heading not required.)

(3)

Place	Date	Hour	Summary of Events and Information	Remarks and references to Appendices
ANNEQUIN·N	22		C.T. Blocks continued. dugout G.3.d.8.6. R.F.A. dugout ANNEQUIN Defences. Revetting [illegible] tanks in CENTRAL KEEP + RESERVE LINE. Repairing bridge at G.3.b.5.1 (damaged by shell fire)	
"	23		Repaired [illegible] at ANNEQUIN BATHS. Church Parade.	
"	24		8 notice boards erected at contaminated streams. revetting of wall tanks. C.T. blocks etc.	
"	25		Continued as above.	
"	26		SANKEY SHELTERS AT ANNEQUIN POSTS. C.T. block dugout at G.3.d.8.6 completed. R.F.A. dugouts. Reconnaissance of Coy Billets	
"	27		As above	
"	28		" "	
"	29		" "	
"	30		Church Parade	

J. [illegible] Capt. R.E. (T)
O/C 409 (Low) Field Coy R.E. (T)

(A9175) Wt W2358/P360 600,000 12/17 D. D. & L. Sch. 52a. Forms/C2118/13

CONFIDENTIAL

WAR DIARY

OF

409th (LOWLAND) FIELD COY. R.E. (T).

from 1st JULY 1918 to 31st JULY 1918

(VOLUME No XLIII)

Secret.

July 1918

409th Lowland F.C.

Army Form C. 2118.

Instructions regarding War Diaries and Intelligence Summaries are contained in F. S. Regs., Part II, and the Staff Manual respectively. Title pages will be prepared in manuscript.

WAR DIARY
or
~~INTELLIGENCE SUMMARY.~~
(~~Erase heading not required.~~)

Vol 43

Place	Date	Hour	Summary of Events and Information	Remarks and references to Appendices
ANNEQUIN Halt near BETHUNE	1/7/18		Work as Forward Coy with Right Bde of Division in Hohenzollern sector.	
			General Distribution of Company RE 2 Sections forward one section Support Battalion locality, one Section making shell proof accommodation for men in own billets.	
			Attached to Company 3 parties of Inf. disposed one party with forward Section one Company with Support locality Section and one Squad on Company dugouts — Capt Rhind acting O.C. during absence of O.C.	
			Work in hand (a) forward, (i) Blocks in Communication Trenches leading into platoon posts & provision of Straight Shoot	
			(ii) Erection of B type shelters for garrison of Keep.	
			(iii) Construction of new platoon post consisting of slit trenches camouflaged & shelters for garrison.	
			(b) Support Locality (i) Strutting cellars occupied by Support Battalion	
			(ii) Technical work on two mined dugouts being made by gunners for their use.	
			Parade for Work section at ½ hour intervals from 8am.	

Gillett

(A9475) Wt W2358/P360 600,000 12/17 D. D. & L. Sch. 52a. Forms/C2118/15

SECRET

Instructions regarding War Diaries and Intelligence Summaries are contained in F. S. Regs., Part II. and the Staff Manual respectively. Title pages will be prepared in manuscript.

July

WAR DIARY — 409th LOWLAND Fd Coy R.E.
or
INTELLIGENCE SUMMARY.
(Erase heading not required.)

Army Form C. 2118.

Place	Date	Hour	Summary of Events and Information	Remarks and references to Appendices
ANNEQUIN North near BETHUNE	2/7/18		Work continued —— 3 Squads Attached Infantry withdrawn and replaced by similar number from Bn of Batt of 2nd Bde	
	3/7/18		Cont'd.	
	4/7/18		Continued above and commenced shaft of mined dugout	
	5/7/18		Continued above — Special part of 12 volunteers for raiding party detached for Training	
	6/7/18		as above add Splinter proof revetting for Water Tanks. (Raiding party returned [illegible] [illegible])	
	7/7/18		2 Sections forward work — Church Parade & Pay	
	8/7/18		All 4 Sections forward — and 3 Squads of Attd Infantry	
			General Employ. Attached Infantry one party night pushing party on light railway. two parties attached to Sections for assistance and carrying. —	
			Work in hand. 1) Revetting of Water Tanks Completed.	
			(2) Reclaiming Old Keeps (a) Trenches & fire bays Revetting (b) Shelters (c) Deep Dugouts	
			(3) Platoon Post Slit trenches	
			(4) Reclaiming blocked entrance to dugout	
			(5) Commenced Work on Mined Dugout for Dressing Station	
			(6) 2 Platoon Posts	

(A9175) Wt W2358/P360 600,000 12/17 D. D. & L. Sch 52a. Forms/C2118/15

SECRET

409 (Lowland) Fd Coy RE — JULY

Army Form C. 2118.

Instructions regarding War Diaries and Intelligence Summaries are contained in F. S. Regs., Part II, and the Staff Manual respectively. Title pages will be prepared in manuscript.

WAR DIARY or INTELLIGENCE SUMMARY.

(*Erase heading not required.*)

Place	Date	Hour	Summary of Events and Information	Remarks and references to Appendices
ANNEQUIN	9/7/18		as above add Russian Saps to site of new O.P.	
East of	10/7/18		as above also extra accommodation in Shelters for garrison.	
BETHUNE	to 17/7/18		Platoon Post Fire [illegible] completed; extra accommodation for garrison completed; [illegible] Platoon Post completed, 2 CT Blocks completed.	
			2 new Platoon Posts commenced	
	15/7/18		New Organisation of Fd Coy Transport Lines brought in —	
			Generally each Coy to detail one subaltern who for general [illegible] and [illegible] is under a 2nd in Cmd selected & detailed by CRE — The subaltern remains responsible to his own O.C. for internal organisation & efficiency but in matter of stable routine has to conform to orders of O.C. detachment — L Kelly [illegible] detailed —	
	14/7/18		Worked in forward area, and handed over all work in hand to 25th Fd Coy RE	
			Work in Reserve Coy Area taken over from 25th Fd Coy	
			Movement Company moved into billets at SAILLY LABOURSE and assumed roll of Reserve Field Coy R.E.	
			2nd in Cmd Capt RHIND [illegible] and [illegible] HQ moved forward —	
			[illegible signature] Major	

(A9175) Wt W2358/P360 600,000 12/17 D. D. & L. Sch 52a. Forms/C2118/15

SECRET

Instructions regarding War Diaries and Intelligence Summaries are contained in F. S. Regs., Part II, and the Staff Manual respectively. Title pages will be prepared in manuscript.

409 (Lowland) Fd Coy RE **WAR DIARY** July
or
INTELLIGENCE SUMMARY.
(*Erase heading not required.*)

Army Form C. 2118.

Place	Date	Hour	Summary of Events and Information	Remarks and references to Appendices
SAILLY LA	17/7/18		Officers & NCO's not previously acquainted with battle stations reconnoitred	
BOURSE			Same — No attached infantry	
S.E. of			Rifle & Kit Inspection — and clean up. Pm Games	
BETHUNE	18/7/18		Works in hand (1) Erecting Shellproof concrete chambers in Chateau Cellars.	
			Work in hand 95%; new shelter commenced.	
			(2) Supervision of Artillery Dugouts.	
			Training etc. Baths all sections,	
		8am	Physical Training.	
		9am	10. Squad Drill 10.15–10.45 Lecture Saluting & other points 11–12 Saluting & Rifle Exercises	
			pm. Games.	
	19/7/18		One section sent to transport lines, one section on works.	
			2 Sections Training. Programme ½ hour Physical Training, 1 hour Squad Drill, 1 hour Gas	
			Equipment Inspection & Lecture pm. 1 hour Explosives followed by organised games for all	
	20/7/18–24/7/18		One section at Transport Lines on Works (no training) chiefly revetment of horse lines at D.E.	
			Sunday on Games pm: Church Service for all.	
			New Jobs Started (1) Clearing Well & erecting Chain Helice Pump (2) Erection of 14 Shelters for TMB in village line.	
			Trainy. Physical Exercises; Map Reading; Knotting & lashing & musketry	

(A9175) Wt W2358/P360 600,000 12/17 D. D. & L. Sch. 52a. Forms/C2118/15

[signature]

Secret

Instructions regarding War Diaries and Intelligence Summaries are contained in F. S. Regs., Part II. and the Staff Manual respectively. Title pages will be prepared in manuscript.

July **WAR DIARY** *or* **INTELLIGENCE SUMMARY.** 409th Lowland Fd Coy RE. Army Form C. 2118.

(Erase heading not required.)

Place	Date	Hour	Summary of Events and Information	Remarks and references to Appendices
SAILLY LA BOURSE	24/7/18		Movement. No 3 Section rejoin Forward Billets by Route March after 5 days at Transport Lines. No 2 Section proceeds by route march to Transport Lines.	
	25/7/18 - 30/7/18		No 2 Section Work at Transport Lines odd jobs round Div HQ chiefly on revetting of H.Q. Horselines.	
			No 4 Sect & Part of No 1 Works. No 3 Sect Training with balance of No 1.	

Training Programme	8 - 8.30	9.15 - 10.15	10.15 - 12	1.30 - 2.30	2.30 - 4
Thursday	Physical Training	Drill Section & Squad	Section Drill & Saluting	Explosives	Organised Games
Friday	"		Explosives	Knotting & Lashing	
Saturday	"	"	Musketry Firing	Football for mats	
Sunday	nil	nil	Church Service at		nil
Monday	P.T.	Squad Drill	Musketry Firing	Lecture Camouflage	Football

Works (1) Concrete shelter in Basement of Chateau Continued.

(2) New Pump (Chain Helice) installed at Well Annequin.

(3) Dugout for Gunners continued.

(4) Sundry odd repair jobs.

(5) Reconnaissances by officers & checking of Property Districts & Returns & Taping out new Trench Line

Secret

Instructions regarding War Diaries and Intelligence Summaries are contained in F. S. Regs., Part II. and the Staff Manual respectively. Title pages will be prepared in manuscript.

July **WAR DIARY** 409 (Lowland) Fd Coy RE

or

INTELLIGENCE SUMMARY.

(Erase heading not required.)

Army Form C. 2118.

Place	Date	Hour	Summary of Events and Information	Remarks and references to Appendices
SAILLY LA BOURSE	30/7/18		Movement	
			No 2 Section by route march to forward billets (8 miles approx)	
			No 4 — — — — to Transport lines Lt Nisbet remained in Charge —	
	31/7/18		No 4 Section Work at Transport Lines	
			No 3 — — Forward.	
			Nos 1 & 2 Training an Squad Drill, Gas Training & Firing Practice & Baths	
			pm. Rifle Inspection, lecture Knotting & Lashing & Games.	
			Transport & Mounted Section	
			Work (1) Other than Rations & [illegible] very little required for works	
			(2) Standings for horse lines had to be made	
			This was all done by Drivers each section doing their own portion	
			(3) Revetting mainly done by drivers assisted by a few Sappers.	
			Grooming Report by ADVS Good on inspection by O.C. on 31/7/18 — There seemed a falling off in condition & grooming of horses and also harness — I attribute it partly to shorter grooming hours and partly to being under a Subaltern since a more senior officer (2nd in Cmd) also partly to change in routine which takes time to assimilate —	

(A9175) Wt W2358/P360 600,000 12/17 D. D. & L. Sch 52a. Forms/C2118/15

31/8/18

[signature]
Major RE OC 409th Lowland Fd Coy RE

Vol 44

CONFIDENTIAL

WAR DIARY

OF

409th (LOWLAND) FIELD COY. R.E. (T)

from 1st AUGUST 1918 to 31st AUGUST 1918

(VOLUME No XLIV.)

Army Form C. 2118.

Instructions regarding War Diaries and Intelligence Summaries are contained in F. S. Regs., Part II. and the Staff Manual respectively. Title pages will be prepared in manuscript.

WAR DIARY
or
INTELLIGENCE SUMMARY.

(Erase heading not required.)

Place	Date	Hour	Summary of Events and Information	Remarks and references to Appendices

D. D. & L., London, E.C.
(A8004) Wt. W1771/M2031 750,000 5/17 Sch. 52 Forms/C2118/14

409TH (LOWLAND) FIELD COMPANY, R.E.

Army Form C. 2118.

Instructions regarding War Diaries and Intelligence Summaries are contained in F. S. Regs., Part II. and the Staff Manual respectively. Title pages will be prepared in manuscript.

WAR DIARY
or
INTELLIGENCE SUMMARY.
(*Erase heading not required.*)

Place	Date	Hour	Summary of Events and Information	Remarks and references to Appendices
SAILLY-LABOURSE	1.8.18	-	Excavating & strengthening cellars at CHATEAU-DES-PRES (F.24.d)	
F.24.c.1.1			Excavating dugout for 115th Batty R.F.A. (L.4.a.6.9)	
(Sheet 44B)			Salving old working material in SAILLY-LABOURSE.	
			Training:- Physical Exercises, Squad Drill, Rifle Exercises & Musketry - a.m.	
			Rifle & Kit Inspections, Games - p.m.	
"	2.8.18		Work as for 1st continued. De-gassing trench at ANNEQUIN (L.5.a.1.9).	
			Pump at SCHOOL YARD NOEUX-LES-MINES (L.13.a.3.0) dismantled. Huts conveyed from MINX YARD	
			to 1st Divl Reception Camp, BOIS D'OLHAIN (Q.8 central)	
			Training - a.m. - as for 1st	
			p.m. - Lecture on camouflage; Bayonet Fighting	

G. [illegible] Findlay
Major R.E.

(A9475) Wt W2358/P360 600,000 12/17 D. D. & L. Sch 52a. Forms/C2118/15

Instructions regarding War Diaries and Intelligence Summaries are contained in F. S. Regs., Part II. and the Staff Manual respectively. Title pages will be prepared in manuscript.

WAR DIARY
or
INTELLIGENCE SUMMARY.
(Erase heading not required.)

Army Form C. 2118.

Place	Date	Hour	Summary of Events and Information	Remarks and references to Appendices
SAILLY-LABOURSE	3-8-18		Work continued at F24.d, L4 a 6.9; L5 a 1.9 & L13 a 3.0.	
F24 C.41			Remainder of huts drawn from MINX YARD transported to Divl Reception Camp. Erection	
(Sheet 44B)			of huts commenced.	
			Stores for erection of Bolder Kiln drawn from MINX YARD & conveyed to site (K18 b 9.5).	
			Erection of Kiln commenced.	
			2 Large trestles made & conveyed to site to be used in fixing charges at Railway	
			Bridge at L.21.a.0.9	
			Training - a.m. Physical Exercises, Squad Drill & Bayonet Fighting.	
			p.m. - Lecture on Explosives & Co-operation of Aircraft with other arms.	
"	4-8-18		Work commenced on T.M. Shelter VILLAGE LINE - HARLEY STREET - (A 20 b 5.5)	
			Church Parade & Recreation.	
"	5-8-18		Work as for 3rd & 4th continued.	
			Bridging exercise - 1 Section (Cyclists).	

[illegible signature]

Instructions regarding War Diaries and Intelligence Summaries are contained in F. S. Regs., Part II. and the Staff Manual respectively. Title pages will be prepared in manuscript.

WAR DIARY
or
INTELLIGENCE SUMMARY.
(Erase heading not required.)

Army Form C. 2118.

Place	Date	Hour	Summary of Events and Information	Remarks and references to Appendices
SAILLY-LABOURSE	6.8.18		As for 5th less Bridging exercise	
			Movement – Relieved 23rd Field Coy R.E. in CAMBRIN Sector & moved forward to billets	
			in ANNEQUIN N. F23.d. central – Sheet 44B	
			Back area work handed over & forward area work reconnoitred & taken over from 23 Fd Coy	
ANNEQUIN	7.8.18		T.M. Shelter – HARLEY STREET completed.	
			CAMBRIN – LA BASSEE Road – Strengthening cellars.	
			RLY EMBANKMENT – (A15.d.0.6) – L.G. post – Shaft to new emplacement.	
			No 6 Siding – (A24 a 3.7) – Straight shaft & C B type shelters	
			WILSON'S TUNNELL (A24 d 2.8) – Russian Saps.	
"	8.8.18		Work as for 7th continued.	
			A15 c.6.4 – L.G. Post E. of LOCK – Driving new shaft to give fire in front of CUINCHY.	
			A20.a.6.15 – Wiring scheme completed.	

[signature]

O.C. 400th (...) Fd. Coy. R.E.

(A9175) Wt W2358/P360 600,000 12/17 D. D. & L. Sch 52a. Forms/C2118/15

Instructions regarding War Diaries and Intelligence Summaries are contained in F. S. Regs., Part II, and the Staff Manual respectively. Title pages will be prepared in manuscript.

WAR DIARY
or
INTELLIGENCE SUMMARY.
(*Erase heading not required.*)

Army Form C. 2118.

Place	Date	Hour	Summary of Events and Information	Remarks and references to Appendices
ANNEQUIN	9.8.18		Work as for 8th continued. Work at No 6 Siding - A24 a 34 - completed.	
"	10.8.18		Work as for 9th continued. Testing charges at Bridges at F30 a 68 & A20 c 8 3	
			A15. c 1 75 - Rifle Section W. of LOCK - Covered trenches from Dugout to Fire position	
			Pump at junction of WILSON'S WAY & WIMPOLE STREET repaired	
"	11.8.18		Work as for 10th continued.	
			A15. c L5 40 - New fire position at TOWER BRIDGE commenced.	
"	12.8.18		Work as for 11th continued.	
			(Area in F23 d 38 & F23 d 54 heavily shelled with 5.9" & 4.2" from 9 to 11 a.m.)	
"	13.8.18		Work as for 12th continued.	
			A15. d 30.55. - RLY EMBKT. at BEXHILL - Existing dugout extended & communicating gallery commenced.	

[signature]
O.C. 409th (LOWLAND) FD. COY. R.E.

Instructions regarding War Diaries and Intelligence Summaries are contained in F. S. Regs., Part II. and the Staff Manual respectively. Title pages will be prepared in manuscript.

WAR DIARY
or
INTELLIGENCE SUMMARY.
(Erase heading not required.)

Army Form C. 2118.

Place	Date	Hour	Summary of Events and Information	Remarks and references to Appendices
ANNEQUIN	14-8-18		Work as for 13th continued.	
			A20.d.56 - Materials collected ready for erection of O.P at Ruin.	
"	15-8-18		Continued as for 14th.	
			Work completed at A15.d.06; A15.c.1.75; A15.c.45.10	
"	16-8-18		A.20.d.56 - O.P. at Ruin completed, also Russian Sap at WILSON'S TUNNEL (A24.d.28). Remainder of work on hand continued.	
			(Casualties - 1 O.R. killed. 1 O.R. died of wounds & 1 O.R. wounded & to hospital).	
"	17-8-18		Work continued as for 16th.	
"	18-8-18		Do 17th. 2/Lieut. W. GRIGOR admitted to hospital (sick).	
"	19-8-18		Work at br. G. Siding completed (A27.a.65.75). Remainder of work on hand continued. Sump dug for NORTON TUBE WELL at MARYLEBONE ROAD (A21.c.8.4).	
"	20-8-18		Work continued as for 19th.	
"	21-8-18		Do " 20th.	

[signature]
Maj. R.E.
O.C. 400th (Lowland) Fd. Coy. R.E.

(A9175) Wt. W2358/P360 600,000 12/17 D. D. & L. Sch. 52a. Forms/C2118/15

Instructions regarding War Diaries and Intelligence Summaries are contained in F. S. Regs., Part II. and the Staff Manual respectively. Title pages will be prepared in manuscript.

WAR DIARY
or
INTELLIGENCE SUMMARY.
(*Erase heading not required.*)

Army Form C. 2118.

Place	Date	Hour	Summary of Events and Information	Remarks and references to Appendices
ANNEQUIN.	22-8-18		All work & billets taken over, & Coy relieved by 157th Field Coy R.E.	
			MOVEMENT:- Coy moved off by Sections at 5 mins intervals No. 1 Section in lead leaving at 11-0 a.m. Entrained at SAILLY-LABOURSE at 12-30 p.m. Detrained RUITZ & marched to Wagon Lines at MAISNIL-LES-RUITZ, arriving 2.45 p.m. Dinners prepared and 6 p.m. Coy complete with Transport moved off by Sections at 100 yards interval.	
			Arrived BAJUS (O.22.a.31 & Sheet 44B) about 7 p.m. - The march from MAISNIL-LES-RUITZ to BAJUS was very trying on the men, the heat being excessive.	
			During the period 1st-21st, Coy Transport was parked at MAISNIL-LES-RUITZ, in conjunction with Transport of 23rd & 26th Field Coys was organized by C.R.E. as "1st DE Wagon Lines" under Capt. J. F. GIBSON. 26th Field Coy R.E. This Detachment ceased to exist on 21st & from that date Coy Transport came under orders of O.C.	
BAJUS. O22.a.31	23-8-18		Inspection of arms & all equipment. Deficiencies noted for re-fitting.	
			Billets cleaned up & improved generally.	
			G. W. [signature] O.C. 409th (Lowland) Fd. Coy. R.E.	

(A9175) Wt W2358/P360 600,000 12/17 D. D. & L. Sch 52a. Forms/C2118/15

Instructions regarding War Diaries and Intelligence Summaries are contained in F. S. Regs., Part II. and the Staff Manual respectively. Title pages will be prepared in manuscript.

WAR DIARY
or
INTELLIGENCE SUMMARY.
(*Erase heading not required.*)

Army Form C. 2118.

Place	Date	Hour	Summary of Events and Information					Remarks and references to Appendices
BATUS			6.0.am	6.15 am	6.45 – 7.30 am	8.45 a.m – 12.0 noon	1.30 p.m – 3.0 p.m.	
SUMMARY OF TRAINING 24th to 30th			REVEILLE.	BISCUIT & TEA.	PHYSICAL EXERCISES.	Infantry Drill, & Rifle Exercises, Communicating Drill, & open order work. Musketry. Firing practices. Range & miniature Target practice. Bridging, Pontooning & Weldon Trestle. Intensive Digging. Explosives & Demolitions. Knotting & Lashing. Map Reading.	Lectures on Bridging. Explosives. Tactical Handling. Reconnaissances & Reports. Use of Tools. Games.	
						L.G. & Cyclist Groups – Special training. BRIDGEING SCHEME & Route March by whole company and rowing & bathing at site.		

[illegible signature]

(A9175) Wt W2358/P360 6,0,000 12/17 D. D. & L. Sch. 51a. Forms/C2118/15.

O.C. 409th (Lowland) Fd. Coy. R.E.

Army Form C. 2118.

Instructions regarding War Diaries and Intelligence Summaries are contained in F. S. Regs., Part II. and the Staff Manual respectively. Title pages will be prepared in manuscript.

WAR DIARY
or
INTELLIGENCE SUMMARY.
(Erase heading not required.)

Place	Date	Hour	Summary of Events and Information	Remarks and references to Appendices
ARRAS.	31.8.18	-	Warning order to move received at 1-15.a.m. Transport moved off by road at 2.0.pm & proceeded with 2nd Bde Transport, arriving at FREVIN CAPELLE about 9.0.pm. remaining there for the night. Dismounted personnel moved out at 3.0.p.m., marched to DIEVAL. Entrained there at 11.0.p.m. Detrained ARRAS. 5.0.a.m. 1.9.18.	

[illegible]
Major RE
(T.F.) R.E.
O.C. 409th (Lowland) Fd. Coy. R.E.

D. D. & L., London, E.C.
(A8001) Wt. W1771/M2031 750,000 5/17 Sch. 52 Forms C2118/14

Vol 45

CONFIDENTIAL

WAR DIARY

OF

409th (LOWLAND) FIELD COY R.E. (T)

from 1st Septr 1918 to 30th Septr 1918

(VOLUME No XLV.)

Army Form C. 2118.

Instructions regarding War Diaries and Intelligence Summaries are contained in F. S. Regs., Part II. and the Staff Manual respectively. Title pages will be prepared in manuscript.

WAR DIARY
or
INTELLIGENCE SUMMARY.

(Erase heading not required.)

Place	Date	Hour	Summary of Events and Information	Remarks and references to Appendices

D. D. & L., London, E.C.
(A8001) Wt. W1771/M2031 750,000 5/17 Sch. 52 Forms C2118/14

Secret 409th Lowland F Coy RE

P.1

Army Form C. 2118.

Instructions regarding War Diaries and Intelligence Summaries are contained in F. S. Regs., Part II, and the Staff Manual respectively. Title pages will be prepared in manuscript.

WAR DIARY or ~~INTELLIGENCE SUMMARY.~~ for Sept

(Erase heading not required.)

Place	Date	Hour	Summary of Events and Information	Remarks and references to Appendices
BAJUS ~~[illegible]~~	3/8/18	1.15a	Recd Warning Order to be ready to move at 2 hrs notice after 8 am	Instructions for [illegible] [illegible]
		2pm	Transport moved off by road	
		3pm	Dismounted personnel moved out dump of [illegible] left at BAJUS under Div arrangements	
		11pm	Dismd personnel entrained DIEVAL (1½ hour journey nominal)	
ARRAS	1/9/18	5am	Arrived ARRAS, breakfasts, sleep	
		12noon	Cyclists moved forward to assist advanced Div HQ. 3pm 1 section [illegible] cyclist reinforcements party	
		5pm	Verbal orders received to move to assembly position behind Canadian Corps	
			Coy to be split into Echelon A & Echelon B latter being moved by Div orders.	
			Roll Reserve Coy from technical work required and part of Div Tactical Reserve	
			In view of possible bridging the Pontoons & Trestle wagon of each company was	
			attached to Reserve Company — other [illegible] to advanced Section to remain forward.	
		10.15pm	Transport arrived by road — Water fed & Drivers meal while being split up	
			into Echelon A & B and loads adjusted. —	
			Dress for this marching order less Haversack & Greatcoat which were dumped in ARRAS and	
			collected later.	
		11.20	Hook in & section Parade 11.30pm moved off to assembly position carrying	
			rations [illegible] for 2 sections forward —	

(A9175) Wt W2358/P566 6,00,000 12/17 D.D.& L. Sch 52a. Forms/C2118/15

P.2

Instructions regarding War Diaries and Intelligence Summaries are contained in F. S. Regs., Part II, and the Staff Manual respectively. Title pages will be prepared in manuscript.

WAR DIARY
or
INTELLIGENCE SUMMARY.
(Erase heading not required.)

Army Form C. 2118.

Place	Date	Hour	Summary of Events and Information	Remarks and references to Appendices
near NEUVILLE VITASSE	2/9/18	2.30 am	1.30 am found line to be crossed between 1½ hrs march considerably delayed by congestion on roads —	
			Selecting a place where pontoons could be drawn in in dark — this in a shelled area was no easy task even although ground had been visited by day before assembly point was known.	
			Breakfast 8am Water & Feed — Very cold at night without greatcoats & men got little sleep.	
			Echelon A. HQ & 1 Limber 4 Sections each with toolcart & pack animal only	
			HQ = OC, Capt, Clerk, Cook, Wheeler, Saddler, Bridging Wagons – 1 limber	
1/40,000 Sheet 51B O 25 b			Echelon B. Technical Wagon, 3 limbers, Mess Cart with CSM, CQMS, Pay Sergt	
		10 am	Moved to move forward about 4 miles arrived 12 noon —	
about ½ mile W of CHERISY			All sappers had to set to & fill in shell holes to allow of pontoons drawing in off road — Feed & Dinners stood by for further move forward.	
			2 officers & NCO mtd. sent forward to reconnoitre Pontoon roads forward	
			Roads practicable & reconnoitred to within about 1000 yds of Infantry — the absence of shelling was very marked — Enemy's aeroplanes were active & destroyed several balloons — Lorries were going into CHERISY.	
			Need for mounted NCO's & officers in reconnoitring roads ahead was very marked	

F3

Army Form C. 2118.

Instructions regarding War Diaries and Intelligence Summaries are contained in F. S. Regs., Part II. and the Staff Manual respectively. Title pages will be prepared in manuscript.

WAR DIARY
or
INTELLIGENCE SUMMARY.
(Erase heading not required.)

Place	Date	Hour	Summary of Events and Information	Remarks and references to Appendices
O 25 b	3/9/18		Night 2/3 very cold in readiness to move forward at once.	
W of HERMIES			Sent back Echelon B limber to bring up greatcoats & officers valises	
			considered necessary to allow men sleeping at nights and keep them fit	
all		4pm	Received verbal orders from CRE that 1st Div will relieve 3rd Div which	
Sheet 57(c)			was on our left and form a defensive flank.	
1/40000			409th Coy to relieve 405th F. Coy RE at O 9 b 96 about 4 miles away.	
			Transport N 3 d – Bridging Wagons rejoin their own companies.	
			Preliminary report of handing over to reach CRE by 5.30pm	
			One section detached complete and placed at disposal of G.O.C. 2 Bde.	
O 9 b 96		6pm	Relief of 405th Coy complete – accommodation rather packed in dugouts	
		6	Detachment sent forward to find forward billets for 1 section which was held	
			in readiness to move forward.	
			Distribution Transport N 3 d, A Echelon Transport about 1 mile behind forward billets	
			HQ & Section at O 9 b 9 6 one Section with Bde at ETERPIGNY. (One OR Wounded)	
	4/9/18		Billets for forward Section found – No 3 Section moved up & settled in in	
			old German dugout – one section reconnoitring crossing of river & commenced work	

(A9175) Wt W2358/P360 600,000 12/17 D. D. & L. Sch 52a. Forms/C2118/15

P.4

Instructions regarding War Diaries and Intelligence Summaries are contained in F. S. Regs., Part II, and the Staff Manual respectively. Title pages will be prepared in manuscript.

Army Form C. 2118.

WAR DIARY
or
INTELLIGENCE SUMMARY.
(Erase heading not required.)

Place	Date	Hour	Summary of Events and Information	Remarks and references to Appendices
near	5th		One section building Bridge.	
MONCHY			One section searching for mines & ready to move forward if required	
le PREUX			one section forward reclaiming wells, improving accommodation &	
0.9.b.9.6			searching for dugouts (Fight for forward dugout claimed by Infantry).	
			one section with Brigade.	
	6th		ditto. spare section salving material for bridging section	
			Orders for move received – Coy to hand over to 572 F Coy – Touch obtained	
			& orders issued about 8.30pm	
	7th	9.30am	Relief complete. Company on move to assemble at N3d at Transport	
			Lines. No orders as to destination then known.	
		2.30pm	Orders recd 10.30am re advance parties, ~~[illegible]~~ transport moved off on	
			20 mile march at 2.30pm arriving 10.30pm. Destination having been altered en route.	
		11.30pm	Dismounted Personnel Embussed and arrived billeting area 4am.	
	8/9/18	4am	No billets available. Slept out in field – got into billets about midday.	
	8th/9th		Orders for move by train recd. Equipment overhauled ready for move	

Remarks: Work of Sect. with Bde
1) Searched all dugouts occupied by 13th Bde.
2) Forward road for troops now forward Infantry accommodation
3) Put 3 wells in working order

[illegible signature]
Capt. [illegible]
OC 409 Lowland Fd Coy

(A9175) Wt W2358/P360 600,000 12/17 D. D. & L. Sch. 52a. Forms/C2118/15

Army Form C. 2118.

(P. 5)

Instructions regarding War Diaries and Intelligence Summaries are contained in F. S. Regs., Part II. and the Staff Manual respectively. Title pages will be prepared in manuscript.

WAR DIARY for Sept
or
INTELLIGENCE SUMMARY.

(*Erase heading not required.*)

Place	Date	Hour	Summary of Events and Information	Remarks and references to Appendices
TILLOY LES HERMAVILLE	10/9/18		Company vacated billets after noon and entrained for an unknown destination – Train at Station due to entrain & move off at 5.50pm	
to			Actually moved at 11pm —	
MARCELCAVE to CHUIGNES	11/9/18		Journey delayed by congestion arrived MARCELCAVE about 4pm and after dinners marched to billets at CHUIGNES.	
	12/9/18		Transport moved out by road to ATHIES at 2pm Dismounted personnel & 2 limbers resting.	
	13/9/18		Transport joined by detached wagons — Dismounted Personnel by bus to vicinity of ATHIES where company bivouaced for night moving forward next day	
	14/9/18		Company moved by route march to near MERAUCOURT and bivouaced	
	15/9/18		Reconnaissance of River Crossings between CULLANCOURT & VERMAND Two sites selected also site for bivouacing —	
		2pm.	Company moved forward 4 miles and settled in new bivouacs, officers in 2 tents	
	16/9/18		No 2 Section working on Div HQ.	
			End of Approach March Division in Line 2nd Bde in Reserve	[signature]

(A9475) Wt W2358/P360 600,000 12/17 D. D. & L. Sch 52a. Forms/C2118/15

Instructions regarding War Diaries and Intelligence Summaries are contained in F. S. Regs., Part II. and the Staff Manual respectively. Title pages will be prepared in manuscript.

WAR DIARY for September
or
INTELLIGENCE SUMMARY.
(Erase heading not required.)

Army Form C. 2118.

(P.6)

Place	Date	Hour	Summary of Events and Information	Remarks and references to Appendices
CAULAINCOURT	16/9/18	7.30am	3 Sections working on Bridges over Omignon river selected on 15th. Tools carried by pack animal. Remaining Section Camp Work & Preparations for Battle	
			Approaches to bridges prepared and timbers collected for Bridges.	
	17th	9am	General parade of Company to explain situation and what was the Company role.	
		9.15am	2 Sections moved out to work on Bridges commenced on 16/9/18.	
			Trestles and roadbearers of one completed – Decking required.	
			1 Section loading special bridging stores & reconnaissance.	
			1 Section moved off 1pm to make a forward crossing over Omignon to be completed by Dawn 18th – It was completed by 5pm 18th	
			All sections reached ~~[illegible]~~ assembly area at dusk and settled down for night in holes behind a bank.	
			Night quiet except for Bombing in vicinity and 2 gas alarms of short duration.	
			Copy of Orders for 17th attached	Copy of Orders for 17th

D. D. & L., London, E.C.
(A8001) Wt. W1771/M2031 750,000 5/17 Sch. 52 Forms/C2118/14

Instructions regarding War Diaries and Intelligence Summaries are contained in F. S. Regs., Part II, and the Staff Manual respectively. Title pages will be prepared in manuscript.

WAR DIARY for Sept
or
INTELLIGENCE SUMMARY.
(Erase heading not required.)

Army Form C. 2118.

(P. 7)

Place	Date	Hour	BATTLE Summary of Events and Information	Remarks and references to Appendices
N.E. of VERMAND	17/18 9/18	17th 9pm	Touch with attacking battalion obtained in evening of 17th/18th	
			Lt Kelly RE & party moved off at dusk to tape left Bde forming up line.	
			Lt Nisbet & party moved off at dusk to tape Right Bde forming up line	
			Both jobs were successfully completed by [illegible] am.	
			No 2 Section on detachment.	Appendix B
	18th	4.30am	Reveille 5am Breakfasts for 1, 2 & 3 Sections No 4 Section Breakfast 7.30am	Role of Sections
		5.20	Zero – final preparations for moving forward. N	
		6 am	Nos 1 & 3 Sections moved off to perform allotted work.	
		9am	No 4 Section moved forward.	
		6.45am	approx Touch obtained with Left Bde HQ on the move near VADENCOURT.	
		7.45am	— — — — Right Bde HQ in MAISSEMY.	
		7.30	approx Communication for foot traffic established between MAISSEMY & VADENCOURT Bend crossing in hand.	
		8am	(approx) orders sent back to send up No 4 Section if not already on move and HQ to be established in VADENCOURT	

Instructions regarding War Diaries and Intelligence Summaries are contained in F. S. Regs., Part II, and the Staff Manual respectively. Title pages will be prepared in manuscript.

WAR DIARY
or
INTELLIGENCE SUMMARY.
(Erase heading not required.)

Army Form C. 2118.

Place	Date	Hour	Summary of Events and Information	Remarks and references to Appendices
VADENCOURT	19th	am	Two Sections working on improving & increasing accommodation	
			Two Sections kept in hand in reserve for case of any special work	
		pm	One forward section out at to improve [illegible]	
			Three Sections returned back for work on new Div HQ	
			worked 5 – 12 midnight	
CAULLAINCOURT	20th		3 Sections work on new Div HQ – No 2 Section remain VADENCOURT	
	21st		1 Section Relieved 9 am by 46th Div and returned for work [illegible] in afternoon	
			3 Section work on Div HQ	
	22nd		All 4 Section on Div HQ in 2 reliefs 6am — 11pm	
	23rd		All 4 Section on — — 6am — 8pm	
	2		Div HQ moved in in evening about 3.30 pm	
	24th		One Sect Div HQ, one sect [illegible] Huts (BATTLE [illegible])	
			2 Section in close reserve working on VERMAND Bridge	
[illegible] Wood near VERMAND	24/25		All 4 Sections in readiness for forward work if required after Battle	
HOLNONCOURT	25th		One Section on VERMAND Bridge completed	
			3 Section on Div HQ	

[illegible signature]

Instructions regarding War Diaries and Intelligence Summaries are contained in F. S. Regs., Part II, and the Staff Manual respectively. Title pages will be prepared in manuscript.

WAR DIARY for Sept
or
INTELLIGENCE SUMMARY.
(Erase heading not required.)

Army Form C. 2118.

Place	Date	Hour	Summary of Events and Information	Remarks and references to Appendices
Caulaincourt	26th		All four Sections work on Div HQ [illegible]	
	27th		One Section detached for work under [illegible] — [illegible]	
			Other sections under 2nd in command moved to site at [illegible] and [illegible]	
	28th		CRE's conference 11am — 3pm [illegible] scheme of attack	
			coming off on 29th —	
			Moved forward No 1 Section [illegible] — saw [illegible] and made arrangements for	
			29th — Night 29th spent in shelter all company fairly comfortable.	
	29th		Role allotted — 1 Section at disposal of [illegible].	
			3 Sections ready to carry out orders from CRE in [illegible] 1st [illegible] Area	
			Bridging Equipment parked under CRE	
	"	4.30	Breakfast for No 2 Section 2/Lt [illegible] and also Lt Kelly as reconnaissance officer	
		5am	Above moved to assembly point at [illegible]	
		8am	Thick fog situation very obscure — Capt [illegible] RE went forward to	
		8am	relieve Lt Kelly RE(?) and carried out an RE Reconnaissance at same	
			time gaining information as to Infantry dispositions which might have been	
			of great value if the fog lifting had not cleared the situation.	

(A9175) Wt W2358/P360 600,000 12/17 D. D. & L. Sch. 52a. Forms/C2118/15

Instructions regarding War Diaries and Intelligence Summaries are contained in F. S. Regs., Part II, and the Staff Manual respectively. Title pages will be prepared in manuscript.

WAR DIARY
or
INTELLIGENCE SUMMARY.
(Erase heading not required.)

Army Form C. 2118.

Place	Date	Hour	Summary of Events and Information	Remarks and references to Appendices
BIHECOURT	29th	2pm	visited Bde found out situation — company & [illegible] to move forward	
		6pm	visited CRE at Div HQ. No move for 29th	
	30th	6am	Reveille 4am Breakfast & [illegible] 5am moved off 5am[illegible] to find billets near PONTRUET	
			Spent till 1.30pm at BELLENGLISE [illegible] with [illegible] & dugouts [illegible] by Infantry	
			Carried out reconnaissance as [illegible]	
			Wells PONTRUET — RIVER OMIGNON — [illegible]	
			Demanded Stores for new Water Point	
			4/10/18 [illegible]	[illegible]

(A9475) Wt W2358/P360 600,000 12/17 D. D. & L. Sch 52a. Forms/C2118/15

Instructions regarding War Diaries and Intelligence Summaries are contained in F. S. Regs., Part II. and the Staff Manual respectively. Title pages will be prepared in manuscript.

WAR DIARY ~~or~~ INTELLIGENCE SUMMARY. Sept 1918

(Erase heading not required.)

Army Form C. 2118.

Appendix B

8

Place	Date	Hour	Summary of Events and Information	Remarks and references to Appendices
			Role allotted to Company and sub-allocation to Sections.	
1) Advance of 2nd Bde was astride [illegible] River — 401st F. Coy was allotted task of establishing communication by footways across river and marsh at [illegible] 3 [illegible] points also to carry out [illegible] reconnaissance of captured area particularly as regards mines —				
2) Sub-allotment. It was decided that main work should be done from North bank but as subsidiary [illegible] Coy [illegible] South bank and also for general reconnaissance one section was detailed for work on the bank remaining three being on North bank also 3 trestle wagons loaded with cork floats —				
No 2 Section on South bank (1) [illegible] of Right battalion forming up line				
			(2) Reconnaissance of vicinity of selected points for crossing and working crossings from South end.	
			(3) General Reconnaissance and search for Mines	
			(4) Touch to be gained with North bank whenever possible	
			Execution of Crossing. Parties of No 2 [illegible] parties of No 1 on North bank and the crossings were thus worked through from both ends simultaneously —	

Actual [illegible] communication was not attained for some time after work commenced which tends to justify independent role allotted [illegible] objection to carrying [illegible] passage of the river after zero. [illegible]

Instructions regarding War Diaries and Intelligence Summaries are contained in F. S. Regs., Part II. and the Staff Manual respectively. Title pages will be prepared in manuscript.

WAR DIARY for September
or
INTELLIGENCE SUMMARY.
(*Erase heading not required.*)

Army Form C. 2118.

Appendix B

Place	Date	Hour	Summary of Events and Information	Remarks and references to Appendices
Roles of 3 Section on Wallbank & section of HQ.				
No 1 Section			— (1) Task find and make crossing in vicinity of R16 d 8.6. (Forming up line)	
			(2) Reconnaissance of strip 500 yds each side of road up to forming up line.	
			This section moved off at 6am as follows (a) Section Officer & party of 6 carrying a few	
			tools sufficient for a temporary crossing (b) Main body (with pack mule carrying a selected	
			assortment of tools suitable for bridging anticipated) followed ½ hour later	
			Execution A place for crossing was selected by Section Officer and work [illegible] on the	
			river about 25' across was crossed by 2 cork float piers and 3 [illegible] piers	
			The track over the marsh being done with Corrugated Iron laying on flat which was found	
			sufficient as a temporary crossing and [illegible] a considerable amount of traffic	
			without it we sank over ankle deep and in places knee deep —	
			Crossing from [illegible] was considerably interrupted by shell fire — [illegible] a casualty [illegible]	
			(2) Area was reconnoitred & report [illegible] in [illegible] mines found but some [illegible]	
			found ready for [illegible] over entrances [illegible] [illegible] were removed.	

(A9375) Wt W2358/P360 600,000 12/17 D. D. & L. Sch 52a. Forms/C2118/15

Instructions regarding War Diaries and Intelligence Summaries are contained in F. S. Regs., Part II. and the Staff Manual respectively. Title pages will be prepared in manuscript.

WAR DIARY
or
INTELLIGENCE SUMMARY.
(Erase heading not required.)

Army Form C. 2118.

Append B

Place	Date	Hour	Summary of Events and Information	Remarks and references to Appendices
VADENCOURT	1		No 3 Section Role (1) Establish Foot Crossing on main road between VADENCOURT & MASSEMY.	
			(2) Reconnoitre from jumping off line to East edge of VADENCOURT 500 yds each side of main road.	
			Section moved forward on No 1 leaving at same time. — Site of work was reached just after enemy lifts and work put in hand — On way up a main party waited for 1/4 hour till enemy shelling lifted — The hour immediately after the enemy lift was the quietest of the day as presumably he had not had time to get back to his heavy guns —	
			Footbridge fit for riders or packmules was put across about a 16 ft span clear of main roadway. — Reconnaissance was carried out and report sent in. One suspected mine dugout — one unfired detonator charge removed from Bridge abutment of demolished bridges — Accommodation for about 80 men was found which was subsequently useful —	
Note.			Technical Work was light but with reconnaissance subalterns to select NCOs with small party full section strength was absorbed —	[initials]

(A9175) Wt W2358/P360 600,000 12/17 D. D. & L. Sch 52a. Forms/C2118/15

Instructions regarding War Diaries and Intelligence Summaries are contained in F. S. Regs., Part II. and the Staff Manual respectively. Title pages will be prepared in manuscript.

WAR DIARY
or
INTELLIGENCE SUMMARY.
(*Erase heading not required.*)

Appendix D

Army Form C. 2118.

Place	Date	Hour	Summary of Events and Information	Remarks and references to Appendices
VADENCOURT	11th		Section No. [illegible] Had to work up to 1st objective when attack was due to move forward at 8.30 am.	
			Role. Crossing of [illegible] at Green Line and reconnaissance of area from VADENCOURT to GREEN Line	
			The section moved off at 2.45 am from assembly point ([illegible] in the same formation as previous sections [illegible])	
			Idea was to obtain touch with other sections at VADENCOURT and if possible see OC for latest information orders failing that carry on previously arranged role	
			Touch was obtained and it moved forward no alteration in role being required	
			Crossing was effected by advance party only main body [illegible] was halted in VADENCOURT and utilised in searching [illegible] Bn HQ for mines and other [illegible] & reports sent in	
			On completion of task first two sections [illegible] ready to move out for any special work.	
			[initials]	

(A9175) Wt W2353/P360 600,000 12/7 D. D. & L. Sch 52a. Forms/C2118/15

Instructions regarding War Diaries and Intelligence Summaries are contained in F. S. Regs., Part II, and the Staff Manual respectively. Title pages will be prepared in manuscript.

WAR DIARY ~~or~~ INTELLIGENCE SUMMARY.

(*Erase heading not required.*)

Army Form C. 2118.

Appx B

Place	Date	Hour	Summary of Events and Information	Remarks and references to Appendices
Action of HQ		(1)	HQ remained at assembly point [illegible] all [illegible] [illegible] [illegible] [illegible] reinforcements formed and ref[illegible]	
		(2)	HQ [illegible] OC, Capt, [illegible] & [illegible] per [illegible] [illegible] or one Clerk	
		(3)	[illegible] OC or [illegible] moved forward with [illegible] [illegible] to [illegible] [illegible] and kept touch with Battalions –	
		(4)	Capt was left in charge with orders to [illegible] [illegible] [illegible] [illegible] [illegible] sent back – but [illegible] [illegible] was NOT [illegible] [illegible] [illegible] [illegible] [illegible] [illegible] [illegible])	
			If no orders recd by 9 am Capt to act as he thought fit [illegible] [illegible] [illegible] [illegible] support Bn HQ –	
			Orders sent back for move arrived about 9.5 am by which time Capt had [illegible] [illegible] [illegible] [illegible] which was just under way.	
		(5)	8.40 am orders sent back ([illegible] 9.5 am) to move HQ to [illegible] – [illegible] was left at assembly point to transmit any messages till 3 hours later.	
	NOTES:		[illegible] were NOT required but might have been and should be with [illegible] – Captain [illegible] at [illegible] point [illegible] [illegible] he would lose [illegible] [illegible] situation changes too rapidly – He is a responsible officer to act on [illegible] points [illegible] [illegible] [illegible] free to be mobile –	
			[illegible] No [illegible] [illegible] [illegible] [illegible] or [illegible] [illegible] [illegible] – [illegible] [illegible] [illegible] [illegible] [illegible] [illegible] for men to [illegible] their coats [illegible] [illegible] [illegible] assembly point	

(A9175) Wt W2358/P360 600,000 12/17 D. D. & L. Sch 52a. Forms/C2118/15

Instructions regarding War Diaries and Intelligence Summaries are contained in F. S. Regs., Part II. and the Staff Manual respectively. Title pages will be prepared in manuscript.

WAR DIARY
or
INTELLIGENCE SUMMARY.
(Erase heading not required.)

Army Form C. 2118.

Vol 46

Place	Date	Hour	Summary of Events and Information	Remarks and references to Appendices
			CONFIDENTIAL	
			WAR DIARY	
			OF	
			409TH (LOWLAND) FIELD COY. R.E. (T)	
			1ST OCTOBER 1918 TO 31ST OCTOBER 1918	
			VOLUME XLVI	

(A9175) Wt W2358/P360 600,000 12/17 D. D. & L. Sch 52a. Forms/C2118/15

Sent for OC

P.1

Army Form C. 2118.

Instructions regarding War Diaries and Intelligence Summaries are contained in F. S. Regs., Part II. and the Staff Manual respectively. Title pages will be prepared in manuscript.

WAR DIARY
or
INTELLIGENCE SUMMARY.

(Erase heading not required.)

Place	Date	Hour	Summary of Events and Information	Remarks and references to Appendices
PONTRUET	1/10/18		No 2 Section Attached to 1st Bde employed on searching dugouts & making Bde & Bn HQ & Water Reconnaissance. No 3 " & Part of No 1 — Preparing Water Point at BERTHAUCOURT for horses & Carts Party No 1 & Capt Rhind road & Water Reconnaissance forward " No 4 & Lt Kelly Tunnel Reconnaissance — found and removed several charges —	Appendix A Plan & detail of work on Water Point
	2/10/18		Nos 1 & 3 Sections Water Point using also 4 wagons Nos 2 & 4 Changed round No 2 going on Water Point in afternoon.	Appendix B — Summary of Reports of Recon[naissance]
	3/10/18		No 1, 2, 3 on Water Point improving troughs & standings.	
	4/10/18		do + 10 Wagons loading party did not turn up loading done by Drivers & some men attached.	
	5/10/18		do + 1 Section of 25th F Coy RE + 70 of 6th Welsh on a 2nd party from 1-6 pm At end of this days work the Temporary water point was capable of dealing with 5,500 horses per hour & 4 filling points for watercarts. Source & bed of stream was wired in and about 70 Notice boards painted & erected A Census of Horses Shewed 20,000 Horses watered single watering = say 10000 horses 120 Water Carts at Standpipe	

[signature]
Major
O.C. 409th (Lowland) Fd. Coy. R.E.

D. D. & L., London, E.C.
(A8004) Wt. W1771/M2031 750,000 5/17 Sch. 52 Forms/C2118/14

Contd

extrication permits.

TRANSPORT.

(1) Pack animals No 1, 3 packed complete for bridging. 9.15 AM

Pack animals No 4 at time ordered by Lt KELLY. (as above)

(2)(a) Toolcarts 1, 2, 3 + 4 Sections 3 p.m.

(b) Limbers do. 3 p.m.

(returning on completion about 11 p.m.)

(c Trestle Wagons as ordered by 2nd in Comd for bridging material, horses remaining forward.

(3) Horses Following will go forward:

O.C. 2. Capt 2. all Section Officers!

SYNCHRONISATION OF WATCHES

Capt SANDFORD will hold himself in readiness to be at H.Q. 1st Inf. B'de at H.5 b 3.3. at 1 p.m. and 7 p.m. and is responsible for passing same on to Officers + CSM

– Watches must be set to correct time

16/9/18 Signed Gulf Findlay Major R.E.

O.C. 409th (Lowland) Field Coy. R.E.

Cy 1st

<u>Special Parties</u>

(1) Sappers Gilmour and Cutsnithly will remain in Camp and act as guides as required.

(2) Capt. SANDFORD will detail two mounted orderlies after noon to proceed to forward billets and learn location of H.Q.

(3) Lt NISBET and party of No 2 Section required to reconnoitre new area.

X. Mtd N.C.O. of No 2 Section to accompany Lt NISBET and learn route.

(4) A party of Q.O.R. detailed by No 2 Section — 9.15 A.M. Work cutting out tin drums, working in two parties, each

X. party to have tools.

(5) Nos 1, 3 & 4 Sections will each detail 1 Junior N.C.O. & 1 Sapper. Parade 9.15 A.M. at disposal of Capt. to learn assembly of cork bridge.

(6) Capt will arrange reconnaissance of approaches to new billets and dumps, by Mtd N.C.O's

X. Will move direct to new billets on completion.

Cont'd

MEALS.

Breakfasts as usual.

Dinners. – Nos 3 + 1 – Haversack Ration

Nos 2 + 4. under Section arrangt.

TEAS. – Nos 1 + 3 in large hollow NORTH of bridging site + limbers to arrive 3.30 p.m.

Breakfast 18/9/18 probably before dawn.

Dinner. Sections to arrange a cold dinner.

GENERAL

(1) Bivouacs of all Sections to be struck + handed in before moving out.

(2) On 18/9/18 packs will not be carried, but will be dumped at assembly point. Haversacks containing Emergency ration and unexpended portion of days ration will be carried, remaining articles as ordered by Section Officers.

(3) Packs containing great coats will be with men on night 17/9/18, also on 18/9/18 situation permitting.

Moving to forward billets packs to be carried on limbers which will be loaded before moving out.

(4) Blankets packed in Sandbag, as Standing Order, one bag per two men, will be left behind to come forward as soon as

Copy

Company Orders for 17-9-18

General Parade 9 a.m. Dress any coats or hats need not be worn. Respirators carried.

Movement. (1) H.Qrs, Nos 1, 2, 3, & 4 Sections less limbers will move to new locations, which will be reached in evening. approx. distance 5 miles.

(2) H.Q. Personnel & Transport & limbers will remain in present billets and be prepared to move on or after 18/9/18 on receipt of orders from H.Q. This detachment will come under orders of Capt SANDFORD R.E. from time H.Q. moves forward.

(3) No 2 Section will be detached from Company as regards billets.

WORKS on 17/9/18.

(a) Nos 1 & 3 Sections Parade 9.15 A.M. Complete Bridge commenced by No 3 Section to day. They will move direct from site of work to new billet area.

(b) No 2 Section less Special Party – 9.15 A.M. at disposal of Captain for loading.

(c) No 4 Section parade at time ordered by Lt Kelly, not before 9.15 A.M. Complete Bridge at R.22a. by dawn 18th and tape out work.

Instructions regarding War Diaries and Intelligence Summaries are contained in F. S. Regs., Part II. and the Staff Manual respectively. Title pages will be prepared in manuscript.

P 2

Army Form C. 2118.

WAR DIARY for Oct
or
INTELLIGENCE SUMMARY.
(Erase heading not required.)

Place	Date	Hour	Summary of Events and Information	Remarks and references to Appendices
PONTRUE	6/10/18	9am	Reveille 9am — Moved back to billets in CAULANCOURT arriving about noon. No 4 Section rejoined company from Bn having spent night at VERMAND — Turn out of mounted section good with about 3 exceptions in HARNESS. Remainder of day rigging up camp till dark.	
CAULANCOURT	7/10/18	09am	Am Free for cleaning up Gas & Rifle Inspection — Gas Officer inspected all helmets. Mounted Section full day in Stables. pm. Football	
	8/10/18	08.30	am. Revetting Stables till 11.30.	
		11.30	one hour Refresher on Pontooning Drill —	
		13.30	Company Sports — fine afternoon — went off excellently and did much to liven men up and prepare them for further tour forward —	
		18.30	Warning Order of possible follow up by bus — prepared list of Tools to carry (a) on man (b) In lorry or bus as H.Q. tools. Pontooning exercise arranged for 9th cancelled.	
	9/10/18	5.30am	Reveille 8.15am Parade for marching out in 2nd Bn Group — Transport by road. Remainder cross country track — March carried out with few checks arriving BELLENGLISE area about 12.30pm. Remainder of daylight settling in ready to move following day —	

Maj. R.E.
O.C. 409th (Lowland) Fd. Coy. R.E.

D. D. & L., London, E.C. (A8001) Wt. W1771/M2031 750,000 5/17 Sch. 52 Forms/C2118/14

Instructions regarding War Diaries and Intelligence Summaries are contained in F. S. Regs., Part II. and the Staff Manual respectively. Title pages will be prepared in manuscript.

WAR DIARY
or
INTELLIGENCE SUMMARY.
(*Erase heading not required.*)

f Oct. P.3

Army Form C. 2118.

Place	Date	Hour	Summary of Events and Information	Remarks and references to Appendices
BELLENGLISE G29 d 0 6	10/10/18	—	No orders for move received — Gas & Rifle Inspection improvement to bivouacs — 42 M.M. recd. for Company Capt Bow, Cpl HUNTER, 2nd Cpl LEGGATE, S/A HUNTER —	
	11/11/18		No orders for move — General parade read out above honours — inspected cycles	
			Cyclist Groups overhauling cycles thoroughly	
			Lewis Guns " overhauling guns & instruction.	
			Rifle " Camp work repairs to [illegible] & Notice Boards.	
FRESNOY LE GRAND	12/11/18	—	Moved by route march to FRESNOY LE GRAND for work on forward roads. Billets found very good also stabling and large quantities of forage.	
	13th 14th 15		Work on Roads in vicinity. Cutting out & filling potholes drainage scraping & relaying pavé — Short hours worked 8 – 1.30 In afternoon football & cleaning up.	
			5pm 15th CRE conference – Plan of attack announced and all details of roles fixed.	
	16th		Work on roads — No 4 Section detached for work under 2nd Bde — orders for attack announced to NCOs at 6 pm. also maps.	

G. E. Knowles(?)
Maj.
O.C. 409th (Lowland) Fd. Coy. R.E.

D. D. & L., London, E.C. (A8004) Wt. W1771/M2031 750,000 5/17 Sch. 52 Forms/C2118/14

October 1918. 409th Lowland Fd Coy RE Army Form C. 2118.

Instructions regarding War Diaries and Intelligence Summaries are contained in F. S. Regs., Part II. and the Staff Manual respectively. Title pages will be prepared in manuscript.

WAR DIARY
or
INTELLIGENCE SUMMARY.
(Erase heading not required.)

Place	Date	Hour	Summary of Events and Information	Remarks and references to Appendices
			Period 17th – 20th BATTLE to reach Oise Canal	
FRESNOY LE GRAND to	16/10/18	2.30pm	No 4 Section moved off to BOHAIN for work under Bde	
BOHAIN	16th	6pm	All NCO's assembled & ground over which we were moving carefully explained on map	
	17/10/18	2.30am	No 2 Section moved forward to BUSIGNY arriving 7am at disposal of RFA to assist in getting forward the guns	
		6.45am	Company less 2 Sections moved forward to BOHAIN arriving by 9am time of assembly.	
			Role of Company (less two Sections) under orders of CRE – O.C. to move A Echelon at his discretion according to situation, keeping in touch with Bde but under orders of CRE.	
			First reports recd about 8.30am that attack was progressing & Bde HQ had moved to VAUX ANDIGNY Quarry – Decided to move up to ~~just the neighbourhood~~ – Placed 2nd in Command to move moving off 10am with orders to rendezvous just Eof of VAUX ANDIGNY where we would stop unless he received further orders there. O.C. went forward with orderlies (cyclist) to find out situation – Company arrived 12 noon – Cook Dinner & Feed	
		2pm	Party out reconnoitring VAUX-ANDIGNY for wells, cellars, etc, mines – Party went forward to see ground and reconnaissance if situation permitted it did NOT	

(A9175) Wt W2358/P360 600,000 12/17 D. D. & L. Sch 52a. Forms/C2118/15

Maj. R.E.
O.C. 409th (Lowland) Fd. Coy. R.E.

Instructions regarding War Diaries and Intelligence Summaries are contained in F. S. Regs., Part II. and the Staff Manual respectively. Title pages will be prepared in manuscript.

WAR DIARY for October
or
INTELLIGENCE SUMMARY.
(Erase heading not required.)

Army Form C. 2118.

Place	Date	Hour	Summary of Events and Information	Remarks and references to Appendices
VAUX ANDIGNY	17/10/18	10pm	1 NCO & 3 men sent out to barricade bridge over railway demolished & dangerous	
			Action of No 2 & 4 Sections in this Day's battle at VAUX ANDIGNY	
			No 2 Section – reconnaissance for crossing place over SELLE RIVER for guns ½ section ramping down and making place practicable for guns which all used it. Remainder of Section NOT employed	
			No 4 Section	
			Marched from BOHAIN 7.30 – to VAUX ANDIGNY NOT required by Bde. Bivouaced for night in trench shelters.	
			"B" Echelon & Bridging Vehicles left at BOHAIN.	
	18/10/18		Further attack in morning – Employment.	
			No 1 Section opening out Spring – No 3 Section improving & repairing wells & searching railway for mines – No 2 Section reported for Bn. repairing holes in road.	
			No 4 Section small party forward assisting Battalion –	
			Reconnaissance General of forward area by O.C. with a view to next move	
			Detailed Search of Railway for mines – Reconnaissance of VAUX MULARONE for wells & mines.	

(A9175) Wt W2358/P360 600,000 12/17 D. D. & L. Sch 52a. Forms/C2118/15

Maj. R.E.
O.C. 409th (Lowland) Fd. Coy. R.E.

46

Instructions regarding War Diaries and Intelligence Summaries are contained in F. S. Regs., Part II. and the Staff Manual respectively. Title pages will be prepared in manuscript.

409th F.C. RE

WAR DIARY or INTELLIGENCE SUMMARY.

for October

(*Erase heading not required.*)

Army Form C. 2118.

Place	Date	Hour	Summary of Events and Information	Remarks and references to Appendices
VAUX ANDIGNY to VALLEE MULATRE	19/10/18		An advance taking place commencing 5-30am to reach Canal – In view of possibility of crossing it was considered advisable to be within working distance of canal –	
		13.30	Paraded Company & Details ... Section & moved into billets in VALLEE MULATRE — Got in touch with Bde	
			Party sent out to make good crossing at [illegible] where preparations for demolition had been made.	
		2.30pm	General mounted reconnaissance of whole of forward area by each of two officers mainly with a view to approach routes for pontoons. Remainder improving & tidying up billets	
	20/10/18		Work on roads south of VALLEE MULATRE – Party on improving billets. No 2 Sect – moved up with Bde HQ to near RIBAUVILLE – cut gaps in hedges & laid out tape avoiding track from Bde to Coy HQ – 3 men wounded in billets	
	21/10/18		Work on road from VALLEE MULATRE to [illegible] – road showing heavy signs of wear. One sect erecting horse troughs – Party reconnoitring railway for mines removed one charge of 100 lbs perdite – Reconnaissance of [illegible] forward area ... Detailed reconnaissance of [illegible] & Guise[?] + RIBAUVILLE for wells & accommodation — 2 men wounded on railway	

G.E. [illegible] Major

Maj. R.E.
O.C. 409th (Lowland) Fd. Coy. R.E.

(A9175) Wt W2358/P360 600,000 12/17 D. D. & L. Sch. 53a. Forms/C2118/15

Instructions regarding War Diaries and Intelligence Summaries are contained in F. S. Regs., Part II. and the Staff Manual respectively. Title pages will be prepared in manuscript.

Army Form C. 2118.

P 4

WAR DIARY
or
INTELLIGENCE SUMMARY.
(Erase heading not required.)

Place	Date	Hour	Summary of Events and Information	Remarks and references to Appendices
Vallée Mulâtre	22/10/18		No 4 Section with 2nd Bde H.Q. — Party from No 1 Section completing railway reconnaissance report — 1 party completing Horse troughs and taking measurements for Heavy Bridge 15 ft span — eventually done by A.T. Coy R.E. Remainder work on roads using 3 limbers for bricks & stone.	Appendix C Reconnaissance
	23/10/18		No 4 Section still detached — 1 squad collecting barrels for bridging. Remainder on roads — Drainage — Rehaunching & reshaping & filling potholes. 4 carts on roads — average of 30% — No 4 Section rejoined midday	
	~~24/10/18~~		Employment of No 4 Section when detached. 22nd Reconnaissance of ground forward — 23rd/24th Taping out jumping off line for Inf Attack — Improvement to Bde, Bn, & Coy H.Q. —	
	25/10/18		All 4 Sections on roads with 5 vehicles. (No 4 from 2 pm).	
	26/10/18		— — — — — (Experiments with Bridges) ~~[illegible]~~	
	27/10/18		Ditto till midday pm free.	
	28/10/18 29/10/18 30/10/18 31/10/18		Ditto Coy joined making portable bridges 23 ft span	

[illegible signature]
Maj. R.E.
O.C. 409th (Lowland) Fd. Coy. R.E.

D. D. & L., London, E.C. (A8001) Wt. W1771/M2031 750,000 5/17 Sch. 52 Forms/C2118/14

Appendix A.

Army Form C. 2118.

Instructions regarding War Diaries and Intelligence Summaries are contained in F. S. Regs., Part II. and the Staff Manual respectively. Title pages will be prepared in manuscript.

WAR DIARY
or
INTELLIGENCE SUMMARY.

(Erase heading not required.)

Place	Date	Hour	Summary of Events and Information	Remarks and references to Appendices
PONTRU WATER POINT.			<u>Police Control Required</u> - of traffic control on approach roads. (1) One man at each water point A, B, C, D & E. —— total five. Main duties:—(1) Organise waiting parties. (2) " watering parties approaching and leaving. (3) See that all hand pumps are continuously manned and troughs kept full. (2) Two men for groups A, B, E, D to organise approaching parties and turn back people going wrong ways. (3) Two men for groups C. & F. and regulating and splitting parties coming in from NORTH so as to divide it evenly between all troughing. See that Source is not polluted. (4) One selected N.C.O. in general charge. <u>Technical Maintenance</u>. Parties required to keep this temporary point in smooth running order, which is essential, if horses are to be kept in condition and clean drinking water supplied. <u>GANG I</u> 1 N.C.O. + 8 men. — Inspection, running repairs + replacements of HAND PUMPS, HOSES, TROUGHS, & STAND PIPES. <u>GANG II</u> 1 N.C.O. + 4 men, and unskilled labour as required. Upkeep of Notice Boards and approaches, bridges, level crossings of swampy places, and fences. <u>GANG III</u> 1 N.C.O. & 6 men. General larger replacements, cleaning out troughs periodically, assisting with engine repairs, filter arrangements round Suctions.	

D. D. & L., London, E.C.
(A8001) Wt. W1771/M2031 750,000 5/17 Sch. 52 Forms/C2118/14

Instructions regarding War Diaries and Intelligence Summaries are contained in F. S. Regs., Part II. and the Staff Manual respectively. Title pages will be prepared in manuscript.

WAR DIARY
or
INTELLIGENCE SUMMARY.
(Erase heading not required.)

Army Form C. 2118.

Place	Date	Hour	Summary of Events and Information	Remarks and references to Appendices
CON'TD				
PONTRU			SUMMARY OF WORK & SCOPE DONE.	
WATER POINT			"A" DRINKING WATER Installing 2 PELAPONE sets with hose	
			8 Hand Pumps with hose.	
			10 Barrels or filters vice roses.	
			STANDING. Standpipes + timber for shed-beds salved.	
			"B" HORSE WATER (1) Temporary erection of 20 troughs.	
			(2) Salving timber and fixing permanent rails.	
			(3) Fixing 20 pumps with hose.	
			Protecting hose under Standing.	
			(4) Installing 4 PELAPONE Sets + erecting Sheds.	
			(5) Standings. Filling in shell holes.	
			(6) Approaches. Ramp over dry bed of stream + later culvert.	
			"C" GENERAL (1) Notice Boards over 70.	
			(2) Loading + unloading above stores + bricks	
			SITUATION. If properly controlled + maintained Horse Water is now satisfactory in	
			dry weather. Drinking Water requires another days work to make it so.	
			at present it is NOT satisfactory.	

(A9175) Wt W2358/P360 600,000 12/17 D. D. & L. Sch 52a. Forms/C2118/15

Instructions regarding War Diaries and Intelligence Summaries are contained in F. S. Regs., Part II. and the Staff Manual respectively. Title pages will be prepared in manuscript.

WAR DIARY
or
INTELLIGENCE SUMMARY.
(Erase heading not required.)

Army Form C. 2118.

Place	Date	Hour	Summary of Events and Information	Remarks and references to Appendices
CONT^D				
PONTRU			SCHEME FOR PERMANENT SUPPLY.	
WATER POINT.			A. PERMANENT.	
			(1) The whole supply could be run from the Source by two 5000 gal. per hour sets with Storage Capacity of — In Troughs 12000 gals. In Tanks 20,000 gals.	
			ASSUMPTION 12000 horses in 6 hrs @ 8 gals. = 80,000 2 Div's (Drinking) · 40,000 120,000	
			Approx. piping — 4" 1000 yds. 2" 500 ft. with fittings	
			(2). Storage Tanks 4 (30 × 30) sited on hill South of River in L between MAISSEMY & PONTRU roads.	
			(3) Troughs remain as at present, cutting out group D entirely + putting it alongside of Group C Water Carts at E & G.	
			B Recommended if expected to last over 3 weeks. On a smaller scale it would save much maintenance to put in 4" Distribution + 2" Service pipes to all troughs and Stand-pipes, which could eventually be incorporated in more permanent Supply Scheme.	

(A9475) Wt W2358/P360 600,000 12/17 D. D. & L. Sch. 52a. Forms/C2118/15

Instructions regarding War Diaries and Intelligence Summaries are contained in F. S. Regs., Part II, and the Staff Manual respectively. Title pages will be prepared in manuscript.

WAR DIARY
or
INTELLIGENCE SUMMARY.
(*Erase heading not required.*)

Army Form C. 2118.

Place	Date	Hour	Summary of Events and Information	Remarks and references to Appendices
CONTD.				
PONTRU	4/10/17		CENSUS. I HORSES. — Note on 8/10/17 between 7 & 8000 horses watered between 5am & 7am	
WATER POINT			GROUP "A" 6,410	
			" "B" (FRENCH.) 3,950 All by 5 hand pumps	
			" "C" 3525	
			" "D" 5,111	
			18,996	
			Estimated broken into stream 500	
			Estimated during night. 100	
			Approx. 20,000.	
			All parties asked were watering twice only.	
			II DRINKING	
			Right round circuit at Group E. 120 Carts. (Many were FRENCH 200 gals)	
			Estimated at River side 60 "	
			Above is I think, rather low, as owing to work some Carts returned the way they entered thus missing count.	
			In addition about 200 dixies were filled with Sterilised Water.	

(A9175) Wt W2358/P360 600,000 12/17 D. D. & L. Sch. 52a. Forms/C2118/15

Instructions regarding War Diaries and Intelligence Summaries are contained in F. S. Regs., Part II. and the Staff Manual respectively. Title pages will be prepared in manuscript.

WAR DIARY
or
INTELLIGENCE SUMMARY.
(Erase heading not required.)

Appendix B.

Army Form C. 2118.

Place	Date	Hour	Summary of Events and Information	Remarks and references to Appendices
			Summary of Reconnaissance Reports sent in 1st Oct – 5th Oct while advancing	
	29/30/9/18		Road Report round PONTRUET ———— Capt RHIND RE(T)	
			Water Report forward of BERTHAUCOURT. – – – do. from observation & summary of Reports.	
	1/10/18		General Reconnaissance from PONTRUET to LETRONQUOY Maj FINDLAY. RE	
			Road, Water reconnaissance of LEVERGIES Area —— 2nd Lt LESSATE RE	
			" " " " BELLENGLISE LEHAUCOURT Area – Capt RHIND RE(T)	
			REPORT with plan of LE TRONQUOY TUNNEL. —— Lt KELLY RE(T)	
			G. C. Findlay Maj RE OC 409 F.C.	
			..........Maj. R.E. O.C. 409th (Lowland) Fd. Coy. R.E.	

D. D. & L., London, E.C. (A8001) Wt. W1771/M2031 750,000 5/17 Sch. 52 Forms/C2118/14

Instructions regarding War Diaries and Intelligence Summaries are contained in F. S. Regs., Part II. and the Staff Manual respectively. Title pages will be prepared in manuscript.

WAR DIARY
or
INTELLIGENCE SUMMARY.
(Erase heading not required.)

Appendix C

Army Form C. 2118.

Place	Date	Hour	Summary of Events and Information	Remarks and references to Appendices
			RECONNAISSANCES of CANAL & Approaches to it	
			24th Immediately after attack by Cpl Bowes — Information obtained re approach roads but military situation did not allow of reaching Canal, area CATILLON	
			25th & 26th/27th By Cpl McLachlan & L/Cpl Stevens with Spr Russell — Approaches to and vicinity of Lock including direct view of bank from short distance	
			28th/29th By Cpl McLachlan & L/Cpl Stevens with Infantry Patrol. Point where road to Lock crosses Stream West of Canal definite information re gap in road —	
			29th/30th [illegible] & Patrick [illegible] vicinity of Lock generally direct view of bank & Stream on West side approaches to canal bank about 200 yds North of Lock and view of Canal. [illegible] Cpl McLachlan & L/Cpl Stevens — reconnaissance of assembly position South of Lock — Road to Lock & Stream just North of Road & possibility of approaching Lock with bridges under cover of Canal Bank — Approach road to Lock reconnoitred throughout length —	

[signature]

Maj. R.E.
O.C. 409th (Lowland) Fd. Coy. R.E.

D. D. & L., London, E.C.
(A8004) Wt. W1771/M2031 750,000 5/17 Sch. 52 Forms/C2118/14

Instructions regarding War Diaries and Intelligence Summaries are contained in F. S. Regs., Part II. and the Staff Manual respectively. Title pages will be prepared in manuscript.

WAR DIARY
or
INTELLIGENCE SUMMARY.
(*Erase heading not required.*)

Army Form C. 2118.

Appendix D p. 1

Place	Date	Hour	Summary of Events and Information	Remarks and references to Appendices
			Lessons in Active Operations from an R.E. point of view from 1st Oct to 31st Oct	
	1		Certain work can be foreseen, many other things cannot be —	
			(a) Foreseen work can & should be allotted to Companies definitely.	
			If small on the area system, if large it may be necessary to allot	
			a definite major task to another Company.	
			(b) Unforeseen including work which is foreseen generally in area but of which	
			the detailed location only is known after the advance.	
			(i) For this ~~[illegible]~~ as the work is to be done at	
			once there is NOT time to refer to Division and such references may	
			entail men sitting idle when useful work could be done at a convenient time	
			when it may have to be done later ~~[illegible]~~ under less suitable conditions —	
			It seems necessary therefore to delegate authority to Company Commanders as was done	
			to undertake such work within certain limits in a given area.	
			(c) As to [illegible] [illegible] [illegible] [illegible] [illegible] [illegible]	
			[illegible] that are [illegible] different from that [illegible] in [illegible]	
			in giving effect to above —	
			[signature] Maj. R.E. O.C. 409th (Lowland) Fd. Coy. R.E.	

(A9475) Wt W2358/P360 600,000 12/17 D. D. & L. Sch. 52a. Forms/C2118/15

Instructions regarding War Diaries and Intelligence Summaries are contained in F. S. Regs., Part II. and the Staff Manual respectively. Title pages will be prepared in manuscript.

409TH (LOWLAND) FIELD COMPANY, R.E.
No. ....
Date ....

WAR DIARY
or
INTELLIGENCE SUMMARY.
(Erase heading not required.)

Army Form C. 2118.

Place	Date	Hour	Summary of Events and Information	Remarks and references to Appendices
			Difficulties – Practice	
			The experience of the recent operations is that from the point of view of [illegible] it is necessary to change infantry at different times and more frequently than the R.E. Also that boundaries alter frequently – also the infantry moving up before considerable R.E. energy has to be expended in reconnaissance – It is therefore desirable not to change with [illegible] unless the information is lost —	
			The greatest difficulty with changing boundaries is overlapping as [illegible] if a man finds his work is being passed over by some one else it tends to [illegible] reconnaissance and consequently loss of work — It also causes doubt as to who should undertake work which leads to hanging back or nothing is more discouraging to men to find they have been turned out for a job and on arrival find some one else has the job —	
			Cases occurred both with Officers of Corps and other units when situation was changing rapidly and boundaries with it and invariably Bdes and RE unit must be prepared for it and recognise it as with infantry.	
			[illegible] Maj R.E. O.C. 409th [illegible]	

(A9175) Wt W2358/P360 600,000 12/17 D. D. & L. Sch 52a. Forms/C2118/15

Instructions regarding War Diaries and Intelligence Summaries are contained in F. S. Regs., Part II. and the Staff Manual respectively. Title pages will be prepared in manuscript.

409TH (LOWLAND) FIELD COMPANY, R.E.
No. ....

WAR DIARY
or
INTELLIGENCE SUMMARY.
(*Erase heading not required.*)

Appendix D

Army Form C. 2118.

Place	Date	Hour	Summary of Events and Information	Remarks and references to Appendices
			Moves & position of RE Company	
Position			In order to keep in touch with situation it is very desirable that Coy HQ and the Company should be in vicinity of Bde HQ in whose area they are working —	
			This position in practice has been found suitable for launching out working parties and reconnaissance parties —	
			On the other hand when Coy HQ got separated by a long distance from Bde HQ it was found very difficult to keep in touch with situation.	
Moves			During movement warfare touch has to be maintained between [illegible] Bde HQ, Rear Echelon of Coy, detached sections for purpose of rations. This involves a heavy drain on strength for orderlies [illegible] —	
			When splitting [illegible] takes place a free use of [illegible] is necessary [illegible] an economy but it is a sufficiently large question to cause detachments & splitting of Company to be considered in this light —	
			Detail With [illegible] 2 [illegible] [illegible] Communication with rear echelon [illegible] [illegible] are often separated [illegible] [illegible] similarly — Also each detachment [illegible] [illegible] gas protection —	

[signature] O.C. 409th (Lowland) Fd. Coy. R.E.

(A9175) Wt W2358/P360 600,000 12/17 D. D. & L. Sch 52a. Forms/C2118/15

Instructions regarding War Diaries and Intelligence Summaries are contained in F. S. Regs., Part II. and the Staff Manual respectively. Title pages will be prepared in manuscript.

Secret

409TH (LOWLAND) FIELD COMPANY, R.E.
No. ....
Date ....

WAR DIARY
or
INTELLIGENCE SUMMARY.
(Erase heading not required.)

Army Form C. 2118.

Appendix 2

Place	Date	Hour	Summary of Events and Information	Remarks and references to Appendices
			Attachment of Sections to Brigades	
			1) From the administrative point of view & communication there is [illegible]	
			To avoid overlapping of work [illegible] within [illegible] one Company when [illegible]	
			or attached company within the same area under different orders is very	
			difficult & involves a considerable amount of extra work & [illegible]	
			~~[illegible] changes~~ and private arrangements with attached sections [illegible]	
			keeps more or less together [illegible] extra work [illegible]	
			When O.C. changes & the section belongs to another Company it is	
			almost impossible to avoid overlapping —	
			2) It is the exception to have all one's officers available — a detached	
			Section or 2 sections ties up a section officer or two often on trivial	
			jobs NOT requiring an officer — the O.C. has not then got all his officers at	
			his disposal and cannot adjust the strain on officers & men evenly; each detachment	
			has to keep in touch with situation which increases officers work —	
			This curtails his latitude for ensuring efficient working of his company and from	
			the company commanders point of view it is not satisfactory and the experience of	
			last operations was that frequently they were not fully employed —	

[illegible signature]
Major R.E.
O.C. 409th (Lowland) Fd. Coy. R.E.

(A9175) Wt W2358/P560 600,000 12/17 D. D. & L. Sch 52a. Forms/C2118/15

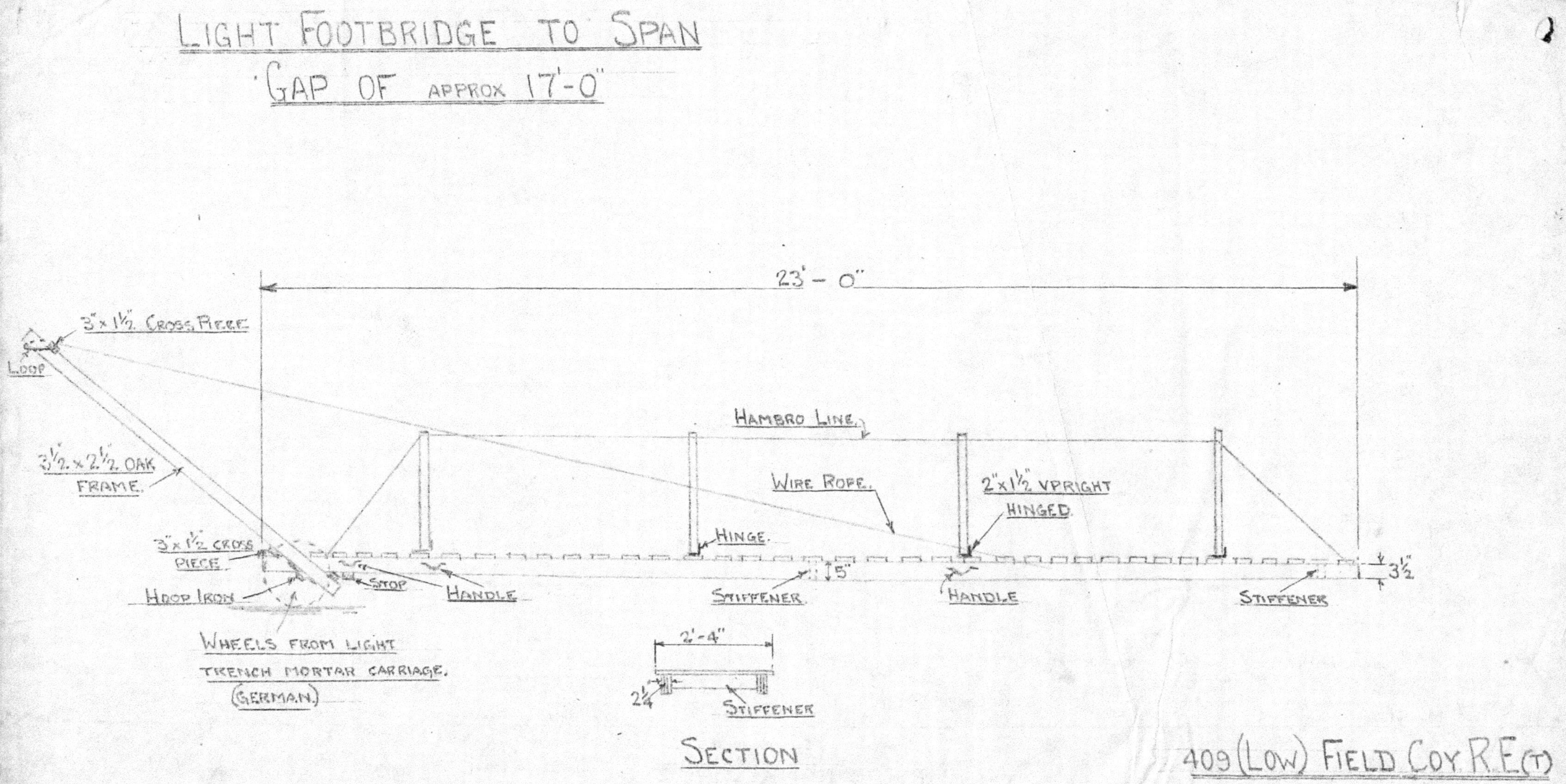
LIGHT FOOTBRIDGE TO SPAN
GAP OF APPROX 17'-0"
23' - 0"
3" x 1½ CROSS PIECE
LOOP
3½ x 2½ OAK FRAME.
HAMBRO LINE.
WIRE ROPE.
2" x 1½" UPRIGHT HINGED.
HINGE.
3" x 1½ CROSS PIECE
HOOP IRON
STOP
HANDLE
5"
STIFFENER
HANDLE
STIFFENER
3½
WHEELS FROM LIGHT TRENCH MORTAR CARRIAGE. (GERMAN.)
2'-4"
2¼
STIFFENER
SECTION
409 (LOW) FIELD COY. R.E. (T)

409th (LOWLAND) Fd Coy RE

1st Div

WAR DIARY for November 1918
or
INTELLIGENCE SUMMARY.
(Erase heading not required.)

Army Form C. 2118.

Instructions regarding War Diaries and Intelligence Summaries are contained in F. S. Regs., Part II. and the Staff Manual respectively. Title pages will be prepared in manuscript.

Vol 47

Place	Date	Hour	Summary of Events and Information	Remarks and references to Appendices
VALLEE-MULATRE N.N.E. of BOHAIN	1/11/18	—	The whole company (less a small party doing essential repairs to roads) employed making 30 bridges for crossing of SAMBRE OISE Canal at the Lock de Bois de l'Abbaye — Capt RHIND superintending all construction — Lt Kelly getting in touch with Battalions over details of covering parties etc.	Detail drawings of bridges — Appendix A Part VII
		5.30pm	Brigade Conference, COs Bns & attached units to discuss and settle outstanding points — Scheme for attack on 4th inst.	
		8pm–10pm	After conference visited CO & went over scheme & settled details of carrying parties with him & Brigadier. Lt Elmslie returned from leave.	
	2/11/18	10.30am	Demonstration under Lt Kelly of bridges & method of placing same. Whole Company employed in making bridges —	
		1.30pm	Final inspection of assembly sites for company & settling of details — Lt Elmslie shewn all details of ground & scheme for whole company which was previously known to Lt Kelly RE & reconnoitred by him — Mounted & dismounted guides taken up to see ground & dump sites. —	
		9pm	Lt Elmslie & Cpl Dow went out on reconnaissance to obtain if possible definite information re best site to place bridges — a thick mist prevented this — Returned about 3am —	

D. D. & L., London, E.C. (A7094) Wt. W1-71/M2031 750,000 5/17 Sch. 52 Forms C2118/14

409 (Lowland) Fd Coy RE

WAR DIARY for November
or
INTELLIGENCE SUMMARY.
(*Erase heading not required.*)

Army Form C. 2118.

P. 2

Instructions regarding War Diaries and Intelligence Summaries are contained in F. S. Regs., Part II. and the Staff Manual respectively. Title pages will be prepared in manuscript.

Place	Date	Hour	Summary of Events and Information	Remarks and references to Appendices
VALLÉE MULÂTRE	3/11/18		Completed making bridges – Loaded same on transport – Delivered to dumps selected near assembly position – Company moved to assembly position near Lock.	Appendix A Pts I–VI Gives all details of crossing
	4/11/18	5.45 – 6.10 6.10 to 8.30 8.30 5? 11.30 am	Passage of Lock de Bois l'ABBAYE. – Maintenance till relieved by 26 Fd Coy RE. Return to Billets in Vallée Mulâtre about 11.30 am; last party 1 pm	
	5/11/18.		Resting – Checking Casualties and tracing missing. – Summary of Casualties Killed 1 off 10 OR. Wounded to hospital 2 off 13 OR Wounded at Duty 1 off 6 OR Total 33 all Ranks 45% of numbers engaged. – Nominal Roll attached.	Appendix A Part VIII
	6/11/18.		Proceeded by route march from VALLÉE-MULÂTRE to FRESNOY-LE-GRAND. Billets good –	
FRESNOY LE GRAND.	7/11/18		Clean up – Rifle & Respirator Inspection, Football in afternoon. –	
"	8/11/18.		Repairs to Own billets & Brigade Billets	
"	9/11/18		ditto	

D. D. & L., London, E.C.
(A8031) Wt. W1771/M2031 750,000 5/17 Sch. 52 Forms C2118/14

409 Lowland Fd Coy RE

App 3

WAR DIARY of November
or
INTELLIGENCE SUMMARY.
(*Erase heading not required.*)

Army Form C. 2118.

Instructions regarding War Diaries and Intelligence Summaries are contained in F. S. Regs., Part II. and the Staff Manual respectively. Title pages will be prepared in manuscript.

Place	Date	Hour	Summary of Events and Information	Remarks and references to Appendices
FRESNOY LE GRAND	10/11/18	10.30 am	Divisional Memorial & Thanksgiving Service attended by Detachment representing all units.	
		11.45 am	Company Memorial Service held by Capt Madian attd unit	
		pm.	Football match v. 26 Fd Coy RE. won 5 goals to nil	
			OC. visited proposed ranges with Bde Major & prepared scheme for developing Ranges	
	11/11/18		All company employed in two groups (a) Making Targets & accessories in camp and 1 Galloway RE. (b) Laying out Range & Firing Point & Supervising Infantry working Party of 120 OR.	
		1.30 pm	General Parade Announced officially the Armistice.	Divisional Concert party performing close by — 2 Sectns held concert in billets —
		pm	Completed Ranges ready for use on Tuesday.	
	12/11/18		Warning order for move recd packing done	
		pm.	Football v. Signals — Result Draw 1 goal all	

[illegible] Capt RE

D. D. & L., London, E.C.
(A6031) Wt. W1771/M2031 750,000 5/17 Sch. 52 Forms C2118/14

Instructions regarding War Diaries and Intelligence Summaries are contained in F. S. Regs., Part II, and the Staff Manual respectively. Title pages will be prepared in manuscript.

WAR DIARY
or
INTELLIGENCE SUMMARY.
(Erase heading not required.)

(P.4)

Army Form C. 2118.

Place	Date	Hour	Summary of Events and Information	Remarks and references to Appendices
			MARCH to RHINE	
FRESNOY LE GRAND	13/11/18	6.40	Reveille — Company moved to billets in SAMBRETON 3 miles W of FAVRIL	
To (20 miles)			Dismounted portion by BUS — Transport by road — Bridging Wagons	
FAVRIL area			stopped empty to Canal OISE-SAMBRE dismantled Bridging Equipment	
			which was in Bridge and rejoined Company at Billets	
SAMBRETON	14/11/18		All Bridging Equipment cleaned up & wagons cleaned & greased —	
			Afternoon Officers & Cpls visited Bridges over canal and there the graves of	
			comrades fallen — the missing man was traced —	
			Interesting talks to inhabitants who were very pleased to be in command	
To	15/11/18	9am	Company marched to billets in farm at main Xroads ½ Mile N.E. of St HILAIRE	
DOMPIERRES area (14 miles)			arriving 5pm — On march a diversion round crater in road had to be made for	
			PONTOONS taking about 1 hour. — No men fell out on march	
			Again outstanding feature was welcome of inhabitants whose unfeigned relief	
			at being again free was most evident.	

(A9175) Wt W2358/P360 600,000 12/17 D. D. & L. Sch. 52a. Forms/C2118/15

Instructions regarding War Diaries and Intelligence Summaries are contained in F. S. Regs., Part II, and the Staff Manual respectively. Title pages will be prepared in manuscript.

WAR DIARY for November
or
INTELLIGENCE SUMMARY.
(*Erase heading not required.*)

Army Form C. 2118.

Place	Date	Hour	Summary of Events and Information	Remarks and references to Appendices
to			MARCH to RHINE (Continued)	
SARS POTERIES 10 mile	16/11/18	9.35	Company vacated billets & moved to SARS POTERIES to billets, all horses in stables — No falling out on march — a very uneventful march arrived 2.30pm — Country shews few positive signs of war this side now except for Craters & Bridges blown by Enemy, even also negative No Cows No horses, No pasture, No implements, inhabitants No Resources necessities only in food & fuel — Again inhabitants very pleased to see us billeting officers much difficulty as each house insisted on drinks & everybody accepting Cups of Coffee their only beverage	
Sunday	17/11/18	am	Resting Cleaning & greasing wagons — 6 pm Church Service (Voluntary) Waiting orders for move following day next. 1st Division now taken its place at head of British Army leading the advance on its portion of front — Certain orders issued regarding Military Precautions to be observed —	

[illegible signatures]

(A9175) W1 W2358/P360 600,000 12/17 D. D. & L. Sch 52a. Forms/C2118/15

Lieut

409 (Lowland) F Coy RE.

WAR DIARY for November
or
~~INTELLIGENCE SUMMARY~~.
(Erase heading not required.)

Army Form C. 2118.

* Instructions regarding War Diaries and Intelligence Summaries are contained in F. S. Regs., Part II. and the Staff Manual respectively. Title pages will be prepared in manuscript.

Place	Date	Hour	Summary of Events and Information	Remarks and references to Appendices
SARS POTERIES.	18/11/18	08.15	Marching out parade – Company proceeded by route march via: DOULERS, BEAUMONT & DONSTIENNES – First British troops to enter village and were given a great welcome. – Mines reported. distance (14 to 16 miles)	
DONSTIENNES	19/11/18	0900	Marching out parade – Company moved by march route via ROGNEE to PRY (distance 8 miles) – 80% of sappers searching for & removing mines	
PRY.	20/11/18		Mtd Section Normal Routine. Dismtd: Rifle inspection Gas inspection & overhaul of equipment. Work on Road	
	21/11/18		Mounted – routine – Stripped harness inspection in afternoon. Ten officers saddlery all officers attended. Dismtd: Cleaning personal & Coy equipment. foot inspection Pay	
	22/11/18		as for 21/11/18 harness being officers & fitting of saddlery	
St AUBIN	23/11/18		Company moved by march route to St AUBIN (10 miles) & halted for night – wagons washed –	
"	24/11/18		Company moved to FTER by march route (10 miles) – STANDARD table for marching out appended:	Appendix B.
FTER.	25/11/18		At FTER – Cleaning up & polishing –	
	26/11/18		Lieut R A GALLOWAY appointed 2nd in Cmd of Coy with acting rank of Capt. Company awarded 2 Bars to MM & 16 Military Medals for work at Bridging Canal	Appendix C. List attached

[signature]

A5834 Wt. W4973/M687 750,000 8/16 D. D. & L. Ltd. Forms/C.2118/13.

409 (Lowland) Fd Coy RE

Instructions regarding War Diaries and Intelligence Summaries are contained in F. S. Regs., Part II. and the Staff Manual respectively. Title pages will be prepared in manuscript.

WAR DIARY for November 1918
or
INTELLIGENCE SUMMARY.
(Erase heading not required.)

Army Form C. 2118.

Place	Date	Hour	Summary of Events and Information	Remarks and references to Appendices
FTER	27/11/18		Cleaning & Polishing Company Equipment to raise it to peace footing – Visit by CRE inspection of Arms	
	28th		ditto – one wagon painted – &	
	29th		am. Cleaning Transport & Equipment pm 6 mile Route March – Limber Painted. Visit by [illegible]	
	30th		Cleaning up Transport & pm. Recreation – Visit by Brig Gen Cmdg 2nd Bde	

30/11/18

[illegible]
Major RE
O.C. 409 [illegible]

D. D. & L., London, E.C.
(A5034) Wt. W1771/M2031 750,000 5/17 Sch. 52 Forms C2118/14

Army Form C. 2118.

Instructions regarding War Diaries and Intelligence Summaries are contained in F. S. Regs., Part II. and the Staff Manual respectively. Title pages will be prepared in manuscript.

WAR DIARY
or
INTELLIGENCE SUMMARY.
(*Erase heading not required.*)

Place	Date	Hour	Summary of Events and Information	Remarks and references to Appendices
			Appendix A Crossing of Oise Sambre Canal	
			at the Lock [illegible]	
			Part I. Reconnaissance, Plan & Preparation	
			Part II. Assembly	
			Part III. Execution	
			A. Advance to first stream & reconnaissance	
			B. Crossing first stream [illegible]	for Infantry
			C. Crossing Canal at Lock [illegible] 17' [illegible]	Lock [illegible]
			D. CROSSING FAR STREAM about 14 ft	
			E. PLACING MULE Bridges	
			Part IV. Maintenance of the Communications	
			Part V. RETURN to BILLETS	
			Part VI. Crossings made by other troops	
			Map	[signature]

(A9175) Wt W2358/P360 600,000 12/17 D. D. & L. Sch 52a. Forms/C2118/15

Instructions regarding War Diaries and Intelligence Summaries are contained in F. S. Regs., Part II. and the Staff Manual respectively. Title pages will be prepared in manuscript.

WAR DIARY
or
INTELLIGENCE SUMMARY.
(Erase heading not required.)

Appendix A
Part I

Army Form C. 2118.

Place	Date	Hour	RECONNAISSANCE PLAN Summary of Events and Information & PREPARATIONS	Remarks and references to Appendices
	Reconnaissance		[illegible] the lock was different from the position as [illegible] the [illegible] and consequently exact information was difficult to obtain —	
			In all 6 close reconnaissances were carried out, 3 by officers, 3 by NCOs — the information [illegible] by them was sufficiently definite to decide on the bridges required and the plan of action —	
	Bridges required		4 [illegible] of [illegible] across [illegible] 8 light [illegible] Bridging [illegible]	
			4 [illegible]	
			2 [illegible] Fete [illegible] 16 / 4 [illegible] Bridges } [illegible]	
			The [illegible] of [illegible] bridges [illegible] streams [illegible] necessary —	
			[illegible] was [illegible] on 30th Nov — Work on these 30 bridges was commenced on	
			31st Nov, [illegible] and finished [illegible] on 3rd [illegible] was available [illegible]	
			[illegible] Capt [illegible] took charge of the [illegible] and [illegible]	
PLAN			[illegible] with infantry was [illegible] in two groups [illegible] 4 [illegible] Stream	
			The distribution of personnel was arranged accordingly — [illegible] Lock / 8 [illegible]	
			Each group was to advance [illegible] and make two [illegible] 4 [illegible] Stream	
			independent crossings at opposite ends of Lock — the section detailed for [illegible] 2 for Lock	
			[illegible] crossings [illegible] passed through [illegible] the sections detailed for [illegible] 4 [illegible] for Lock	
			the first crossings [illegible] bridges [illegible] 6 [illegible] Bridges	
			followed by [illegible] BRIDGES — the plan was explained in detail to all NCOs [illegible] [illegible]	

[illegible]

Instructions regarding War Diaries and Intelligence Summaries are contained in F. S. Regs., Part II. and the Staff Manual respectively. Title pages will be prepared in manuscript.

WAR DIARY
or
INTELLIGENCE SUMMARY.
(Erase heading not required.)

Appendix A
Part II
ASSEMBLY

Army Form C. 2118.

Place	Date	Hour	Summary of Events and Information	Remarks and references to Appendices
			(1) Transport of Bridges to Site	
			4 wagons left under Capt RHIND at 3.30pm [illegible] party	
			The bridges were dumped as arranged [illegible] at X 5 d 7.2	
			and X 6 b [illegible] by 6pm	
			Loading party left [illegible]	
			(2) Remainder of Sappers	
			(a) Paraded 7pm [illegible] with 1 tool cart, 1 limber, 4 wagons with BERTHON Boats [illegible]	
			marched to Bn HQ [illegible]	
			[illegible] arrived dump 9.30pm.	
			(b) Off loaded BERTHON Boats [illegible]	
			[illegible]	
			[illegible]	
			of 23 and officer [illegible]	
			(c) [illegible] Capt RHIND [illegible]	
			(d) [illegible] Breakfast [illegible] 4.30 am [illegible]	
			[illegible]	

(A9475) Wt W2358/P360 600,000 12/17 D. D. & L. Sch 52a. Forms/C2118/15

BERTHON Boats were available [illegible]
all officers were [illegible]

O.C. 409th (Lowland) Fd. Coy. R.E.

P 1

Appendix (A)

Part III (A).

[illegible] Stream [illegible] of Canal [illegible]

Army Form C. 2118.

Instructions regarding War Diaries and Intelligence Summaries are contained in F. S. Regs., Part II. and the Staff Manual respectively. Title pages will be prepared in manuscript.

WAR DIARY
or
INTELLIGENCE SUMMARY.
(Erase heading not required.)

Place	Date	Hour	Summary of Events and Information	Remarks and references to Appendices
[illegible]	[illegible]	0530	Two minutes before zero the Machine Gun barrage from South opened up followed	
			half a minute later by M.G. from the North	
		0545	Artillery barrage opened punctually and fell on line of canal and near bank.	
			The lights were excellent with the exception of one gun on right which was	
			dropping about 100 yds short at [illegible] 05.20 (marked 1 on plan attached)	
			The [illegible] edging towards the North after passing through the gap	
			in [illegible] —	
Start			The Southern party under Capt [illegible] and the 4 Sprs 238 troops under Capt [illegible]	
			were well away at zero and were 50 to 100 yds ahead of the Infantry —	
		0548	At 5.48 the barrage was still on the canal at 5.49 it lifted and fell behind	
		0549	the [illegible] buildings inspection of the ground afterwards confirmed the accuracy of the	
			lift —	
			Simultaneously with this lift the Southern party moved forward to the canal	
			bank — for about half a minute the area was unshelled then the enemy	
			barrage came down [illegible] about 5.50 200 yds clear of canal with [illegible]	
			on the canal bank — up to this time the Southern party had few casualties 2 or 3 men	
			slightly wounded and Capt [illegible] severely wounded by the time he had got his bridges through the	
			[illegible] We will now leave this party with bridges just reaching stream and the [illegible]	
			Northern Group the leading parties of party had just reached the canal bank with [illegible] casualties.	

(A9475) Wt W2358/P360 600,000 12/17 D. D. & L. Sch 52a. Forms/C2118/15

Instructions regarding War Diaries and Intelligence Summaries are contained in F. S. Regs., Part II, and the Staff Manual respectively. Title pages will be prepared in manuscript.

WAR DIARY
or
INTELLIGENCE SUMMARY.
(Erase heading not required.)

Appendix [illegible] Part III C

Army Form C. 2118.

Place	Date	Hour	Summary of Events and Information	Remarks and references to Appendices
			Northern Group consisting of 4 light bridges and 2 ~~heavy~~ 23ft bridges under Lt [illegible]	
			" 2 12ft " under Lt Kelly M.C. R.E.	
			This party also moved out punctually at Zero – they had to cross a small stream & Lt [illegible] had arranged to temporarily utilise two of his light bridges to enable passage of ~~heavy~~ 23ft bridges.	
			These were placed and the first bridge under Cpl [illegible] crossed, the second bridge was just on the point of crossing when an Enemy shell passing over the heads of the leading team put out of action the whole section officer (Lt [illegible]) Sergt. and the whole team except one man. Also the 4 men with the 16ft bridge, thus [illegible] half the bridges from the Northern Group — the remaining two 16ft bridges [illegible] 23ft [illegible] followed by the 23ft bridge moved straight on. Still a 2nd shell [illegible] two men carrying a 16ft bridge [illegible] with the remaining 16ft bridge followed by the 23ft bridge still proceeded till they reached the stream.	x [illegible]
Reconnaissance			It was at once evident that owing to obstructions such fallen trees and barbed wire that it was not possible to find a place where 2 16ft bridges could go in side by side [illegible] was at once sent back to hurry up the 23ft bridges — the far bank was examined & found to be covered with barbed wire to South of Ruined house — the bank was then examined just North of ruined house and a suitable place found for 2 23ft bridges side by side [illegible] the point was free from wire or debris — This point was decided on for passage of both bridges — [illegible] fitted to find a [illegible] across the first 23ft bridge [illegible] The details of first crossing taking place during above reconnaissance [illegible] in Part III (13)	

(A9175) Wt W2358/P360 600,000 12/17 D. D. & L. Sch 52a. Forms/C2118/15

Army Form C. 2118.

Appendix A
Part III B
Crossing of [illegible] Stream West of Canal

WAR DIARY
or
INTELLIGENCE SUMMARY.
(Erase heading not required.)

Instructions regarding War Diaries and Intelligence Summaries are contained in F. S. Regs., Part II, and the Staff Manual respectively. Title pages will be prepared in manuscript.

Place	Date	Hour	Summary of Events and Information	Remarks and references to Appendices
[illegible]	[illegible]		The first three bridges* of the Southern party arrived close behind the infantry carrying party and simultaneously with the infantry carrying party the first bridge was placed [illegible] working across up to the north — The other two bridges of this party were [illegible] 50ft [illegible] and placed shortly after as a combined bridge 	[illegible]
[illegible]			The first two in these infantry scrambled across the stream followed by the others over the bridges, and advanced over the barbed wire up the bank and silenced the enemy post in the [illegible] at the top of the bank which had been causing considerable trouble & casualties by bombs — the first enemy post was a Sussex [illegible] who [illegible] them forward throughout even when they fell back and it is largely due to them that the bridging was able to proceed — [illegible] party of infantry had worked their way along the road and along the bank from the South —	
			While this was going on the first 16ft bridge* of the Northern party arrived and was placed across the stream enabling the first 23 foot bridge* of the Southern party to be dropped across it and placed enabling the first canal bridge to be got over it — A few minutes later this single 23' bridge was supplemented by a [illegible] 23' bridge [illegible]	[illegible]

(A9175) Wt W2358/P360 600,000 12/17 D. D. & L. Sch 52a. Forms/C2118/15

Instructions regarding War Diaries and Intelligence Summaries are contained in F. S. Regs., Part II. and the Staff Manual respectively. Title pages will be prepared in manuscript.

Appendix A
Part III B (cont)

P.4

Army Form C. 2118.

WAR DIARY
or
INTELLIGENCE SUMMARY.
(Erase heading not required.)

Place	Date	Hour	Summary of Events and Information	Remarks and references to Appendices
About 5.51 to 6 am			While the bridging of the first stream was in progress the infantry suffered heavy casualties chiefly in the places marked C - - C - - C and withdrew a second time. They fell back including some who were across the first stream. They then came forward a third time and remained till the bridge was over — their steadiness and determination to get over this time seemed to be largely due to the personal influence of their Commanding Officer† who remained by the bridge over the first stream.	†Lt Col Johnson DSO MC.
			At the second withdrawal Lt Kelly offered to try a crossing by the boats 200 yds up the canal but I told him I could NOT spare the men and get the main crossing over and asked him to do everything he could to push along the long bridges this he did most ably encouraging & cheering on the men and getting assistance when required from the infantry a task which his excellent friendliness with them previously much facilitated.	
About 5.51 to 6.35 am.			Throughout he proved what was wanted next & saw that it was got ~~up~~ assisting himself — the last thing I saw him doing before he was killed was spacing out the bridge on the lock on completion he drew his men back for a short rest ~~[illegible]~~ on the bank ~~before~~ while he collected a large carrying party for the main bridges — throughout he rendered most gallant and valuable ~~[illegible]~~ services	

[signature]
Maj. RE
[illegible]

(A9475) Wt. W2358/P363 600,000 12/17 D. D. & L. Sch. 52a. Forms/C2118/15

Army Form C. 2118.

Instructions regarding War Diaries and Intelligence Summaries are contained in F. S. Regs., Part II. and the Staff Manual respectively. Title pages will be prepared in manuscript.

WAR DIARY
or
INTELLIGENCE SUMMARY.
(Erase heading not required.)

[illegible] Crossing the Lock

Place	Date	Hour	Summary of Events and Information	Remarks and references to Appendices
[illegible]	[illegible]		[illegible]	[illegible]
		06.13	[illegible]	
			[illegible]	
	6.35		[illegible]	
			THIS COMPLETED SIX INFANTRY [illegible] BRIDGES [illegible]	

(A9175) Wt W2358/P369 600,000 12/17 D. D. & L. Sch 52a. Forms/C2118/15

Appendix A

1st [illegible]

CROSSING of [illegible]

Army Form C. 2118.

Instructions regarding War Diaries and Intelligence Summaries are contained in F. S. Regs., Part II. and the Staff Manual respectively. Title pages will be prepared in manuscript.

WAR DIARY
or
INTELLIGENCE SUMMARY.
(Erase heading not required.)

Place	Date	Hour	Summary of Events and Information	Remarks and references to Appendices
			[illegible] the [illegible] bridges were over the lock 2nd Lt [illegible] with a 12th [illegible]	
			and 2/Lt White + 2nd Lt [illegible] + with a [illegible] bridge [illegible] and placed them over the	* [illegible]
			[illegible] [illegible] [illegible]	[illegible]
			with the [illegible] bridges [illegible] by [illegible] + [illegible]	[illegible]
			[illegible] and [illegible] the [illegible]	[illegible]
			the [illegible] bridge [illegible]	
			The [illegible]	
			and the [illegible] of the [illegible]	
			NCOs [illegible]	
			of 2/Lt White ——	
			THIS completes the Infantry Crossings	
			[illegible]	
			The [illegible]	
			[illegible] across the [illegible] BRIDGES ——	
			[signature illegible]	

(A9475) Wt W2358/P360 6[illegible]0,000 12/17 D. D. & L. Sch 52a. Forms/C2118/15

Appendix B [illegible]

Army Form C. 2118.

Instructions regarding War Diaries and Intelligence Summaries are contained in F. S. Regs., Part II, and the Staff Manual respectively. Title pages will be prepared in manuscript.

WAR DIARY
or
INTELLIGENCE SUMMARY.
(*Erase heading not required.*)

[illegible]

Place	Date	Hour	Summary of Events and Information	Remarks and references to Appendices
			[illegible]	
			(1) [illegible]	
			(2) [illegible]	
			(3) [illegible] 15 [illegible]	
[illegible]			[illegible]	

[illegible] R.E.

Army Form C. 2118.

WAR DIARY

or

INTELLIGENCE SUMMARY.

(Erase heading not required.)

Instructions regarding War Diaries and Intelligence Summaries are contained in F. S. Regs., Part II. and the Staff Manual respectively. Title pages will be prepared in manuscript.

Place	Date	Hour	Summary of Events and Information	Remarks and references to Appendices
		[illegible]	[illegible]	
			[illegible]	
			[illegible]	
			[illegible]	
			[illegible]	
Part VI			[illegible]	
		[illegible]	[illegible]	
[illegible]		[illegible]	[illegible]	
			[illegible]	
			[illegible]	
			[illegible]	

[illegible]

[illegible]

(A9175) Wt W2358/P360 600,000 12/17 D. D. & L. Sch. 52a. Forms/C2118/15

Appendix "A" Part VII

Light Footbridge to Span Gap of approx 17'-0".

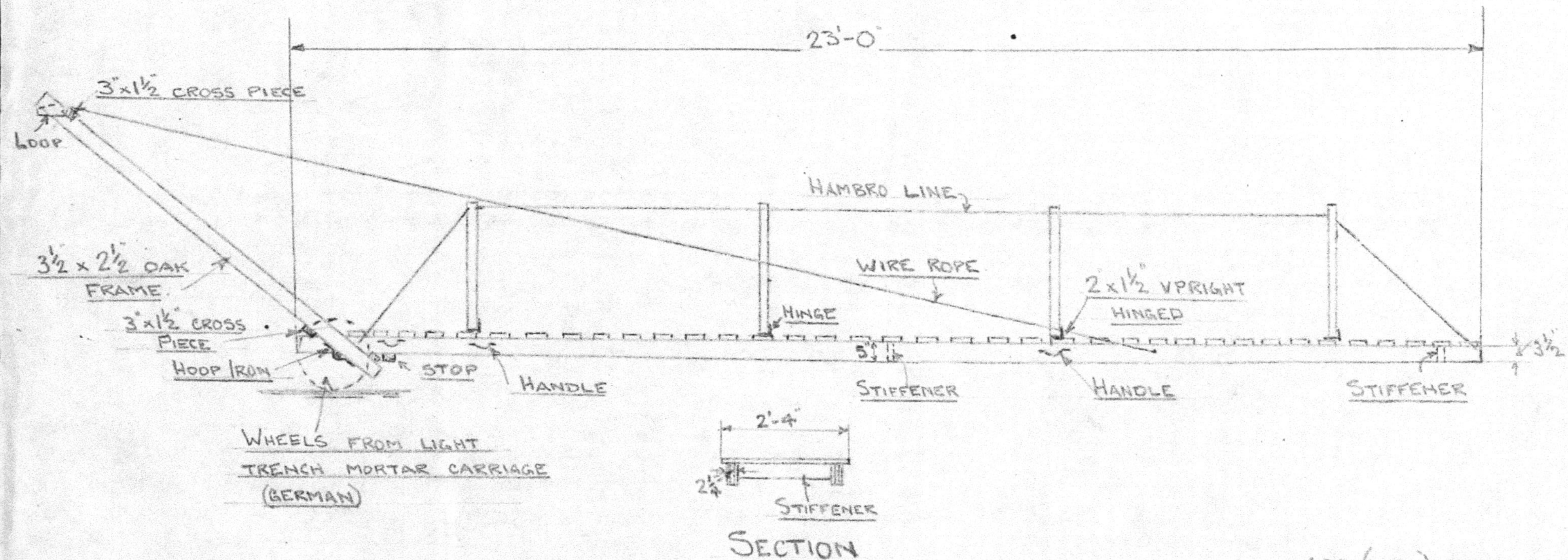

409 (Low) Field Co. RE. (T)

Appendix 'A' - Part VII

Timber Bridge to take Cavalry in Single File

Bridge built in two parts for convenience of transport.

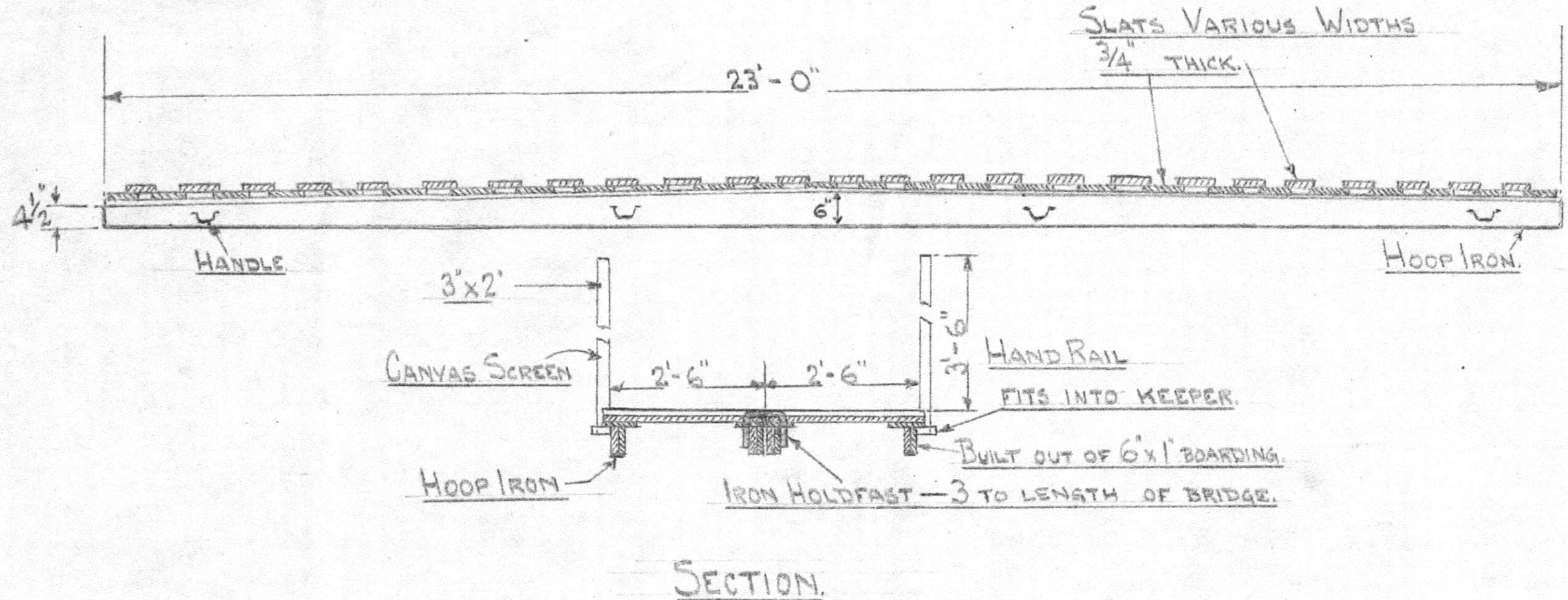

409 (Low) Field Coy. R.E. (T)

2-11-18.

409th (Lowland) Field Coy. R.E.(T)
Appendix "A" Part VIII
Nominal Roll of Casualties on
4th Novr 1918

	Lieut. Kelly. J.L.	Killed in Action
412702	L/Cpl. Miller. J.E	" "
412496	Spr. Adair. R.	" "
262717	" Hudson. W.	" "
412544	" McDougall. B	" "
145126	" Wilson J	" "
412750	" Meikle. A.J.	" "
207916	" Buckmaster. R	" "
412129	" Stirling. J.	" "
180809	" Miller S.	" "
412131	" Taylor. W.	Missing
	Capt. Rhind. W.	Wounded
	II Lieut. Elmslie. N.A.	"
412003	Sergt. Rankin. G.	"
412197	Cpl. Hunter. J.	"
412079	" McLachlan R.	"
412634	L/Cpl. Gibson. G.	"
412516	Spr. Miller. P.	"
412850	" Moodie C	"
412684	" Patrick. D	"
412855	" Pitcaithly. J	"
412538	Spr. McDougall. A.	Wounded
454495	" Saunders. J.H.	"
412847	" Guest. J.	"
457827	" Morris. H	"
412249	" Robertson. L.	"
478420	" Parrott. J.A.	"
	Major G. de C. E. Findlay.	Wounded (at duty)
412110	Spr. Frame. J.	" "
486934	" Purbehouse. J.	" "
532685	" Wheeler. W.L.	" "
466283	" Rischmiller. J.H.	" "
466382	" Hargreaves. J.	" "
342247	" Martin. W.R.	" "

IX C

LIST [illegible] AWARDS.

412064	Spr.	STEVENSON. A	(M.M)
412079	"	McLACHLAN. R	(")

AUTHY IX CORPS No N.R./716 d/21 11/18

AWARDED BAR TO M.M.

412093	2/Cpl (a/Cpl)	CHAPMAN. W.
412092	L/Cpl (a/2/Cpl)	WHITE. J.
412238	Spr. (a/L/Cpl)	SCOTT. J.
412146	" "	WELLS. W.
412845	" "	CAMPBELL. J.
412364	" "	RUSSELL. R.
412634	" "	GIBSON. G.
412703	" "	BEATTIE. J.
412181	2/Cpl (a/Cpl)	STEVEN. G.
412122	L/Cpl	FARQUHARSON. C.
413043	Spr.	ANDERSON. S.
412211	" (a/L/Cpl)	KAY. J.
412334	L/Cpl (a/2/Cpl)	GRAHAM. J.
412410	Spr.	FRAME. J. F
412148	Driver	HOGG. J.
412494	Spr.	GILMOUR. J.

AUTHY IX CORPS No H.R./176 d/21 11/18

Instructions regarding War Diaries and Intelligence Summaries are contained in F. S. Regs., Part II, and the Staff Manual respectively. Title pages will be prepared in manuscript.

WAR DIARY

or

~~INTELLIGENCE SUMMARY.~~

(Erase heading not required.)

Appendix B

Army Form C. 2118.

Place	Date	Hour	Summary of Events and Information	Remarks and references to Appendices

STANDARD MARCHING OUT times to cater for changes in orders frequently received late at night.

	Men	Drivers	Officers	Billeting Party
Reveille	06.00	06.30	06.30	06.00
1st Stables	06.10			
Breakfast	06.45	07.15	07.15	06.30
Wagons packed by		08.30		
Billets ready for inspection		08.45		
Parade				
(Personnel & Transport drawn up ready to move off)		07.10		07.00

NOTE. On receipt of actual orders above table is advanced or retarded so many minutes or hours.

Above table accompanied by standard calling times for Cooks etc. to avoid avoidable disturbance of sleep.

2/11/18

[illegible signatures]

Army Form C. 2118.

Instructions regarding War Diaries and Intelligence Summaries are contained in F. S. Regs., Part II. and the Staff Manual respectively. Title pages will be prepared in manuscript.

WAR DIARY
or
~~INTELLIGENCE SUMMARY.~~
(Erase heading not required.)

Place	Date	Hour	Summary of Events and Information	Remarks and references to Appendices
			CONFIDENTIAL.	
			WAR DIARY of. 409th (LOWLAND) FIELD COY. R.E.	
			for.	
			DECEMBER 1918	

D. D. & L., London, E.C.
(A5001) Wt. W1771/M2031 750,000 5/17 Sch. 52 Forms C2118/14

Secret

409 Lowland F Coy RE

Instructions regarding War Diaries and Intelligence Summaries are contained in F. S. Regs., Part II. and the Staff Manual respectively. Title pages will be prepared in manuscript.

WAR DIARY
or
~~INTELLIGENCE SUMMARY.~~
(Erase heading not required.)

for December 1918

Army Form C. 2118.

Place	Date	Hour	Summary of Events and Information MARCH to RHINE	Remarks and references to Appendices
FTER	1/12/18		Marched from FTER to ROSTENNE and stopped night.	Note All horses in excellent condition on 20/12 and transport rather heavy for
ROSTENNE	2/12/18		" " ROSTENNE to LAVYS via DINANT & stopped night	
LAVYS	3/12/18		" " LAVYS to BRIQUEMONT	
BRIQUEMONT	4th		Resting at BRIQUEMONT. Cleaning up personal and Company	
	5th		Equipment — Check of all harness & Kit Inspection.	
	6			
	7th			
	8th		Church Parade — Football officers v. Sergts.	
HAVERSIN	9th		Proceeded by march route arriving about 1pm very bad	
HOTTON	10th		Moved to HOTTON for night 14 miles.	
	11th		Moved to NY billets in Farm & Chateau.	
	12th		Dancing in evening Cleaning up Kit inspection billeting drawn with horses	
	13th		Concert in evening	
	14th		VAUXCHAVANNE very dirty plenty accomodation — transport left on	
	15th		COMTE. Clean (road) 1 mile away	
	16th		MALDINGREM crossed the frontier into Germany village dirty — Company complimented on its turn out	
	17th		CIERREUX stopped 1 night took trade tests.	
	18th		Moved to EIMERSCHEID	
	19th		Moved ... KONIGSBURG HUTTE	
	20th		rested same place	

[signature] Major RE

D. D. & L., London, E.C. (A7001) Wt. W1271/M2031 750,000 3/17 Sch. 52 Forms C2118/14

Secret. 409th (Lowland) Field Co RE.

Instructions regarding War Diaries and Intelligence Summaries are contained in F. S. Regs., Part II. and the Staff Manual respectively. Title pages will be prepared in manuscript.

WAR DIARY for December 1918.
or
~~INTELLIGENCE SUMMARY.~~

(*Erase heading not required.*)

Army Form C. 2118.

Place	Date	Hour	Summary of Events and Information	Remarks and references to Appendices
	21st		Marched to SCHMIDTHEIM. and remained for night. Good billets and Stables.	
	22nd		Marched to EICHERSCHEID and remained for night. Transport sent under Brigade Orders via SCHONAN to avoid Steep Climb N. of HOLZMULHEIM. Very good billets and Stables.	
	23rd		Dismounted branch marched to winter quarters OBER-DREES via KIRSPENICH and FLAMERSHEIM. Transport marched brigaded via KUCHENHEIM on account of heavy grade East of KIRSPENICH. Coy. came under orders of CRE. on arrival.	
OBER-DREES.	24th	–	Resting. Additional billets found.	
	25th	–	Resting. All men in good billets and horses under cover, mostly in Stables. Short Combined Christmas Service of 3 Field Coys. in Recreation Hall. Company Christmas Dinner held in Recreation Room in Evening. Combined Do (Officers' Mess opened on Christmas Evening)	
	26th	–	Cleaning up personal Equipment.	
	27th 28th		Cleaning section vehicles and equipment. 28th 1 OR. to England for dispersal (Long service) (Chiseldon Centre)	Afternoons free for recreation
	29th		Church Parade. 6 OR. to England for release as Coalminers – Duddingston Centre	
	30th		Cleaning Coy. Equipment. Inspection of horses by D.A.D.V.S. 1st Div.	
	31st		Started training – physical drill, rifle exercises. Work on Coy. Transport.	R A Galloway Capt RE. a/OC. Coy

D. D. & L., London, E.C. (A5091) Wt. W1-71/M2031 750,000 5/17 Sch. 52 Forms C2.118/14

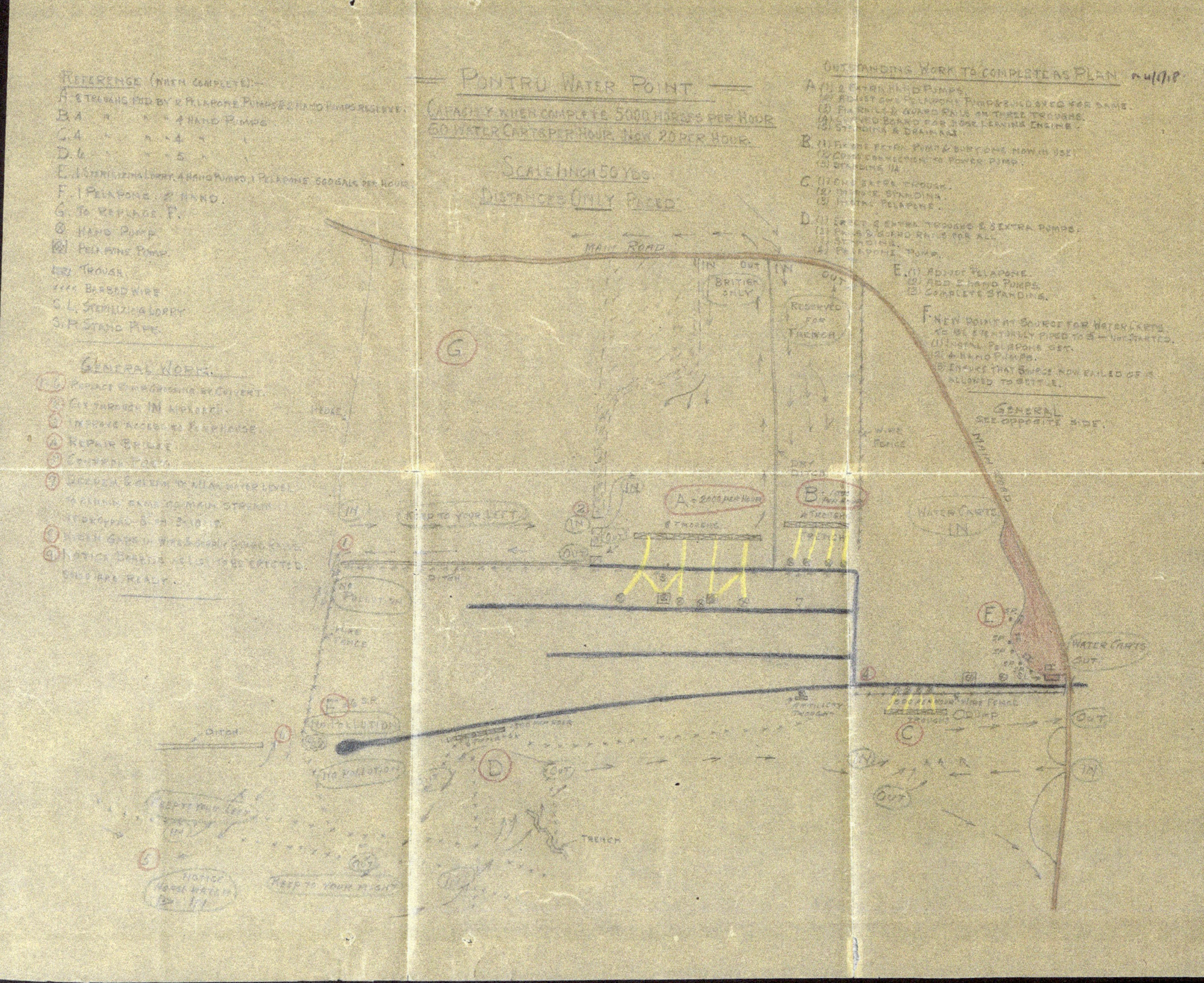

PONTRU WATER POINT
CAPACITY WHEN COMPLETE 5000 HORSES PER HOUR
60 WATER CARTS PER HOUR. NOW 20 PER HOUR.
SCALE 1 INCH 50 YDS.
DISTANCES ONLY PACED
REFERENCE (WHEN COMPLETE):-
A. 8 TROUGHS FED BY 2 PELAPONE PUMPS & 2 HAND PUMPS RESERVE.
B. 4 " " " 4 HAND PUMPS
C. 4 " " " 4 " "
D. 6 " " " 5 " "
E. 1 STERILIZING LORRY. 4 HAND PUMPS. 1 PELAPONE. 600 GALS PER HOUR.
F. 1 PELAPONE. 2 HAND.
G. TO REPLACE F.
HAND PUMP
PELAPONE PUMP.
TROUGH.
BARBED WIRE
S.L. STERILIZING LORRY
S.P. STAND PIPE.
GENERAL WORK.
REPAIR BRIDGE
OUTSTANDING WORK TO COMPLETE AS PLAN
E. (1) ADJUST PELAPONE.
(2) ADD 2 HAND PUMPS.
(3) COMPLETE STANDING.
F. NEW POINT AT SOURCE FOR WATER CARTS
GENERAL
SEE OPPOSITE SIDE.
MAIN ROAD
IN
OUT
BRITISH ONLY
RESERVED FOR FRENCH
A = 2000 per hour
8 TROUGHS
WATER CARTS IN
WATER CARTS OUT
KEEP TO YOUR LEFT
KEEP TO YOUR RIGHT
WIRE FENCE
DRY DITCH
DITCH
TRENCH

Instructions regarding War Diaries and Intelligence Summaries are contained in F. S. Regs., Part II. and the Staff Manual respectively. Title pages will be prepared in manuscript.

WAR DIARY
or
INTELLIGENCE SUMMARY.
(Erase heading not required.)

Army Form C. 2118.

98 4

Place	Date	Hour	Summary of Events and Information	Remarks and references to Appendices
			CONFIDENTIAL.	
			WAR DIARY of 409th (LOWLAND) FIELD COY. R.E.	
			for	
			JANUARY 1919.	

D. D. & L., London, E.C.
(A8031) Wt. W1771/M2031 750,000 5/17 Sch. 52 Forms C2118/14

Confidential

409th (Lowland) Field Co R.E.

Instructions regarding War Diaries and Intelligence Summaries are contained in F. S. Regs., Part II. and the Staff Manual respectively. Title pages will be prepared in manuscript.

WAR DIARY
or
~~INTELLIGENCE SUMMARY.~~

(Erase heading not required.)

January 1919

Army Form C. 2118.

Place	Date	Hour	Summary of Events and Information	Remarks and references to Appendices
OBER-DREES, GERMANY Sheet Germany 2L 1/100,000 9.B.45.75.	1st to 21st		Company Employed in Training as under (a) Military – Physical Drill, Ceremonial, Route Marchs (once per week), Lectures on map reading, use of prismatic Compass, Etc. with practical work (b) Technical – Tradesmen eg Carpenters, blacksmith, bricklayers, & painters working under D.E. Workshops Officer to brush up trades. (c) Educational – Classes in English, History, Geography, Civics, Germany, Shorthand, Building Construction, Internal Combustion Engines Etc. under D.E. Education Officer. Classes varying from 11 hrs to 12.30 hrs. daily and 14 hrs to 16 hrs on Mondays, Wednesdays and Fridays. (d) Recreational – Chiefly football, organised by Coy. Sports Committee. Occasional Matches D.E. v Other units arranged by D.E. Sports Officer	

D. D. & L., London, E.C.
(A7093) Wt. W1771/M2031 750,000 5/17 Sch. 52 Forms C2118/14

Confidential

(2)

409th (Lowland) Field Coy RE

WAR DIARY
or
~~INTELLIGENCE SUMMARY.~~
(Erase heading not required.)

January 1919

Army Form C. 2118.

Instructions regarding War Diaries and Intelligence Summaries are contained in F. S. Regs., Part II. and the Staff Manual respectively. Title pages will be prepared in manuscript.

Place	Date	Hour	Summary of Events and Information	Remarks and references to Appendices
OBER-DREES	1st to 21st		Reconnaissance. Several reconnaissances were carried out for all information of a military nature in an allotted portion of the Divisional Area.	
			Work. Painting signs on walls at entrances of villages in 2nd Brigade Area.	
			Cadre Strength. 1st Div H.Q. issued Cadre Strength for Field Coy. of 4 Officers and 128 O.R.	
			Demobilisation. Occasional allotments for dispersal were received. Owing to this and fact that men on leave were being granted extension of 14 days in connection with demobilisation, ration strength had fallen to approx. 140 O.R. by 21st inst.	
			J. Galloway Capt RE O/C Coy. 21/1/19.	

2353 Wt. W2544/1454 700,000 5/15 D. D. & L. A.D.S.S./Forms/C. 2118.

Confidential

(3)

Army Form C. 2118.

409th (Lowland) Field Coy. R.E.

WAR DIARY
or
~~INTELLIGENCE SUMMARY.~~

January 1919.

Instructions regarding War Diaries and Intelligence Summaries are contained in F. S. Regs., Part II. and the Staff Manual respectively. Title pages will be prepared in manuscript.

(Erase heading not required.)

Place	Date	Hour	Summary of Events and Information	Remarks and references to Appendices
OBER-DREES	1st to 31st		48 HOURS LEAVE TO HOSTEL. — A Hostel was opened up at COLOGNE to accommodate Officers N.C.O.s & men of the 1st Divn. to allow better facilities for visiting places of interest in, and around COLOGNE. An allotment for O.Rs was absorbed by this Coy. from 23rd to 25th inclusive. Very satisfactory reports of the Hostel and its advantages have been obtained.	
			LEAVE. Passes to visit places of interest are granted after duty on Tuesdays, Thursdays, Saturdays & Sundays; advantage of which is being freely taken to places in Divisional Area.	
	22nd to 31st		Training, Reconnaissance, Education, etc. carried out as shown from 1st to 21st.	

W. Illingworth Lt RE.
a/O.C. Coy.

D. D. & L., London, E.C.
(A7001) Wt. W1771/M2031 750,000 5/17 Sch. 52 Forms C2118/14

Vd 50

CONFIDENTIAL

WAR DIARY

OF

409th (LOWLAND) FIELD COY. R.E. (T.)

from 1st FEBY. 1919 to 28th FEBY. 1919

(VOLUME No. L.)

409th (Lowland) Fd Coy R.E.

Instructions regarding War Diaries and Intelligence Summaries are contained in F. S. Regs., Part II. and the Staff Manual respectively. Title pages will be prepared in manuscript.

WAR DIARY for February 1919.
or
~~INTELLIGENCE SUMMARY.~~
(Erase heading not required.)

Army Form C. 2118.

Place	Date	Hour	Summary of Events and Information	Remarks and references to Appendices
OBER DREES	1/2/19 to 11/2/19		2nd Lt Grigor R.E. continued acting as O.C. General programme 1st to 28th Feb. 1) Educational Training Classes in varies subjects were continued and as many tradesmen as possible were given an opportunity of getting their hand in in a fortnight course at the Workshops run by the CRE. 2) Works. only odd jobs of a small nature involving a few men and Sign Painting. Officers Mess for Battalion started at KIRCHEIM. 3) Games. A full programme during latter half of month of Div Engineer Teams — This unit providing more than half the football team which carried through into the final for the Divisional Cup. — General football almost impossible owing to wet state of ground. The Indoor & outdoor Games Committees reconstituted after having become broken up by demobilisation of some members A whist drive held & a concert 4) Leave & Passes. Good facilities given to men to get about and see the Country. (i) Travelling free (ii) Divisional Hotel @ 1mk per day available for all on leave to COLOGNE for food & accomodation is appreciated. — Leave slowed up partly owing to low numbers & partly as the majority of men were awaiting demobilisation & therefore not eligible. COLOGNE 48 hours leave restricted to those about to be demobilised within the Divn	

D. D. & L., London, E.C.
(10340) Wt W5300/P713 750,000 3/18 E 2688 Forms/C2118/16.

Instructions regarding War Diaries and Intelligence Summaries are contained in F. S. Regs., Part II. and the Staff Manual respectively. Title pages will be prepared in manuscript.

WAR DIARY

or

~~INTELLIGENCE SUMMARY.~~

(Erase heading not required.)

Army Form C. 2118.

Place	Date	Hour	Summary of Events and Information	Remarks and references to Appendices
			5) Internal Economy. Billets good — Sanitary arrangements improved & latrines provided — but like in France every house has its midden used for all purposes.	
			Horses all Stabled	
	11/2/19		2nd Lt Grigor handed over to Lieut Smith and proceeded on leave	
	12/2/19 to 15/2/19		Lt Smith a/O.C. unit.	
	15/2/19		Maj G. Findlay returned off leave and resumed command —	
	16/2/19.	8.45 am	General Parade & Rifle Inspection — found men well turned out & arms in good condition. also Billets and Interior Economy was satisfactory.	
	16th to 28th		General Programme continued — Mounted portion exercise daily for horses not on works	
	20/2/19		Volunteers for Army of Occupation — 14 men volunteered for extra year.	
	20/2/19		General explanation to company on state of Demobilisation, Duties of Army of Occupation, Methods of Reenlisting or volunteering for one year.	

D. D. & L., London, E.C.
(10340) Wt W5300/P713 750,000 3/18 E 2688 Forms/C2118/16.

Army Form C. 2118.

WAR DIARY
or
~~INTELLIGENCE SUMMARY.~~
(Erase heading not required.)

Instructions regarding War Diaries and Intelligence Summaries are contained in F. S. Regs., Part II. and the Staff Manual respectively. Title pages will be prepared in manuscript.

Place	Date	Hour	Summary of Events and Information	Remarks and references to Appendices
OBERDREES.	26/2/19		Leaving farewell concert with 23rd & 26th Fd Coy in Recreation hall – on occasion of their changing billets with 75th & 76th Fd Coys pending return to home.	
	27/2/19		Final of 1st Div. Sports – football Tug of War & Boxing.	
			Followed by farewell Officers meeting at dinner preparatory to the 1st Division as at present formed being broken up.	
	28/2/19		23rd & 26th Fd Coys changed places with 75th & 76th Fd Coys ———	
			1/3/19.	
			J. A. C. Hindley Maj. RE. O.C. 409th Lowland Fd Coy RE.	

D. D. & L., London, E.C.
(10340) Wt W5300/P713 750,000 3/18 E 2688 Forms/C2118/16.

War Diary for 409 Fly[illegible] March

Instructions regarding War Diaries and Intelligence Summaries are contained in F. S. Regs., Part II. and the Staff Manual respectively. Title pages will be prepared in manuscript.

WAR DIARY
or
~~INTELLIGENCE SUMMARY.~~
(Erase heading not required.)

Army Form C. 2118.

Vol 51

Place	Date	Hour	Summary of Events and Information	Remarks and references to Appendices
1/3/19 OBERDREES	1/3/19		Works & Education Classes & Usual Stable Routine —	
	2/3/19		Church Service. Div. Engineers parade	
	3/3/19		Usual routine & works and Tool Cart inspection.	
	4/3/19		Usual afternoon Company photograph taken —	
	5/3/19		Distribution of Company approx strength 156 [illegible] open [illegible] & others on [illegible]	
			leaving 128 with unit.	
	5			
	10/3/19		Company on Special employ including O.C. Company [illegible] 50.	
			Mounted including 20 sappers acting as Drivers 45 These sappers [illegible] in charge of [illegible] [illegible]	
			Workshops & Hutting & Education 25 Party on instruction in Workshop [illegible]	
			Available for General Duties 10 to 20 [illegible] for [illegible] [illegible] in [illegible] Company cookhouse, repairs to transport.	
	11/3/19		Lecture by O.C. on (a) Demobilisation & present position (b) Raw Materials & Employment.	
	12/3/19		Continue Works, Demobilisation, Education, 4 or 5 wagons out daily on 20 mile journey [illegible] for	
	5			
	17/3/19		Keeping horses fit — ~~[illegible]~~ 19/3/19 [illegible] to build [illegible] HQ offices & [illegible]	
			Scouts — [illegible]	

D. D. & L., London, E.C.
(10340) Wt W5300/P713 750,000 3/18 E 2688 Forms/C2118/16.

War Diary March 19 [illegible]

Instructions regarding War Diaries and Intelligence Summaries are contained in F. S. Regs., Part II. and the Staff Manual respectively. Title pages will be prepared in manuscript.

WAR DIARY
or
INTELLIGENCE SUMMARY.
(Erase heading not required.)

Army Form C. 2118.

Place	Date	Hour	Summary of Events and Information	Remarks and references to Appendices
OBERDREES & [illegible]	1/3/19		20 [illegible] — [illegible] by lorry & rail — [illegible] Horse [illegible] with [illegible] — [illegible] for [illegible] — Temporarily [illegible] [illegible] [illegible] — Officers [illegible] material for Hut	
	1/3/19 to 31/3/19		(a) Commenced Hut for [illegible] Officers. [illegible] supply of [illegible] [illegible] 4.6 — [illegible] shortage of [illegible] [illegible] by unskilled labour — Size 50 x 24 with [illegible] 8 x 24 [illegible] [illegible] [illegible] nearly —	
			(b) Reinforcements arrived as under. 17 OR for 157 Fd Coy 24/3/19; 25 OR — 23 Fd Coy 24/3/19; 12 ORs 427 Fd Coy 28/3/19; 15 OR 26 Fd Coy 29/3/19	
			(c) Demobilisation continued & company gradually [illegible] with [illegible] [illegible] adopted all [illegible] [illegible] section & each section built up by [illegible] as reinforcements arrive — Regard unit as a NEW COMPANY.	

[illegible signature]

Maj. R.E.

O.C. 409th (Lowland) Fd. Coy. R.E.

1/4/19

D. D. & L., London, E.C.
(10340) Wt W5300/P713 750,000 3/18 E 2688 Forms/C2118/16.

Army Form C. 2118.

Instructions regarding War Diaries and Intelligence Summaries are contained in F. S. Regs., Part II. and the Staff Manual respectively. Title pages will be prepared in manuscript.

WAR DIARY
or
INTELLIGENCE SUMMARY.
(Erase heading not required.)

Place	Date	Hour	Summary of Events and Information	Remarks and references to Appendices
March.	23rd		Military training carried on as last month.	
			Recreational training – Plenty of football matches were played – The 76th Field Coy went to COLOGNE and were beaten 4-0 by 433rd Fd. Coy.	
	31st		Work in progress. Erection of a Divisional Nissen hut started.	
			Rifle range at WITTERSCHLICK.	
			Painting of signboards for Div^l area.	
			Sentry boxes & latrines made at BORNHEIM.	
			On this date – 75th Fd. Coy moved from NIEDERDREES to TRIPPELSDORF.	
			76th " " " OBERDREES " MERTEN.	
			409th " " " SECHTEM " RÖSBERG.	
			Also DE.H.Q moved from OBERDREES to RÖSBERG chateau.	
April.	2nd		Football fields made near RÖSBERG and MERTEN.	
			Education classes started again under Lt. Brown. A number of books for this purpose received from England.	
			23rd & 26th Fd. Coys wasting rapidly to cadre strength (B).	
			Wire received from Div: altering cadre B to cadre A.	
	9th		Demobilisation receives a new impetus and 409th, 76th & 75th have got rid of most releasable men.	
			[illegible] Lt. RE. A/Adjt. Western D.E.	

D. D. & L., London, E.C. (A5031) Wt. W1771/M2031 750,000 5/17 Sch. 52 Forms C2118/14

Secret.

409th Fd Coy R.E.

WAR DIARY
or
~~INTELLIGENCE SUMMARY~~.
(Erase heading not required.)

Army Form C. 2118.

Instructions regarding War Diaries and Intelligence Summaries are contained in F. S. Regs., Part II. and the Staff Manual respectively. Title pages will be prepared in manuscript.

Place	Date	Hour	Summary of Events and Information	Remarks and references to Appendices
SECHTEM.	1/4/19		Work on Divl. H.Q. Hut for Offices in progress — party 30 Saps. 9 Infantry All structure complete Glazing & fitting of windows & doors in hand. Advance party sent to new billets in RÖSBERG to make latrines. One Section on detachment with 1st Bde. 26 Sappers attached to mounted Section for training to allow of release of Drivers	[initials]
	2/4/19 } 3/4/19 }		Continued as above	
	4/4/19.		H.Q. & No. 3 Section moved into new billets at Rösberg { Harness & Animals did not permit of move of whole unit together. } No 1 & 4 Section continue work as above	
	5/4/19.		No 4 Section took over work & billets from No 2 Section on detachment with 1st Bde at BORNHEIM No. 2 " rejoined Company at Rösberg. No 1 Sect. completed Div H.Q. Hut.	
	6/4/19.		No 1 " moved to billets at Rösberg. — Lecture on temperance.	
	7/4/19. - 15/4/19		No 1. 2. 3 Section — Company Cookhouse, Workshops & Div H.Q. Work —	
	16/4/19 - 17/4/19		No 1. 2. Sections — Drill & training prior to going on detachment.	
	18/4/19		No 3 Section moved to HEIMERZHEIM, on detachment with R.A. for work on Cookhouses latrines etc — This period closed the reforming of the Company except drivers — N.C.O.'s promoted to fill all vacancies and Sections reformed on trade basis as men arrived — All reinforcements on arrival split up evenly by trades to all 4 sections so as to break up old inter unit feeling and leave the way clear to form a new Company spirit	[signature] Maj R.E.

D. D. & L., London E.C.
(10342) Wt W5300/P713 700,000 3/18 E. 688 Forms/C2118/16.

Instructions regarding War Diaries and Intelligence Summaries are contained in F. S. Regs., Part II. and the Staff Manual respectively. Title pages will be prepared in manuscript.

WAR DIARY

or

~~INTELLIGENCE SUMMARY.~~

(Erase heading not required.)

Army Form C. 2118.

Place	Date	Hour	Summary of Events and Information	Remarks and references to Appendices
RÖSBERG GERMANY	19/4/19		4 O.R. proceeded on demobilization. Major G. de C. E. FINDLAY D.S.O. M.C. took over duties of a/C.R.E. WESTERN DIVISION. CAPT. P.C.E. FIELDS-CLARKE took over duties of O.C. 409 Field Co. R.E.	
"	do		No 4 Sect. on detachment at BORNHEIM continued work for 1st WESTERN BDE. on Cookhouses, Latrines, Incinerators &c.	P.F.C.
			Nos 1, 2 & 3 Sections on work for Divl. H.Q. EICHOLZ CHATEAU, ~~[illegible]~~ DIVL. SIGNAL SCHOOL, & WIDDIG, Cookhouses, Incinerators &c. 12 O.R. working with Divl. Engrs. Workshops. Work on Coy. Cookhouse, Incinerator &c continued. 17 Sappers attached to mounted Section doing duty as drivers. No 3 Sect. proceeded to HEIMERZHEIM on detachment for work for Divl. Artillery	
"	20/4/19		3 O.R. proceeded on demobilization. Work of Sections continued as on previous day	P.F.C.
"	21/4/19		Work of Sections continued as above.	P.F.C.
"	22/4/19		Do.	P.F.C.
"	23/4/19		Do. 1 O.R. proceeded on demobilization.	P.F.C.
"	24/4/19		Do.	P.F.C.
"	25/4/19		Do.	P.F.C.
"	26/4/19		No 2 Section proceeded to BORNHEIM to relieve No 4 Sect. who returned to H.Q. at RÖSBERG. No 3 Section proceeded to MORENHOVEN for work on Latrines, Cookhouses &c for 104 Bde. R.F.A.	P.F.C.
"	27/4/19		4 drivers transferred to 75th Field Co. R.E. 1 O.R. proceeded on demobilization. No work done. Voluntary Church Parade at 18.00 hrs.	P.F.C.
"	28/4/19		Work for 1st Western Bde. continued by No 2 Sect. Work for 104 Bde. R.F.A. continued by No 3 Sect. Nos 1 & 3 Sects. continued work at EICHOLZ, for D. E. Workshops, Signal School & Coy. Cookhouse.	P.F.C.
"	29/4/19		Do Do	P.F.C.
"	30/4/19		Do Do	P.F.C.
			The weather for the period 19/4/19 to 30/4/19 was showery with cold winds.	P.F.C.

(A9175) Wt W2358/P360 600,000 12/17 D. D. & L. Sch. 52a. Forms/C2118/15

409th Fd Coy RE

WAR DIARY for May 1919
or
INTELLIGENCE SUMMARY.
(*Erase heading not required.*)

Army Form C. 2118.

Instructions regarding War Diaries and Intelligence Summaries are contained in F. S. Regs., Part II. and the Staff Manual respectively. Title pages will be prepared in manuscript.

Place	Date	Hour	Summary of Events and Information	Remarks and references to Appendices
ROSBERG	1/5/19		General Distribution of Company	
			No 2 Section with 1st Bde. – erecting latrines Cookhouses etc	
			No 3 " " Div Art " " "	
			HQ No 1 & 4 Section at ROSBERG on odd works Div HQ & Transport & Guards	
			Leave beginning to flow freely approx 30 men away strength 200 approx	
			Maj Gen Cl Hundley acting CRE – Capt R.E. Fields Clarke O/C	
			Civil Procession & Demonstrations being held troops prohibited from attending.	
	2/5/19		Education. Classes during working hours closed down – ~~voluntary~~ owing to men being required for works and other duties.	
	3/5/19		Normal Works	
	4/5/19		Voluntary Church Parade –	
	5/5/19		Steel Helmets withdrawn for Painting	
	6–15/5/19		Usual Routine & Works	
	16/5/19		13 promotions in the company to fill vacancies	
	17/5/19		Reposting of NCO to Sections	
	18/5/19		Football match at HEMMERICH v 1st Fd Ambulance Won –	
	21/5/19 23/5/19 24/5		23rd Cadre moving to entraining point Teams & Drivers for half their transport supplied.	

D. D. & L., London, E.C.
(10340) Wt W5300/P713 750,000 3/18 Sch. 2688 Forms/C2118/16.

409 Field Coy RE

WAR DIARY of May
or
INTELLIGENCE SUMMARY.
(Erase heading not required.)

Army Form C. 2118.

Instructions regarding War Diaries and Intelligence Summaries are contained in F. S. Regs., Part II. and the Staff Manual respectively. Title pages will be prepared in manuscript.

Place	Date	Hour	Summary of Events and Information	Remarks and references to Appendices
Rosberg	25/5 to 30/5/19		Continued Works as usual — No 2 & 3 Sections rejoined from detachment. Preparations for training in hand.	
	31/5/19		All four Sections paraded for Works.	
			Jobs completed during the month	
			HQ & 2 Section: Poultry farm Div HQ. Cookhouse & Oven Div HQ. " " Div Troops. Incinerator " ". Sand Bath for mules. Canteen. Picket Line. 2 Canvas Tanks at WALDORF with roofs. Supervision of Inf Working Parties & Requisition Services for Water Supply of Rosberg Marten Sechten — Waldorf — HEMMERICH	
			No 3 Section: Completed Latrines for 15 Bn. " " 104th Bn. " Cookhouse ". " Ablution Benches ". " 3 weirs on stream for refilling points. Improved Ration Stage & Shed for Supply Dump.	
			No 2 Sect – 1 Bn: 11 meat safes. Latrines brought up to 5%. Baths at Waldorf erected & water connections. Wash Downs at BORNHEIM & at HERSEL. 4 Cookhouse Sheds complete. 2 ovens in hand —	

(Signed) [illegible] Major RE

D. D. & L., London, E.C.
(10340) Wt W5300/P713 750,000 3/18 E 2688 Forms/C2118/16.

Instructions regarding War Diaries and Intelligence Summaries are contained in F. S. Regs., Part II. and the Staff Manual respectively. Title pages will be prepared in manuscript.

Copy No 1

Army Form C. 2118.

WAR DIARY
or
INTELLIGENCE SUMMARY.
(Erase heading not required.)

Place	Date	Hour	Summary of Events and Information	Remarks and references to Appendices
			409th Fd Coy RE	
			June 1919	
			TRAINING	(a) Diary (b) Appendix A (c) Appendix B

D. D. & L., London, E.C.
(10340) Wt W5300/P713 750,000 3/18 Sch 2688 Forms/C2118/16.

409th Fd Coy R.E.

WAR DIARY *for June 1919*
or
INTELLIGENCE SUMMARY.
(*Erase heading not required.*)

Army Form C. 2118.

Instructions regarding War Diaries and Intelligence Summaries are contained in F. S. Regs., Part II. and the Staff Manual respectively. Title pages will be prepared in manuscript.

Place	Date	Hour	Summary of Events and Information	Remarks and references to Appendices
ROSBERG	1/6/19	—	Church Parade in DINING HALL. —	
—	2/6/19		Company commenced on a Months Training Programme all officers except Captain were present.	
			The main objects were (1) To get company together as an organised whole (previously there were always over half away on leave & detachment) and get them quickened & fit & uniform and capable of working together.	
			(2) Technical Training for Officers NCO's & O.R.	
			Factors Effecting Training: (a) Officers (1) Two of subalterns had NOT been fully trained or required training as well as opportunity of training their sections.	
			(2) We were responsible for handling of a daily digging party of 100 – 260 men requiring sometimes two officers to start parties	
			(b) NCO's. All had been recently promoted into their ranks, some were known others coming from other units, their experience & knowledge still had to be found out	
			(c) Men. Had been thrown together from about 14 different units and some were experienced some not, some had one way and some another.	
			(d) Strength of Sections on works averaged approx 8 & 14 this meant frequently grouping them and very difficult to find men for odd jobs without entirely stopping training of Section.	

D. D. & L., London, E.C.
(10340) Wt W5300/P713 750,000 3/18 E 2688 Forms/C2118/16.

409th Field Coy RE.

Instructions regarding War Diaries and Intelligence Summaries are contained in F. S. Regs., Part II. and the Staff Manual respectively. Title pages will be prepared in manuscript.

WAR DIARY for June
or
INTELLIGENCE SUMMARY.
(Erase heading not required.)

Army Form C. 2118.

p 2

Place	Date	Hour	Summary of Events and Information	Remarks and references to Appendices
			PROGRAMME: A syllabus was drawn up at CRE's conference and based on that weekly programmes were prepared – these were subsequently modified according to progress made, weather, special days then had to be modified and the final training carried out is shewn on attached Appendix A.	Training programme – Appendix A attached
			Notes & Opinions on First Week.	
			(a) Physical Training carried out under CSM is very valuable for quickening men up & getting them alert.	
			(b) Drill is valuable for getting men together and moving to an order and good for Officers & NCOs giving definite orders.	
			(c) Pontoon & Trestle assembly was necessary on dry land first as many had never laid out & assembled a Weldon Trestle & all ~~many~~ were rusty and required a rub up – before attempting it over water.	
			(d) Musketry – On the whole positions aiming & trigger pressing were very fair and it was evident that they had been taught; firing at short range shewed necessity for practise and in my opinion emphasises the fact that Royal Engineers have more than enough to do to keep efficient in their rifles and that the LEWIS GUN except one Anti-aircraft is an encumbrance ——— and should be withdrawn.	
			(e) Explosives training previously very fair.	

[signature]

D. D. & L., London, E.C. (10340) Wt W5300/P713 750,000 3/18 E 2688 Forms/C2118/16.

409th Fd Coy RE

Army Form C. 2118.

Instructions regarding War Diaries and Intelligence Summaries are contained in F. S. Regs., Part II. and the Staff Manual respectively. Title pages will be prepared in manuscript.

WAR DIARY for June 1919
or
INTELLIGENCE SUMMARY.

(Erase heading not required.)

Place	Date	Hour	Summary of Events and Information	Remarks and references to Appendices
Rosberg	8th to 15.		Notes on Second Weeks Training. (a) Wiring most had had previous experience many had NOT been taught or used the G.H.Q. system which I have found in practice gives good results – all present have now been so trained. (b) Digging one day on this was NOT wasted as proper use of shovel & pick is very important. On same tasks it was found that the Sappers took less than half the time that the young infantry did. (c) Erection of Steel Shelter. Some men had not previously used them. (d) Sandbag revetment – even trained men sometimes must fill batter & not keep tops level (e) Pack up of whole company & move out – Required and the only way of satisfactorily ensuring that the unit is mobile – (f) Bridge & Road Reconnaissances made by officers.	

[illegible]

D. D. & L., London, E.C.
(10340) Wt W5300/P713 750,000 3/18 E 2688 Forms/C2118/16.

409th Fd Coy RE

Instructions regarding War Diaries and Intelligence Summaries are contained in F. S. Regs., Part II. and the Staff Manual respectively. Title pages will be prepared in manuscript.

WAR DIARY for June
or
INTELLIGENCE SUMMARY.

(Erase heading not required.)

Army Form C. 2118.

Place	Date	Hour	Summary of Events and Information	Remarks and references to Appendices
Rosbey	15th & 21st June		Notes on 3rd Weeks Training	
			(a) Completed 1st cycle of wiring, Support, firing 10 rds + one mornings digging on pipe track.	
			(b) Wiring. All men trained in GHQ system for Low Wire Entanglement + Concertina Wire. All section completed their night wiring and showed result of good system by making sound obstacles with joints correctly made	
			(c) Demolitions All section had previously had 3 hrs on details of jointing and use of explosives (during training on Wet Days) – An officer gave a lecture bringing in some more advanced points followed by demonstration of actual connecting up placing firing + examination of results of charges on timber earth wall, mine, steel rail pipe representing a gun	
			(d) BRIDGEING. The estimate of the gap over water with marshy banks varied from 30 to 60 feet – It was 70 ft and gave a good idea to those taking part of the size of gap company equipment can bridge – Work was done from one edge – one party under an officer was placed in charge of 1st trestle. the remainder – – – of the two pontoon formed into a raft – Bridging was from one side only. The farther trestle was built on the raft and launched from cantilever over the end – the difficulties encountered were (i) manoeuvring raft into exact position (ii) holding the trestle upright till lashed + staged – 	
			Conclusion Should NOT be used for a far shore trestle but might have to be used on submerged banks in mid stream when pontoons cd NOT be floated over so as to put it in centre of raft – It is almost impossible to ensure keeping the raft still without anchor ropes – and a mistake on the part of a party involves considerable risks of accident – with anchor ropes a useful method.	GWH

D. D. & L., London, E.C.
(10340) Wt W5300/P713 750,000 3/18 E 2688 Forms/C2118/16.

409th Fd Coy RE

p5

WAR DIARY for June
or
INTELLIGENCE SUMMARY.
(Erase heading not required.)

Army Form C. 2118.

Instructions regarding War Diaries and Intelligence Summaries are contained in F. S. Regs., Part II. and the Staff Manual respectively. Title pages will be prepared in manuscript.

Place	Date	Hour	Summary of Events and Information	Remarks and references to Appendices
Rosberg	23rd 27th		Notes on 4th Weeks training This week was reserved mainly for Schemes and it was hoped to either go under canvas for it or to have several days out with meals out — Uncertainty of signing Peace and canvas not being available caused me to abandon the away from home part — the question of games & sports for which we had a good ground also was a consideration — Very unsettled weather only allowed of one whole day out with meals cooked out but except for variety the places available for Bridging ~~Trestle~~ were very suitable giving every variety. Footbridges Perhaps the type that has been more useful by Fd Coys than any other. The numbers available only allowed of two types being used DRY GAP This had uneven footings & a cleft with a stream in centre — Points brought out in scheme were (1) Section at each site of bridge (2) Selection of & use of material at hand & careful preparation to reduce transport & cooly labour to minimum. (3) Spacing trestles to suit gap & leave stream clear & suit material (3) Various types of trestle — Doffed & lashed. Legs worn & tob dug [illegible] & legs of different length (4) Allowance for sinkage — finishing approaches bracing (5) Watching effect of transport at crossing. EXECUTION of Work 3 Officers with 3 parties (a) Preparation of footings (b) North 3 trestles & 3 bays (c) South 2 — & 3 bays Time 40 mins = 3.5 mins per foot run.	GOH

D. D. & L., London, E.C.
(10340) Wt W5300/P713 750,000 3/18 E 2688 Forms/C2118/16.

409th Fd Coy R.E.

Instructions regarding War Diaries and Intelligence Summaries are contained in F. S. Regs., Part II. and the Staff Manual respectively. Title pages will be prepared in manuscript.

WAR DIARY for June
or
INTELLIGENCE SUMMARY.
(Erase heading not required.)

Army Form C. 2118.

Place	Date	Hour	Summary of Events and Information	Remarks and references to Appendices
Rosberg	23 / 25 /6/19		Dry Gap Scheme. Involved all horses of Company out – Each Section Officer was responsible for the transport allotted him. Forming Company picquet line watering & feeding & grooming.	
			BRIDGEING SCHEME. Wet Gap. 9ft.	
			Scheme was set to subaltern was – At 8.30 hrs I showed him the Gap and gave him Centre line and told him that the Coy (40 men), Coy Bridging equipment tool carts & 2 wagons with timber sufficient for 2 11 ft bays approx on board wd be on site by 9.30 hrs – Conditions gap ct be measured assuming one man ct swim across otherwise no man or material was to cross except in a boat –	
			Officer decided to erect one cillon & 2 pontoons from near shore & 1 trestle from far shore which was ferried over with pontoon – an officer with his section was given this job – The 3rd officer was given the two trestles to design & construct – The bottom was a muddy one.	
			Points brought out: (1) Quick design of trestle & measurement of double section, (2) making a plank trestle out of what was to hand (3) Value of adjustable transom on mud bottom & value of slipper, strength of nailed joints. (4) Need of strong foot ropes & adjustment of trestle before weight is put on it and it is sunk in mud, (5) Allowance for sinking of floating part of bridge – (6) Use of short timbers in baulking	
			The bridge stood transport without distortion – Time 4 hrs for 40 men or 2/3 man hours per ft. Dismantling & packing – 1½ or 2/3 –	
				[signature]

(10340) Wt W5300/P713 750,000 3/18 E 2888 Forms/C2118/16. D. D. & L., London, E.C.

409th F. Coy R.E.

Instructions regarding War Diaries and Intelligence Summaries are contained in F. S. Regs., Part II. and the Staff Manual respectively. Title pages will be prepared in manuscript.

WAR DIARY for June
or
INTELLIGENCE SUMMARY.
(*Erase heading not required.*)

~~R.E.~~ p7 Army Form C. 2118.

Place	Date	Hour	Summary of Events and Information	Remarks and references to Appendices
			General Notes on Training	
			It is of very great value to a company commander to get all his officers and men the majority of his company together — the training technical enables even trained men to rub up rusty parts and quite a number shew up rusty in many things.	
			The greatest value is getting them together as a company & games assist greatly in this —	
			The following subjects were not touched.	
			(a) Rafts (b) Derricks Shears etc (c) Lewis Gun (d) Musketry could only be touched on & shooting left much room for improvement. (e) Gas Masks were used in all the Bridging Schemes but more time was required for training in quickness of adjustment.	
	28/6/19		Allotted for Sports owing to death of Sergt Hickman Sports and concert were postponed & the funeral took place in afternoon.	
	29/6/19		Sunday Free	
	30/6/19		Company Sports (a) Commenced 10hrs finished 17.00 – Weather cold & threatening rain otherwise all went well — (b) After tea Officers and NCO's of O.E. Jumping & tent pegging.	
			END of TRAINING PERIOD.	
			G. W. Findlay Major R.E. OC 409 F Coy RE	

D. D. & L., London, E.C.
(10340) Wt W5300/P713 750,000 3/18 E 2688 Forms/C2118/16.

App A

TRAINING CARRIED OUT in JUNE 1919

Army Form C. 2118.

WAR DIARY
or
INTELLIGENCE SUMMARY.
(Erase heading not required.)

Instructions regarding War Diaries and Intelligence Summaries are contained in F. S. Regs., Part II. and the Staff Manual respectively. Title pages will be prepared in manuscript.

Place	Date	~~Hour~~ Day	Summary of Events and Information: 1st WEEK.				Afternoon		Remarks and references to Appendices
RÖSBERG	1/6/19		← Sunday	Church Parade →			AFTERNOON.		
	2/6/19	Mon.	6.30 – 7.00 Physical Training preceded by Cup of Tea	8.45 – 9.30 Squad Drill & Saluting	930 – 10.15 Rifle Exercises	1030 – 12.30. Kit & Gas helmet inspection	14 to 16.45 (a) Clean Wagons & Company Sports Gear (b) Officers & NCO's Musketry & Communication Drill.		
	3/6/19	Tues		8.00 hr — 11 KINGS BIRTHDAY PARADE march to SECHTEM & BACK 5 miles			Free Games.		
	4/6/19	Wed.	Physical training	0845 — 10.30 Section Drill & Saluting (under Cbn)		10.45 — 12.30 No 1 & 3 Pontoon Drill; No 2 & 4 Trestle Drill	Games		
		Thurs	Physical Training	8.45 – 9.30 ~~Section Drill~~; 9.30 – 10.15 ~~Company Drill~~; Explosives		No 2 & 4 Pontoon Drill; No 1 & 3 Trestle Drill	No 2 & 4 ~~[illegible]~~ Cleaning Wagons & ~~[illegible]~~ preparation of Material ~~Muscle [illegible]~~	Wet Day	
		Friday	P.T.	8.45 – 930 Section Drill; 930 – 10.15 Company Drill		10.30 — 12.30 No 2 & 4 Trestle Drill; No 1 & 3 Pontoon "	No 2 & 4 Dismantling Bridge; No 1 & 3 Aiming, Position & Trigger Pressing	CE IX Corps inspected Company on Training	
		Sat.	P.T.	9.30 – 12.30 Nos 1 & 3 Trestle Bridging Drill; 9.30 – 10.30 Nos 2 & 4 Musketry Aiming etc; 10.30 – 12.30 — Pontoon Drill			← Games →	[signature] Major RE O.C. 409 Fd Coy RE	

D. D. & L., London, E.C.
(10340) Wt W5300/P713 750,000 3/18 E 2688 Forms/C2118/16.

TRAINING CARRIED OUT in JUNE 1919

Army Form C. 2118.

6

Instructions regarding War Diaries and Intelligence Summaries are contained in F. S. Regs., Part II. and the Staff Manual respectively. Title pages will be prepared in manuscript.

WAR DIARY
or
INTELLIGENCE SUMMARY.
(Erase heading not required.)

Place	Date	Hour	2nd Week	Summary of Events and Information: Forenoon	Afternoon	Remarks	Remarks and references to Appendices
Rosberg	8/6/19		Sunday				
	9/6/19	Monday	(Whit)	Holiday. Games Officers & NCOs v. rest & Tip & Run.			
	10/6/19	Tuesday	6.30–7.00 Physical Training	Nos 2 & 3 Section Digging Pipe Track. Nos ~~1 & 4~~ – Wiring Drill & Preparation of Materials 1 – Erection of Shelter C Type & Sandbag revetment.	Tool Carts – Baths 7.	Mounted Branch Riding drill daily	
	11/6/19	Wed.	P.T.	Nos 2 & 3 Section Digging Pipe Track 1 Wiring Drill. 4 Erection of Shelter & Sandbag Revetment	Games		
	12/6/19	Thurs		Company Packed up & move out complete 5.45–6.45 Loading Bridging Equipment 7.00 Breakfast 8.30 All Wagons Packed by. 8.45 Section Parade. 9.30 General Parade March Out 2 miles – Map Reading – Return	Cleaning Wagons & Offloading Bridging Equipment	Officers 2 Bridge & Road Reconnaissance.	
	13/6/19	Friday		8.15 – 11.30 No 3 Sandbag Revetment, No 2 Wiring (Tool Carts) 8.15 – 12.30 No 4 Digging 8 No 1 Deposits.	12.00 – 15.45 Explosives All sections		
	14/6/19	Sat		(a) Trip up RHINE for Roll (b) Camp Work			

(10340) Wt W5300/P713 750,000 3/18 E 2688 Forms/C2118/16. D. D. & L., London, E.C.

409th Fld Coy R.E. Training carried out in June 1919

WAR DIARY
or
INTELLIGENCE SUMMARY.
(Erase heading not required.)

Army Form C. 2118.

Instructions regarding War Diaries and Intelligence Summaries are contained in F. S. Regs., Part II. and the Staff Manual respectively. Title pages will be prepared in manuscript.

Place	Date	Hour	Summary of Events and Information — 3rd Week Forenoons	Afternoon	Remarks	Remarks and references to Appendices
Rosbury	15/6/19	Sun.	Voluntary Church Service			
	16/6/19	Mon.	8.30–7.00 Physical Training No 1 Sect. Musketry Firing 10 rds No 2 " Sandbag Revetment & Steel Shelter No 3 " Wiring (Apron) No 4 " Dugouts	Gas Drill & Inspection all sections H.Q. & Drivers		
	17/6/19	Tues	ditto No 1 & 4 Sect. at disposal of Lt Goldfinch for Preparing Demolitions No 3 Dugouts & Musketry. No 2 Wiring (Low Wire & Concertina)	Demolitions (a) Lecture on ground (b) Demonstration	About 50 lbs guncotton used and all went off successfully.	
	18/6/19	Wed	ditto No 1 Sect. Digging Pipe Track No 2 – Dugouts & Musketry 10 rds No 3 & 4 Wiring (Low Wire & Concertina)	Cricket		
	19/6/19	Thurs	ditto No 1 Sect. Wiring (Low Wire & Concertina) No 2 3 4 at disposal of Capt. Making hurdles, overhauling & [illegible] equipment & wagons	No 2 & 3 at disposal of Capt. No 1 & 4 night Wiring	About 60 yds done in pitch dark in a wood work entirely by feel — Result a good job —	
	20/6/19	Fri.	No 2 & 3 loading Bridging Wagons Nos 1 2 3 4 Sects = 40 OR (a) Marched to Pont put equipment into bridge (b) Dismantling (8.45 – 13.00 hrs)	Baths & Clothing [illegible]	Note It took about 2½ hrs NOT fast but first time over water and many points were learned	
	21/6/19	Sat	No — 8 – 12.30 1½ hours Baths 1½ .. Dismantling Wire Fence 2 – Knotting & lashing & use of Spars & Tackle	Games Match v Signals Cricket	[signature]	

D. D. & L., London, E.C.
(10340) Wt W5300/P713 750,000 3/18 E 2688 Forms/C2118/16.

TRAINING Carried Out in June 1919

WAR DIARY
or
INTELLIGENCE SUMMARY.
(*Erase heading not required.*)

Army Form C. 2118. (4

Instructions regarding War Diaries and Intelligence Summaries are contained in F. S. Regs., Part II. and the Staff Manual respectively. Title pages will be prepared in manuscript.

4th Week

Place	Date	Hour	Summary of Events and Information — Forenoon	Afternoon	Remarks.	Remarks and references to Appendices
	Sun 22/6/19	Sunday				
	Monday 23/6/19	6.30–7.00 Physical Drill + Loading Wagon	8.45 – 12.45 hrs Footbridging over water + Dismantling (a) Lashed Stakes [illegible] (b) Piles + plankway cantilevered out	2–4.30 1 + 4 Sect. under Capt Hepburn [illegible] wagons etc. 20.30–23.30 2 + 3 S Night wiring	One fence excellent other very good —	
	Tuesday 24/6/19	6.30–7.00 1 + 4 [illegible] Pontoons	8.30 – 17 hrs BRIDGEING SCHEME Dry Gap → (a) A gap was selected + section measured by Subaltern + design for bridge got out previous evening gap 60 ft (b) Material nearly felled trees from a wood, chesses + lashings + dogs + (c) Execution two junior Subalterns each given half; find material build together		Work commenced — [illegible] 11 hrs bridge ready 4 hrs Toolcarts were passed over also a [illegible] wagon — Dismantled	
	25/6/19	Wed	2 Sections under another Subaltern dismantled. 2 Section dismantled [illegible] + odd jobs round Camp wagons etc.	Games		
	26/6/19	Thurs	7.30–8.30 hrs Loading Bridging Equipment; 8.30 Complete Turn Out of Company Transport. 9 hrs No 1 2 3 4 section parade; BRIDGEING 95 ft Water Gap + Dismantling		Note – Toolcart limber + all horses passed over bridge.	
	27/6/19	Fri.	Baths and Preparation for Sports (including erection of obstacle course)			
	28/6/19	Sat	Allotted for Sports postponed to Monday owing to Casualty		[signature]	

End of Training Period

D. D. & L., London, E.C.
(10340) Wt W5300/P713 750,000 3/18 E 2688 Forms/C2118/16.

Appendix B

Army Form C. 2118.

Instructions regarding War Diaries and Intelligence Summaries are contained in F. S. Regs., Part II. and the Staff Manual respectively. Title pages will be prepared in manuscript.

WAR DIARY
or
INTELLIGENCE SUMMARY.

(*Erase heading not required.*)

Place	Date	Hour	Summary of Events and Information	Remarks and references to Appendices

Materials over and above Equipment used in Training.

	Used	Fit for use again
~~1000~~ Sandbags	1000	80%
Pickets Long	100	80%
Short	150	80%
Barbed Wire Coils	18	100%
Cartridges Dummy	1000	100%
Bullseye Targets	100	0%
Figure Targets	100	0%
Aiming Discs	12	100%
Coil 2" Rope	1	Cut into lashings
Poles Long	100	80%
Poles Brushwood	80	100%
Section Clyde Shelter	1	100%

Timber	Ft.	Fit for use again
8 x 3	500	90%
10 x 1½"	150	90%
5 x ¾"	100	20%
3 x 2	150	90%

used for Mining Frames, Tripods, Bridging & Decking.

[illegible]

D. D. & L., London, E.C.
(10340) Wt W5300/P713 750,000 3/18 £ 2688 Forms/C2118/16.

Confidential

409th F. Coy R.E.

Army Form C. 2118.

Instructions regarding War Diaries and Intelligence Summaries are contained in F. S. Regs., Part II. and the Staff Manual respectively. Title pages will be prepared in manuscript.

WAR DIARY for July 1919
or
INTELLIGENCE SUMMARY.
(Erase heading not required.)

Place	Date	Hour	Summary of Events and Information	Remarks and references to Appendices
Rosberg. Germany	1/7/19		Training Completed – Men on odd jobs, overhaul & cleaning of all Bridging Equipment and wagons	
	2/7/19.		Officers taking over work from 76th F Coy RE	
	3/7/19		Movement. Nos 1 & 3 Sections moved into billets at ALFTER & BORNHEIM for work in 2nd & 1st Bde Areas.	
	4/7/19		Commemoration of Signing of Peace – holiday. – Cricket Match v. 76th Coy RE.	
	5/7/19.		(a) 50 OR on Rhine Trip. (b) Remainder on Works.	
	6/7/19		Church Parade for C of E @ 10-30 hrs.	
	7/7/19		Inspection of Technical Wagon by O.C. — Maj FINDLAY & CSM DOW proceeded to Paris for the Victory March. Capt Foster Clarke assumed temporary command & took over imprest a/c.	
	8/7/19 – 19/7/19		Daily Works chiefly small jobs to improve comfort of Divisional Units and erection of tanks for water supply. 18/7/19 Maj Findlay returned from Paris and reassumed command. Imprest remained with Capt Foster Clarke. CSM Dow.	
			Works in hand – Officers Mess, Roof of Hut, Tanks, Recreation Hut, Cookhouse Ovens Latrines, Baths & Delouser, Incinerator – Partitions	

G. W. Findlay
Maj RE

D. D. & L., London, E.C.
(10340) Wt W5300/P713 750,000 3/18 E 2688 Forms/C2118/16.

409th Fd Coy RE

Instructions regarding War Diaries and Intelligence Summaries are contained in F. S. Regs., Part II. and the Staff Manual respectively. Title pages will be prepared in manuscript.

WAR DIARY for July
or
INTELLIGENCE SUMMARY.

(*Erase heading not required.*)

Army Form C. 2118.

(2)

Place	Date	Hour	Summary of Events and Information	Remarks and references to Appendices
~~13/7/19~~ Rosbeck	20/7/19		Sunday Cricket Match v. 75 Fd Coy RE	
	22/7/19		Harness Inspection by O.C. 2.30 pm of HQ No 2 & [illegible] sections. a section 75 Fd Coy RE	
	23/7/19 21/7/19 ~~25~~/7/19		Works as for first fortnight continued ———	
			Owing to the scattered nature of the work it has not been found possible to carry out any Educational Training	
			25/7/19. Gol E Findlay Major R.E. OC 409 Fd Coy RE	
	25/7/19.		Transfers etc: Capt: Field Clarke R.E and IInd Lt. Thatcher posted to 567 A.T. Coy: R.E.	
			IInd Lt. [illegible] R.E. joined 409th (Low) Fd Coy: from 75th Fd Coy: R.E. and took over No 1 Section.	
	26/7/19.		Major Findlay, V.C., D.S.O., M.C., R.E proceeded to U.K. on leave. Lieut W. Geiger R.E. assumed temporary command & took over impress a/cs.	

D. D. & L., London, E.C.
(10340) Wt W5300/P713 750,000 3/18 E 2688 Forms/C2118/16.

3.

409th Fd. Coy: R.E.

Army Form C. 2118.

WAR DIARY for July.
or
INTELLIGENCE SUMMARY.
(*Erase heading not required.*)

Instructions regarding War Diaries and Intelligence Summaries are contained in F. S. Regs., Part II. and the Staff Manual respectively. Title pages will be prepared in manuscript.

Place	Date	Hour	Summary of Events and Information	Remarks and references to Appendices
RÖSBERG	27/7/19 28/7/19		Work in Div: area chiefly minor repairs & renewals.	
	29/7/19		Transferred six "S" mules to Remount Depot COLOGNE.	
	30/7/19 31/7/19.		As for 27/7/19.	
			L. Geiger Lt: R.E. of O.C. 409th Fd Coy: R.E.	
			31/7/19.	

D. D. & L., London, E.C.
(10340) Wt W5300/P713 750,000 3/18 E 2688 Forms/C2118/16.

409'

Army Form C. 2118.

WAR DIARY
or
INTELLIGENCE SUMMARY.
(*Erase heading not required.*)

Instructions regarding War Diaries and Intelligence Summaries are contained in F. S. Regs., Part II. and the Staff Manual respectively. Title pages will be prepared in manuscript.

Place	Date	Hour	Summary of Events and Information	Remarks and references to Appendices
			WAR DIARY for. AUGUST. 409th H Coy R.E.	

D. D. & L., London E.C
(10340) Wt W3300/P713 750,000 3/18 E 688 Forms/C2118/16.

409th Fd Coy RE

Instructions regarding War Diaries and Intelligence Summaries are contained in F. S. Regs., Part II. and the Staff Manual respectively. Title pages will be prepared in manuscript.

WAR DIARY for Aug 1919.
or
INTELLIGENCE SUMMARY.
(Erase heading not required.)

Army Form C. 2118

Place	Date	Hour	Summary of Events and Information	Remarks and references to Appendices
Rasberg. Germany.	1/8/19		Distribution Maj Findlay on leave Lt Grigor a/OC. till 12th Aug. No1 Sect. at Oberdrees Div Art. Area; No3 Sect in Bornheim 1st Bde Area; HQ No 2&4 at Rasberg.	
			Works as usual	
	2/8/19		Saturday mornings available when reqd for Military Training and Administration.	
			10.00 hrs Gas Helmet Inspection.	
	3/8/19		Church Parade.	
	4/8/19 – 8/8/19		Works in Areas — Repairs & alterations to Coolhouses buildings [illegible] etc. Supervision of Water Supply Scheme, Baths & Delousers. Tiles on Div HQ. Roof!	
			Preliminary orders for move home recd — No 1&3 Section withdrawn – rejoin HQ.	
	9/8/19.		Baths & Pay. & Cleaning up & repairing vehicles. — Maj Findlay resumed Command 18th [illegible]	
	10 & 11th		Continued cleaning up & putting by equipment no longer reqd.	
	12th & 13th		Special orders for packing issued.	
	14th		(a) Packing commenced under Lt Goldfinch & 2Lt Fea. (b) Lt Grigor with Lt Gibbs i/c Preparing all Harness & Vehicles for Packing & return of horses. Toolcart which was 1st in Corps Horse Show being prepared for Army Horse Show. (c) General Kit Inspection	
	15th		Packing Continued & Cricket.	
	16th		Packing Cont & Baths — State of Coy. Strength 147 — Half horses returned	

D. D. & L., London, E.C. (A8031) Wt. W1371/M2031 750,000 5/17 Sch. 52 Forms C2118/14

409th Fd Coy RE.

Instructions regarding War Diaries and Intelligence Summaries are contained in F. S. Regs., Part II. and the Staff Manual respectively. Title pages will be prepared in manuscript.

WAR DIARY for Aug.
or
INTELLIGENCE SUMMARY.
(Erase heading not required.)

Army Form C. 2118.

P. 2.

Place	Date	Hour	Summary of Events and Information	Remarks and references to Appendices
Raberg Germany	17/8/19		3 Bridging Wagons + 3 Tool Carts packed ready for Embarkation - proceeded to Bonn Station & were parked under a Guard.	
	18/8/19.		All horses returned to Remount Depot leaving unit with 12 mules. Army Horse Show, in which unit toolcart was 4th out of 8 toolcarts left in the final after eliminating trials –	
	19/8/19.		All 6 pairs of mules out returning ~~Supplies~~ Ordnance Stores & taking 2/3 of remaining transport to Bonn two journeys.	
	20/8/19.		All mules out taking remaining transport to Bonn – completed move	
	21/8/19.		Lt Goldfinch & 8 O.R. took over charge of Equipment at Bonn entrained with it and proceeded to port of Embarkation – Evening continued company Concert – Col Sankey C.R.E. addressed the party & thanked all ranks for their very excellent behaviour & discipline during the period of occupation –	
	22/8/19		one section duty remainder free. Afternoon Cricket Officers & N.C.O. v. rest.	
	23/8/19		Advance party Lt Grigor & 2 O.R. left for U.K.	
	24th 25 26th		Necessary fatigues by 1 section. Remainder free All Stores packed up & company marched to SECHTEM Station by 10.13 hrs for entraining Moving off for U.K at 15.13 hrs or shortly after.	[illegible]

D. D. & L., London, E.C. (10340) Wt W5300/P713 750,000 3/18 E. 688 Forms/C2118/16.

War 409th Fld Coy RE

Instructions regarding War Diaries and Intelligence Summaries are contained in F. S. Regs., Part II. and the Staff Manual respectively. Title pages will be prepared in manuscript.

WAR DIARY for August
or
INTELLIGENCE SUMMARY.

(Erase heading not required.)

Army Form C. 2118.

P3

Place	Date	Hour	Summary of Events and Information	Remarks and references to Appendices
In train from Germany to RHYLL U.K.	26 to 29th.		Leaving Sechtem at 16 hrs approx – Tea was made en route water being obtained by men from engines houses etc along railway during unforseen stoppages.	
			Train arr. at Charleroi about 3 or 4 hrs late at approx 9 hrs – Breakfast washing & latrine arrangements were waiting and were satisfactory.	
			Halt Repas arranged for 1 hr at 12 hrs was cut out as time not suitable.	
			Train arrived about 6 hrs late at next Halte Repas namely about 13 hrs when Dinners were served arrangements satisfactory.	
			Tea was again made en route as before –	
			Halt Repas at Mons at 1.30 hrs vice 16 hrs previous day –	
			Train arrived Calais 07 hrs. 28/8/19 Breakfasts served in Camp. & proceed to boat embarking about 10.30 hrs. Arr. England about 12 hrs. L/Goldfinch and party were at Calais having completed tob & handed over all equipment –	
			Train left for RHYLL at 15.30 hrs. arriving at 2 hrs after a very smooth quick and well arranged journey compared with the other side.	
			Met by Advance party & settled into Camp.	
	29th 12 hrs 30		Dinners then drawing camp furniture.	
	Note		With the very late running of trains the Kitchen Truck is far better than Halte Repas –	
			11	
			Gilbert Cay Major OC 409th Fld Coy RE	

D. D. & L., London E.C
(10346) Wt W5300/P713 750,000 3/18 E 688 Forms/C2118/16.

409 F Coy

P-4

Army Form C. 2118.

Instructions regarding War Diaries and Intelligence Summaries are contained in F. S. Regs., Part II. and the Staff Manual respectively. Title pages will be prepared in manuscript.

WAR DIARY f Aug.
or
INTELLIGENCE SUMMARY.

(Erase heading not required.)

Place	Date	Hour	Summary of Events and Information	Remarks and references to Appendices
30/8/19 Kinmel Park Camp	30/8/19		Preparations for Demobilising 60 men — drawing Camp Utensils	
	3/8/19		ditto	
			1/9/19	

G. W. Hadley
Maj RE
Maj. R.E.
O.C. 409th (Lowland) F.D. Coy. R.E.

D. D. & L., London E.C
(10340) Wt W5300/P713 750,000 3/18 E 686 Forms/C2118/16.

Camp HQ

Herewith last number of 409th Fd Coy RE War Diary.

1/10/19

G de C E Findlay
Maj RE.
O.C. 409 Fd Coy RE

Instructions regarding War Diaries and Intelligence Summaries are contained in F. S. Regs., Part II. and the Staff Manual respectively. Title pages will be prepared in manuscript.

WAR DIARY Sept.
or
INTELLIGENCE SUMMARY.
(Erase heading not required.)

Western 1 DIV

Army Form C. 2118.

Place	Date	Hour	Summary of Events and Information	Remarks and references to Appendices
Kinmel Pk Camp Nr. Wales	1/9/19		Demobilised 56 O.R.	
	2/9/19	–	" 1 O.R.	
			– 1 O.R. – Usual parties – Football match v. 45 R.F.C.R.S. won.	
	3/9/19	–	Rifle Inspection and Drill and Fatigues – Wet Afternoon.	
	4/9/19	–		
	5/9/19	–	Rifle Inspection Drill & Fatigues	
	6/9/19	–	ditto.	
	7/9/19	–	Church Parade.	
	8/9/19	–	Preparation for Demobilisation of Camp.	
	9/9/19	–	Drill & Fatigues & handing in of equipment etc.	
	10/9/19	–	" " " " " " "	
	11/9/19	–	41 men Demobilised – leaving paper strength of 54. with 18 on leave	
	12/9/19	–	1 " " Centre ... concert.	
	13/9/19	–	Fatigues.	
	14/9/19	–		
	15/9/19	–		
	16/9/19		5 men proceed on Demob.	

D. D. & L., London E.C. (10349) Wt W5300/P713 750,000 3/18 E 688 Forms/C2118/16.

409th Fld Coy RE

WAR DIARY Sept.
or
INTELLIGENCE SUMMARY.
(Erase heading not required.)

Army Form C. 2118.

Instructions regarding War Diaries and Intelligence Summaries are contained in F. S. Regs., Part II. and the Staff Manual respectively. Title pages will be prepared in manuscript.

Place	Date	Hour	Summary of Events and Information	Remarks and references to Appendices
Kinmel Pk	15/9/19	—	Arrangements for Civic Reception & handing in.	
	16/9/19	—	Handing in AOD Stores Boards on Office etc.	
	17/9/19	—	" — — — — Fatigues — awaiting orders to dispatch personnel.	
	18/9/19	—	Continue Strength 4 Off. 1 WO 7 Sgts 7 Cpls 29 O.R. —	
	19/9/19	—	4 men Demobbed — Preparing Statement of Cost Accounts — For a unit just about to be disbanded this appears an absolute waste of time & paper —	[illegible]
	20/9/19	—	Received warning of moving on Monday.	
	21/9/19	-	Awaiting orders as warning cancelled.	
	22/9/19	17.30 hr	recd orders to catch train at 7.00 hr reveille 4.15 hr.	
	23/9/19		To Newark 10 OR leaving 4 officers & 13 OR awaiting orders for disposal of officers. To Aldershot 9 OR.	
	24/9/19		1 OR Demobilised — All books &c to close and dispatched.	
	25/9/19		Officers & Batmen awaiting orders —	
	30/9/19		As all personnel other than Officers Batmen & mess staff have been disbanded this is last entry to Diary of 409th Fld Coy RE CLOSED.	[illegible] Capt RE Cmdg 409 Fld Coy RE

D. D. & L., London E.C. (10346) Wt W5300/P713 750,000 3/18 E 688 Forms/C2118/16.

www.ingramcontent.com/pod-product-compliance
Lightning Source LLC
Chambersburg PA
CBHW081422300426
44108CB00016BA/2278
* 9 7 8 1 4 7 4 5 0 2 4 0 5 *